NAUSICAÄ
Of The Valley Of The Wind

6

HAYAO MIYAZAKI

Nausicaä of the Valley of the Wind
Volume 6

STORY & ART BY HAYAO MIYAZAKI

Translation /Matt Thorn
Translation Assist — Editor's Choice Edition /Kaori Inoue & Joe Yamazaki
Touch-up Art & Lettering /Walden Wong
Design /Izumi Evers
Editor — 1st Edition /Annette Roman
Editor — Editor's Choice Edition /Elizabeth Kawasaki

Managing Editor /Masumi Washington
Editor-in-Chief /Alvin Lu
Production Manager /Noboru Watanabe
Sr. Director of Licensing & Acquisitions /Rika Inouye
Vice President of Sales /Joe Morici
Vice President of Marketing /Liza Coppola
Executive Vice President /Hyoe Narita
Publisher /Seiji Horibuchi

Printed in Canada

Published by VIZ, LLC
P.O. Box 77010
San Francisco CA 94107

Editor's Choice Edition

10 9 8 7 6 5 4 3 2 1

First printing, July 2004
First English edition, April 1996 & August 1997

www.viz.com

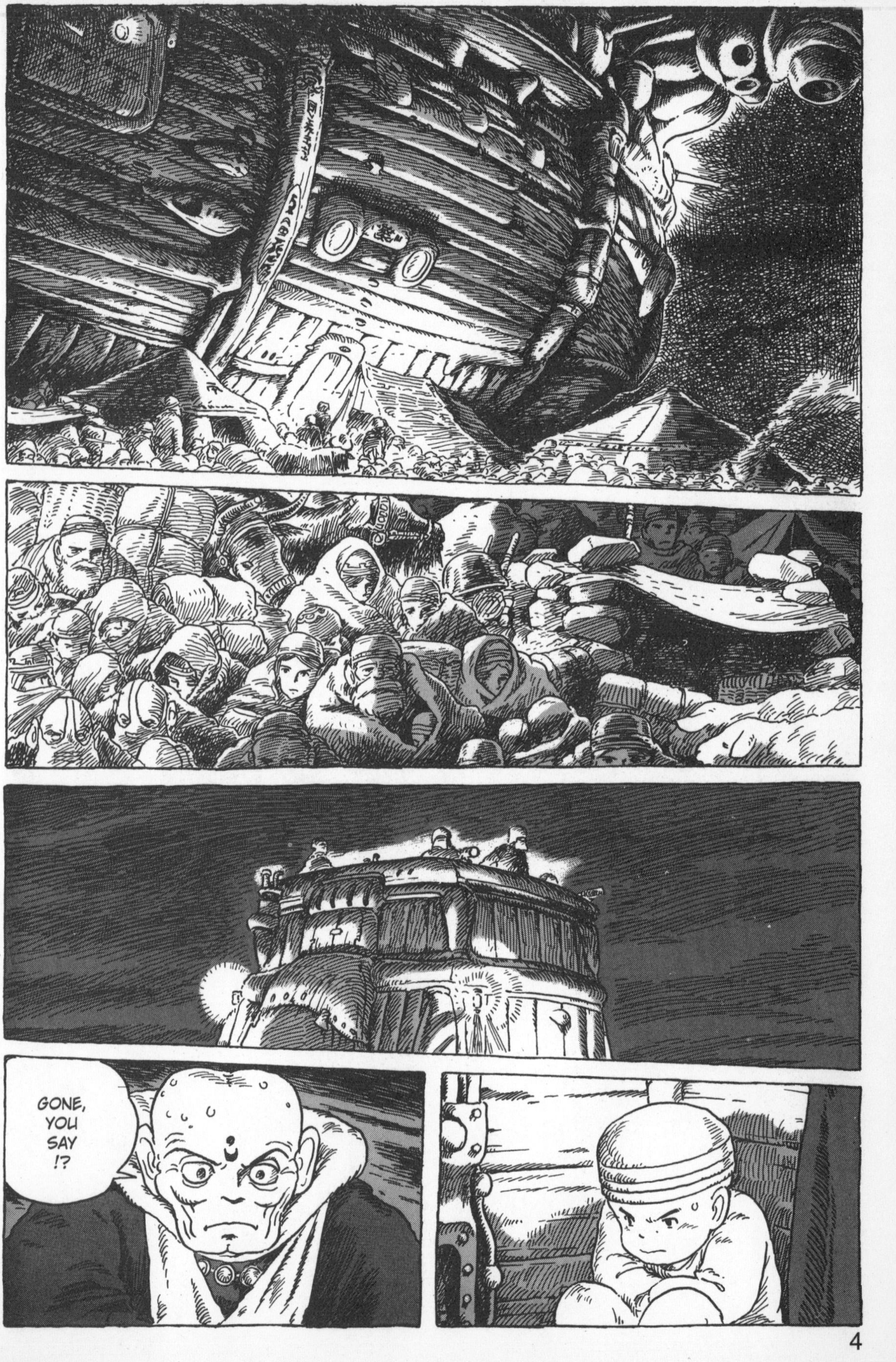
GONE, YOU SAY !?

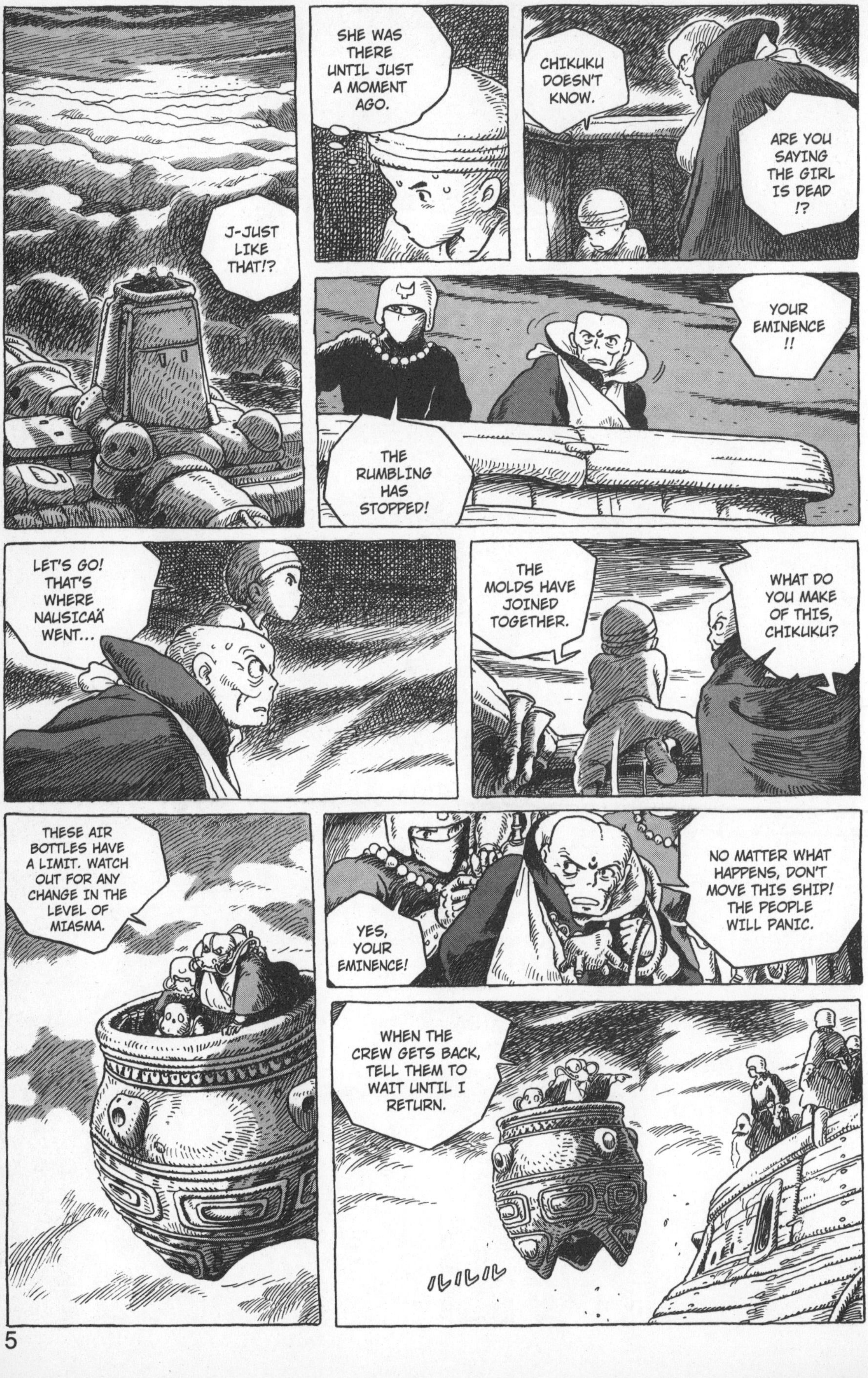
ARE YOU SAYING THE GIRL IS DEAD !?
CHIKUKU DOESN'T KNOW.
SHE WAS THERE UNTIL JUST A MOMENT AGO.
YOUR EMINENCE !!
THE RUMBLING HAS STOPPED!
J-JUST LIKE THAT!?
WHAT DO YOU MAKE OF THIS, CHIKUKU?
THE MOLDS HAVE JOINED TOGETHER.
LET'S GO! THAT'S WHERE NAUSICAÄ WENT...
NO MATTER WHAT HAPPENS, DON'T MOVE THIS SHIP! THE PEOPLE WILL PANIC.
YES, YOUR EMINENCE!
WHEN THE CREW GETS BACK, TELL THEM TO WAIT UNTIL I RETURN.
ルルルル
THESE AIR BOTTLES HAVE A LIMIT. WATCH OUT FOR ANY CHANGE IN THE LEVEL OF MIASMA.

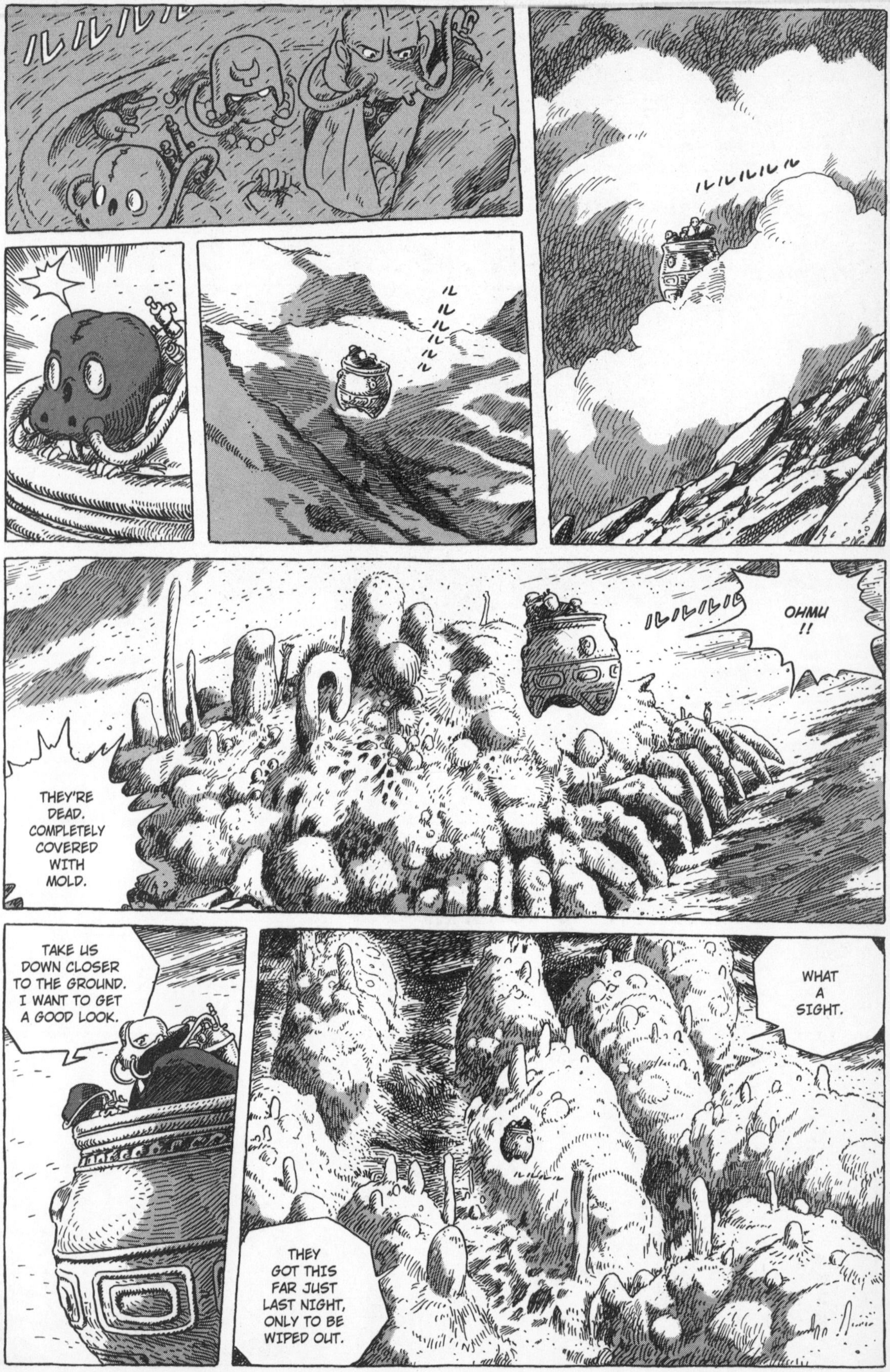
ルルルルルル
ルルルルル
ルルルルルル
ルルルルル
OHMU !!
THEY'RE DEAD. COMPLETELY COVERED WITH MOLD.
WHAT A SIGHT.
THEY GOT THIS FAR JUST LAST NIGHT, ONLY TO BE WIPED OUT.
TAKE US DOWN CLOSER TO THE GROUND. I WANT TO GET A GOOD LOOK.

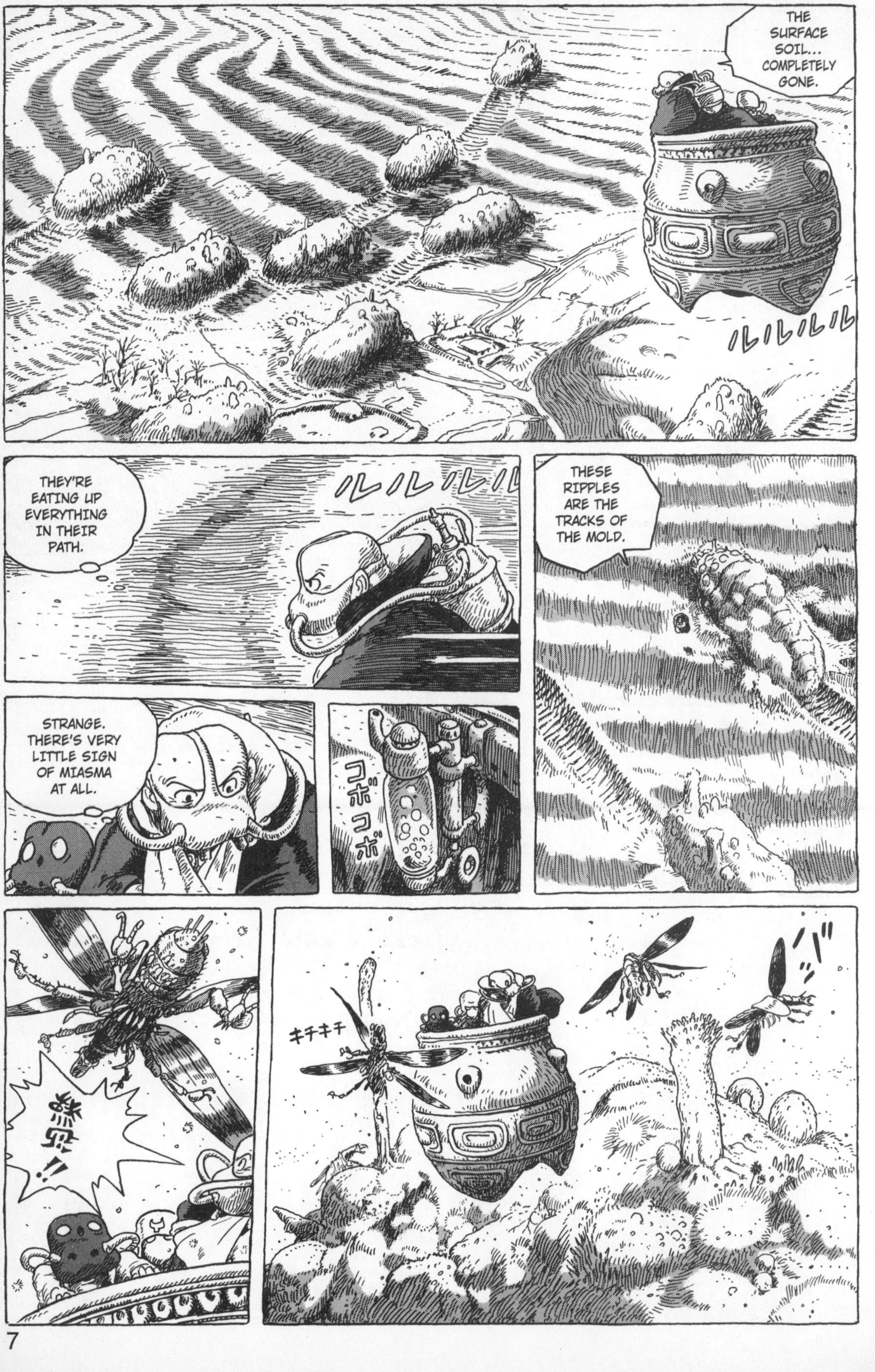

THE SURFACE SOIL... COMPLETELY GONE.
ルルルルル
THESE RIPPLES ARE THE TRACKS OF THE MOLD.
THEY'RE EATING UP EVERYTHING IN THEIR PATH.
ルルルルル
コポコポ
STRANGE. THERE'S VERY LITTLE SIGN OF MIASMA AT ALL.
キチキチ

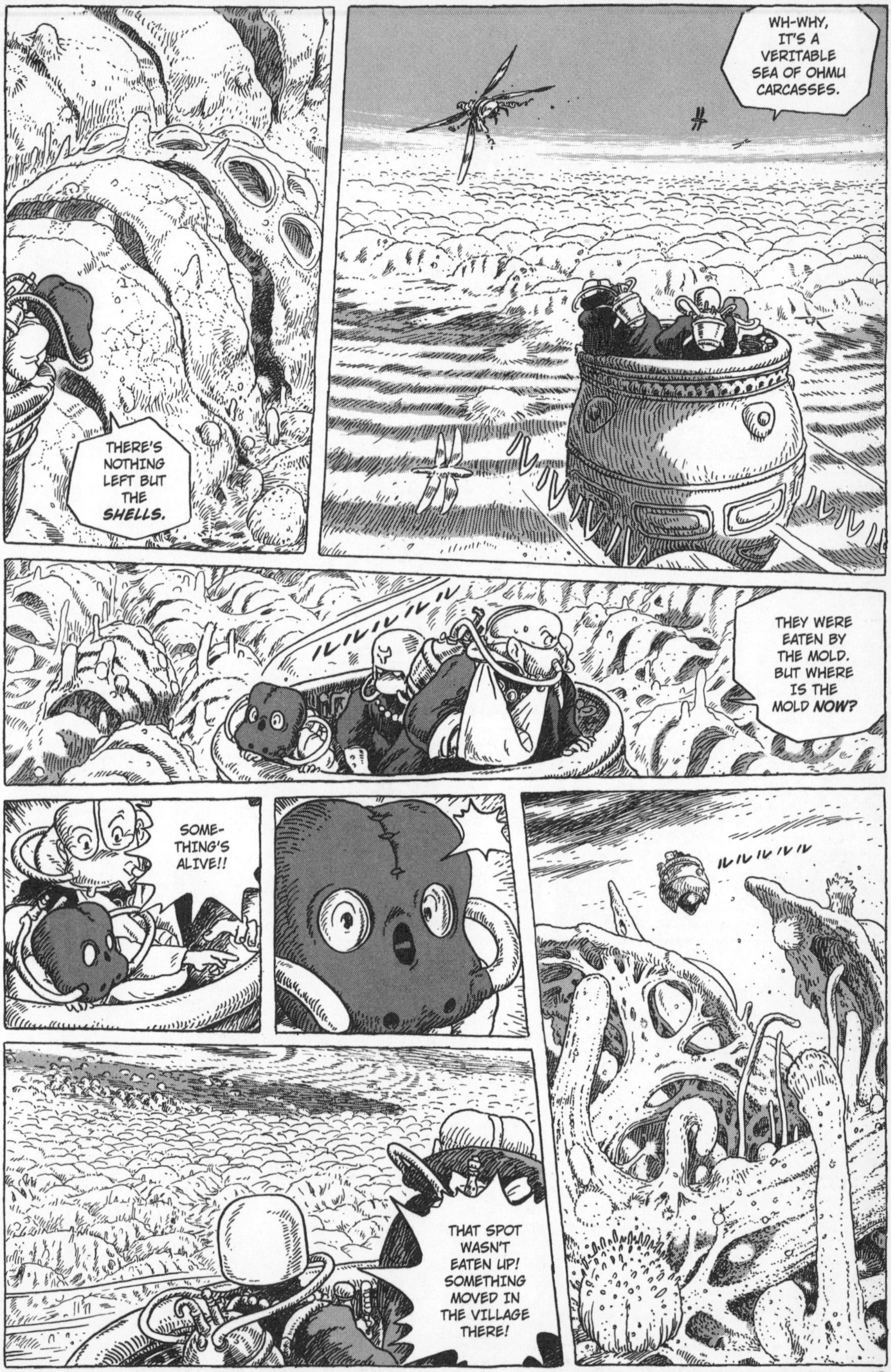
WH-WHY, IT'S A VERITABLE SEA OF OHMU CARCASSES.
ルルルル
THERE'S NOTHING LEFT BUT THE SHELLS.
THEY WERE EATEN BY THE MOLD. BUT WHERE IS THE MOLD NOW?
ルルルルルル
ルルルルル
SOME-THING'S ALIVE!!
THAT SPOT WASN'T EATEN UP! SOMETHING MOVED IN THE VILLAGE THERE!

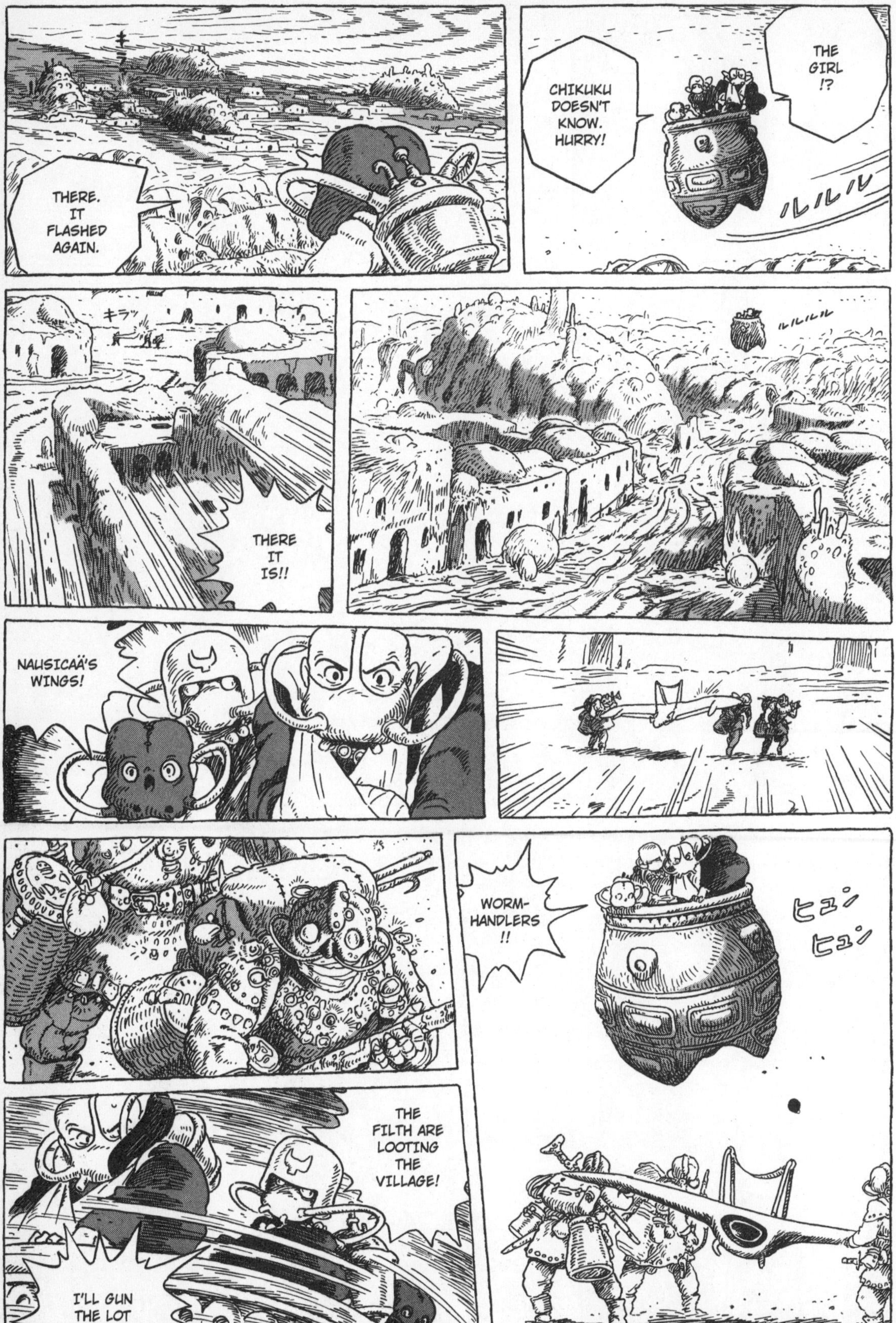
THE GIRL !?
CHIKUKU DOESN'T KNOW. HURRY!
ルルルル
THERE. IT FLASHED AGAIN.
ルルルル
キラッ
THERE IT IS!!
NAUSICAÄ'S WINGS!
WORM-HANDLERS !!
ヒュン ヒュン
THE FILTH ARE LOOTING THE VILLAGE!
I'LL GUN THE LOT OF THEM DOWN!!

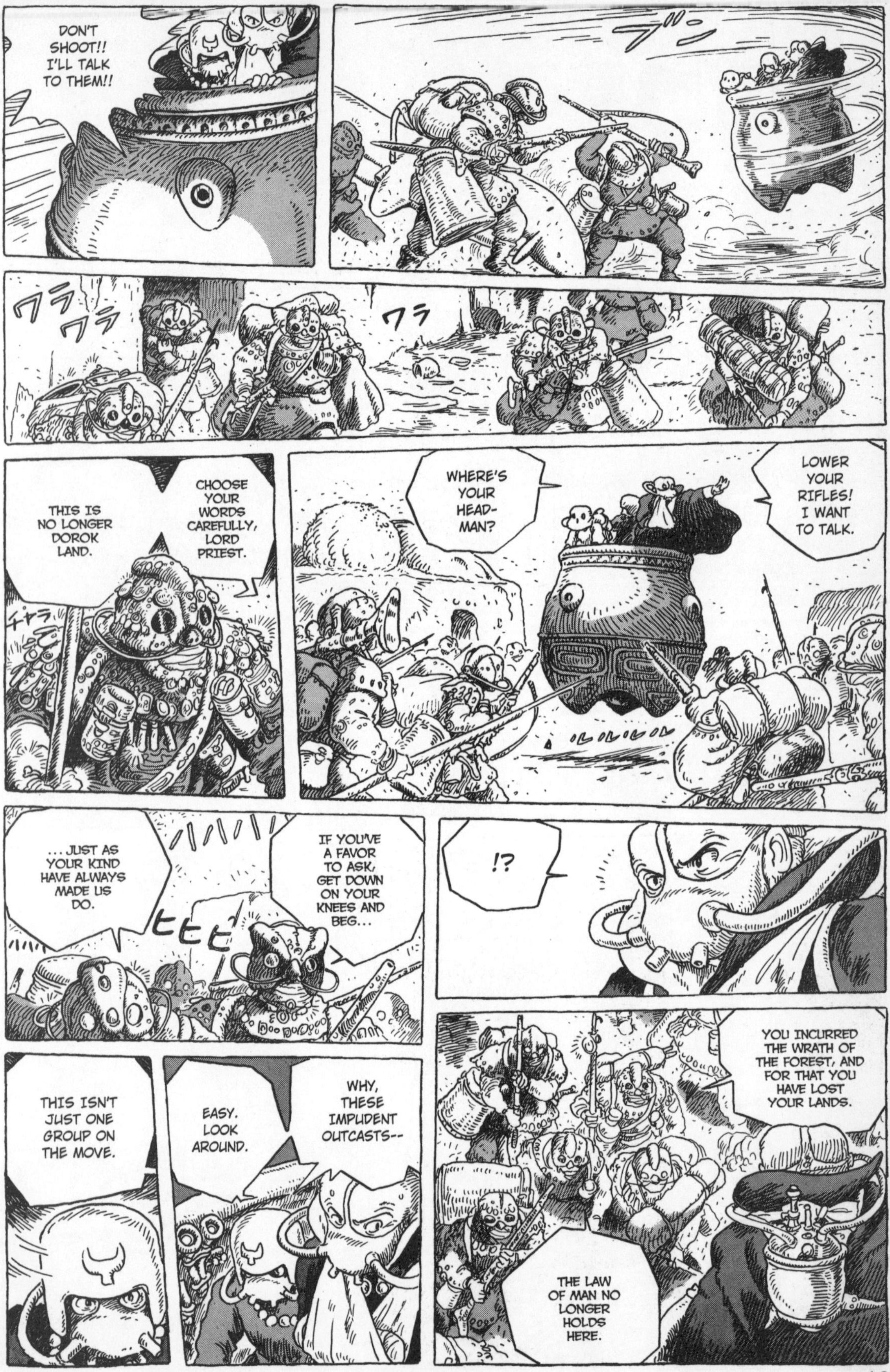
DON'T SHOOT!! I'LL TALK TO THEM!!
ワラ ワラ
ワラ
LOWER YOUR RIFLES! I WANT TO TALK.
WHERE'S YOUR HEAD-MAN?
CHOOSE YOUR WORDS CAREFULLY, LORD PRIEST.
THIS IS NO LONGER DOROK LAND.
!?
IF YOU'VE A FAVOR TO ASK, GET DOWN ON YOUR KNEES AND BEG...
...JUST AS YOUR KIND HAVE ALWAYS MADE US DO.
YOU INCURRED THE WRATH OF THE FOREST, AND FOR THAT YOU HAVE LOST YOUR LANDS.
THE LAW OF MAN NO LONGER HOLDS HERE.
WHY, THESE IMPUDENT OUTCASTS--
EASY. LOOK AROUND.
THIS ISN'T JUST ONE GROUP ON THE MOVE.

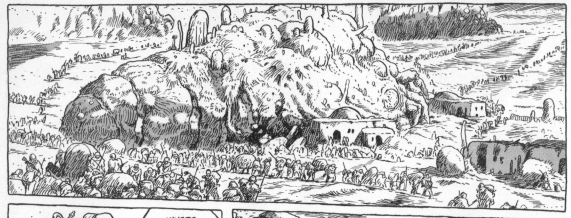

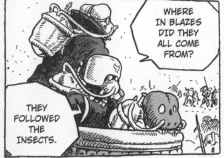

WHERE IN BLAZES DID THEY ALL COME FROM?
THEY FOLLOWED THE INSECTS.
THEY DON'T SEEM THE LEAST BIT AFRAID OF THE MOLD. COULD IT BE THEY JUST DON'T KNOW?
WAIT! YOU THERE WITH THE BASKET!
EMINENCE !!
WHAT ARE YOU HIDING IN THERE? LET ME LOOK INSIDE!!

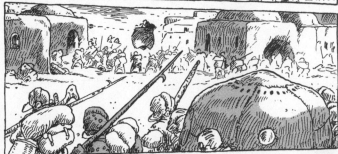

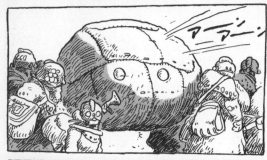

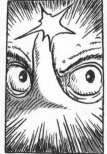

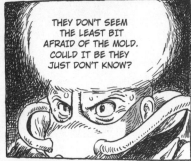

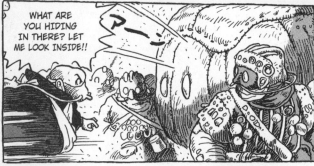

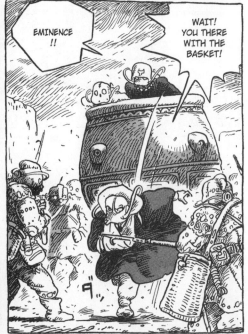

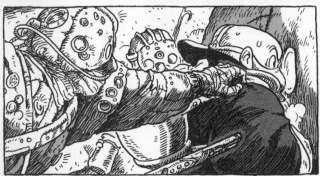

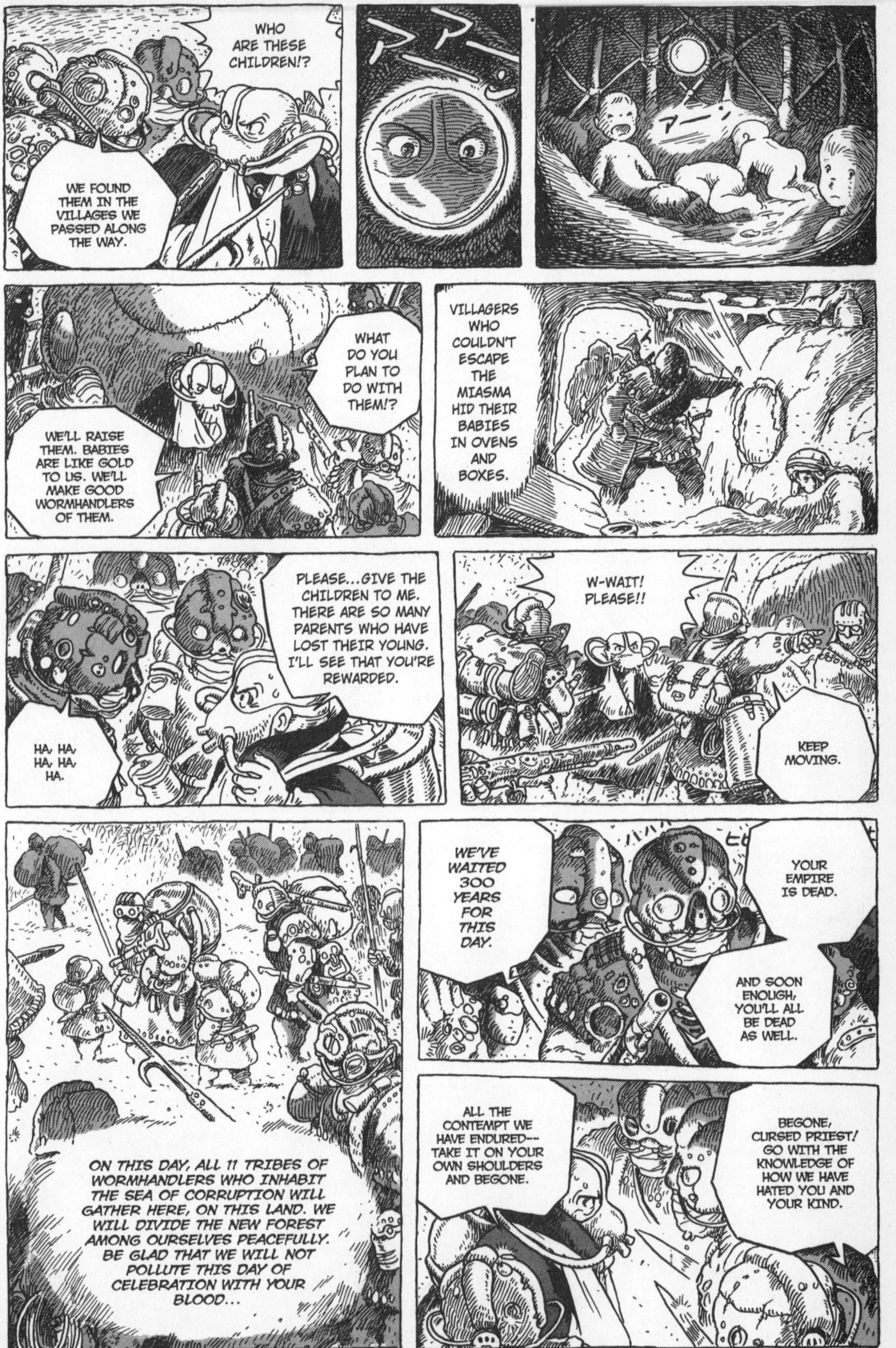
アー
WHO ARE THESE CHILDREN!?
WE FOUND THEM IN THE VILLAGES WE PASSED ALONG THE WAY.
VILLAGERS WHO COULDN'T ESCAPE THE MIASMA HID THEIR BABIES IN OVENS AND BOXES.
WHAT DO YOU PLAN TO DO WITH THEM!?
WE'LL RAISE THEM. BABIES ARE LIKE GOLD TO US. WE'LL MAKE GOOD WORMHANDLERS OF THEM.
W-WAIT! PLEASE!!
KEEP MOVING.
PLEASE...GIVE THE CHILDREN TO ME. THERE ARE SO MANY PARENTS WHO HAVE LOST THEIR YOUNG. I'LL SEE THAT YOU'RE REWARDED.
HA, HA, HA, HA, HA.
YOUR EMPIRE IS DEAD.
WE'VE WAITED 300 YEARS FOR THIS DAY.
AND SOON ENOUGH, YOU'LL ALL BE DEAD AS WELL.
BEGONE, CURSED PRIEST! GO WITH THE KNOWLEDGE OF HOW WE HAVE HATED YOU AND YOUR KIND.
ALL THE CONTEMPT WE HAVE ENDURED--TAKE IT ON YOUR OWN SHOULDERS AND BEGONE.
ON THIS DAY, ALL 11 TRIBES OF WORMHANDLERS WHO INHABIT THE SEA OF CORRUPTION WILL GATHER HERE, ON THIS LAND. WE WILL DIVIDE THE NEW FOREST AMONG OURSELVES PEACEFULLY. BE GLAD THAT WE WILL NOT POLLUTE THIS DAY OF CELEBRATION WITH YOUR BLOOD...

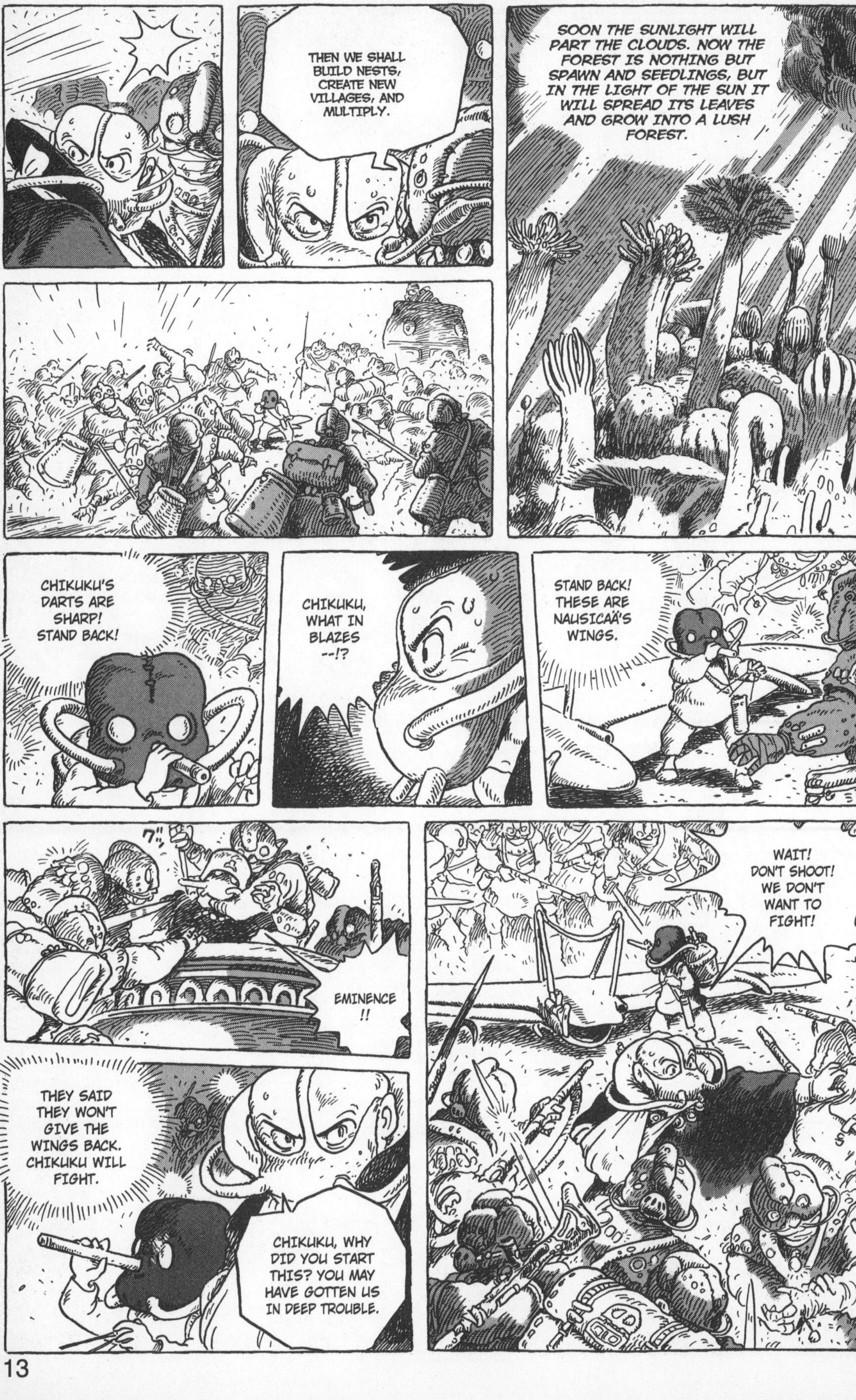
SOON THE SUNLIGHT WILL PART THE CLOUDS. NOW THE FOREST IS NOTHING BUT SPAWN AND SEEDLINGS, BUT IN THE LIGHT OF THE SUN IT WILL SPREAD ITS LEAVES AND GROW INTO A LUSH FOREST.
THEN WE SHALL BUILD NESTS, CREATE NEW VILLAGES, AND MULTIPLY.
STAND BACK! THESE ARE NAUSICAÄ'S WINGS.
CHIKUKU, WHAT IN BLAZES --!?
CHIKUKU'S DARTS ARE SHARP! STAND BACK!
WAIT! DON'T SHOOT! WE DON'T WANT TO FIGHT!
EMINENCE !!
THEY SAID THEY WON'T GIVE THE WINGS BACK. CHIKUKU WILL FIGHT.
CHIKUKU, WHY DID YOU START THIS? YOU MAY HAVE GOTTEN US IN DEEP TROUBLE.

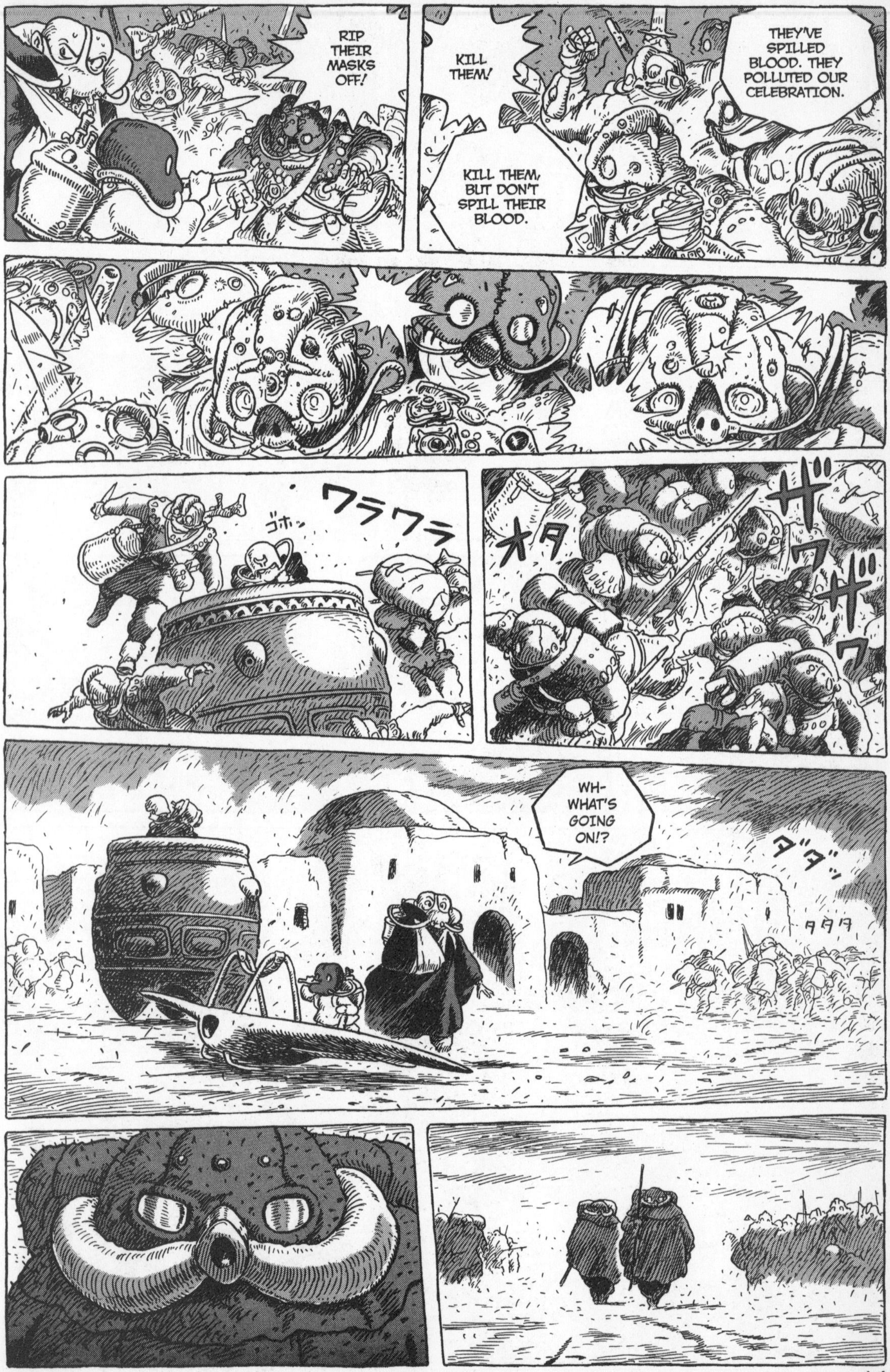
THEY'VE SPILLED BLOOD. THEY POLLUTED OUR CELEBRATION.
KILL THEM!
KILL THEM, BUT DON'T SPILL THEIR BLOOD.
RIP THEIR MASKS OFF!
ザワザワ
オタ
ワラワラ
ゴホッ
WH- WHAT'S GOING ON!?
ダダッ
タタタ

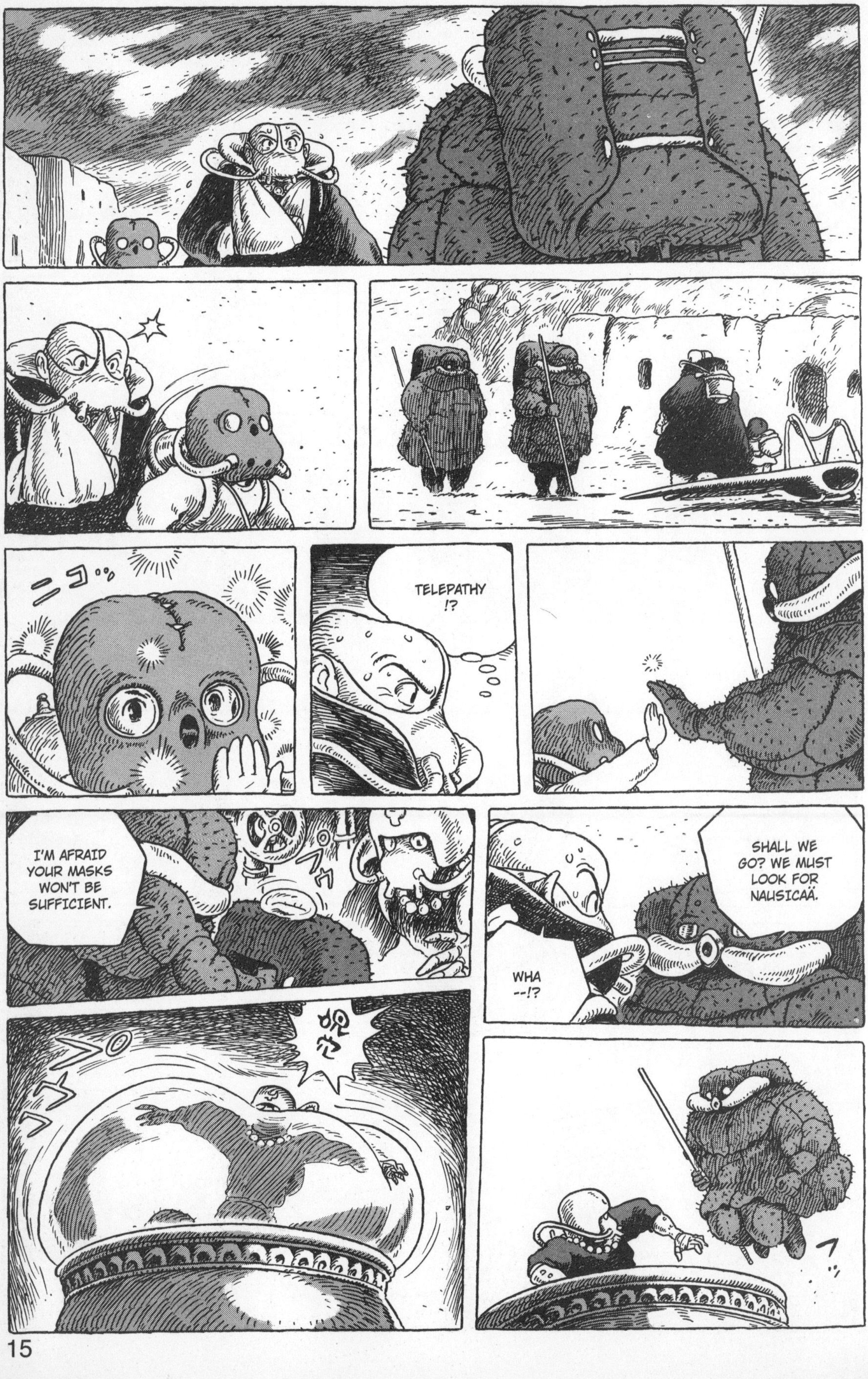
TELEPATHY !?
ニコッ
SHALL WE GO? WE MUST LOOK FOR NAUSICAÄ.
WHA --!?
I'M AFRAID YOUR MASKS WON'T BE SUFFICIENT.

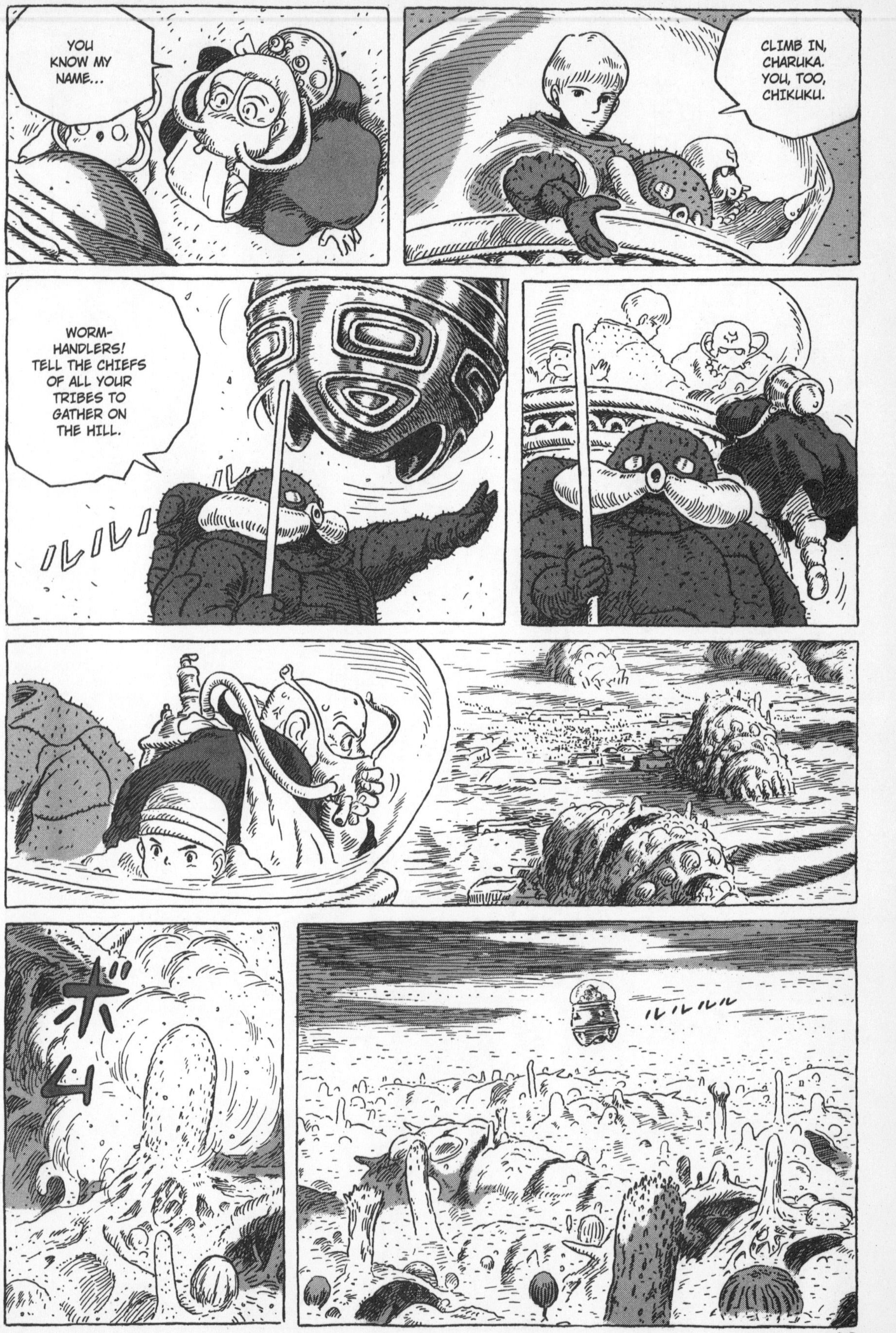

CLIMB IN, CHARUKA. YOU, TOO, CHIKUKU.
YOU KNOW MY NAME...
WORM-HANDLERS! TELL THE CHIEFS OF ALL YOUR TRIBES TO GATHER ON THE HILL.
ルルル
ルルルル
ボム

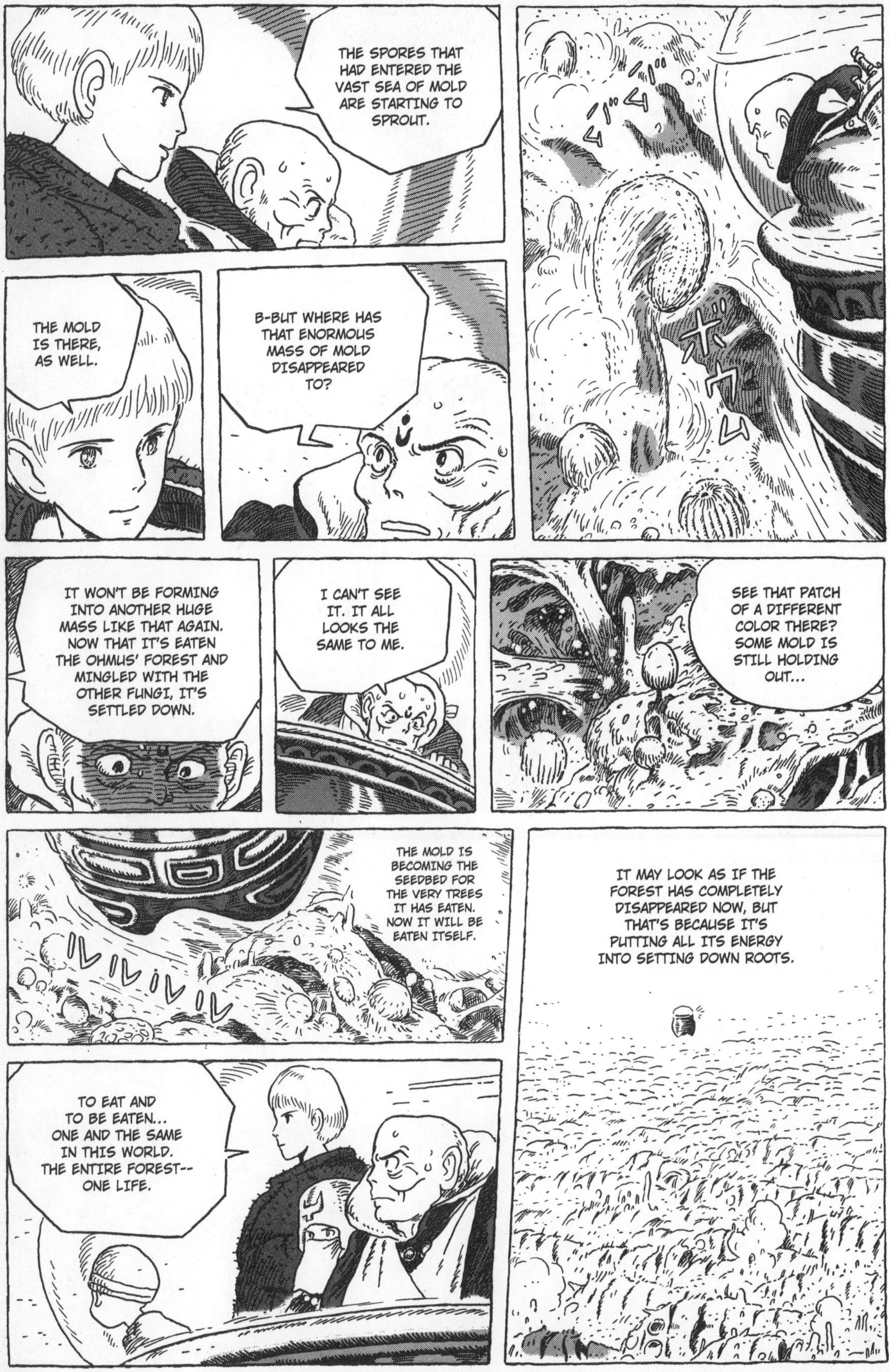
THE SPORES THAT HAD ENTERED THE VAST SEA OF MOLD ARE STARTING TO SPROUT.
B-BUT WHERE HAS THAT ENORMOUS MASS OF MOLD DISAPPEARED TO?
THE MOLD IS THERE, AS WELL.
SEE THAT PATCH OF A DIFFERENT COLOR THERE? SOME MOLD IS STILL HOLDING OUT...
I CAN'T SEE IT. IT ALL LOOKS THE SAME TO ME.
IT WON'T BE FORMING INTO ANOTHER HUGE MASS LIKE THAT AGAIN. NOW THAT IT'S EATEN THE OHMUS' FOREST AND MINGLED WITH THE OTHER FUNGI, IT'S SETTLED DOWN.
IT MAY LOOK AS IF THE FOREST HAS COMPLETELY DISAPPEARED NOW, BUT THAT'S BECAUSE IT'S PUTTING ALL ITS ENERGY INTO SETTING DOWN ROOTS.
THE MOLD IS BECOMING THE SEEDBED FOR THE VERY TREES IT HAS EATEN. NOW IT WILL BE EATEN ITSELF.
TO EAT AND TO BE EATEN... ONE AND THE SAME IN THIS WORLD. THE ENTIRE FOREST-- ONE LIFE.

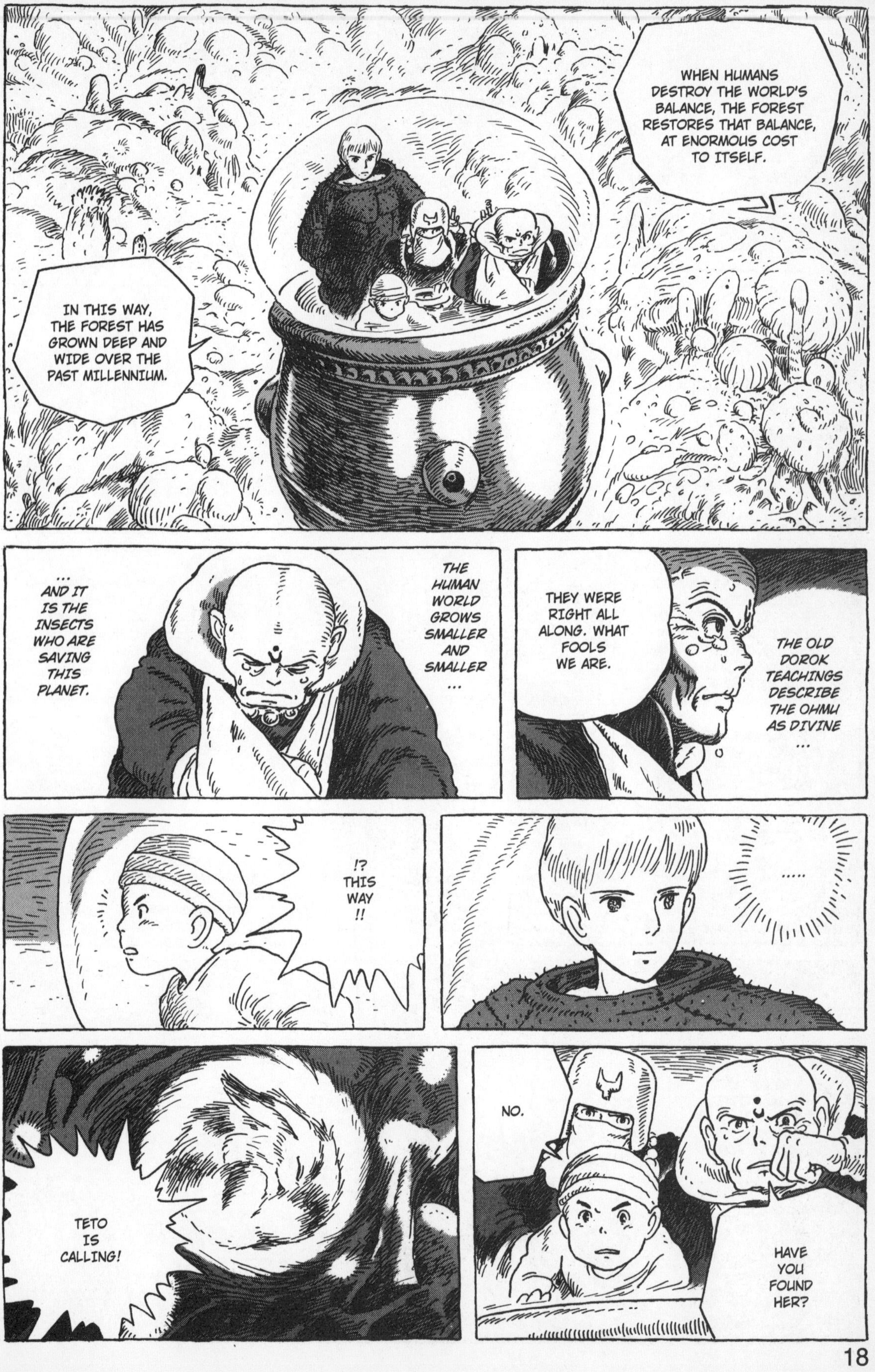
WHEN HUMANS DESTROY THE WORLD'S BALANCE, THE FOREST RESTORES THAT BALANCE, AT ENORMOUS COST TO ITSELF.
IN THIS WAY, THE FOREST HAS GROWN DEEP AND WIDE OVER THE PAST MILLENNIUM.
THE OLD DOROK TEACHINGS DESCRIBE THE OHMU AS DIVINE ...
THEY WERE RIGHT ALL ALONG. WHAT FOOLS WE ARE.
THE HUMAN WORLD GROWS SMALLER AND SMALLER ...
... AND IT IS THE INSECTS WHO ARE SAVING THIS PLANET.
.....
!? THIS WAY !!
HAVE YOU FOUND HER?
NO.
TETO IS CALLING!

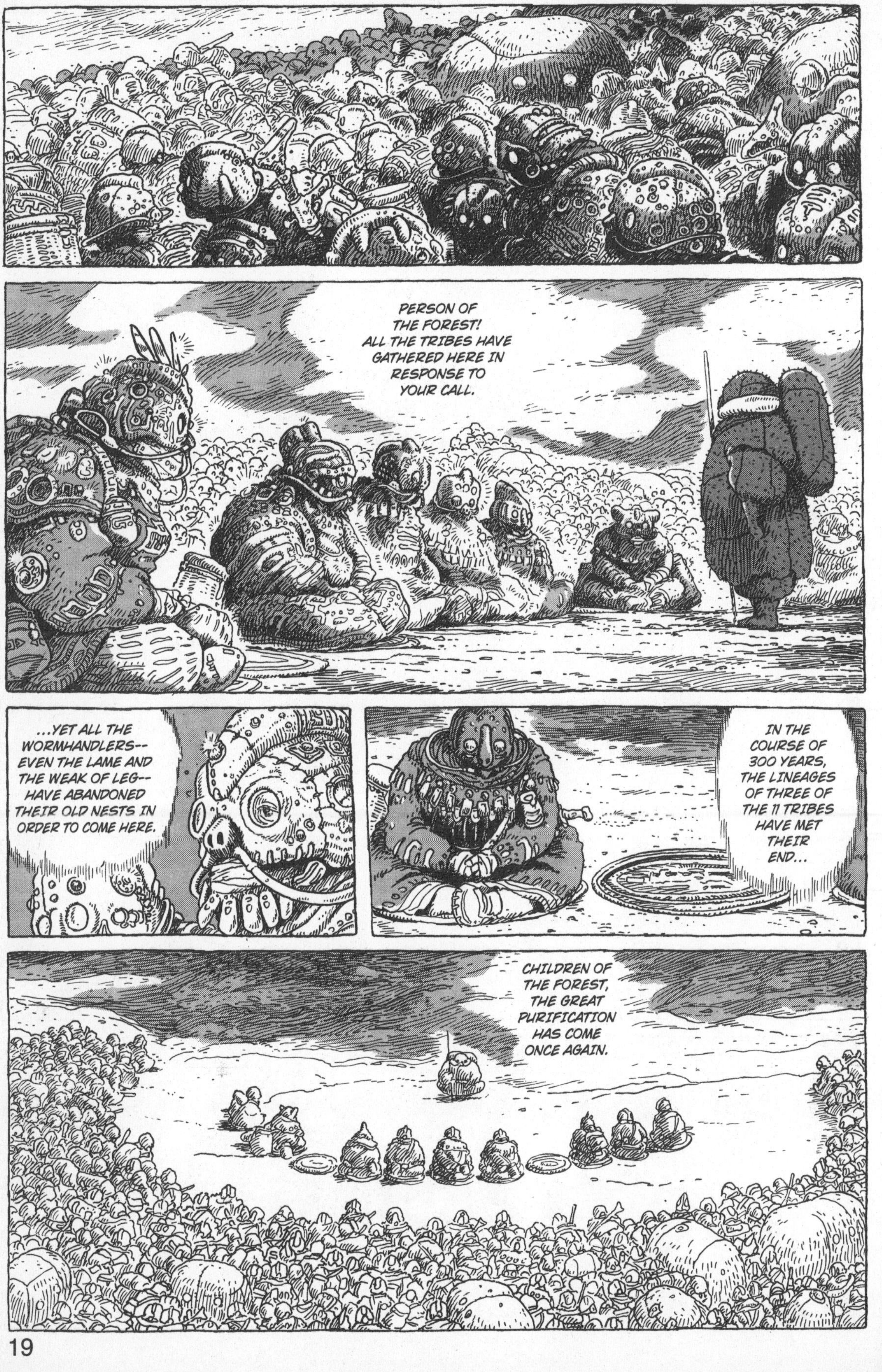
PERSON OF THE FOREST! ALL THE TRIBES HAVE GATHERED HERE IN RESPONSE TO YOUR CALL.
IN THE COURSE OF 300 YEARS, THE LINEAGES OF THREE OF THE 11 TRIBES HAVE MET THEIR END...
...YET ALL THE WORMHANDLERS-- EVEN THE LAME AND THE WEAK OF LEG-- HAVE ABANDONED THEIR OLD NESTS IN ORDER TO COME HERE.
CHILDREN OF THE FOREST, THE GREAT PURIFICATION HAS COME ONCE AGAIN.

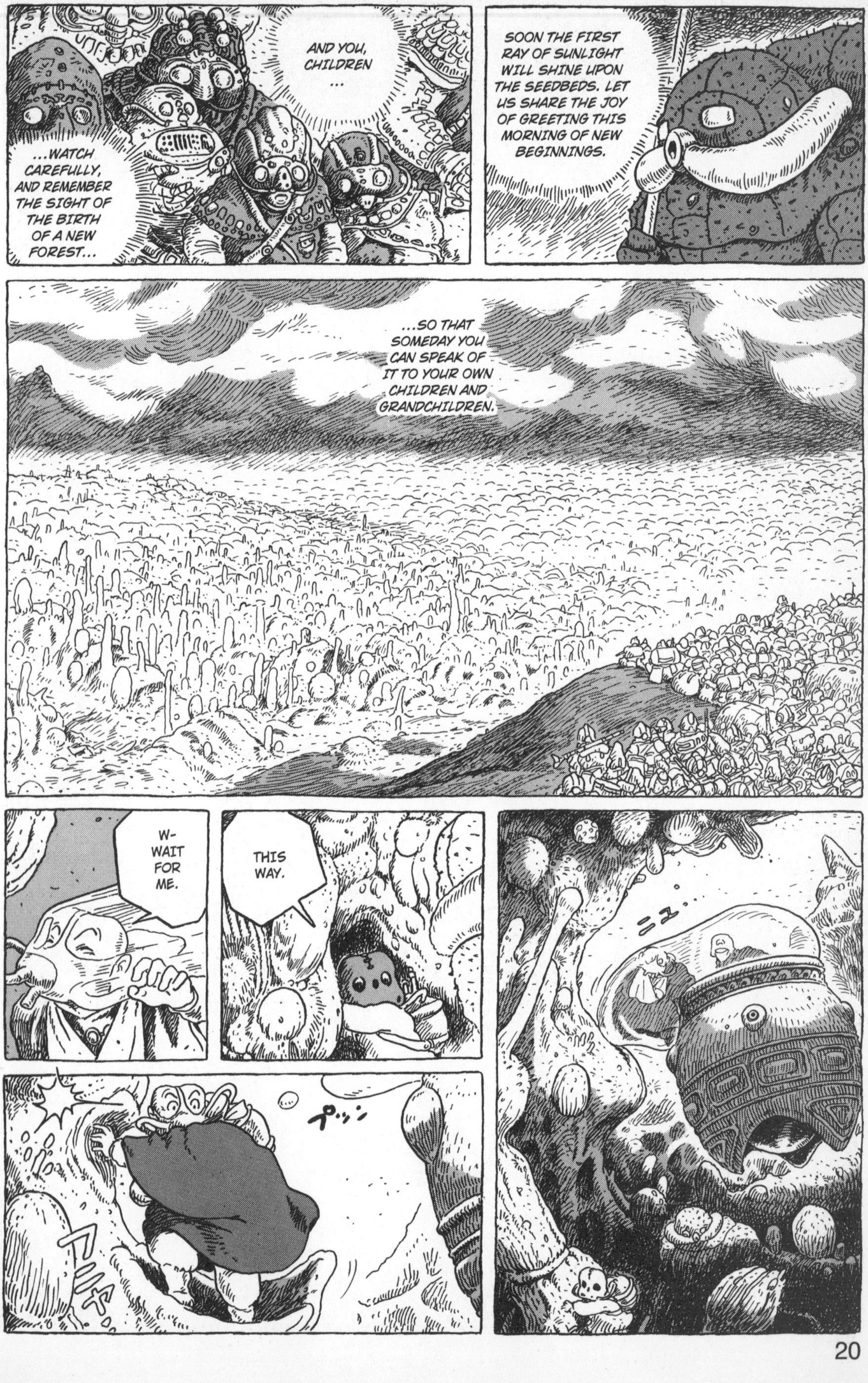
SOON THE FIRST RAY OF SUNLIGHT WILL SHINE UPON THE SEEDBEDS. LET US SHARE THE JOY OF GREETING THIS MORNING OF NEW BEGINNINGS.
AND YOU, CHILDREN ...
...WATCH CAREFULLY, AND REMEMBER THE SIGHT OF THE BIRTH OF A NEW FOREST...
...SO THAT SOMEDAY YOU CAN SPEAK OF IT TO YOUR OWN CHILDREN AND GRANDCHILDREN.
THIS WAY.
W-WAIT FOR ME.

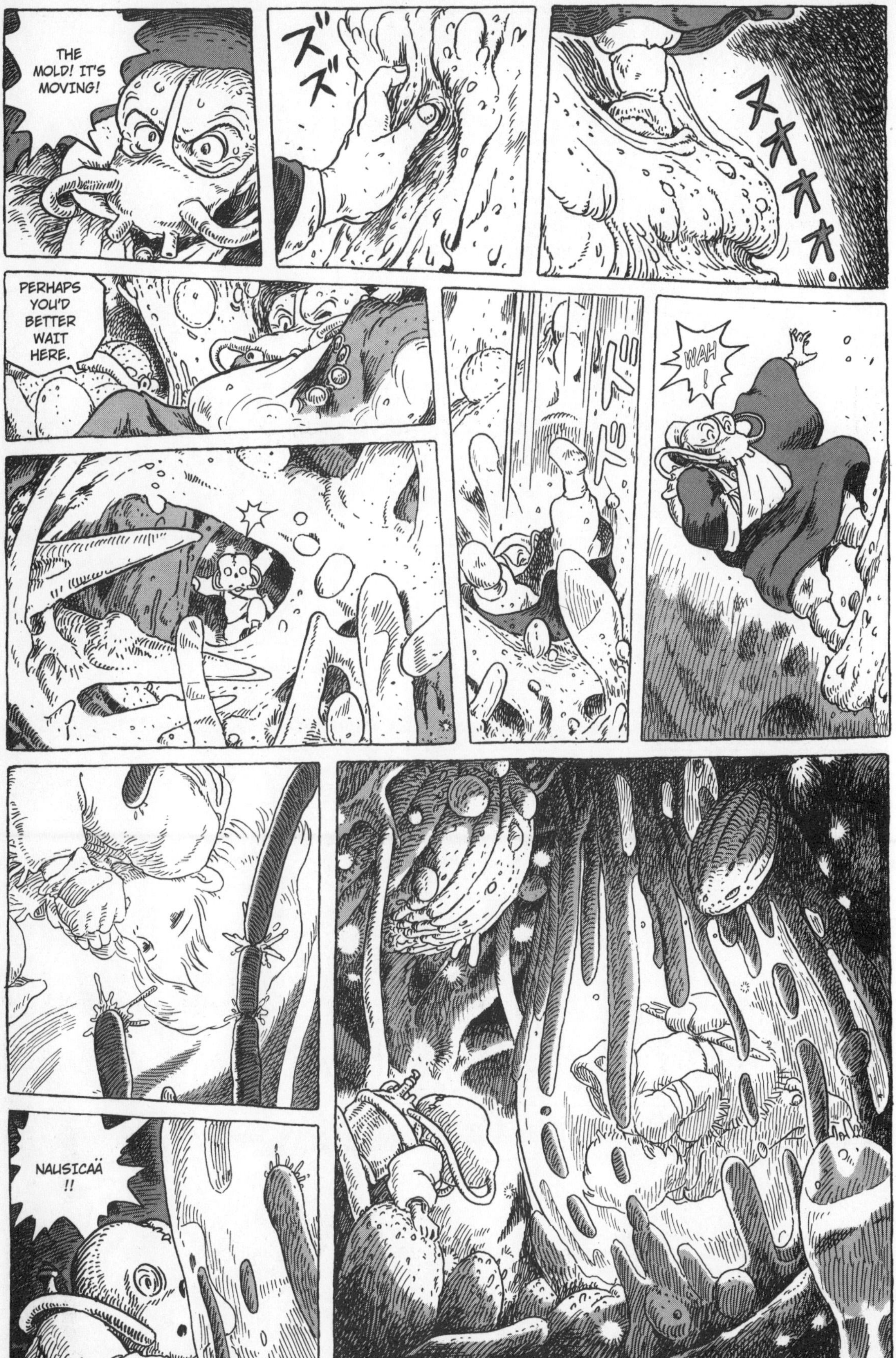
ヌォォォォォ
ズズ
THE MOLD! IT'S MOVING!
WAH!
ドド
PERHAPS YOU'D BETTER WAIT HERE.
NAUSICAÄ!!

UNH-H-H!

NAUSICAÄ!!

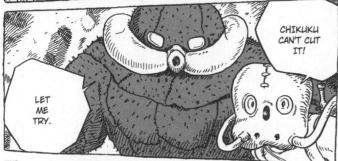

CHIKUKU CAN'T CUT IT!

LET ME TRY.

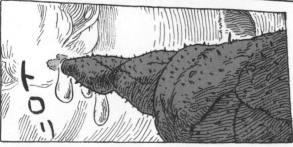

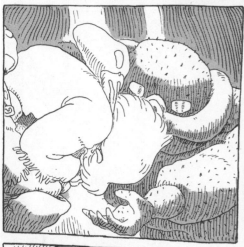

22

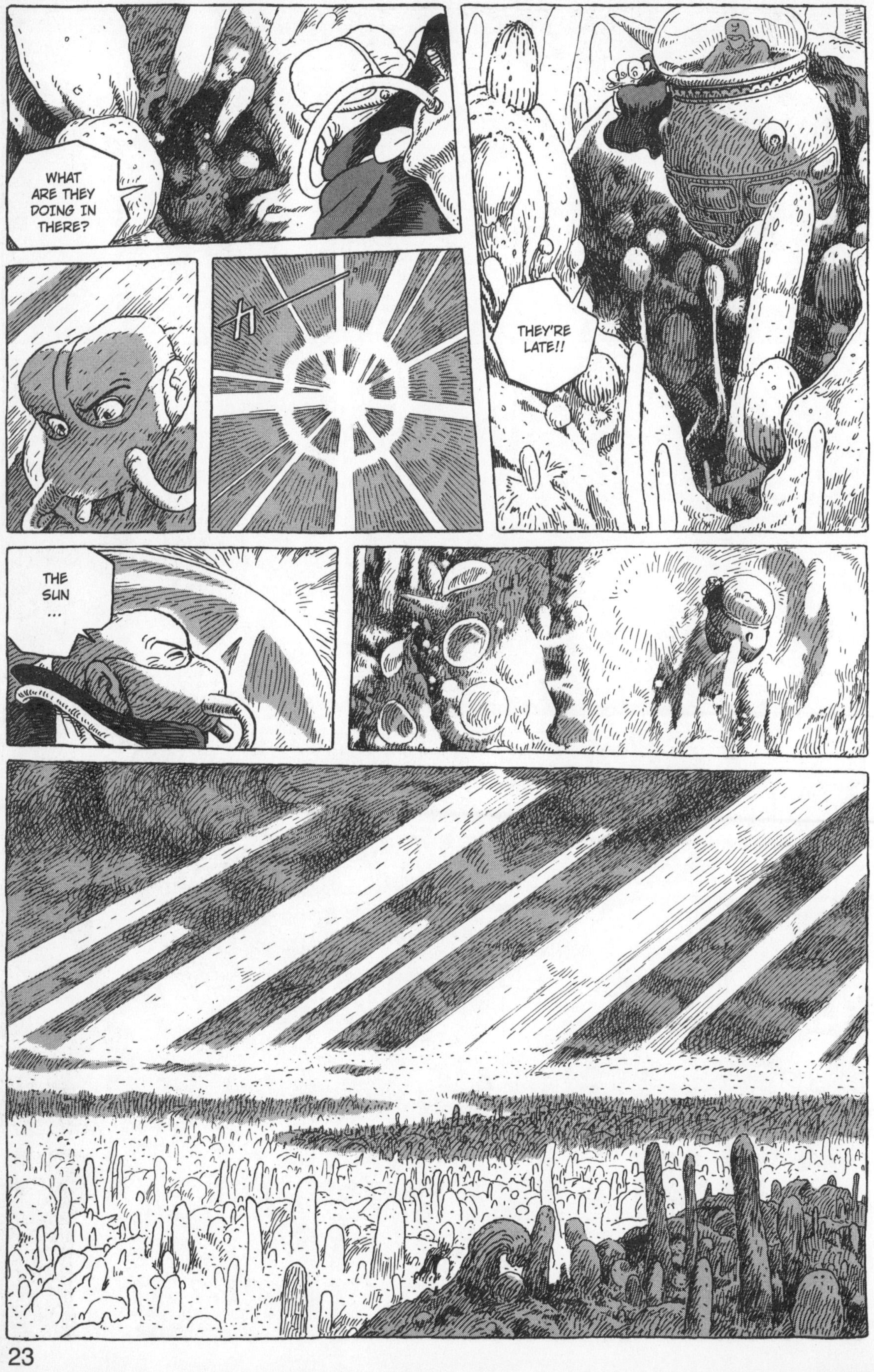
THEY'RE LATE!!
WHAT ARE THEY DOING IN THERE?
カ
THE SUN ...

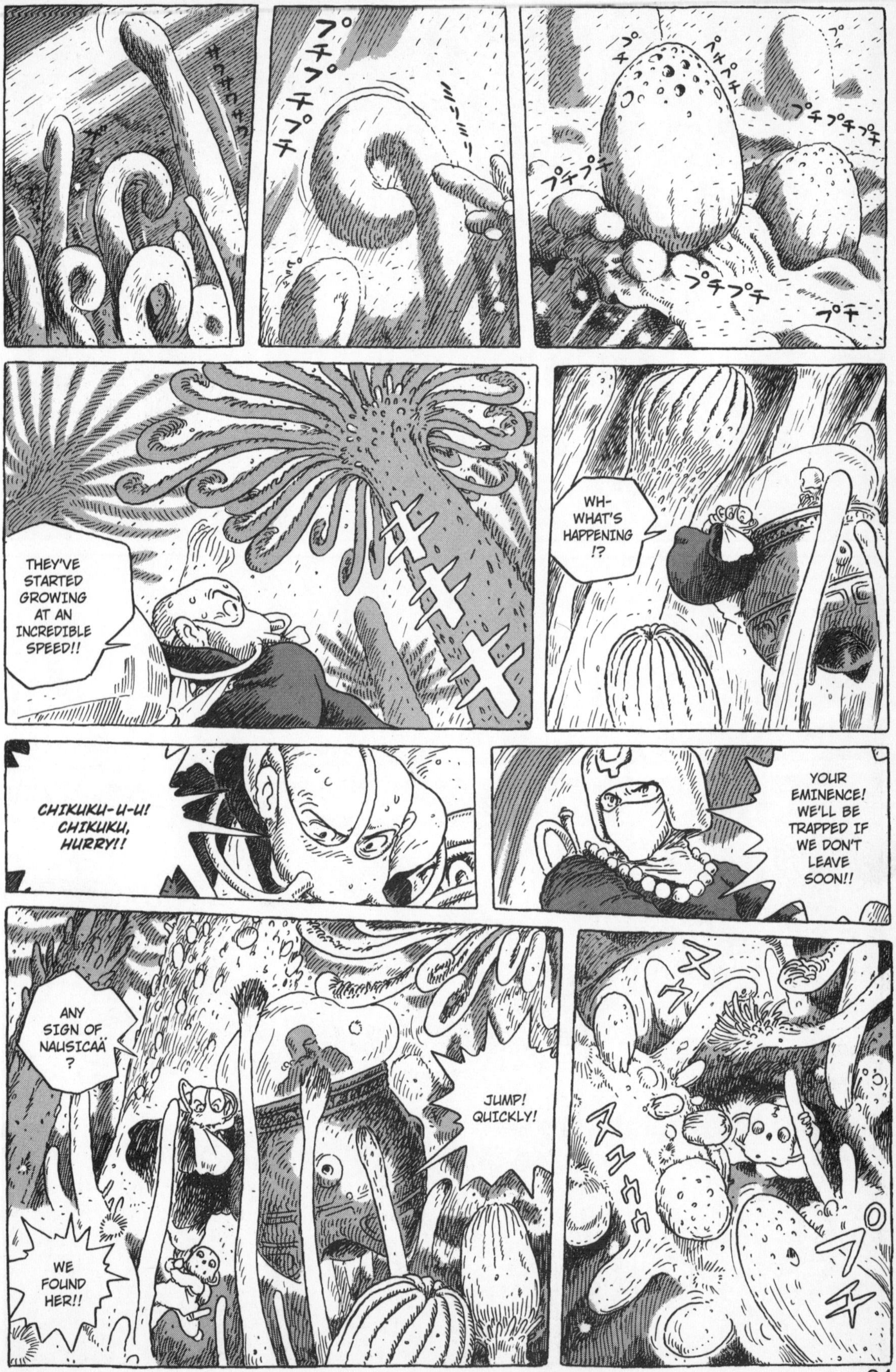
プチプチ
プチプチプチプチ
プチプチ
プチプチ
プチ
プチプチプチプチ
ミリミリ
サワサワサワ
WH- WHAT'S HAPPENING !?
THEY'VE STARTED GROWING AT AN INCREDIBLE SPEED!!
YOUR EMINENCE! WE'LL BE TRAPPED IF WE DON'T LEAVE SOON!!
CHIKUKU-U-U! CHIKUKU, HURRY!!
プチ
ANY SIGN OF NAUSICAÄ?
JUMP! QUICKLY!
WE FOUND HER!!

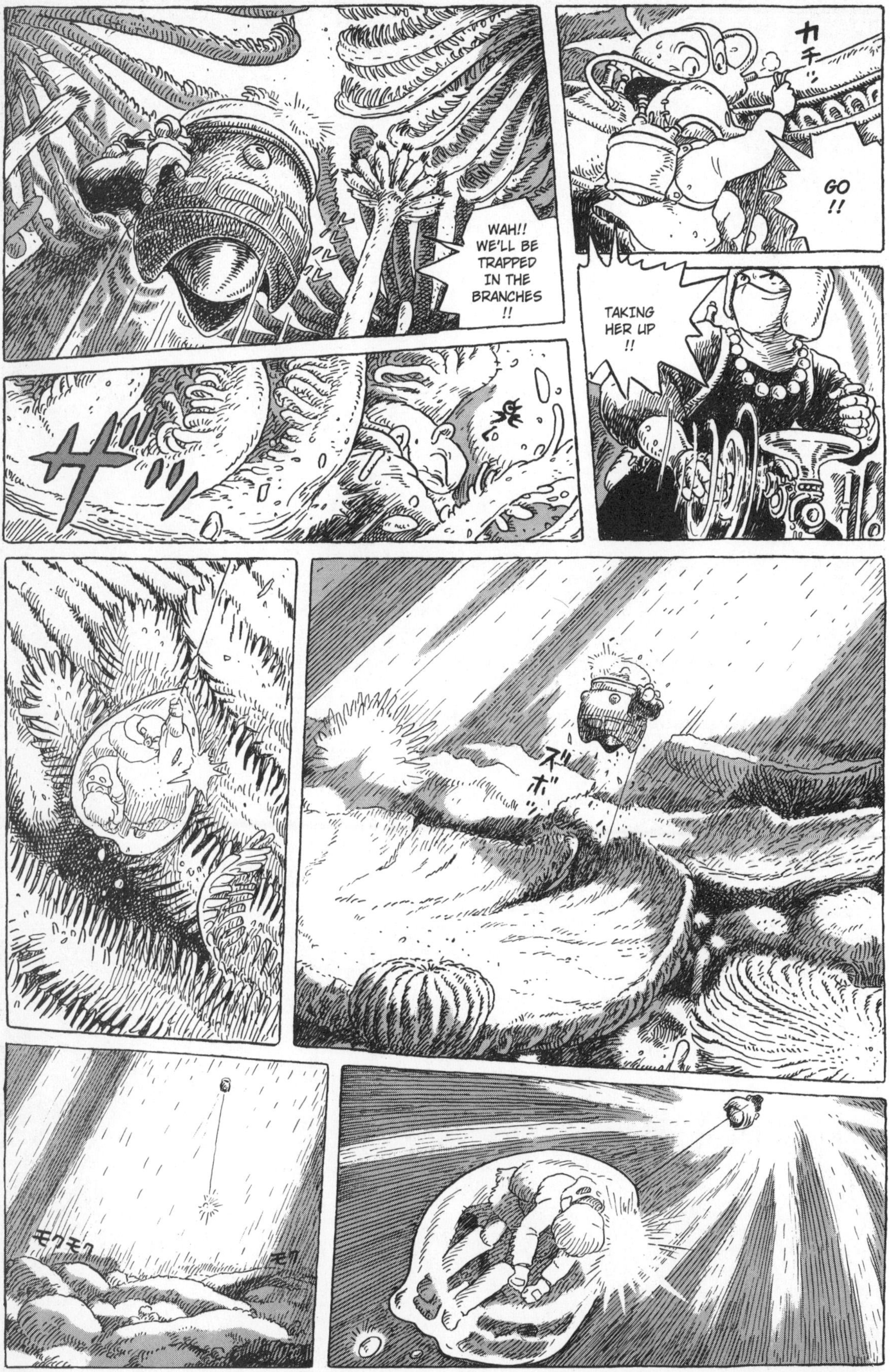
カチッ
GO!!
TAKING HER UP!!
WAH!! WE'LL BE TRAPPED IN THE BRANCHES!!
ズボッ
モク
モクモク

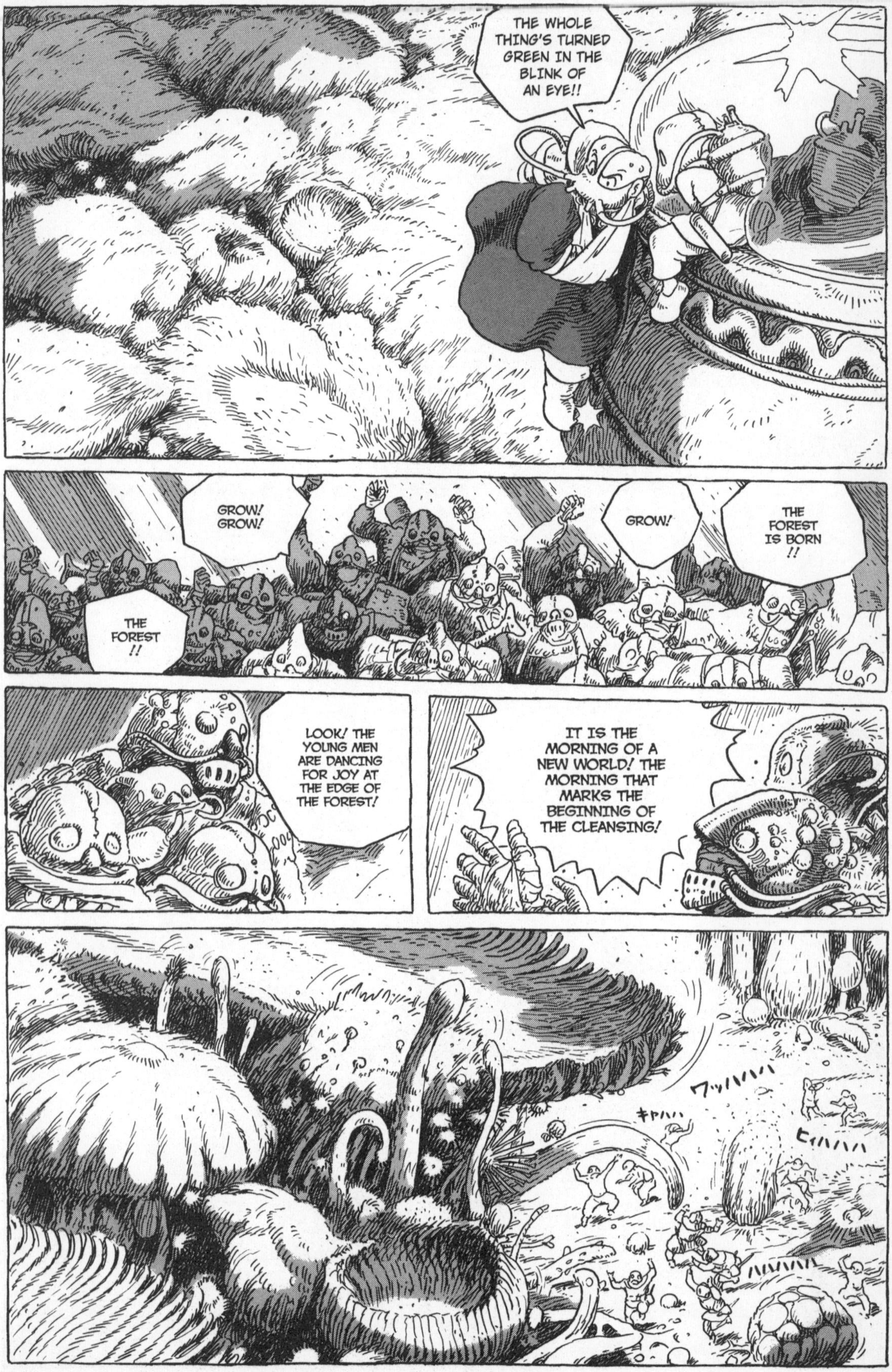
THE WHOLE THING'S TURNED GREEN IN THE BLINK OF AN EYE!!
THE FOREST IS BORN!!
GROW!
GROW! GROW!
THE FOREST!!
IT IS THE MORNING OF A NEW WORLD! THE MORNING THAT MARKS THE BEGINNING OF THE CLEANSING!
LOOK! THE YOUNG MEN ARE DANCING FOR JOY AT THE EDGE OF THE FOREST!
ワッハハハ
ヒィハハハ
キャハハ
ハハハハハ

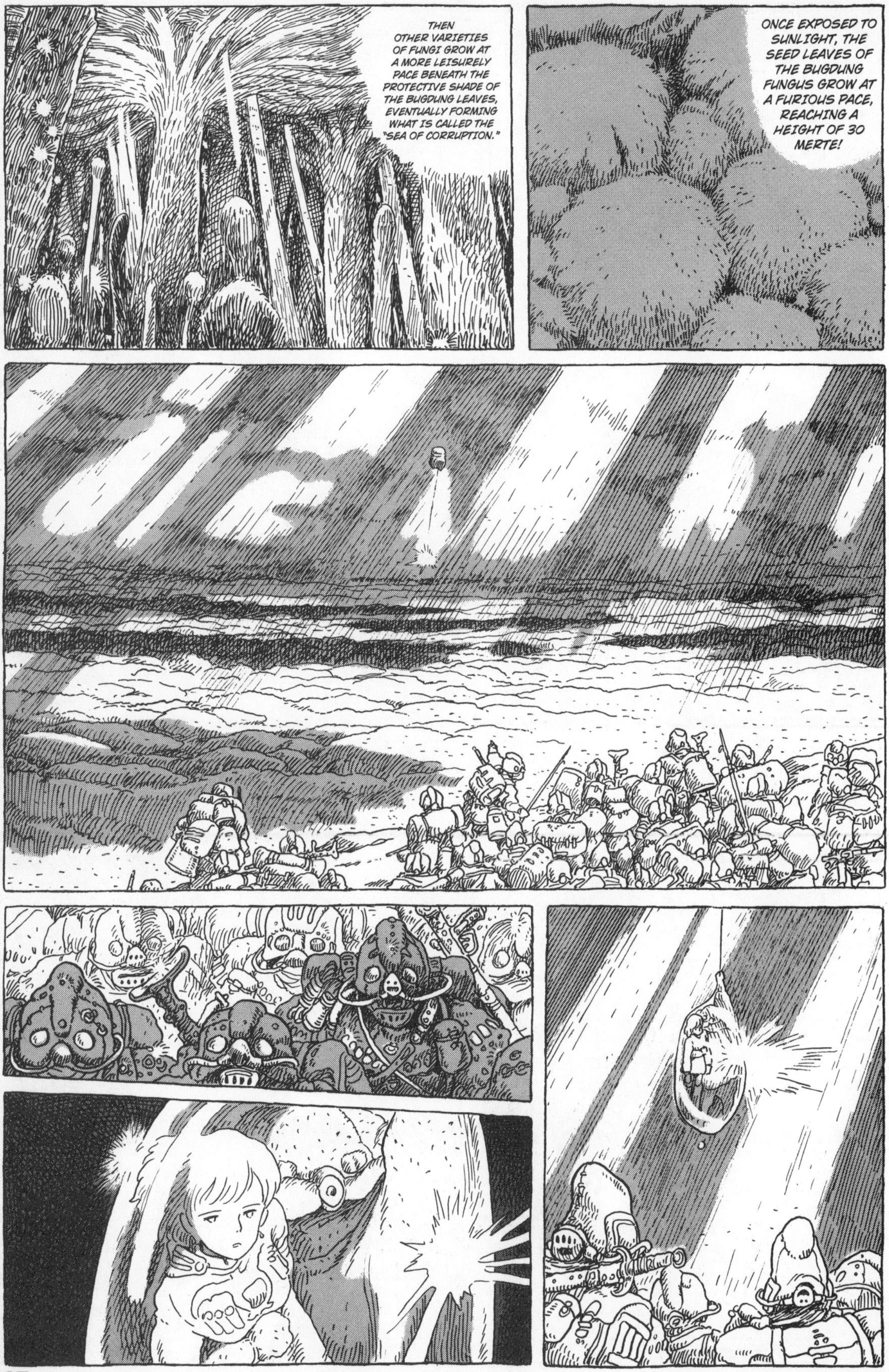
ONCE EXPOSED TO SUNLIGHT, THE SEED LEAVES OF THE BUGDUNG FUNGUS GROW AT A FURIOUS PACE, REACHING A HEIGHT OF 30 MERTE!
THEN OTHER VARIETIES OF FUNGI GROW AT A MORE LEISURELY PACE BENEATH THE PROTECTIVE SHADE OF THE BUGDUNG LEAVES, EVENTUALLY FORMING WHAT IS CALLED THE "SEA OF CORRUPTION."

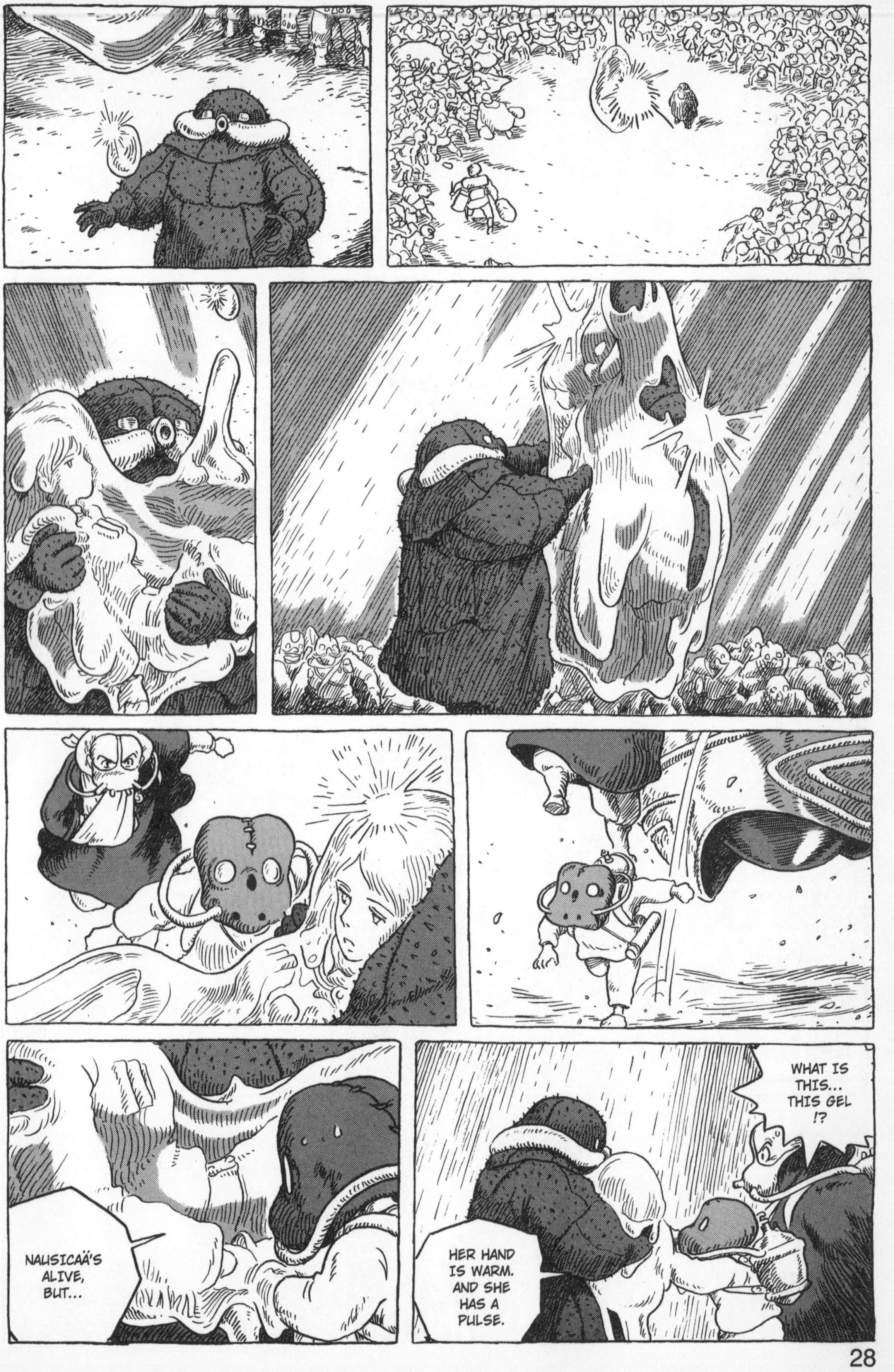
WHAT IS THIS... THIS GEL !?
HER HAND IS WARM. AND SHE HAS A PULSE.
NAUSICAÄ'S ALIVE, BUT...

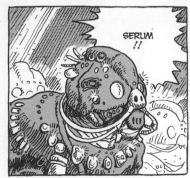

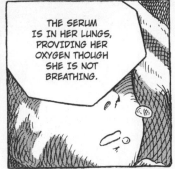

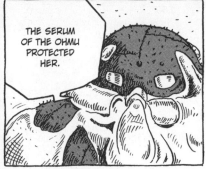

THE SERUM OF THE OHMU PROTECTED HER.
THE SERUM IS IN HER LUNGS, PROVIDING HER OXYGEN THOUGH SHE IS NOT BREATHING.
SERUM !!
CHIKUKU KNOWS. NAUSICAÄ TRIED TO HELP THE OHMU CALM THE MOLD.
SHE WANTED TO BECOME PART OF THE FOREST ALONG WITH THE OHMU.
SO THE OHMU TOOK HER AWAY...
NAUSICAÄ IS ALIVE, BUT SHE'S NOT HERE.
CHIKUKU IS SAD.
NO, CHIKUKU. THE OHMU WRAPPED NAUSICAÄ IN SERUM PRECISELY BECAUSE THEY DID **NOT** WANT TO TAKE HER AWAY.
S-SO THIS IS SERUM ...
THIS IS THE FIRST I'VE EVER SEEN IT. WHAT A BLESS'D DAY!
WE BEG YOU, PLEASE GIVE THIS HONORED PERSON TO US. WE SHALL MAKE HER THE GUARDIAN DEITY OF OUR PEOPLE.
PEOPLE OF THE FOREST, THIS HONORED PERSON IS THE FOREST IN HUMAN FORM. SHE STANDS AT THE CENTER OF BOTH WORLDS.

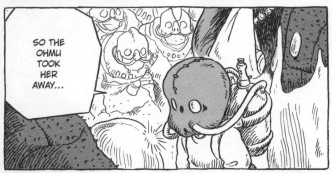

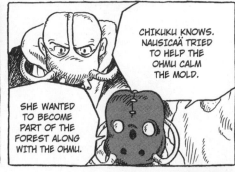

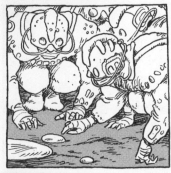

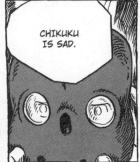

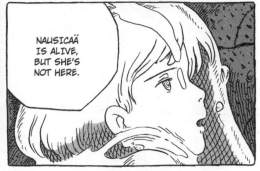

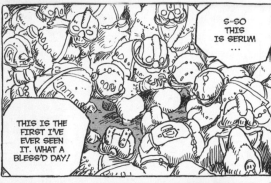

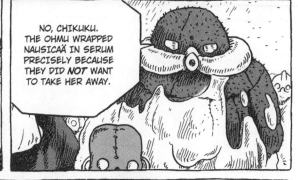

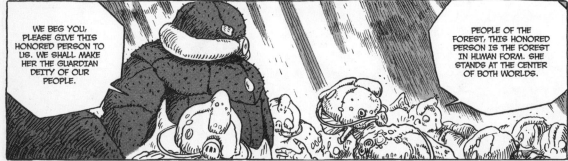

WE WHO HAVE LONG BEEN DESPISED AS AN OUTCAST PEOPLE AT LAST HAVE A RAY OF HOPE!
THEY SAY THAT WITH THE SERUM ONE CAN LIVE WITHOUT THESE CURSED MASKS!!
CAN IT BE THAT THE PAINFUL CENTURIES WE'VE SPENT, DENIED OUR OWN DEITY, HAVE FINALLY COME TO AN END!?
GIVE HER TO US!
PEOPLE OF THE FOREST! GIVE HER TO US!!
AH! SHE'S SMILING IN THE MIDST OF THIS MIASMA... AND WITHOUT A MASK!
BEAUTIFUL. OUR DEITY IS BEAUTIFUL!
LET ME SEE!
CHARUKA, THIS IS DANGEROUS. GET NAUSICAÄ'S WINGS, QUICKLY!!
LET US SEE HER!
EASY! DON'T PUSH!
BY THE BUILDING TO YOUR LEFT.
I-- SEE THEM!
GIVE US THE SERUM!!
MOVE ASIDE! LET ME THROUGH!!

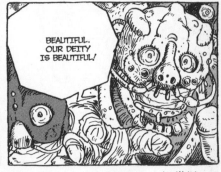

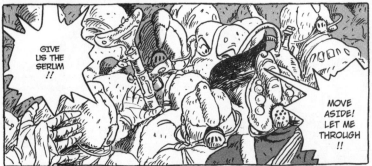

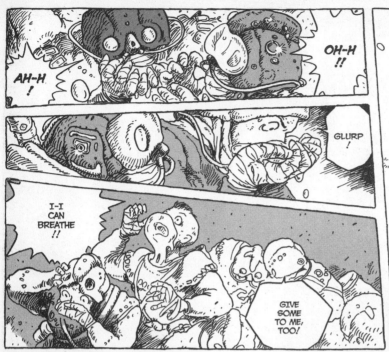

SERUM!!
OH-H!!
AH-H!
GLURP!
I-I CAN BREATHE!!
GIVE SOME TO ME, TOO!
NO!! WHERE ARE YOU TAKING HER!?
GIVE US MORE SERUM!!
GIVE US BACK OUR DEITY!!
HEAR ME, CHILDREN OF THE FOREST.
THIS GIRL TRIED TO FOLLOW THE OHMU WHEN THEY TURNED THEMSELVES TO FOREST IN ORDER TO SAVE THE MOLD.
THE OHMU CHERISHED HER LIFE, AND WRAPPED HER IN SERUM TO KEEP HER FROM BECOMING FOREST. BUT THEY OPENED THEIR HEART TO HER.
I DO NOT KNOW WHAT THIS GIRL SAW INSIDE THE OHMU AS SHE LAY WRAPPED IN SERUM.
THERE ARE THOSE WHO HAVE ACHIEVED SYMPATHY WITH THE OHMU, BUT NONE HAVE EVER PEERED INTO THE ABYSS THAT IS THE HEART OF THE OHMU.

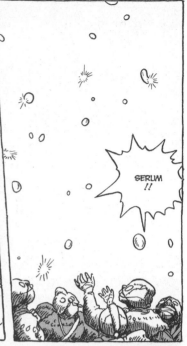

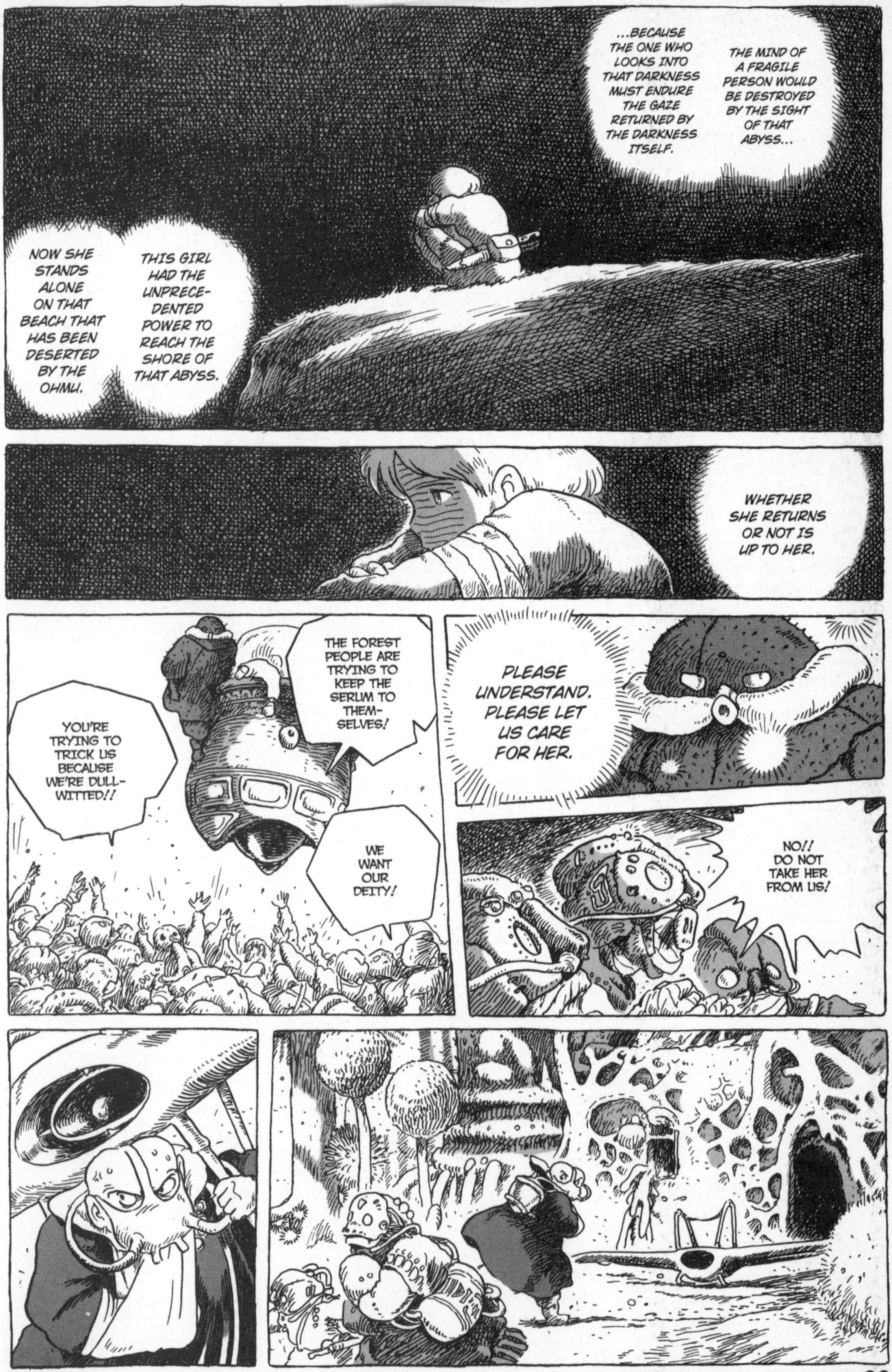

THE MIND OF A FRAGILE PERSON WOULD BE DESTROYED BY THE SIGHT OF THAT ABYSS...
...BECAUSE THE ONE WHO LOOKS INTO THAT DARKNESS MUST ENDURE THE GAZE RETURNED BY THE DARKNESS ITSELF.
THIS GIRL HAD THE UNPRECE-DENTED POWER TO REACH THE SHORE OF THAT ABYSS.
NOW SHE STANDS ALONE ON THAT BEACH THAT HAS BEEN DESERTED BY THE OHMU.
WHETHER SHE RETURNS OR NOT IS UP TO HER.
PLEASE UNDERSTAND. PLEASE LET US CARE FOR HER.
NO!! DO NOT TAKE HER FROM US!
THE FOREST PEOPLE ARE TRYING TO KEEP THE SERUM TO THEM-SELVES!
YOU'RE TRYING TO TRICK US BECAUSE WE'RE DULL-WITTED!!
WE WANT OUR DEITY!

WE'RE NOT AFRAID OF THE FOREST PEOPLE!!

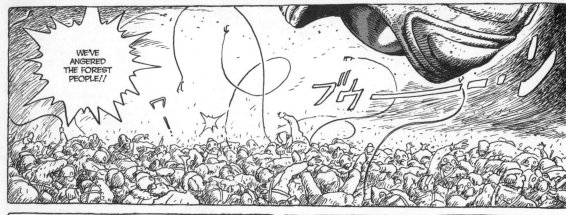

WE'VE ANGERED THE FOREST PEOPLE!!

HEY !!

TH-THEY TOOK HER AWAY...

WH-WHAT WILL WE DO!? THEY'VE TAKEN HER AWAY!

OUCH.

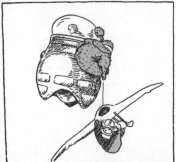

ILILILIL

WE WERE CARELESS. WE SHOULDN'T HAVE SHOWN HER TO THEM, GIVEN THEM HOPE.

POOR SOULS. THEIR KNOWLEDGE OF A BETTER WORLD-- IT CAN ONLY CAUSE THEM PAIN.

ルルル

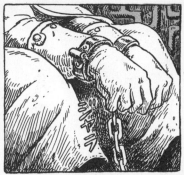

TSST!
TSST!
TSST!

STUFF 'EM
UP GOOD.
THEY'VE A
BIG BATTLE
AHEAD OF 'EM!

TSST!
TSST!

35

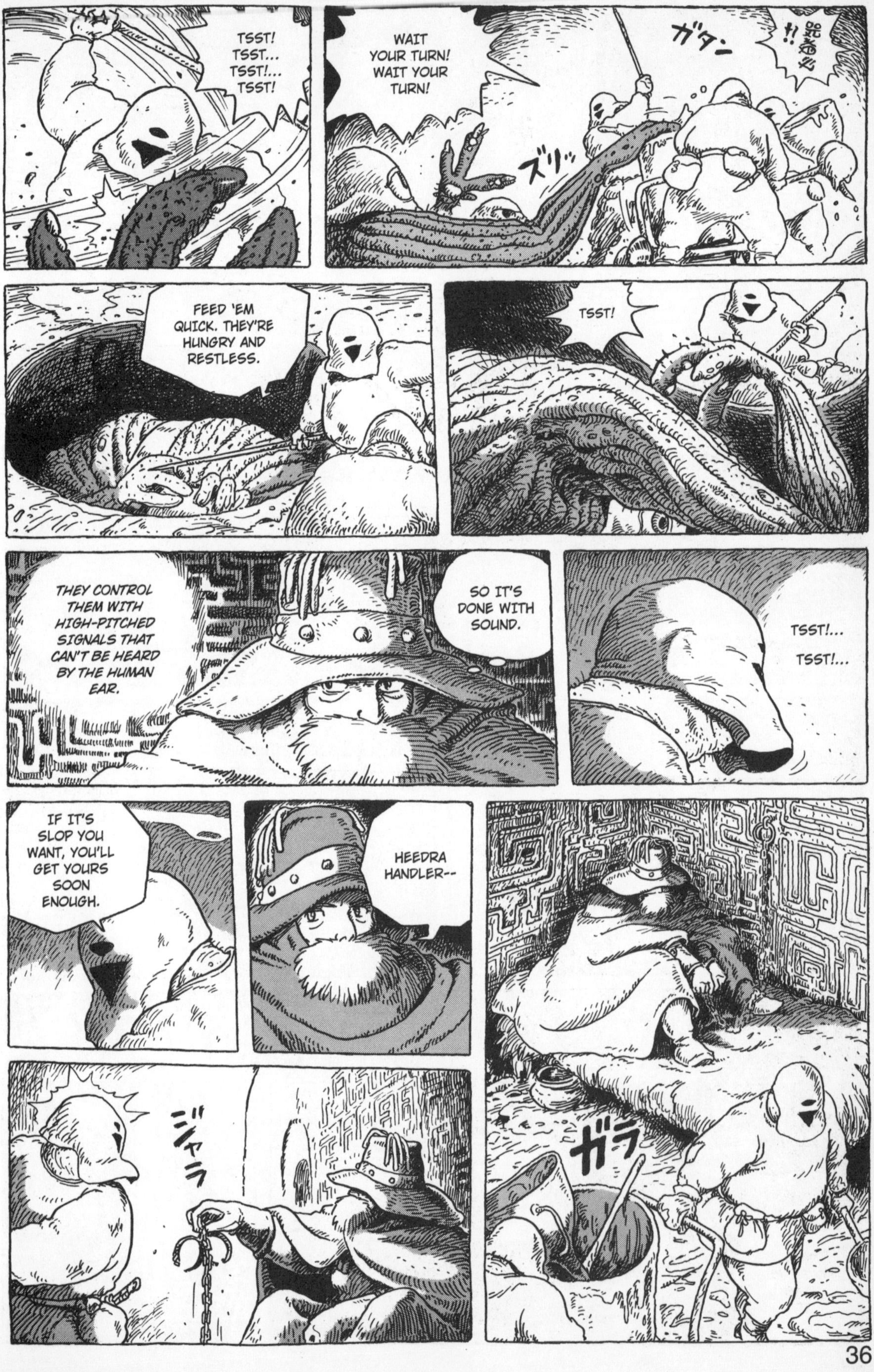
WAIT YOUR TURN! WAIT YOUR TURN!
ガタン
ズリッ
TSST! TSST!... TSST!... TSST!
TSST!
FEED 'EM QUICK. THEY'RE HUNGRY AND RESTLESS.
TSST!... TSST!...
SO IT'S DONE WITH SOUND.
THEY CONTROL THEM WITH HIGH-PITCHED SIGNALS THAT CAN'T BE HEARD BY THE HUMAN EAR.
ガラ
HEEDRA HANDLER--
IF IT'S SLOP YOU WANT, YOU'LL GET YOURS SOON ENOUGH.
ジャラ

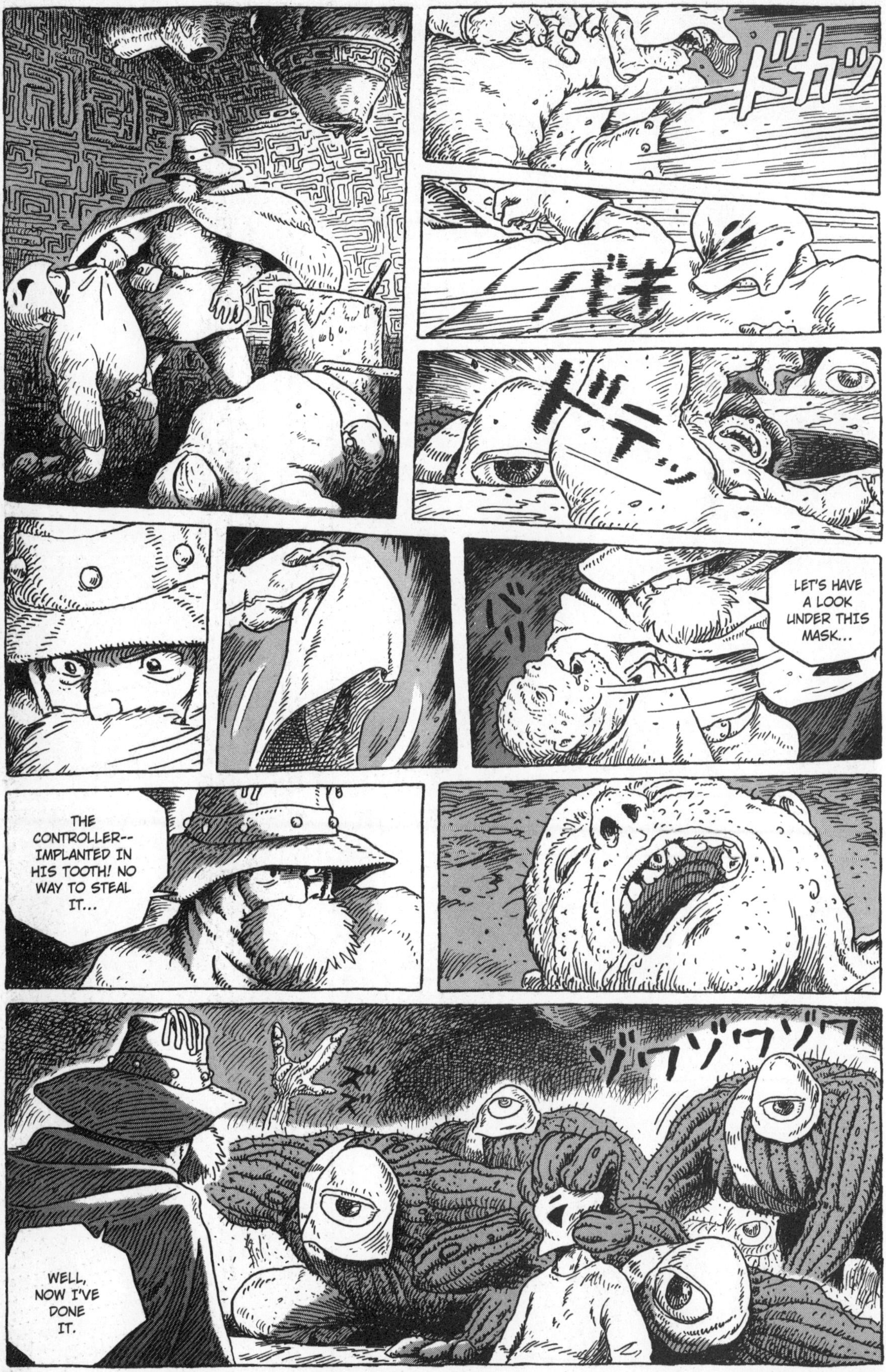
ドカッ
バキ
バリ
LET'S HAVE A LOOK UNDER THIS MASK...
THE CONTROLLER--IMPLANTED IN HIS TOOTH! NO WAY TO STEAL IT...
ゾワゾワゾワ
ズズ
WELL, NOW I'VE DONE IT.

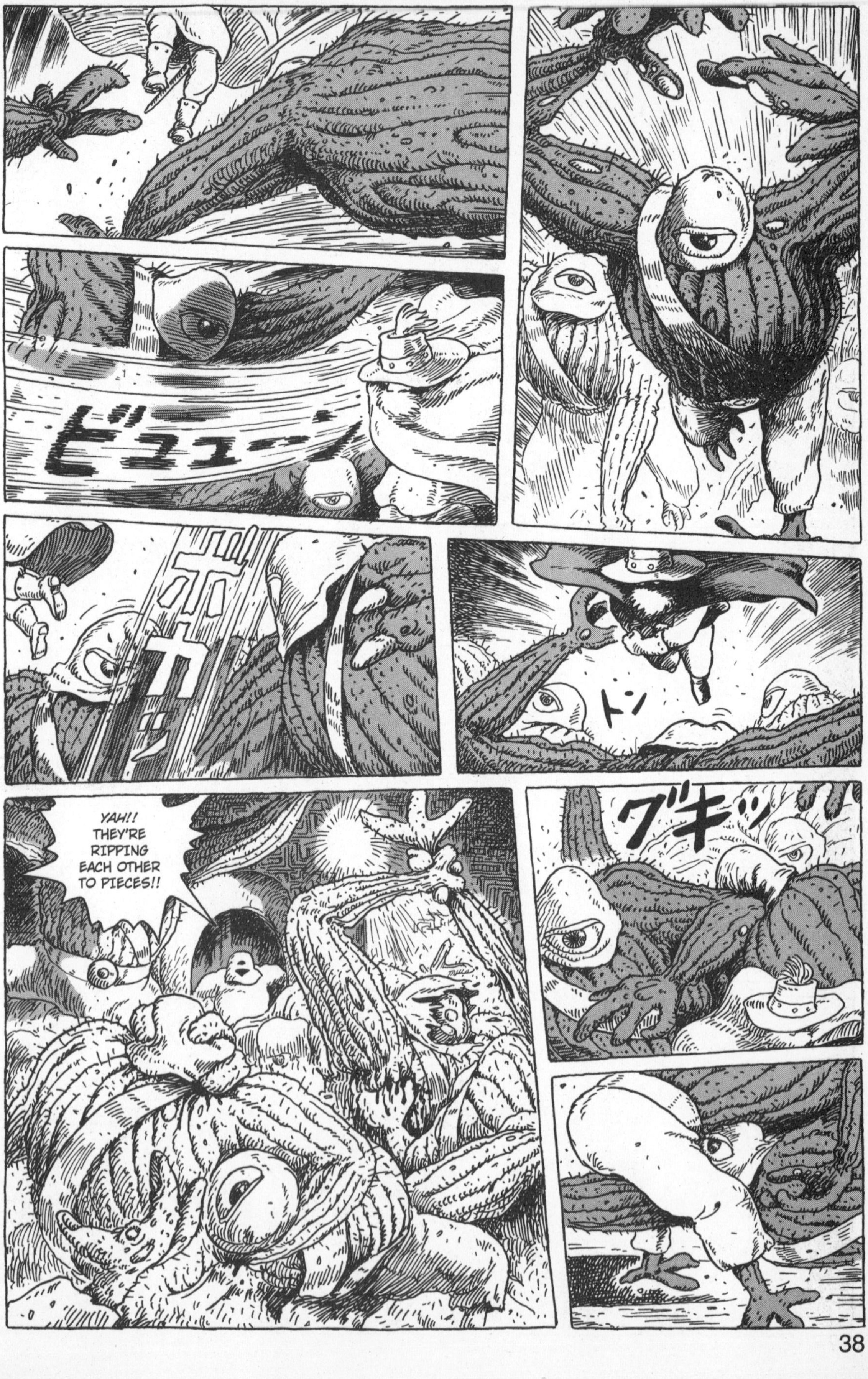
ビュユーン
トン
ボカッ
グキッ
YAH!! THEY'RE RIPPING EACH OTHER TO PIECES!!

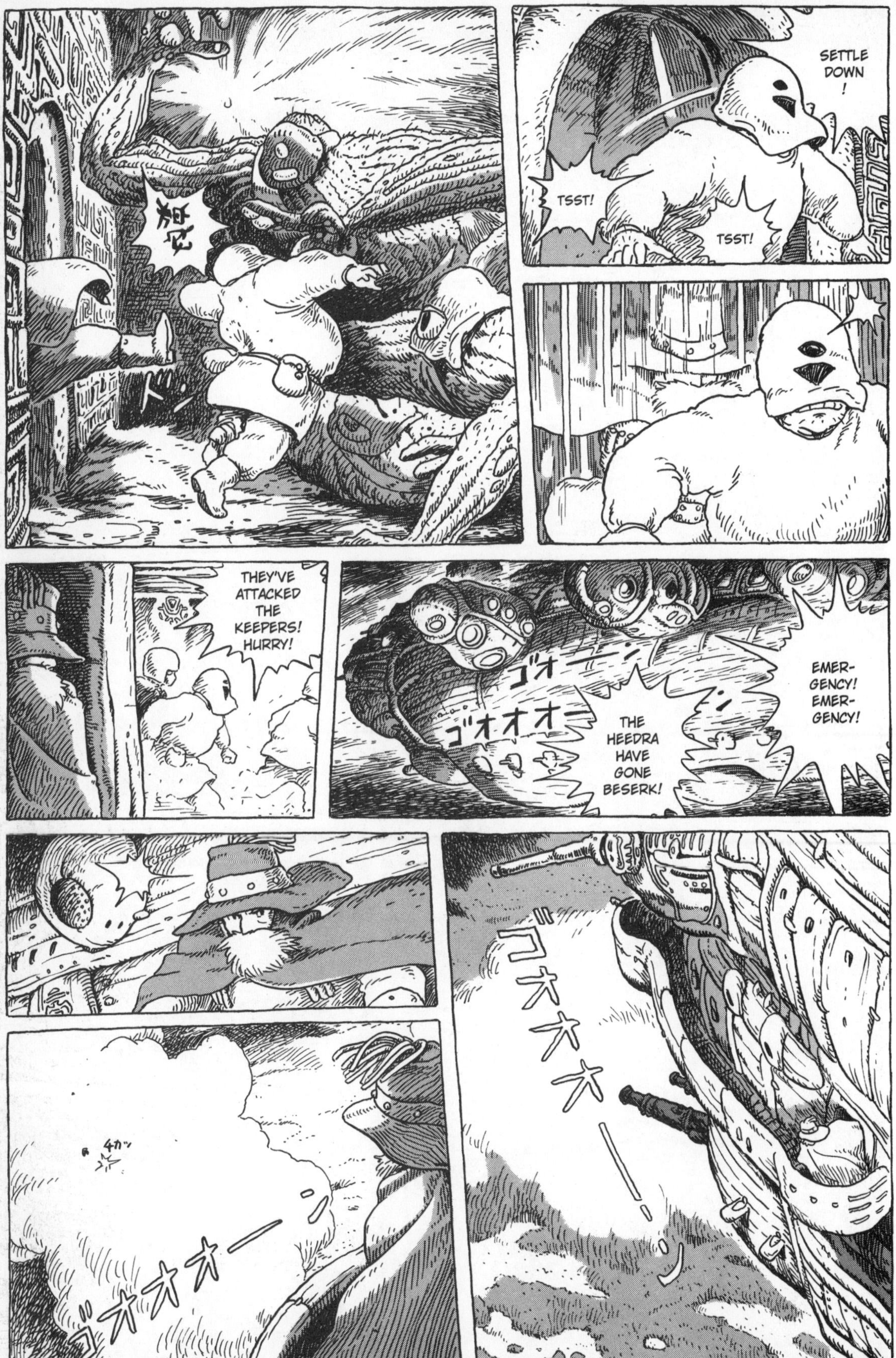
SETTLE DOWN!
TSST!
TSST!
THE HEEDRA HAVE GONE BESERK!
EMERGENCY! EMERGENCY!
THEY'VE ATTACKED THE KEEPERS! HURRY!

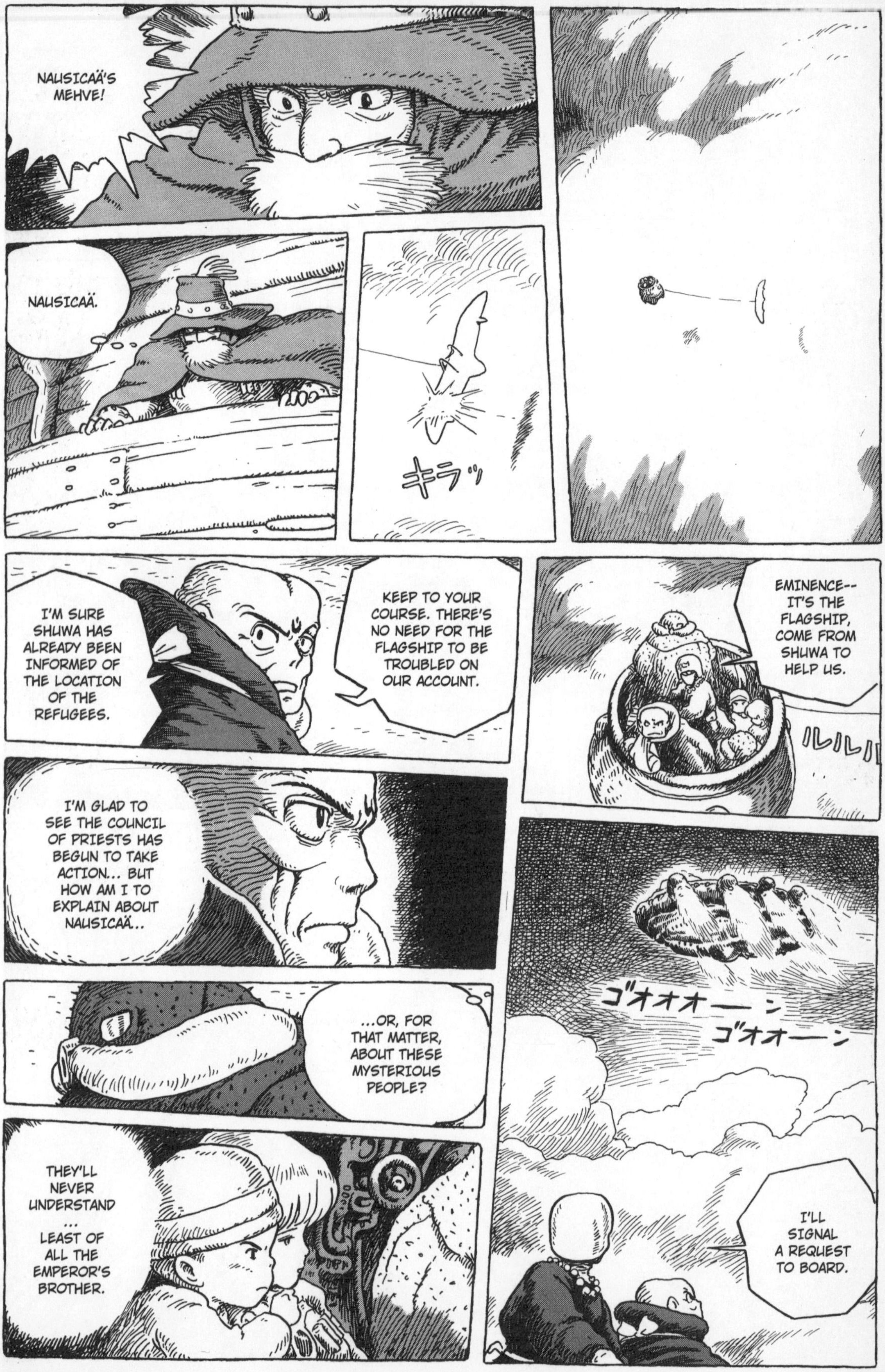

NAUSICAÄ'S MEHVE!
キラッ
NAUSICAÄ.
EMINENCE-- IT'S THE FLAGSHIP, COME FROM SHUWA TO HELP US.
ルルル
ゴオオオーン
ゴオオーン
I'LL SIGNAL A REQUEST TO BOARD.
KEEP TO YOUR COURSE. THERE'S NO NEED FOR THE FLAGSHIP TO BE TROUBLED ON OUR ACCOUNT.
I'M SURE SHUWA HAS ALREADY BEEN INFORMED OF THE LOCATION OF THE REFUGEES.
I'M GLAD TO SEE THE COUNCIL OF PRIESTS HAS BEGUN TO TAKE ACTION... BUT HOW AM I TO EXPLAIN ABOUT NAUSICAÄ...
...OR, FOR THAT MATTER, ABOUT THESE MYSTERIOUS PEOPLE?
THEY'LL NEVER UNDERSTAND ... LEAST OF ALL THE EMPEROR'S BROTHER.

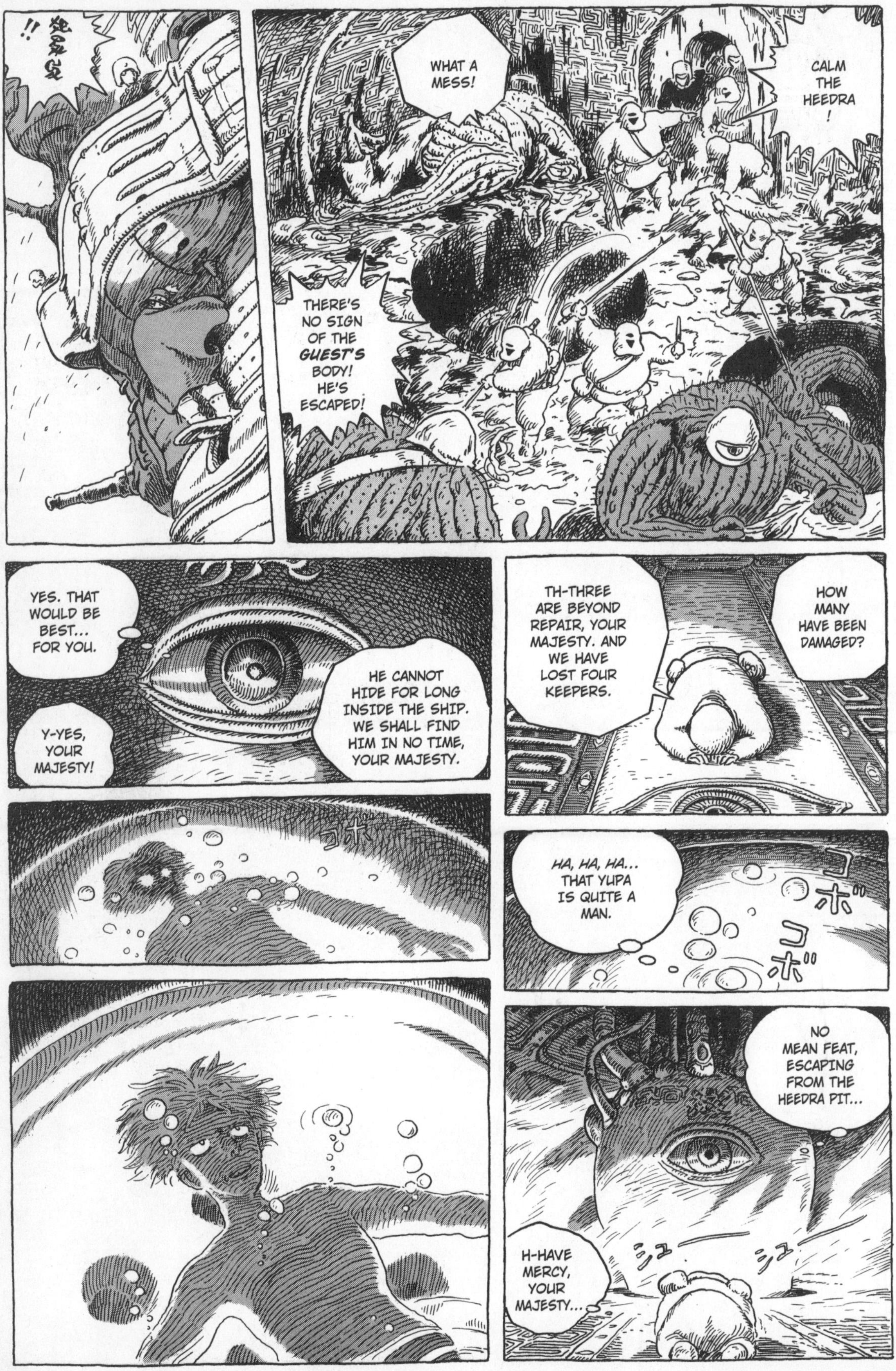
CALM THE HEEDRA!
WHAT A MESS!
THERE'S NO SIGN OF THE GUEST'S BODY! HE'S ESCAPED!
HOW MANY HAVE BEEN DAMAGED?
TH-THREE ARE BEYOND REPAIR, YOUR MAJESTY. AND WE HAVE LOST FOUR KEEPERS.
HE CANNOT HIDE FOR LONG INSIDE THE SHIP. WE SHALL FIND HIM IN NO TIME, YOUR MAJESTY.
YES. THAT WOULD BE BEST... FOR YOU.
Y-YES, YOUR MAJESTY!
HA, HA, HA... THAT YUPA IS QUITE A MAN.
NO MEAN FEAT, ESCAPING FROM THE HEEDRA PIT...
H-HAVE MERCY, YOUR MAJESTY...

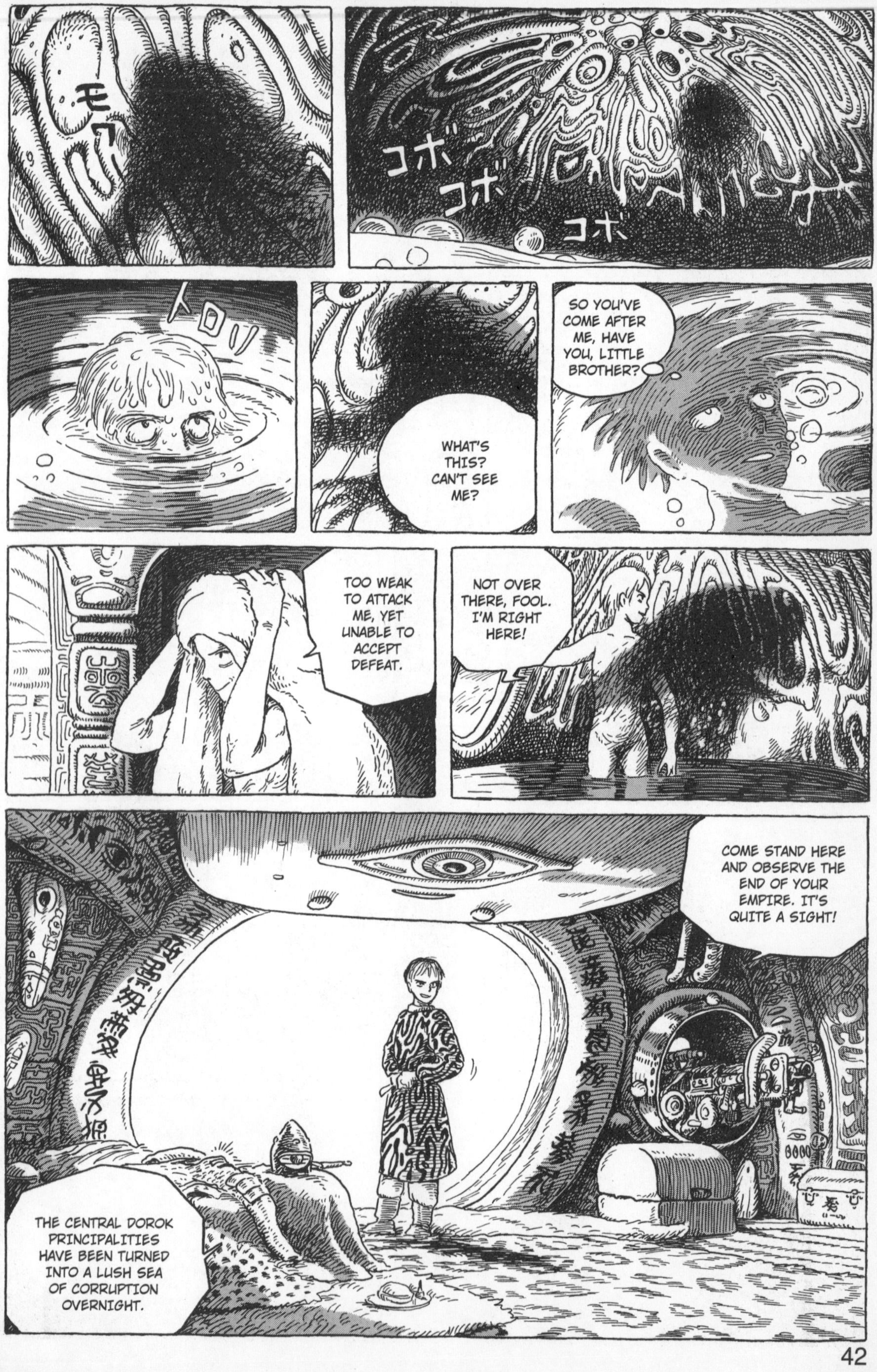
コボ
コボ
コボ
モワ
SO YOU'VE COME AFTER ME, HAVE YOU, LITTLE BROTHER?
WHAT'S THIS? CAN'T SEE ME?
トロリ
NOT OVER THERE, FOOL. I'M RIGHT HERE!
TOO WEAK TO ATTACK ME, YET UNABLE TO ACCEPT DEFEAT.
COME STAND HERE AND OBSERVE THE END OF YOUR EMPIRE. IT'S QUITE A SIGHT!
THE CENTRAL DOROK PRINCIPALITIES HAVE BEEN TURNED INTO A LUSH SEA OF CORRUPTION OVERNIGHT.

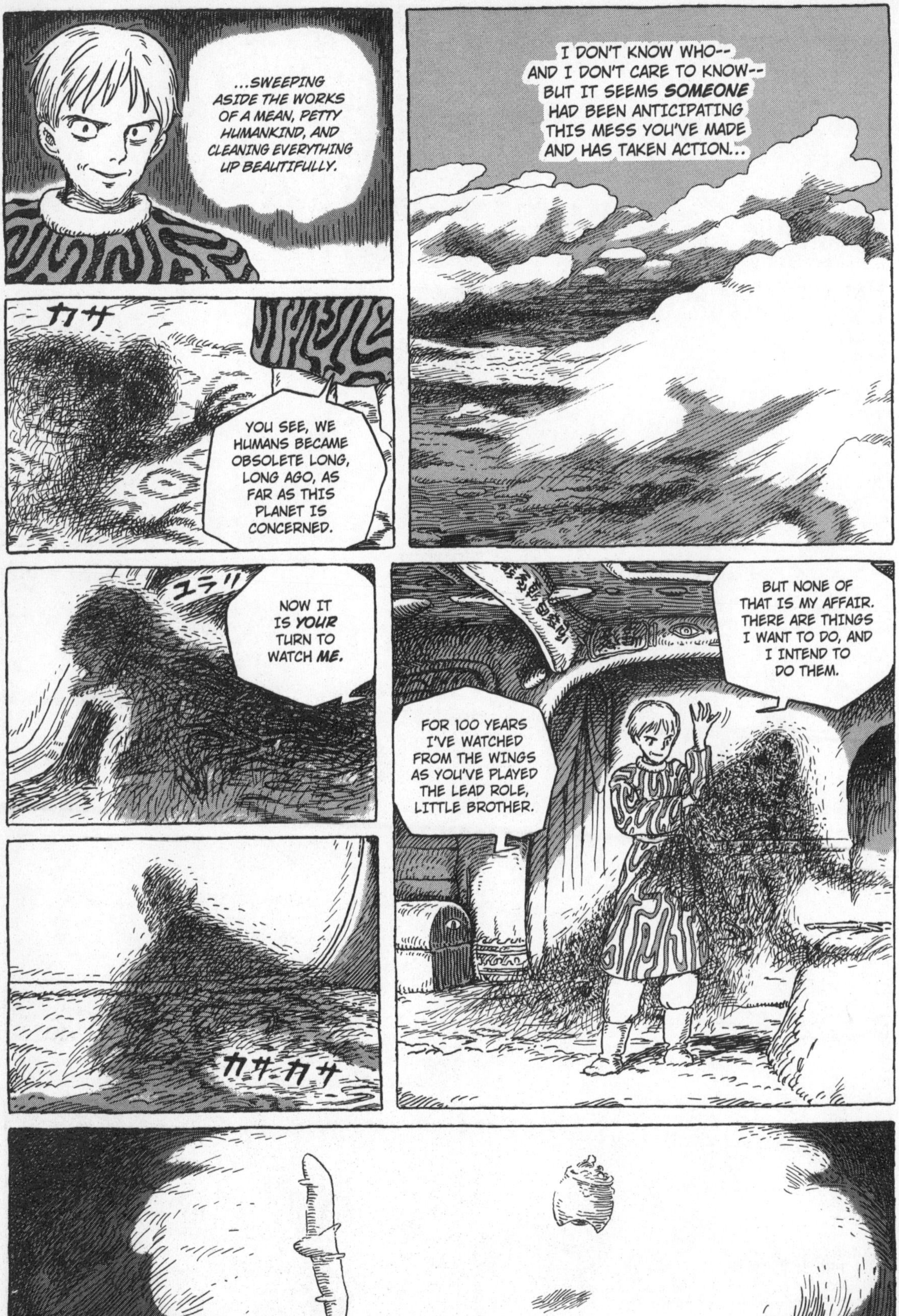

I DON'T KNOW WHO-- AND I DON'T CARE TO KNOW-- BUT IT SEEMS **SOMEONE** HAD BEEN ANTICIPATING THIS MESS YOU'VE MADE AND HAS TAKEN ACTION...
...SWEEPING ASIDE THE WORKS OF A MEAN, PETTY HUMANKIND, AND CLEANING EVERYTHING UP BEAUTIFULLY.
カサ
YOU SEE, WE HUMANS BECAME OBSOLETE LONG, LONG AGO, AS FAR AS THIS PLANET IS CONCERNED.
BUT NONE OF THAT IS MY AFFAIR. THERE ARE THINGS I WANT TO DO, AND I INTEND TO DO THEM.
FOR 100 YEARS I'VE WATCHED FROM THE WINGS AS YOU'VE PLAYED THE LEAD ROLE, LITTLE BROTHER.
ユラリ
NOW IT IS ***YOUR*** TURN TO WATCH ***ME.***
カサカサ

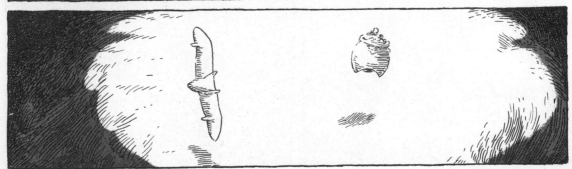

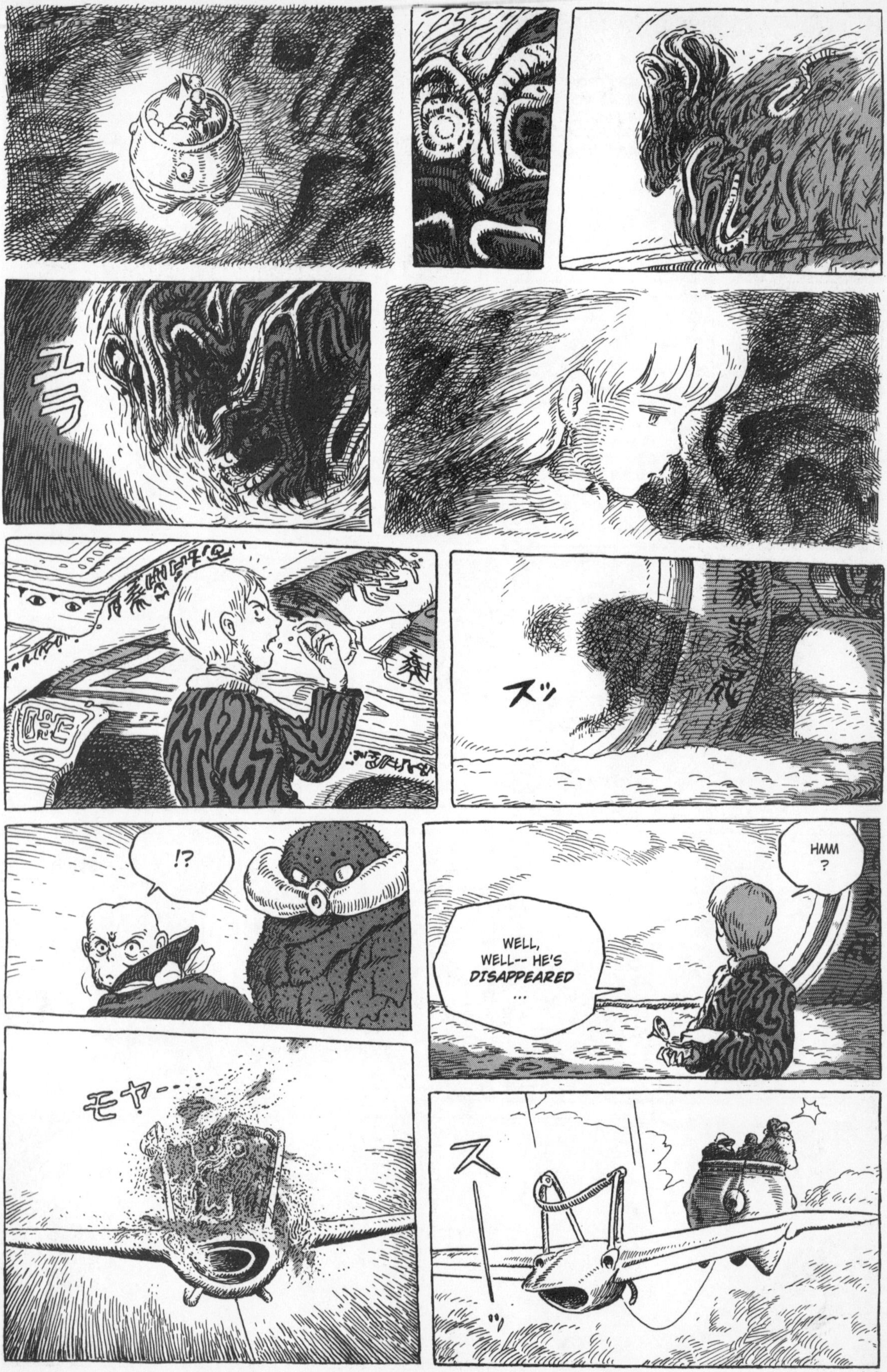
ユラ
ズッ
HMM ?
WELL, WELL-- HE'S DISAPPEARED ...
!?
ス
モヤー

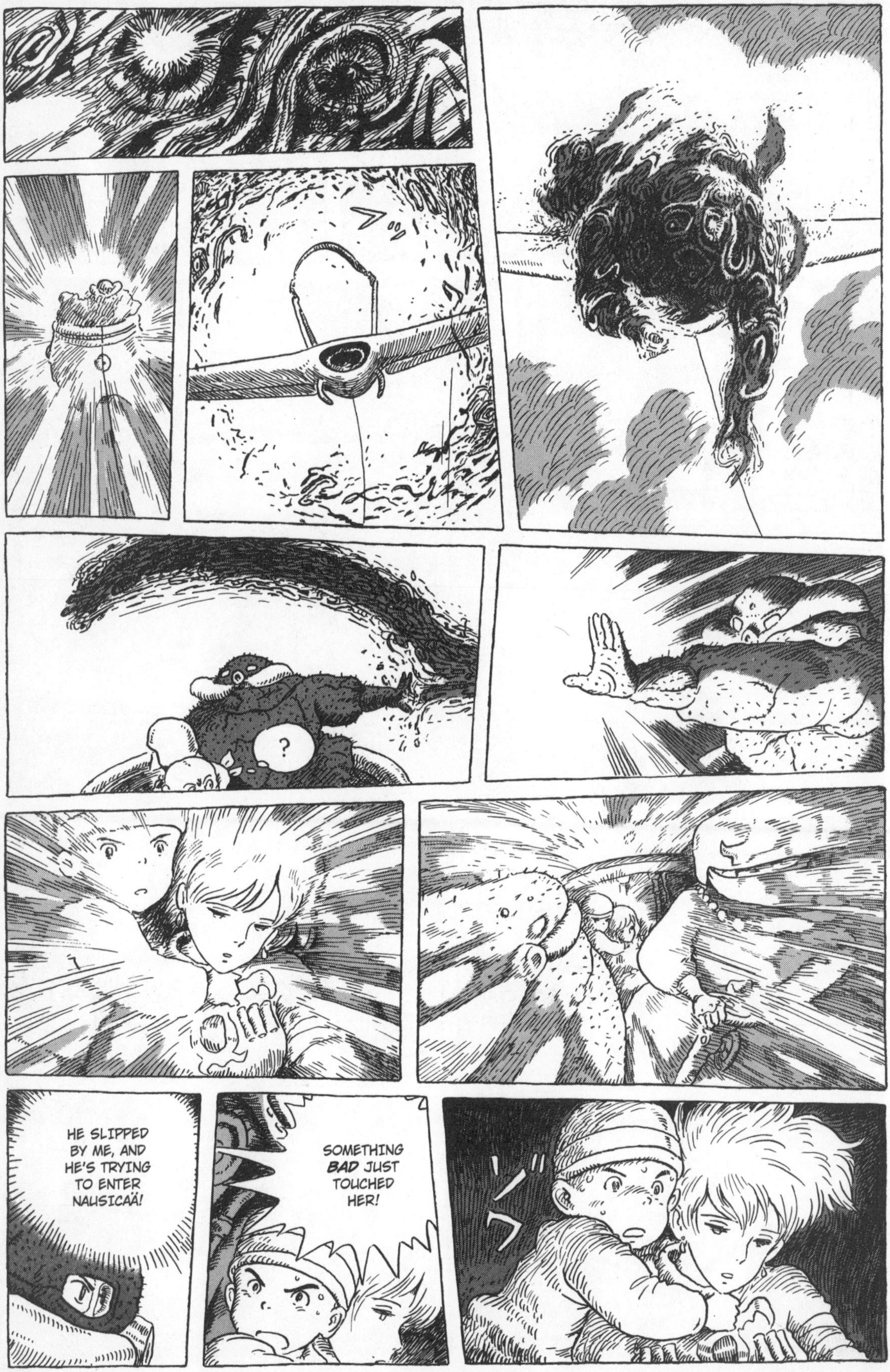
?
SOMETHING **BAD** JUST TOUCHED HER!
HE SLIPPED BY ME, AND HE'S TRYING TO ENTER NAUSICAÄ!

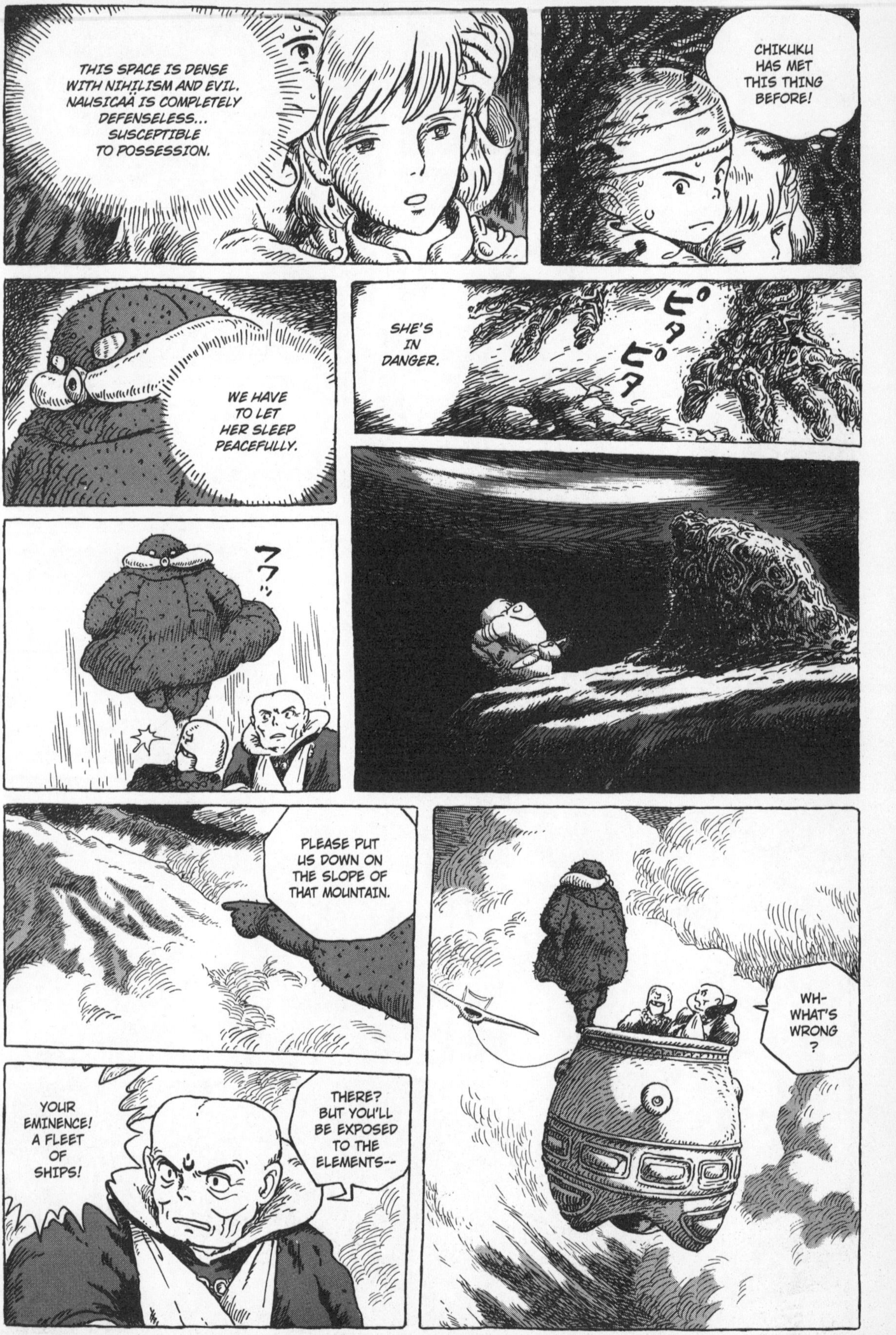
CHIKUKU HAS MET THIS THING BEFORE!
THIS SPACE IS DENSE WITH NIHILISM AND EVIL. NAUSICAÄ IS COMPLETELY DEFENSELESS... SUSCEPTIBLE TO POSSESSION.
ピタ ピタ
SHE'S IN DANGER.
WE HAVE TO LET HER SLEEP PEACEFULLY.
フワッ
WH- WHAT'S WRONG ?
PLEASE PUT US DOWN ON THE SLOPE OF THAT MOUNTAIN.
THERE? BUT YOU'LL BE EXPOSED TO THE ELEMENTS--
YOUR EMINENCE! A FLEET OF SHIPS!

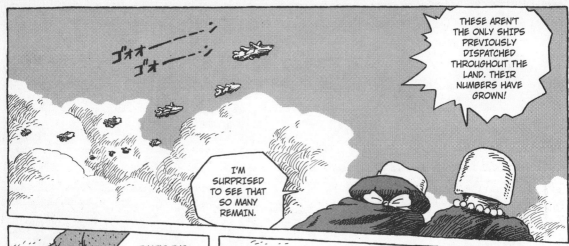

THESE AREN'T THE ONLY SHIPS PREVIOUSLY DISPATCHED THROUGHOUT THE LAND. THEIR NUMBERS HAVE GROWN!
ゴオーーーン
ゴオーーン
I'M SURPRISED TO SEE THAT SO MANY REMAIN.
ゴオオオオーーン
オオーーン
NOW WE'LL BE ABLE TO EVACUATE THE REFUGEES ON THE MOUNTAIN, YOUR EMINENCE.
THAT'S THE COMMAND SHIP OF THE EASTERN MILITARY PARISH AT THE HEAD.
COULD IT BE THAT THE COASTAL REGIONS HAVE ESCAPED DAMAGE?
ゴオオオオ
THE FLAGSHIP IS TURNING, YOUR EMINENCE.
HMPH.
ヴッ
I WAS HOPING TO LET THAT CURSED LITTLE BROTHER OF MINE SEE THIS, BUT HE'S DISAPPEARED.
ゴオオオオ
オーンオーン
ウァーンウァーン

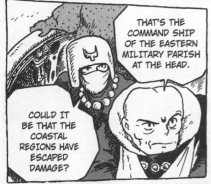

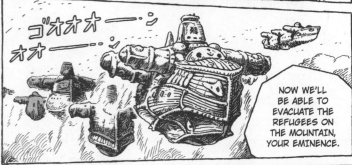

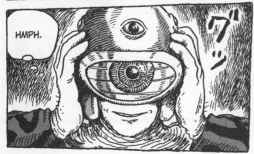

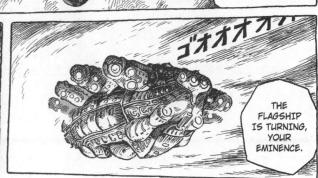

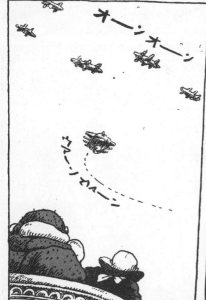

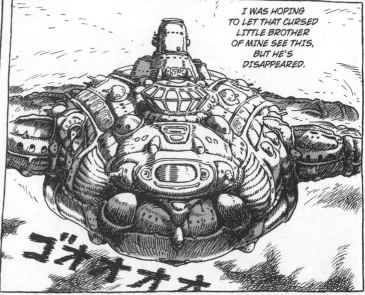

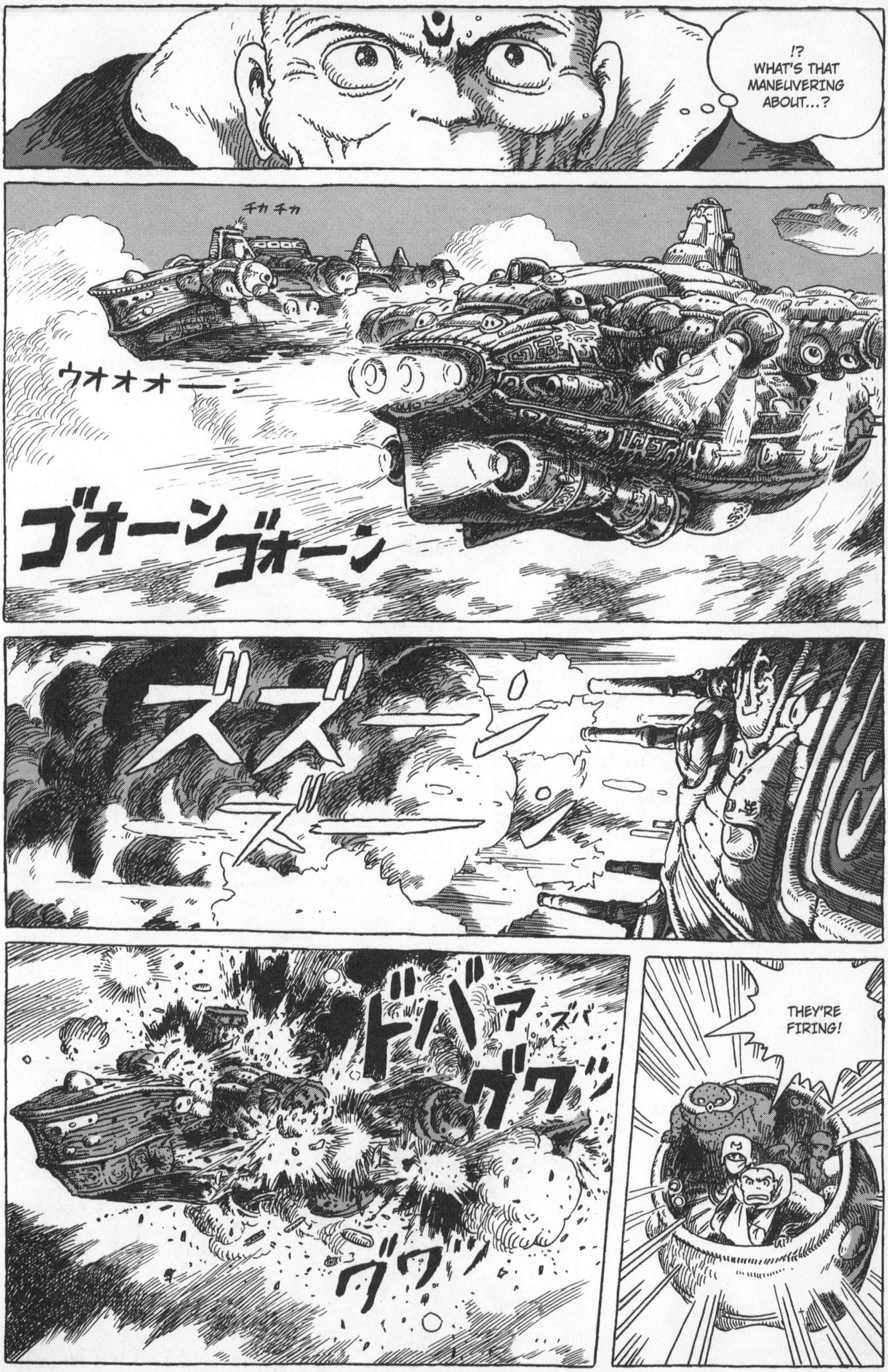
!? WHAT'S THAT MANEUVERING ABOUT...?
チカチカ
ウオオオー
ゴオーン
ゴオーン
ズズーン
THEY'RE FIRING!
ドバァ
ズバ
グワ
グワ

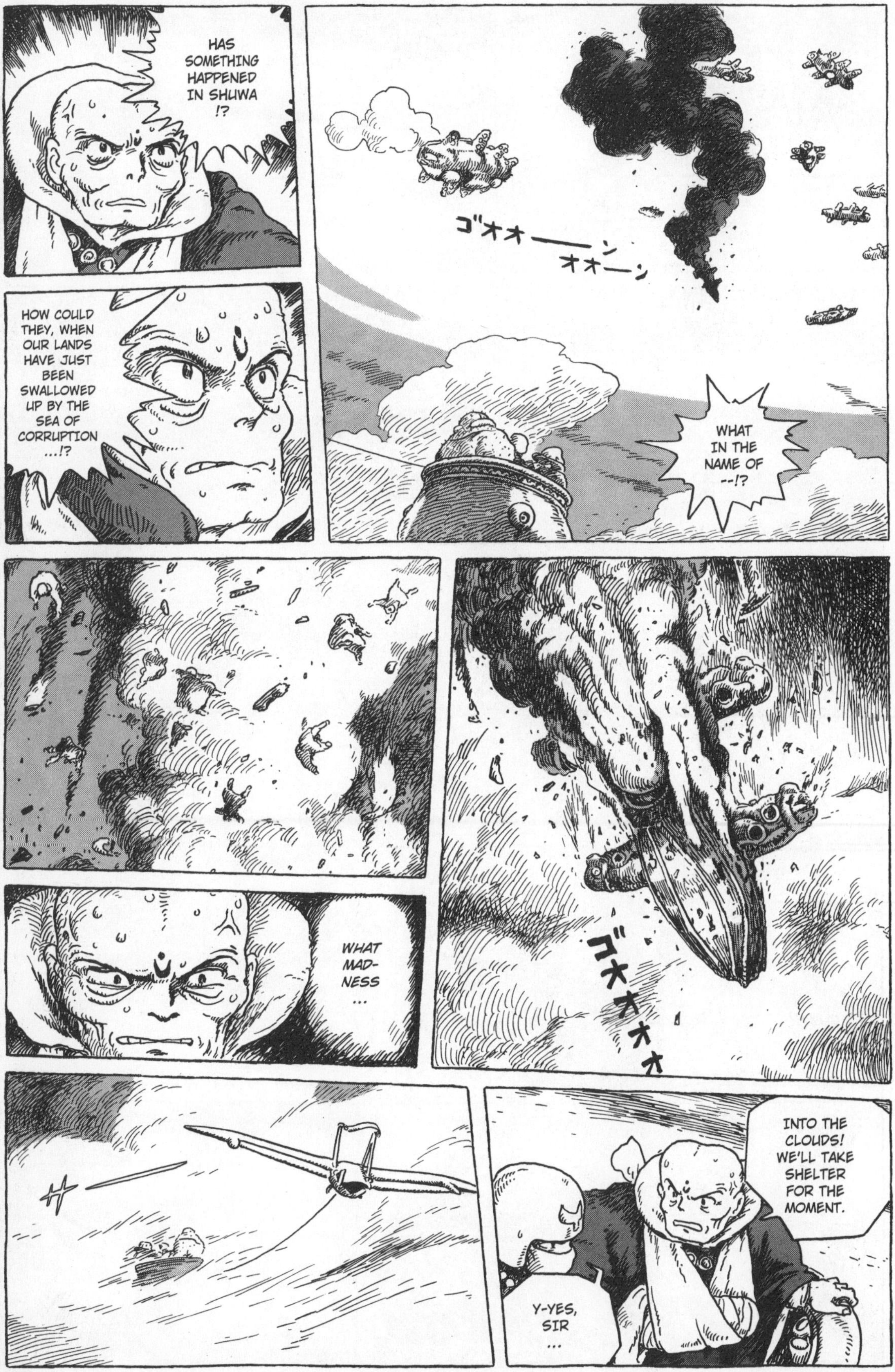
ゴオオーーーン
オオーーン
WHAT IN THE NAME OF --!?
HAS SOMETHING HAPPENED IN SHUWA !?
HOW COULD THEY, WHEN OUR LANDS HAVE JUST BEEN SWALLOWED UP BY THE SEA OF CORRUPTION ...!?
ゴオオオオオ
WHAT MAD-NESS ...
INTO THE CLOUDS! WE'LL TAKE SHELTER FOR THE MOMENT.
Y-YES, SIR ...

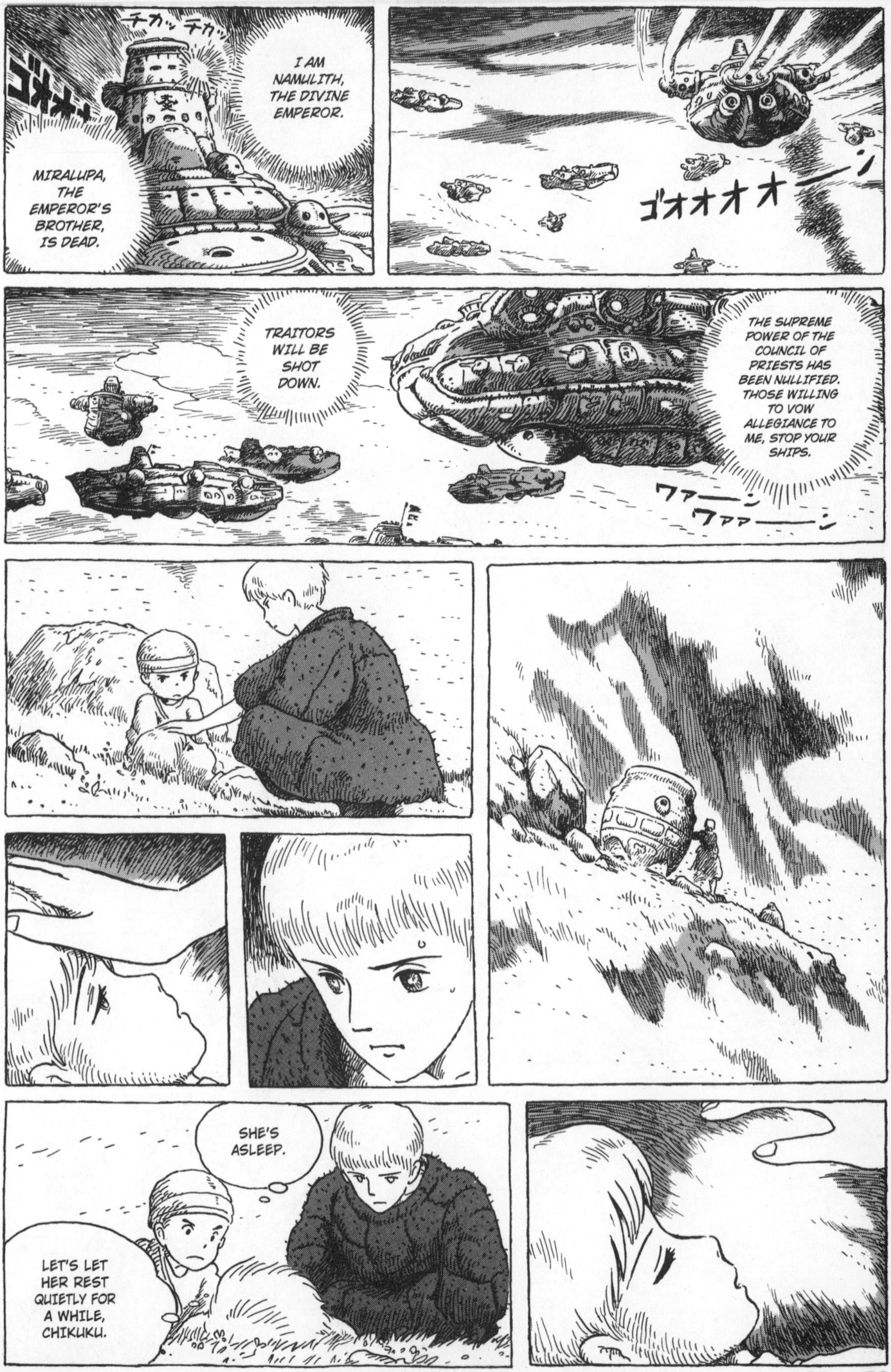
ゴオオオオーーン
チカッチカッ
I AM NAMULITH, THE DIVINE EMPEROR.
MIRALUPA, THE EMPEROR'S BROTHER, IS DEAD.
THE SUPREME POWER OF THE COUNCIL OF PRIESTS HAS BEEN NULLIFIED. THOSE WILLING TO VOW ALLEGIANCE TO ME, STOP YOUR SHIPS.
TRAITORS WILL BE SHOT DOWN.
ワァーン
ワァァーーン
SHE'S ASLEEP.
LET'S LET HER REST QUIETLY FOR A WHILE, CHIKUKU.

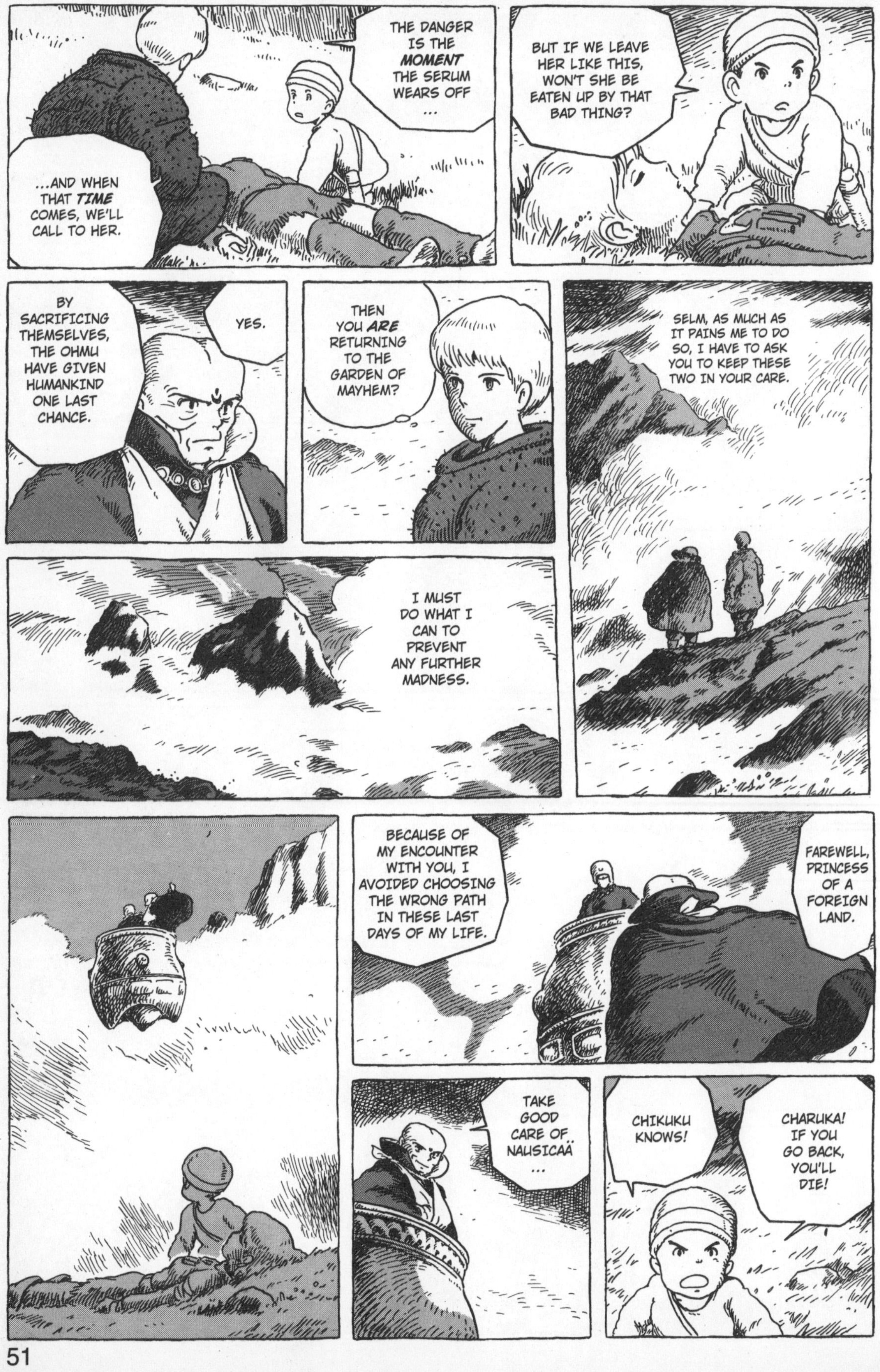

BUT IF WE LEAVE HER LIKE THIS, WON'T SHE BE EATEN UP BY THAT BAD THING?
THE DANGER IS THE ***MOMENT*** THE SERUM WEARS OFF ...
...AND WHEN THAT ***TIME*** COMES, WE'LL CALL TO HER.
SELM, AS MUCH AS IT PAINS ME TO DO SO, I HAVE TO ASK YOU TO KEEP THESE TWO IN YOUR CARE.
THEN YOU ***ARE*** RETURNING TO THE GARDEN OF MAYHEM?
YES.
BY SACRIFICING THEMSELVES, THE OHMU HAVE GIVEN HUMANKIND ONE LAST CHANCE.
I MUST DO WHAT I CAN TO PREVENT ANY FURTHER MADNESS.
FAREWELL, PRINCESS OF A FOREIGN LAND.
BECAUSE OF MY ENCOUNTER WITH YOU, I AVOIDED CHOOSING THE WRONG PATH IN THESE LAST DAYS OF MY LIFE.
CHARUKA! IF YOU GO BACK, YOU'LL DIE!
CHIKUKU KNOWS!
TAKE GOOD CARE OF NAUSICAÄ ...

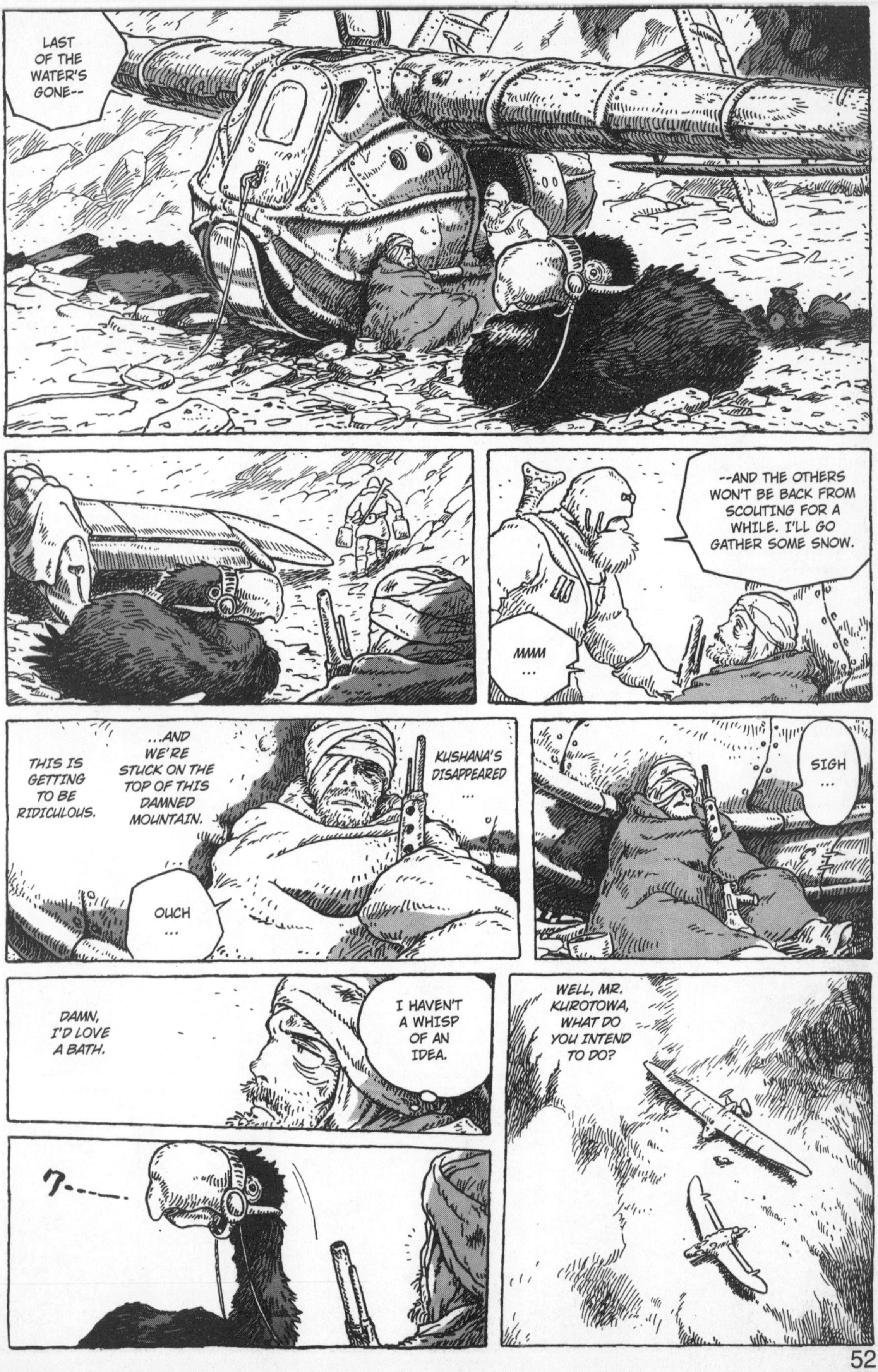
LAST OF THE WATER'S GONE--
--AND THE OTHERS WON'T BE BACK FROM SCOUTING FOR A WHILE. I'LL GO GATHER SOME SNOW.
MMM ...
THIS IS GETTING TO BE RIDICULOUS.
...AND WE'RE STUCK ON THE TOP OF THIS DAMNED MOUNTAIN.
KUSHANA'S DISAPPEARED ...
OUCH ...
SIGH ...
DAMN, I'D LOVE A BATH.
I HAVEN'T A WHISP OF AN IDEA.
WELL, MR. KUROTOWA, WHAT DO YOU INTEND TO DO?

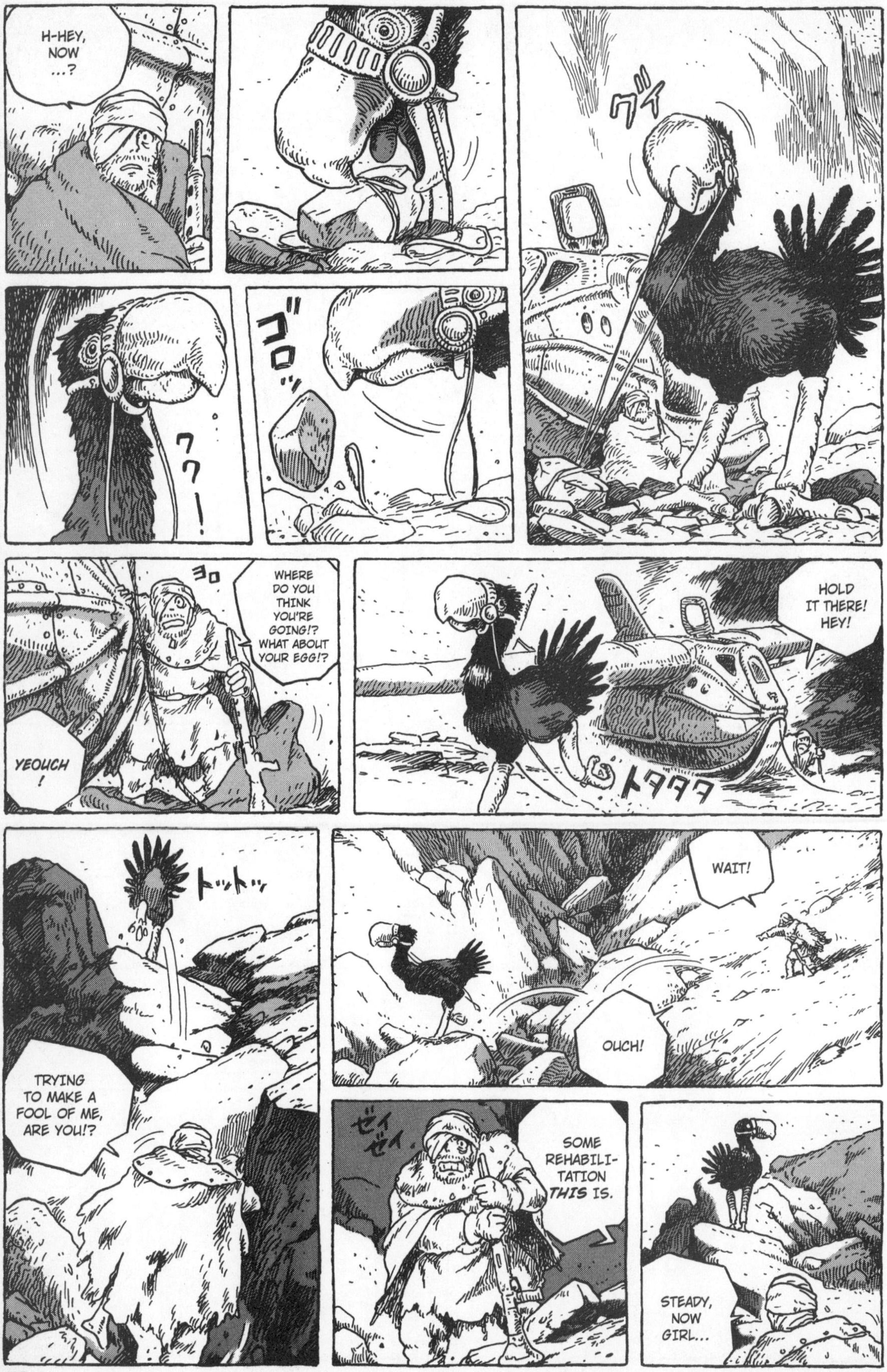
グイ
H-HEY, NOW ...?
ゴロッ
ワクー!
HOLD IT THERE! HEY!
トタタタ
ヨロ
WHERE DO YOU THINK YOU'RE GOING!? WHAT ABOUT YOUR EGG!?
YEOUCH!
WAIT!
OUCH!
STEADY, NOW GIRL...
ゼイゼイ
SOME REHABILITATION THIS IS.
トットッ
TRYING TO MAKE A FOOL OF ME, ARE YOU!?

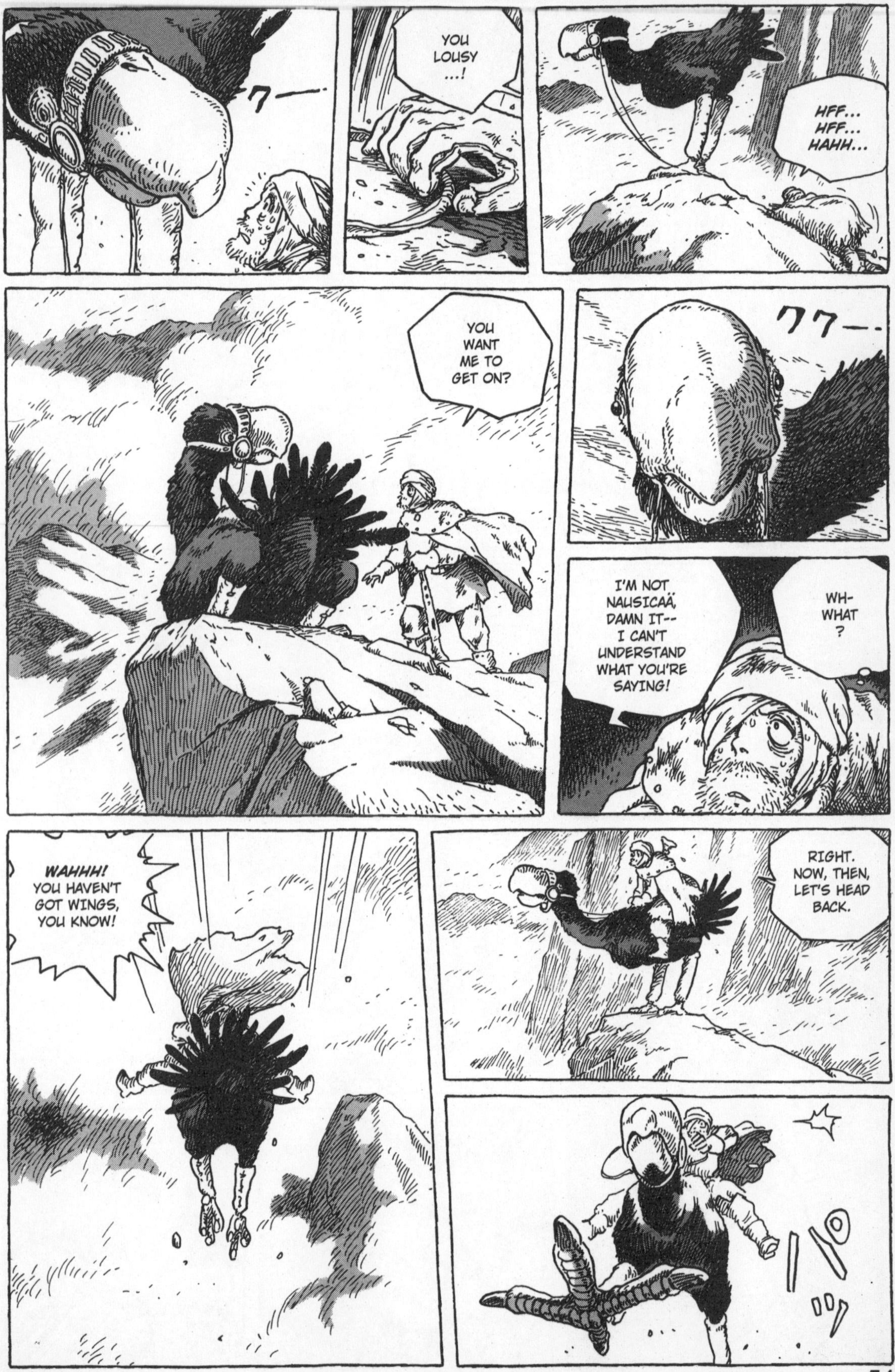
HFF...
HFF...
HAHH...
YOU LOUSY ...!
ク—
クク—
WH-WHAT?
I'M NOT NAUSICAÄ, DAMN IT-- I CAN'T UNDERSTAND WHAT YOU'RE SAYING!
YOU WANT ME TO GET ON?
RIGHT. NOW, THEN, LET'S HEAD BACK.
WAHHH! YOU HAVEN'T GOT WINGS, YOU KNOW!

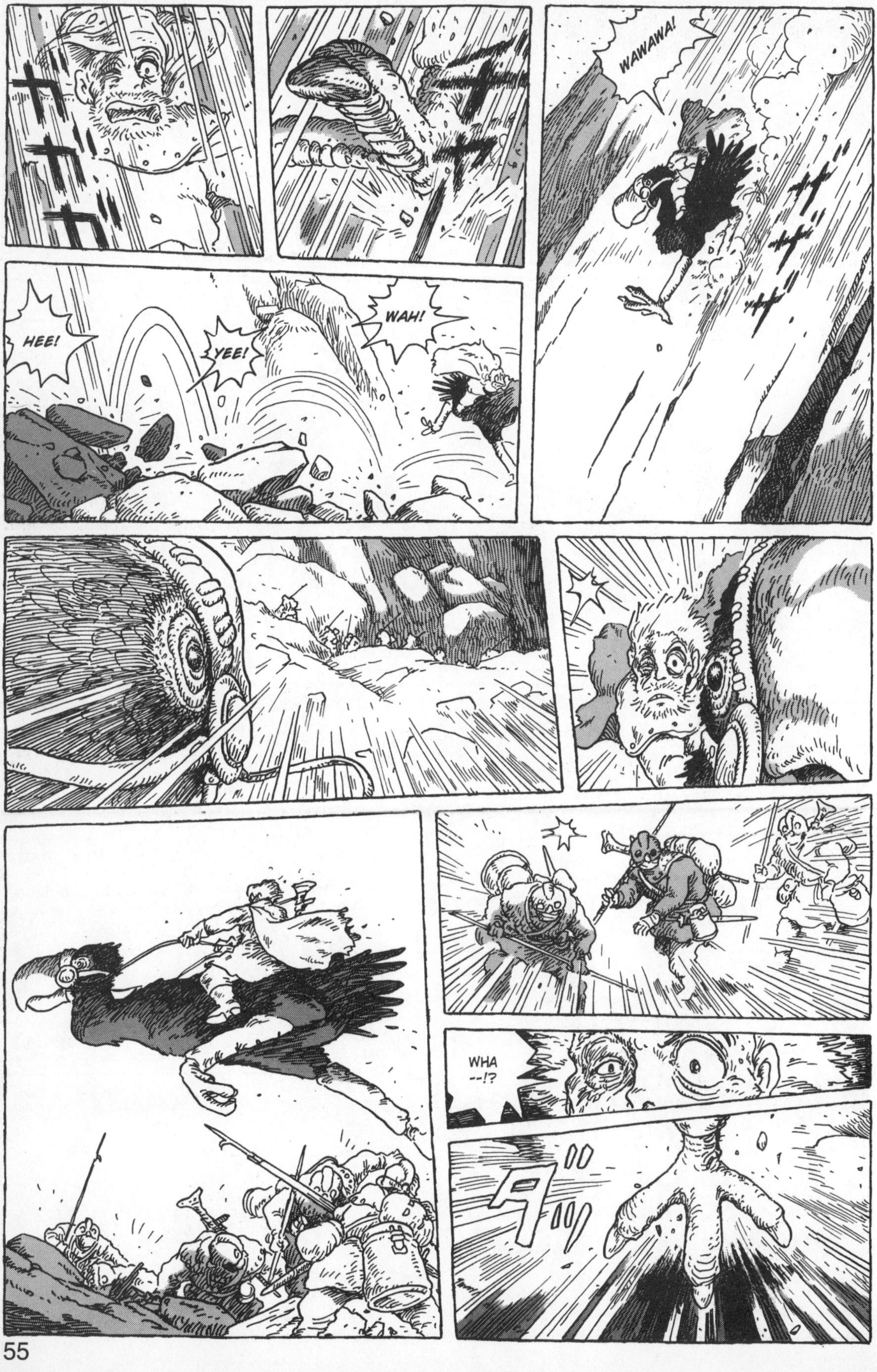
WAWAWA!
HEE!
YEE!
WAH!
WHA
--!?

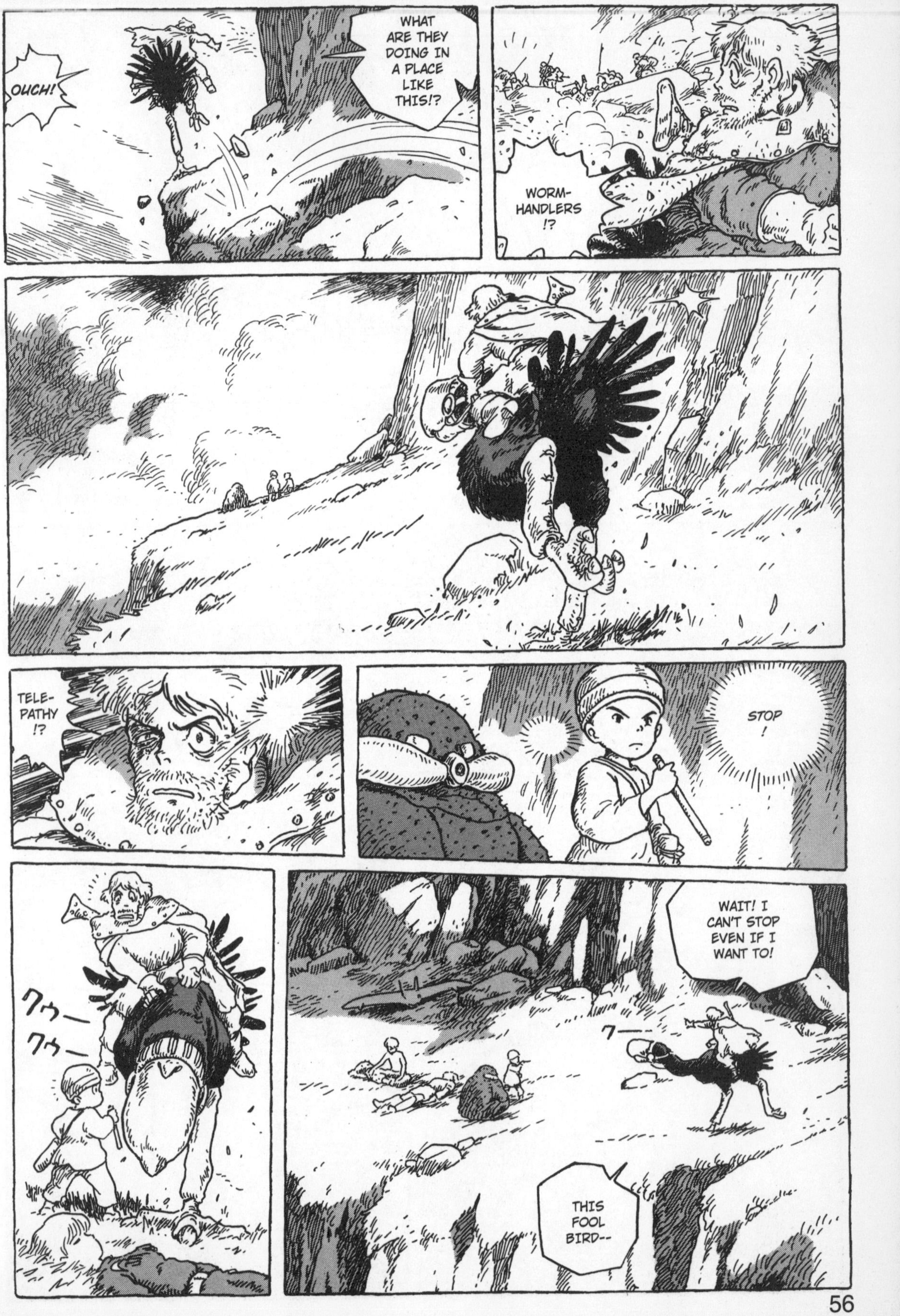
WORM-HANDLERS !?
WHAT ARE THEY DOING IN A PLACE LIKE THIS!?
OUCH!
STOP !
TELE-PATHY !?
WAIT! I CAN'T STOP EVEN IF I WANT TO!
ワー
THIS FOOL BIRD--
クウー
クウー

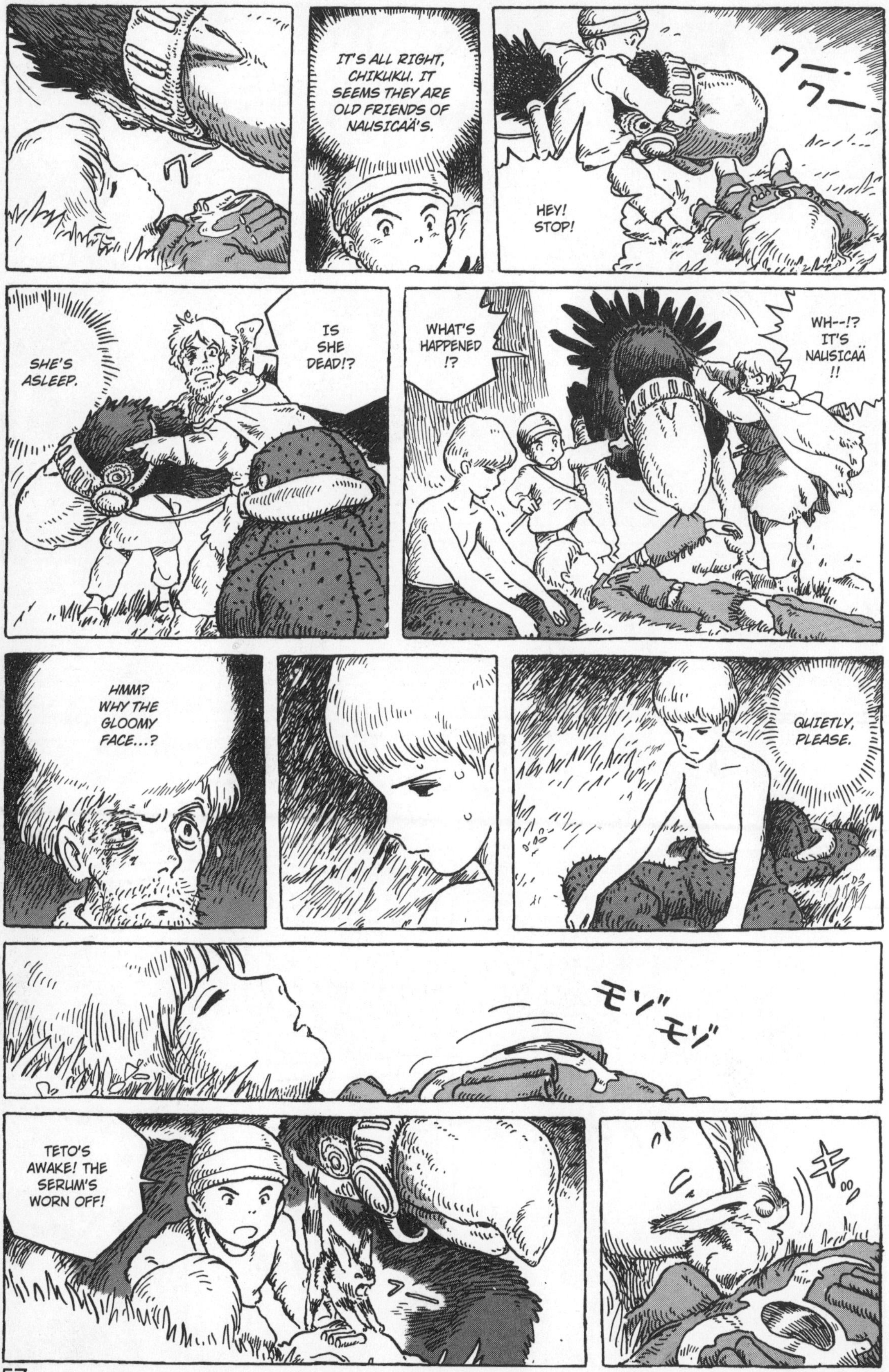
クー
クー
HEY! STOP!
IT'S ALL RIGHT, CHIKUKU. IT SEEMS THEY ARE OLD FRIENDS OF NAUSICAÄ'S.
WH--!? IT'S NAUSICAÄ !!
WHAT'S HAPPENED !?
IS SHE DEAD!?
SHE'S ASLEEP.
QUIETLY, PLEASE.
HMM? WHY THE GLOOMY FACE...?
モゾモゾ
TETO'S AWAKE! THE SERUM'S WORN OFF!

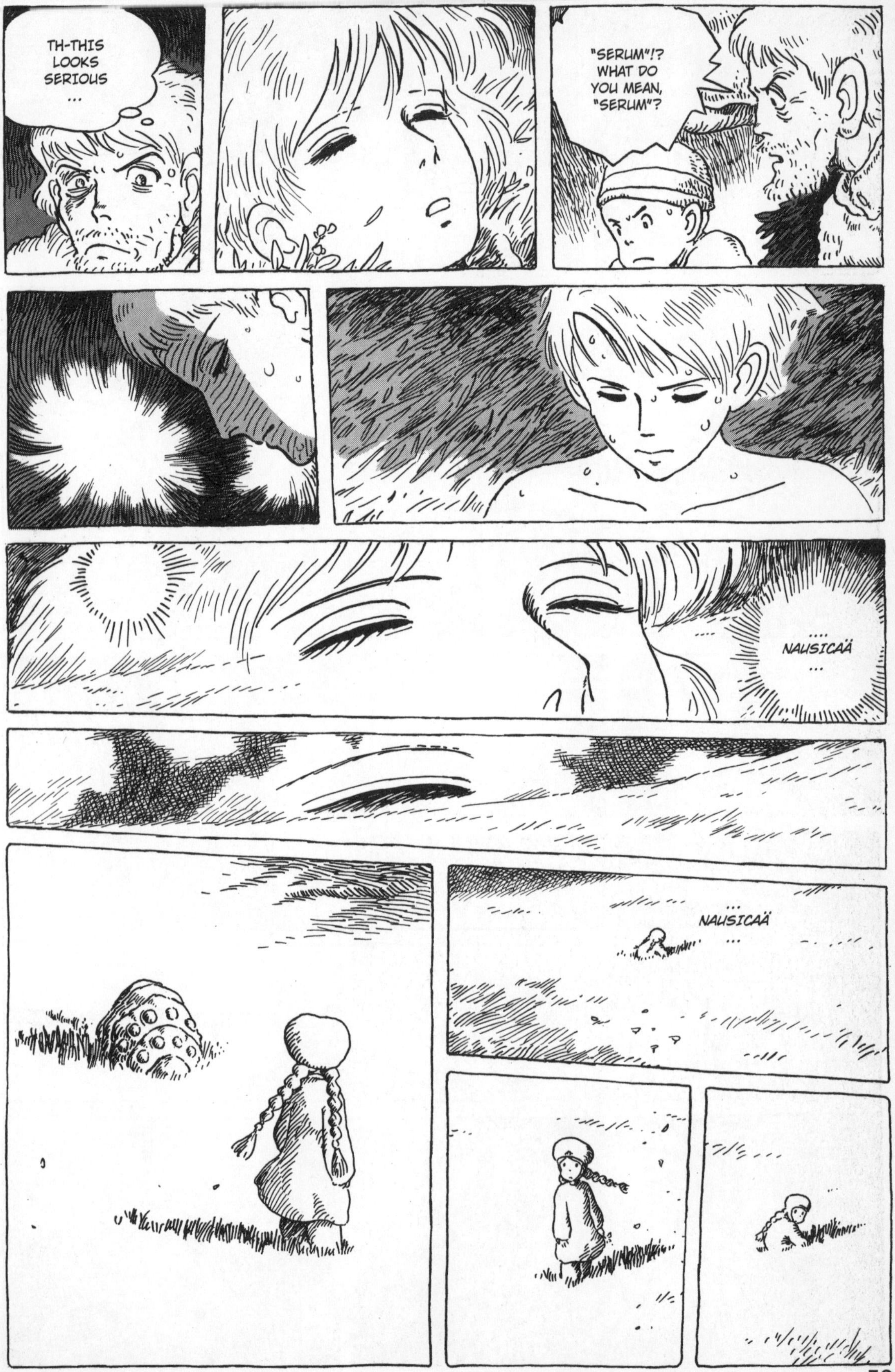
"SERUM"!? WHAT DO YOU MEAN, "SERUM"?
TH-THIS LOOKS SERIOUS ...
.... NAUSICAÄ ...
... NAUSICAÄ ...

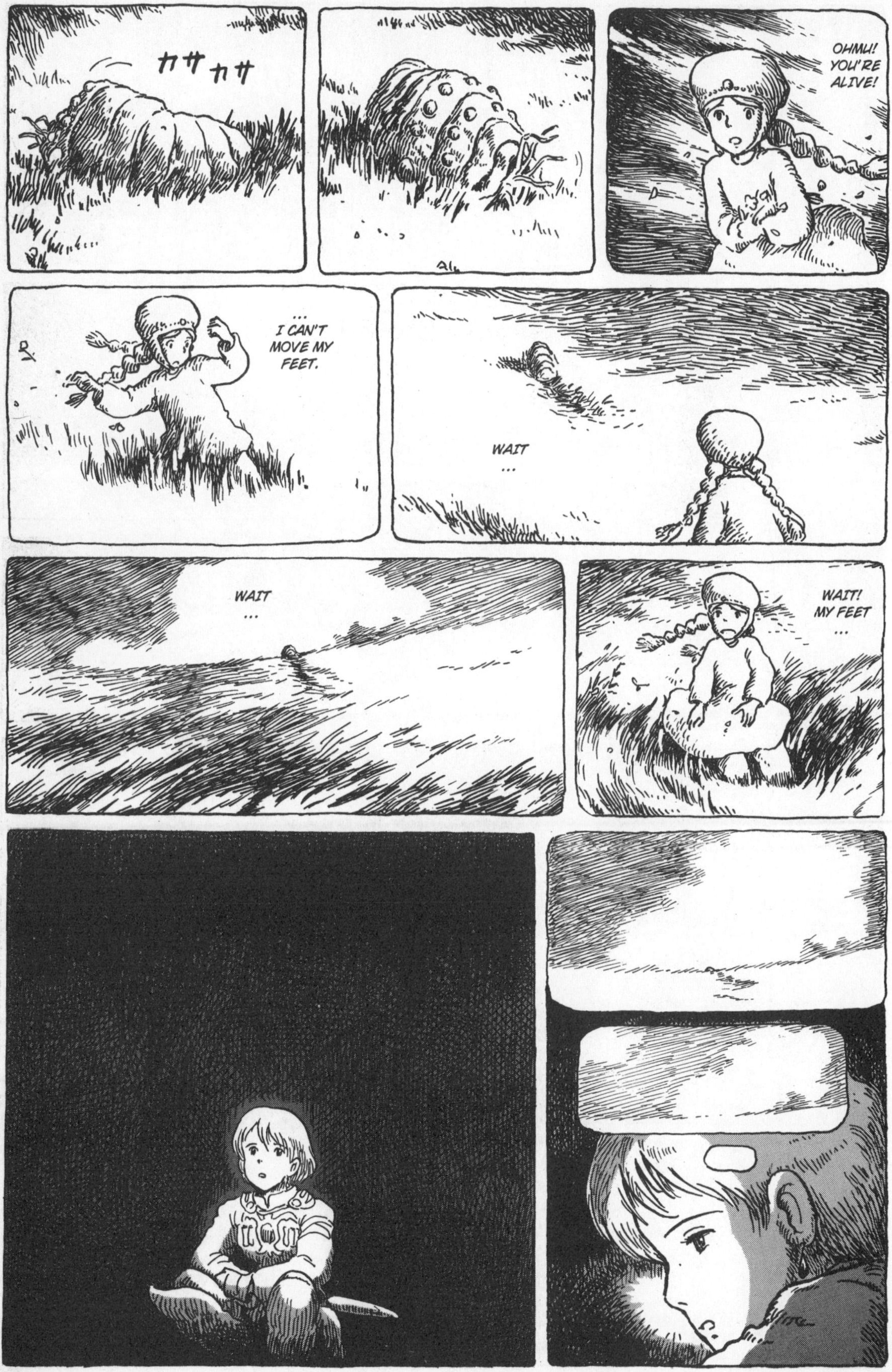
OHMU! YOU'RE ALIVE!
カサカサ
WAIT ...
... I CAN'T MOVE MY FEET.
WAIT! MY FEET ...
WAIT ...

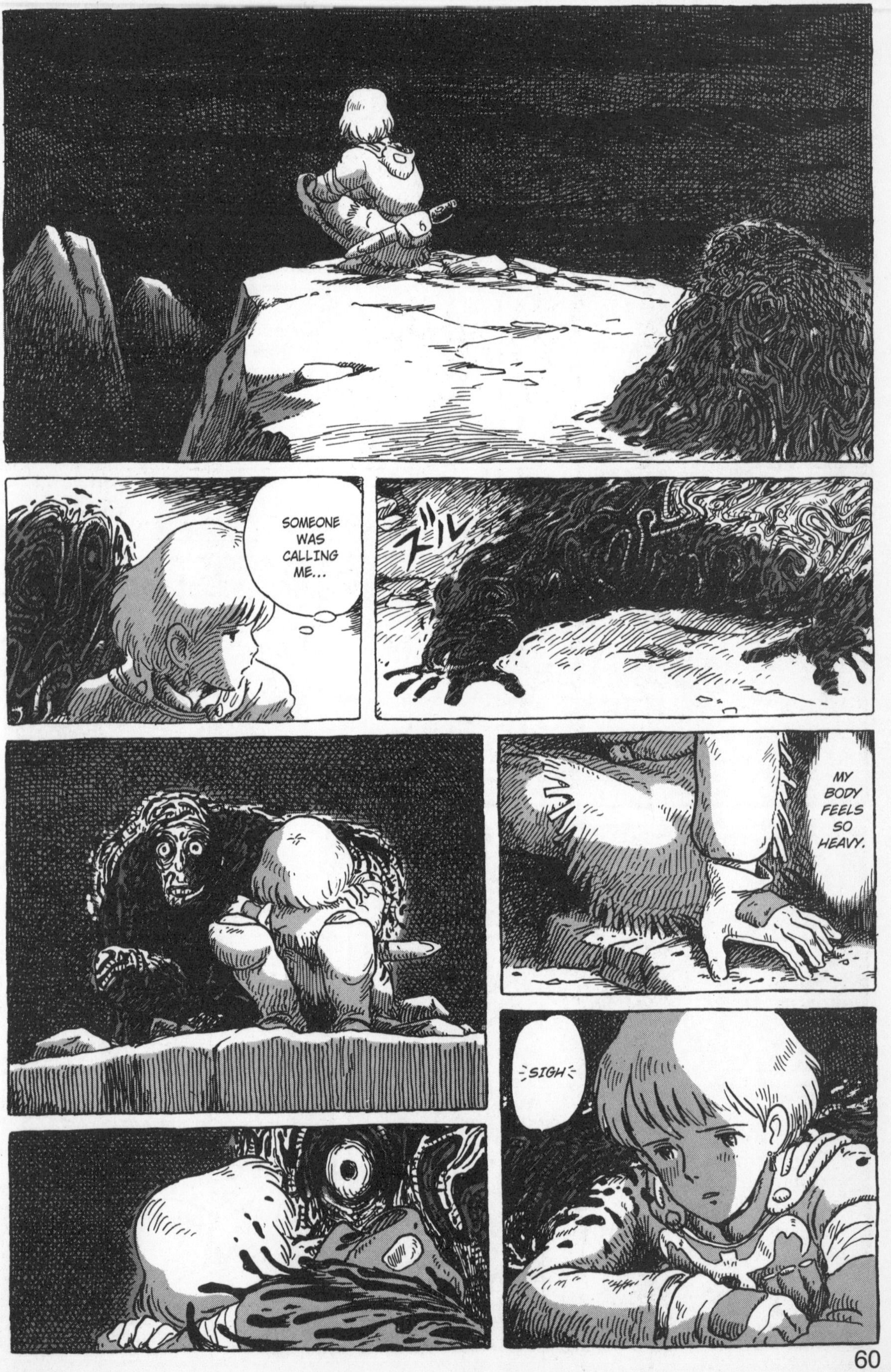
ズル
SOMEONE WAS CALLING ME...
MY BODY FEELS SO HEAVY.
SIGH

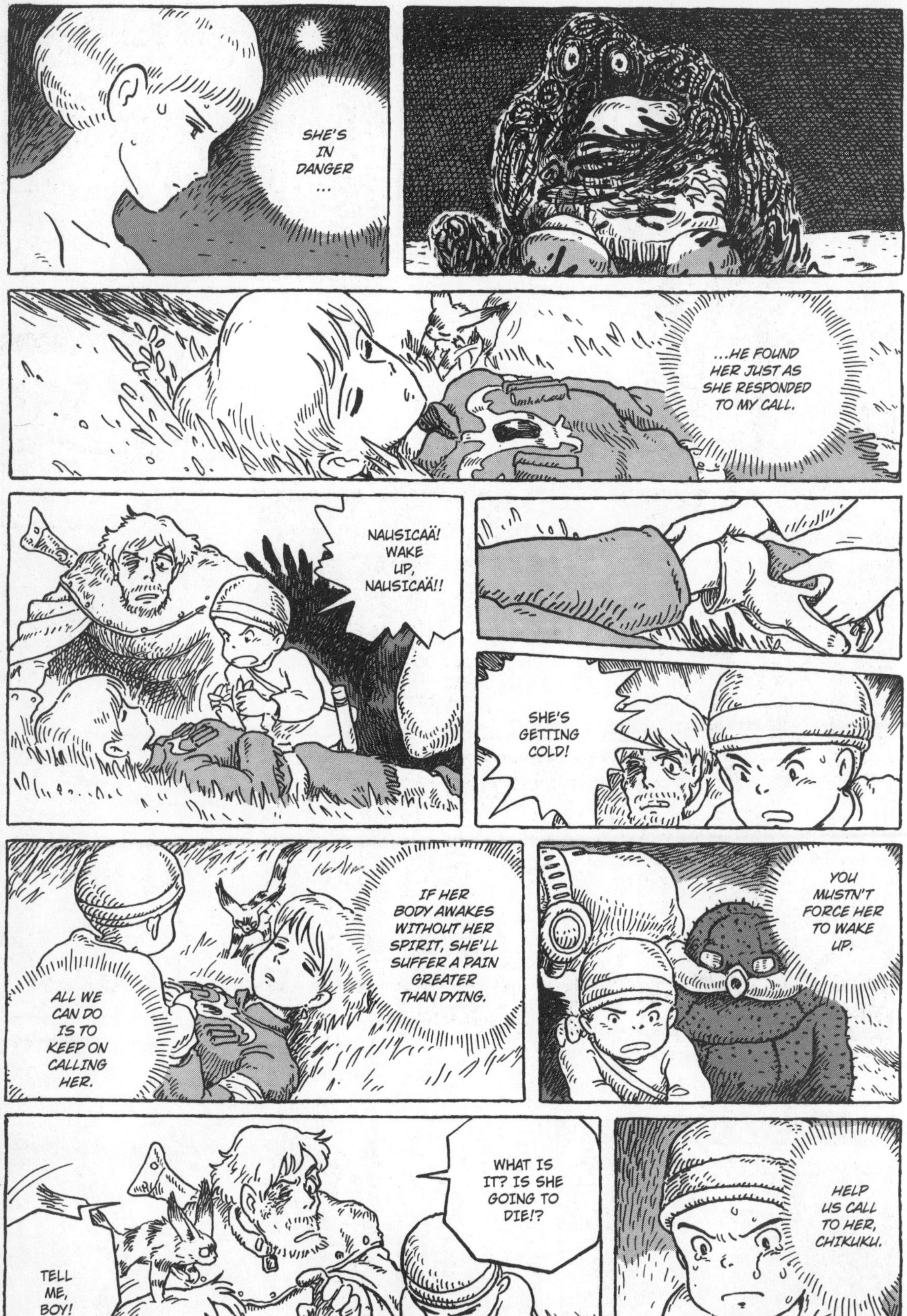
SHE'S IN DANGER ...
...HE FOUND HER JUST AS SHE RESPONDED TO MY CALL.
SHE'S GETTING COLD!
NAUSICAÄ! WAKE UP, NAUSICAÄ!!
YOU MUSTN'T FORCE HER TO WAKE UP.
IF HER BODY AWAKES WITHOUT HER SPIRIT, SHE'LL SUFFER A PAIN GREATER THAN DYING.
ALL WE CAN DO IS TO KEEP ON CALLING HER.
HELP US CALL TO HER, CHIKUKU.
WHAT IS IT? IS SHE GOING TO DIE!?
TELL ME, BOY!

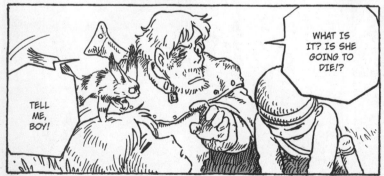

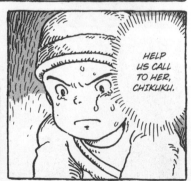

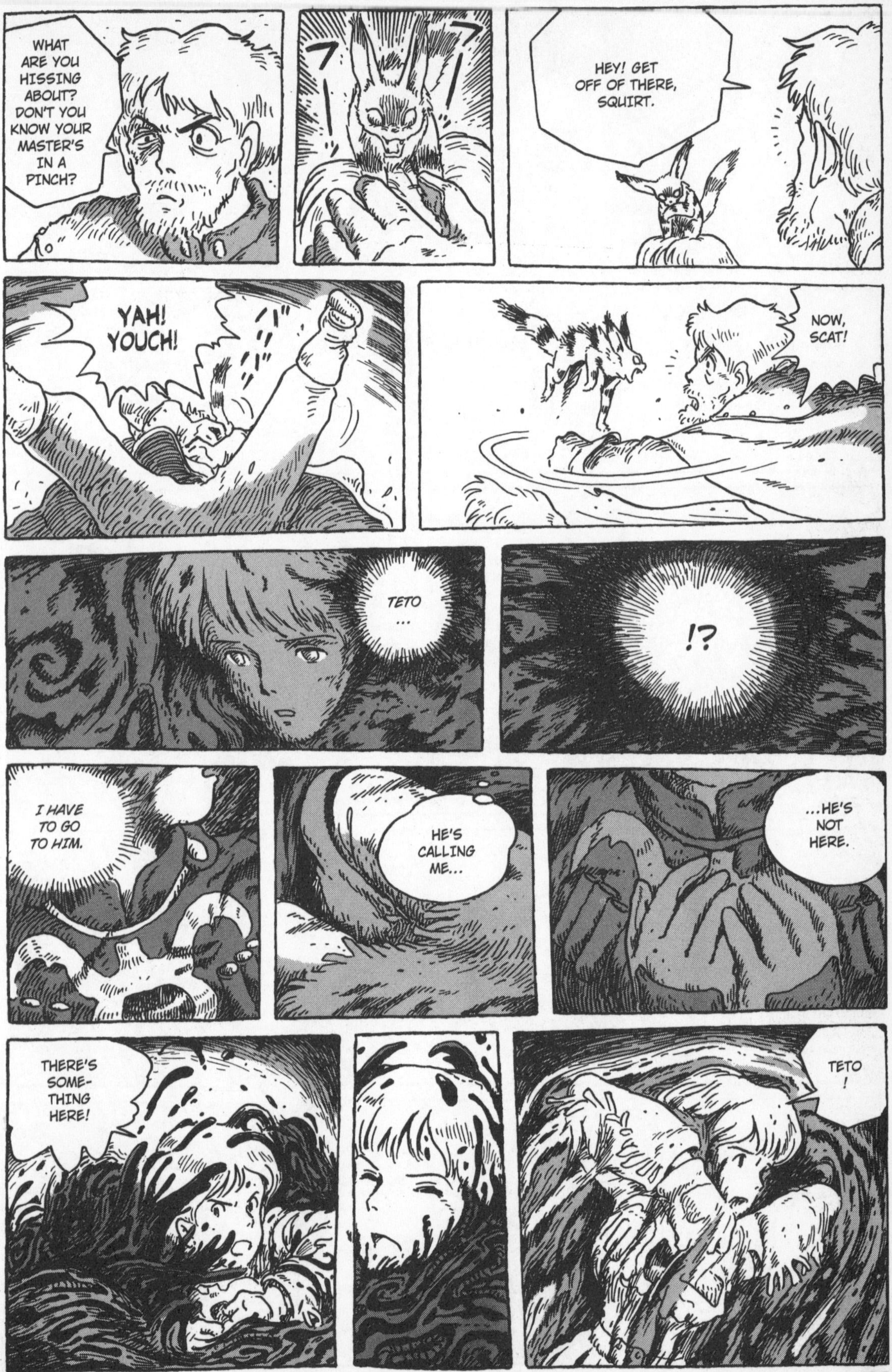
HEY! GET OFF OF THERE, SQUIRT.
WHAT ARE YOU HISSING ABOUT? DON'T YOU KNOW YOUR MASTER'S IN A PINCH?
NOW, SCAT!
YAH! YOUCH!
!?
TETO ...
...HE'S NOT HERE.
HE'S CALLING ME...
I HAVE TO GO TO HIM.
TETO !
THERE'S SOME-THING HERE!

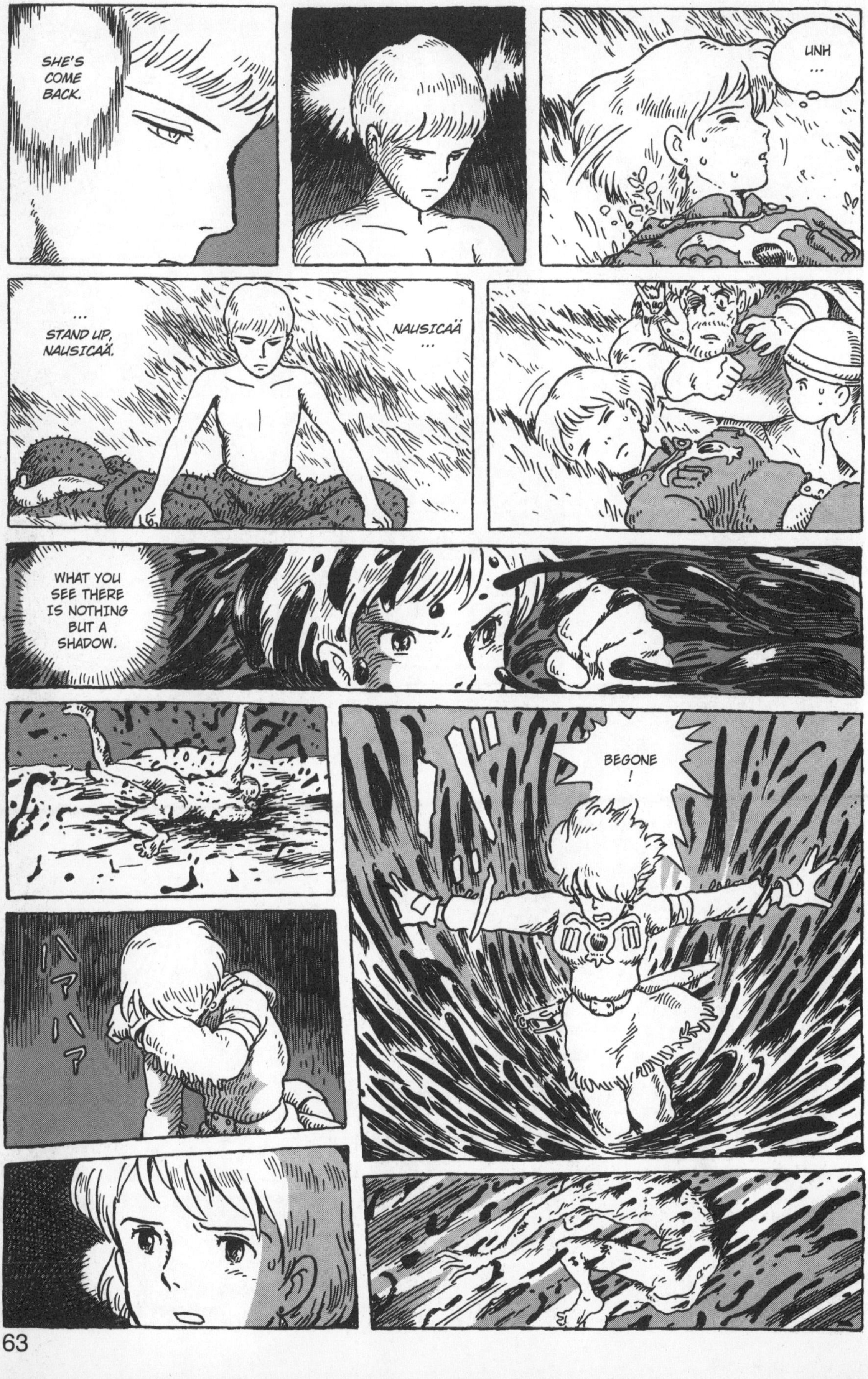
UNH ...
SHE'S COME BACK.
NAUSICAÄ ...
... STAND UP, NAUSICAÄ.
WHAT YOU SEE THERE IS NOTHING BUT A SHADOW.
BEGONE !
ハァハァ

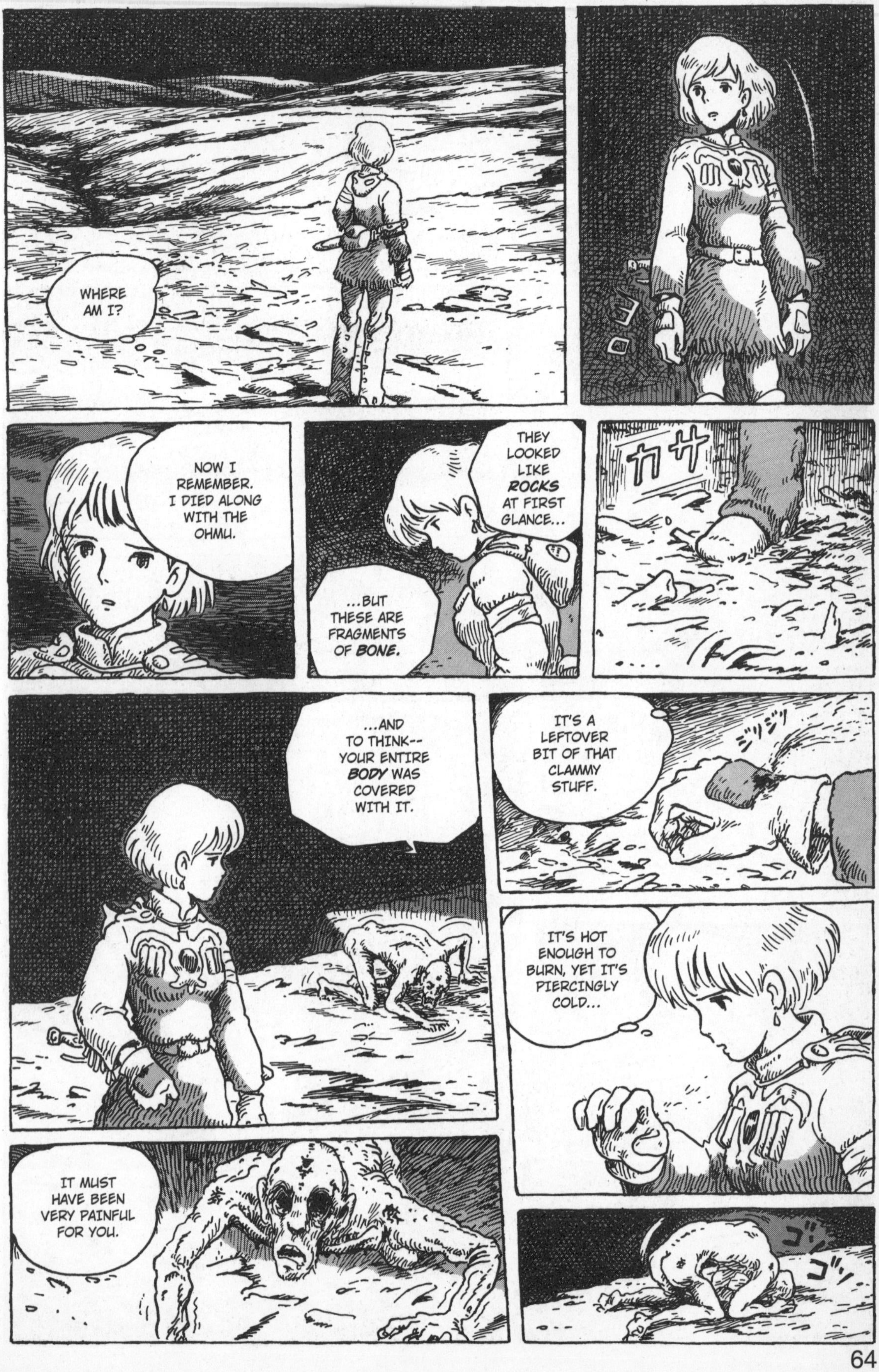
WHERE AM I?
カサ
THEY LOOKED LIKE *ROCKS* AT FIRST GLANCE...
...BUT THESE ARE FRAGMENTS OF *BONE.*
NOW I REMEMBER. I DIED ALONG WITH THE OHMU.
IT'S A LEFTOVER BIT OF THAT CLAMMY STUFF.
IT'S HOT ENOUGH TO BURN, YET IT'S PIERCINGLY COLD...
...AND TO THINK-- YOUR ENTIRE *BODY* WAS COVERED WITH IT.
IT MUST HAVE BEEN VERY PAINFUL FOR YOU.

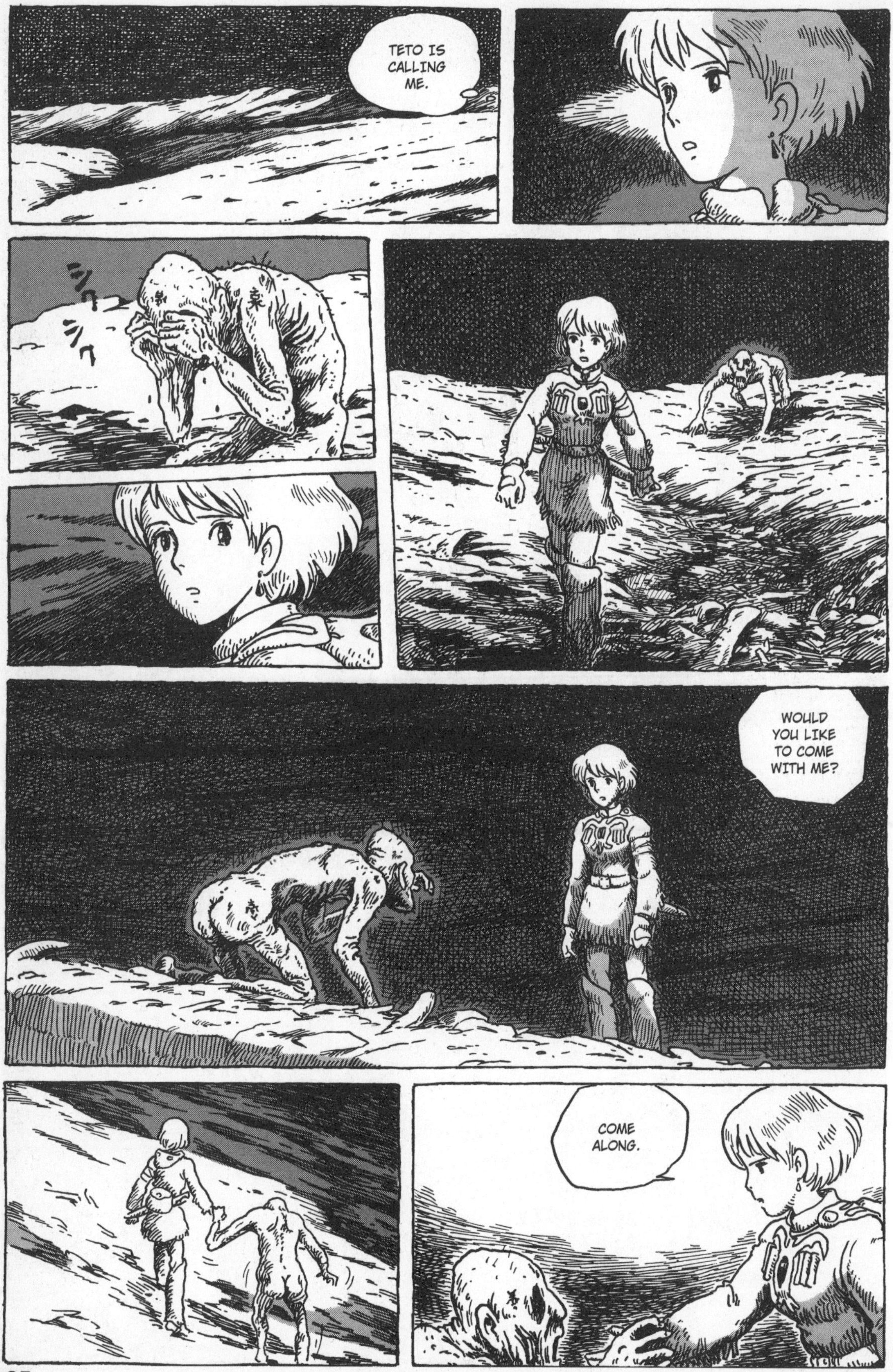
TETO IS CALLING ME.
シク シク
WOULD YOU LIKE TO COME WITH ME?
COME ALONG.

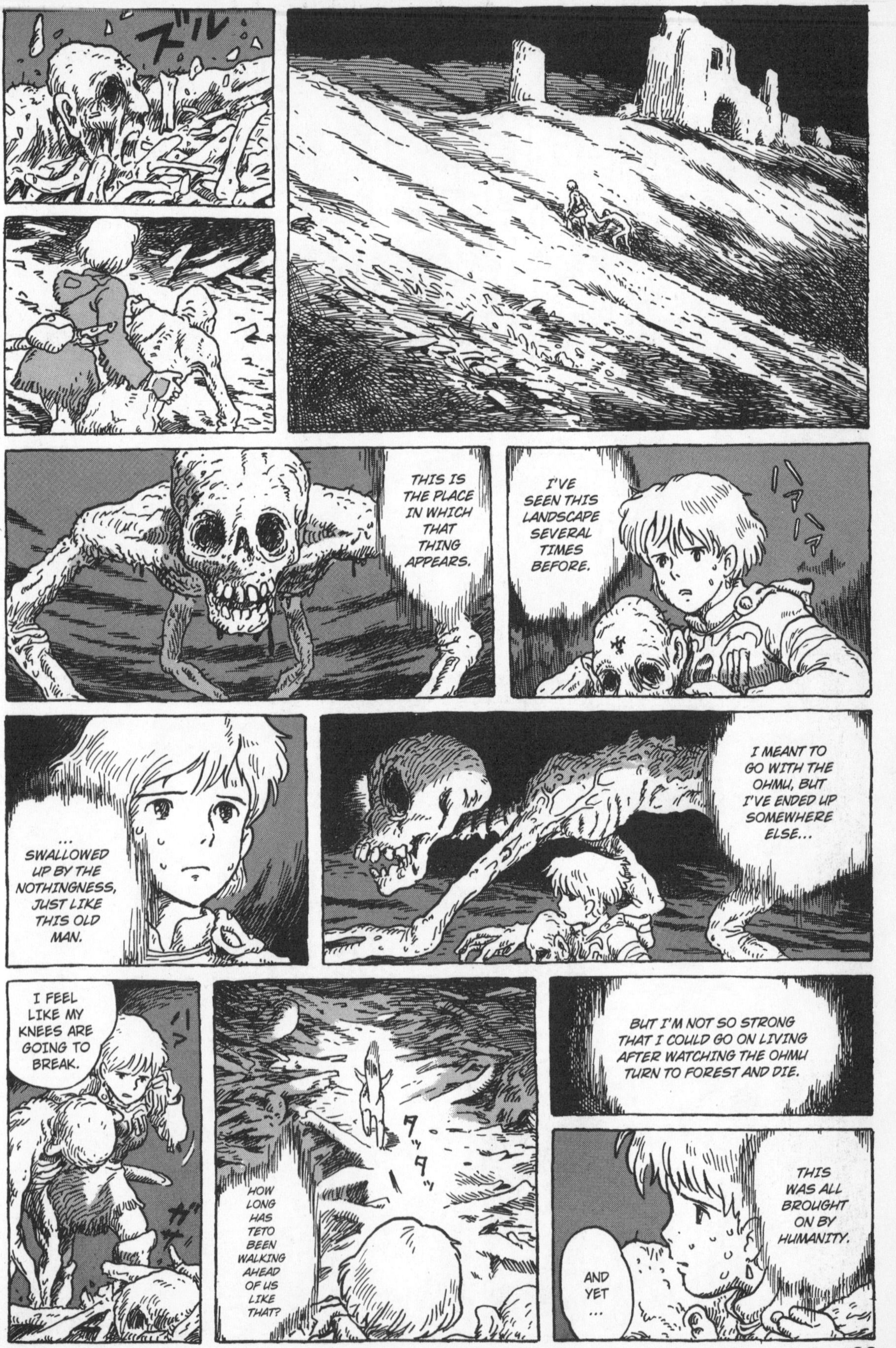
ズル
I'VE SEEN THIS LANDSCAPE SEVERAL TIMES BEFORE.
ハァハァ
THIS IS THE PLACE IN WHICH THAT THING APPEARS.
I MEANT TO GO WITH THE OHMU, BUT I'VE ENDED UP SOMEWHERE ELSE...
...SWALLOWED UP BY THE NOTHINGNESS, JUST LIKE THIS OLD MAN.
BUT I'M NOT SO STRONG THAT I COULD GO ON LIVING AFTER WATCHING THE OHMU TURN TO FOREST AND DIE.
THIS WAS ALL BROUGHT ON BY HUMANITY.
AND YET ...
HOW LONG HAS TETO BEEN WALKING AHEAD OF US LIKE THAT?
I FEEL LIKE MY KNEES ARE GOING TO BREAK.

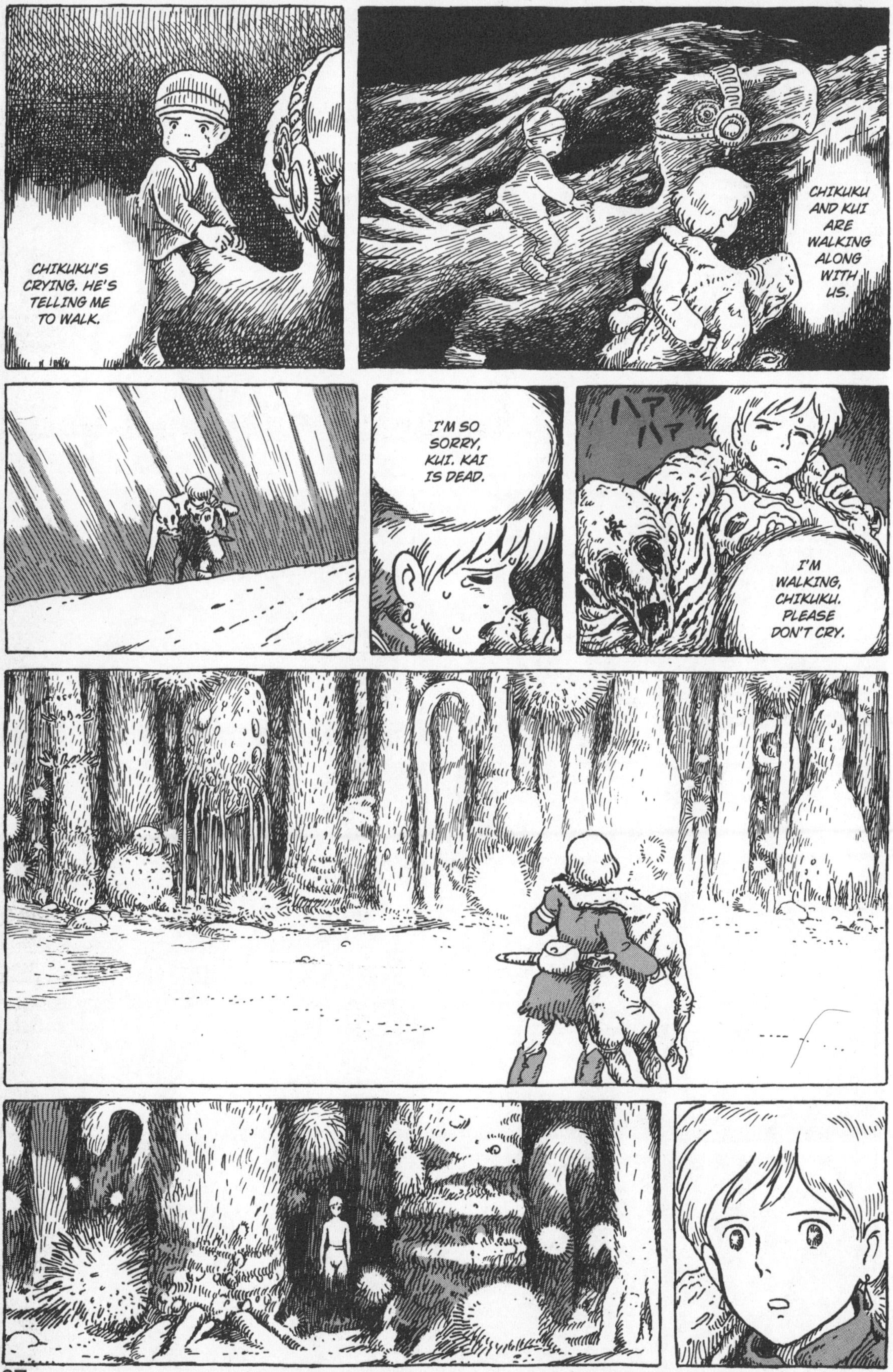
CHIKUKU AND KUI ARE WALKING ALONG WITH US.
CHIKUKU'S CRYING. HE'S TELLING ME TO WALK.
ハア ハア
I'M WALKING, CHIKUKU. PLEASE DON'T CRY.
I'M SO SORRY, KUI. KAI IS DEAD.

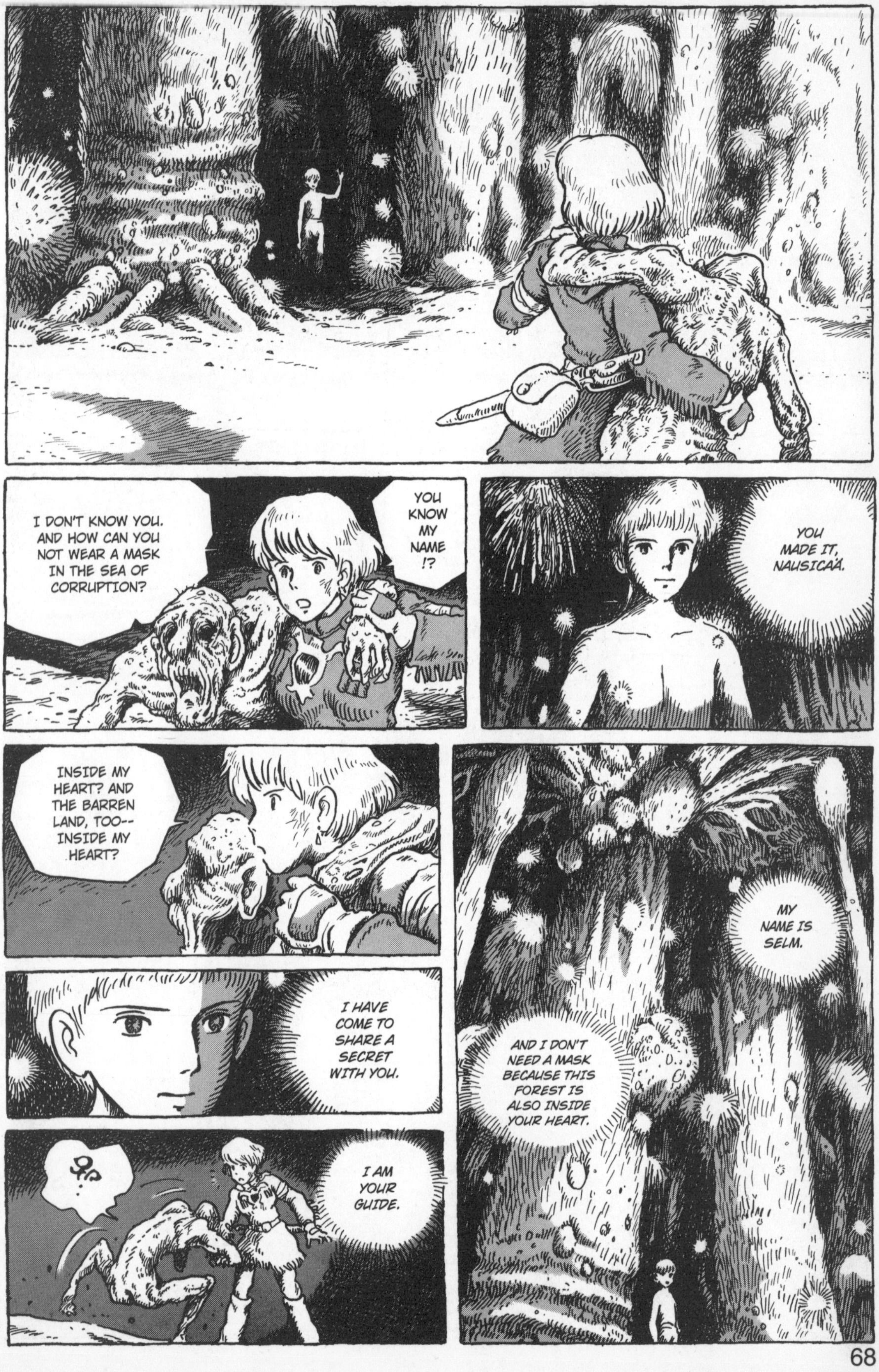
YOU MADE IT, NAUSICAÄ.
YOU KNOW MY NAME !?
I DON'T KNOW YOU. AND HOW CAN YOU NOT WEAR A MASK IN THE SEA OF CORRUPTION?
MY NAME IS SELM.
AND I DON'T NEED A MASK BECAUSE THIS FOREST IS ALSO INSIDE YOUR HEART.
INSIDE MY HEART? AND THE BARREN LAND, TOO-- INSIDE MY HEART?
I HAVE COME TO SHARE A SECRET WITH YOU.
I AM YOUR GUIDE.
?!

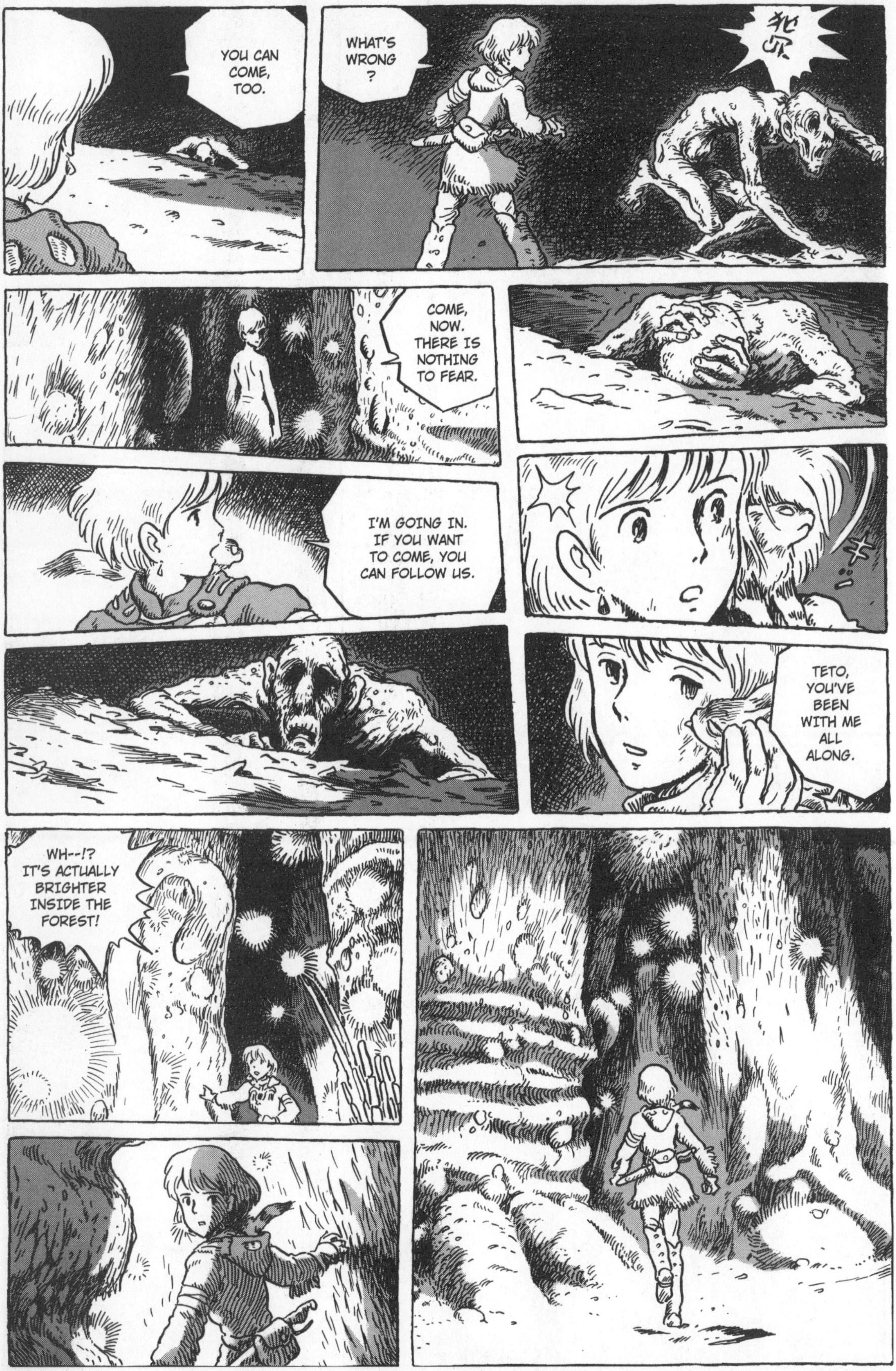
WHAT'S WRONG ?
YOU CAN COME, TOO.
COME, NOW. THERE IS NOTHING TO FEAR.
I'M GOING IN. IF YOU WANT TO COME, YOU CAN FOLLOW US.
TETO, YOU'VE BEEN WITH ME ALL ALONG.
WH--!? IT'S ACTUALLY BRIGHTER INSIDE THE FOREST!

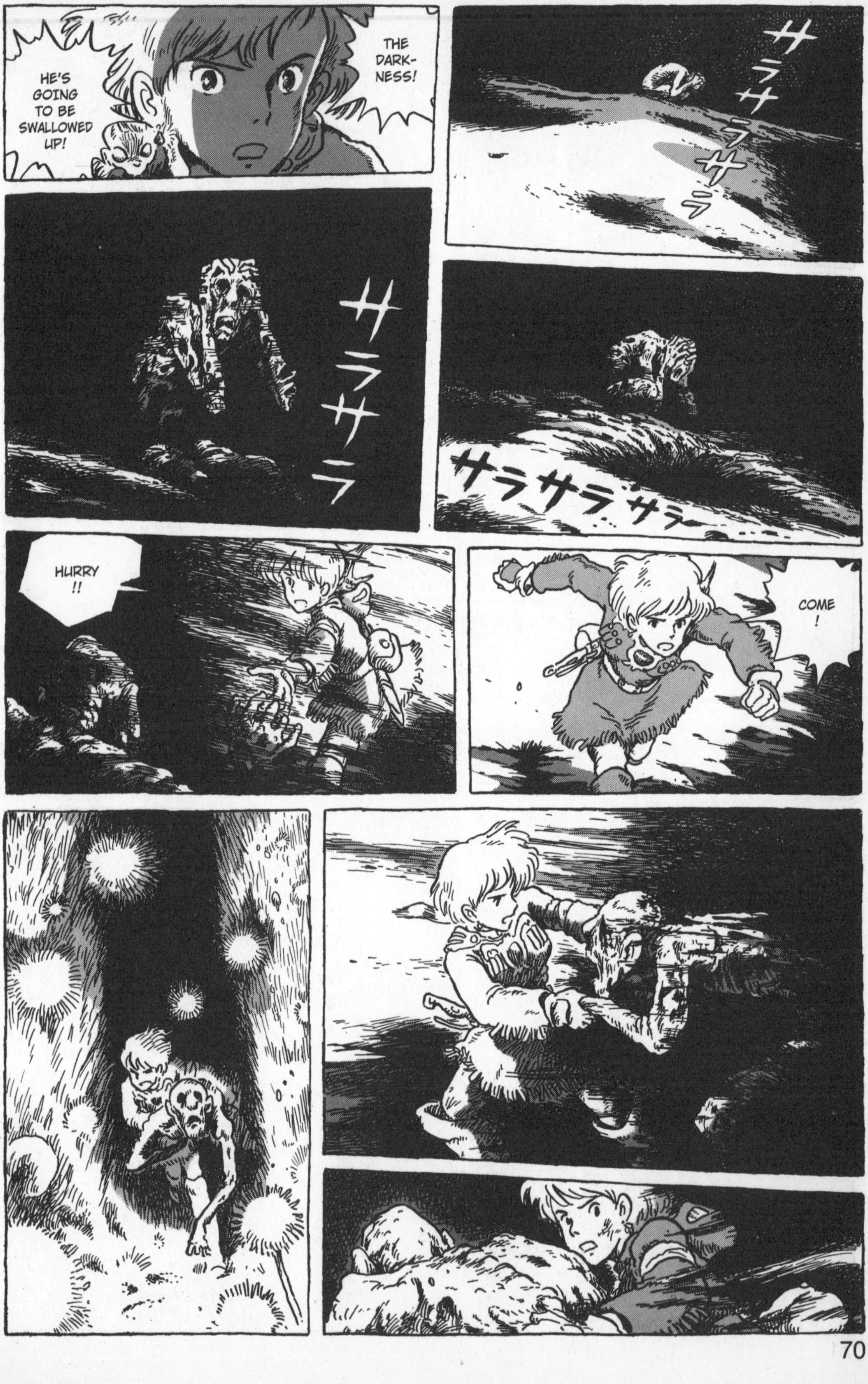
サラサラサラ
THE DARKNESS!
HE'S GOING TO BE SWALLOWED UP!
サラサラサラサラ
サラサラ
COME!
HURRY!!

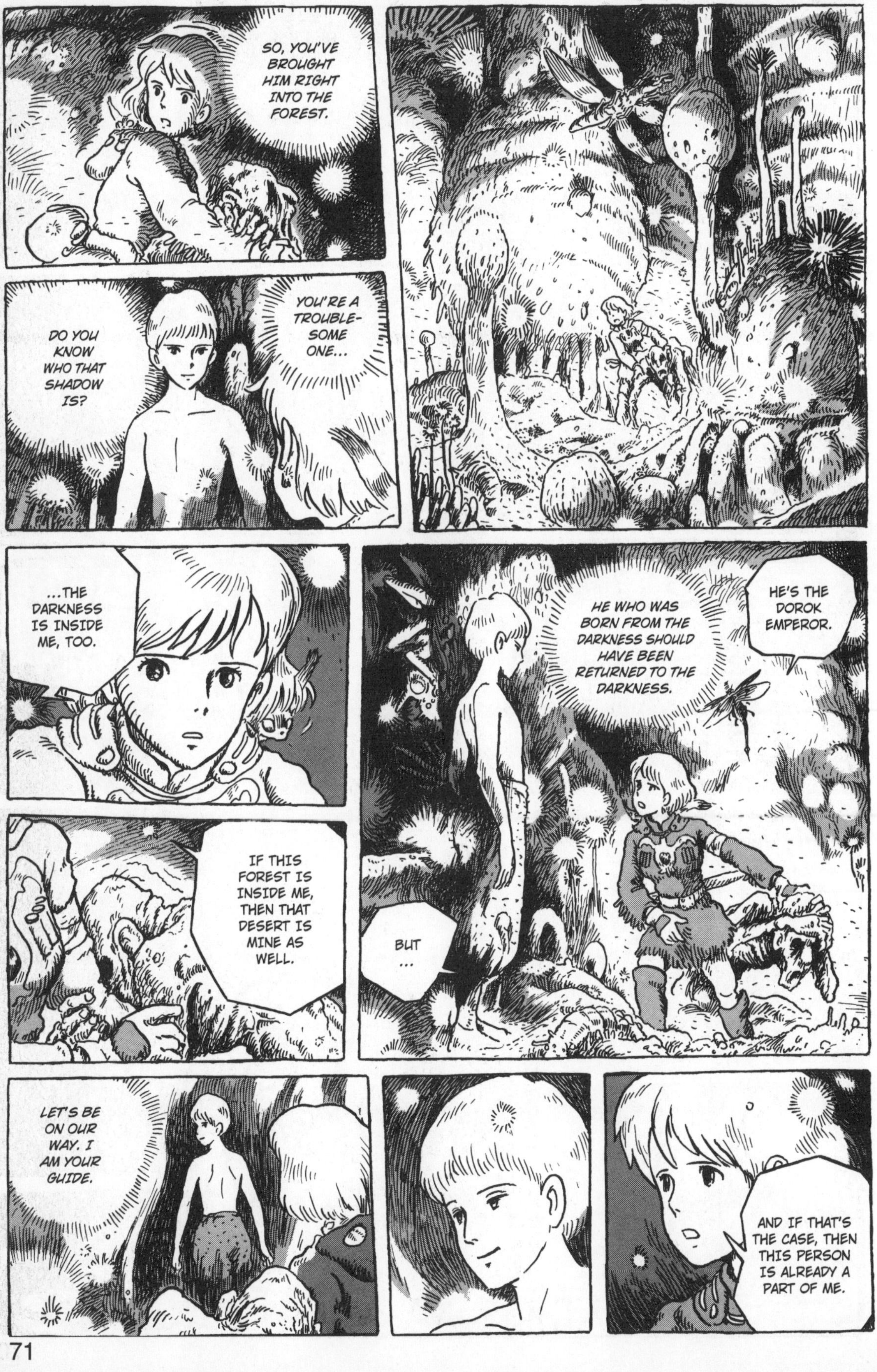
SO, YOU'VE BROUGHT HIM RIGHT INTO THE FOREST.
YOU'RE A TROUBLE-SOME ONE...
DO YOU KNOW WHO THAT SHADOW IS?
HE'S THE DOROK EMPEROR.
HE WHO WAS BORN FROM THE DARKNESS SHOULD HAVE BEEN RETURNED TO THE DARKNESS.
BUT ...
...THE DARKNESS IS INSIDE ME, TOO.
IF THIS FOREST IS INSIDE ME, THEN THAT DESERT IS MINE AS WELL.
AND IF THAT'S THE CASE, THEN THIS PERSON IS ALREADY A PART OF ME.
LET'S BE ON OUR WAY. I AM YOUR GUIDE.

SO MANY SPORES ...

...WHO WOULD THINK THAT MIASMA WAS SO FRAGRANT?

WHAT A MYSTERIOUS PERSON.

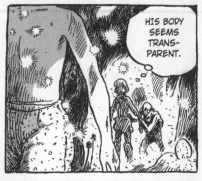

HIS BODY SEEMS TRANSPARENT.

AHH ...

I RECOGNIZE THESE SCARS!

THIS IS THAT OHMU.

IT'S A LONG JOURNEY.

LET'S CATCH A RIDE.

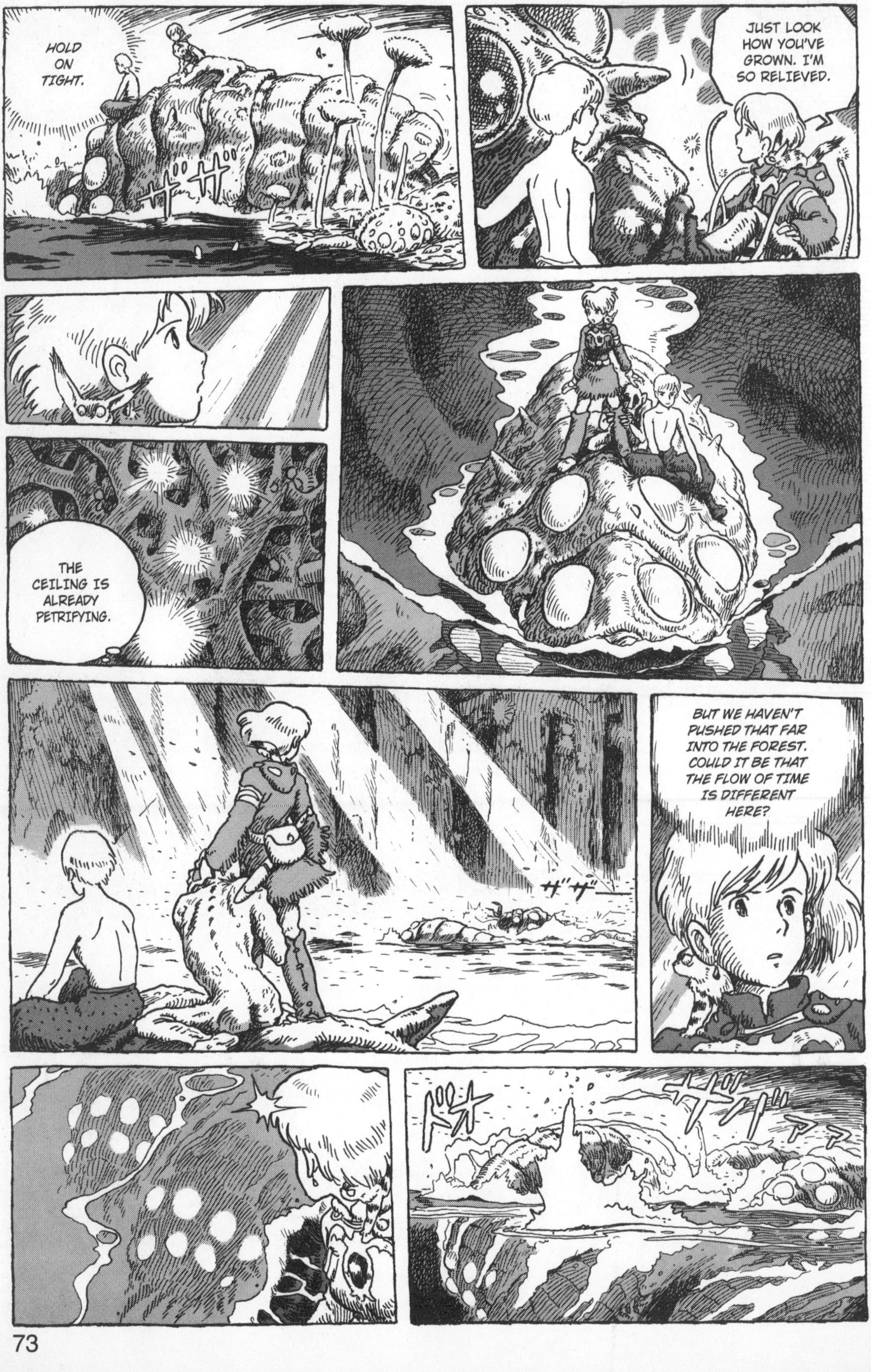
JUST LOOK HOW YOU'VE GROWN. I'M SO RELIEVED.
HOLD ON TIGHT.
THE CEILING IS ALREADY PETRIFYING.
BUT WE HAVEN'T PUSHED THAT FAR INTO THE FOREST. COULD IT BE THAT THE FLOW OF TIME IS DIFFERENT HERE?

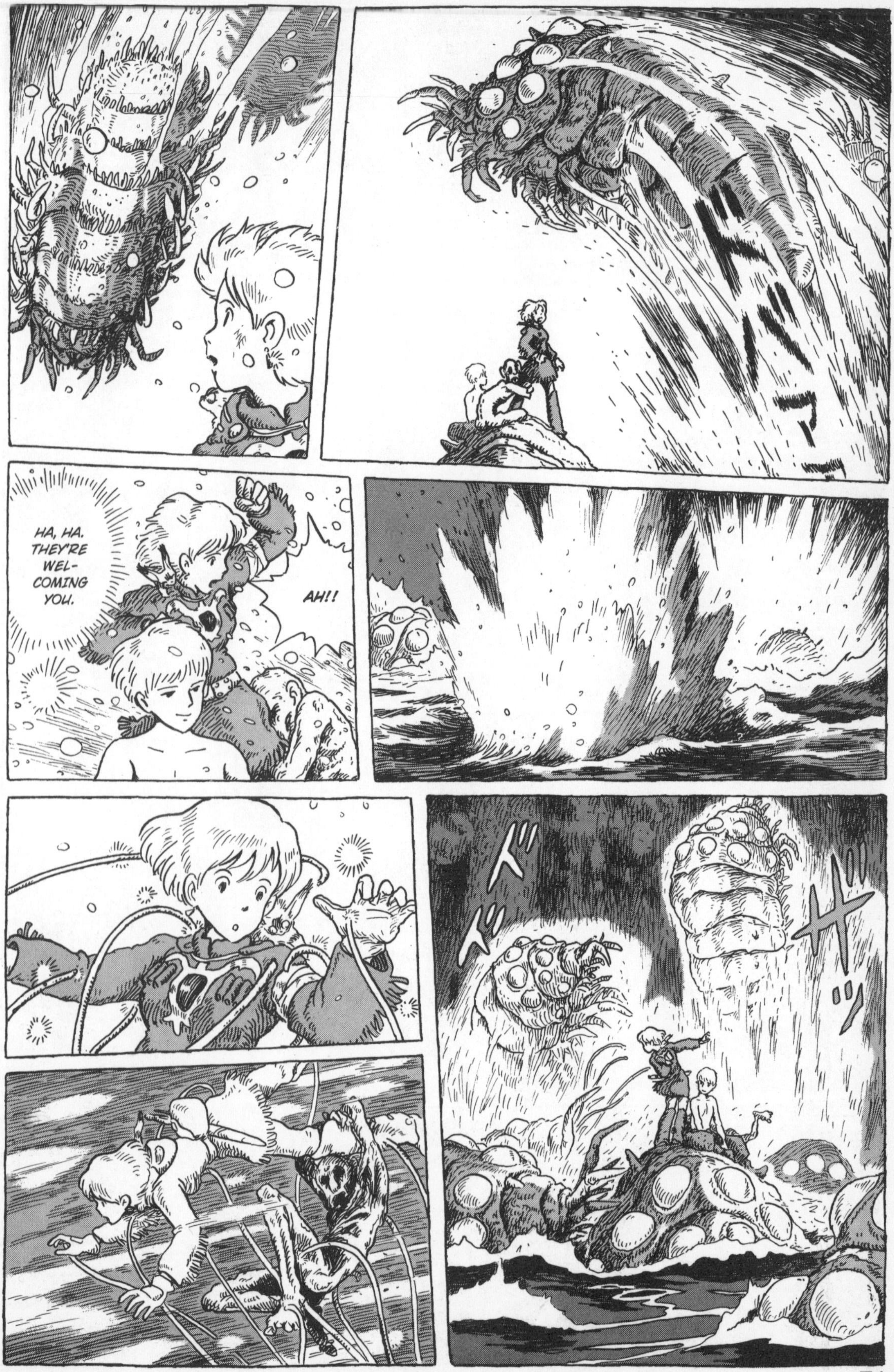
AH!!
HA, HA. THEY'RE WEL-COMING YOU.

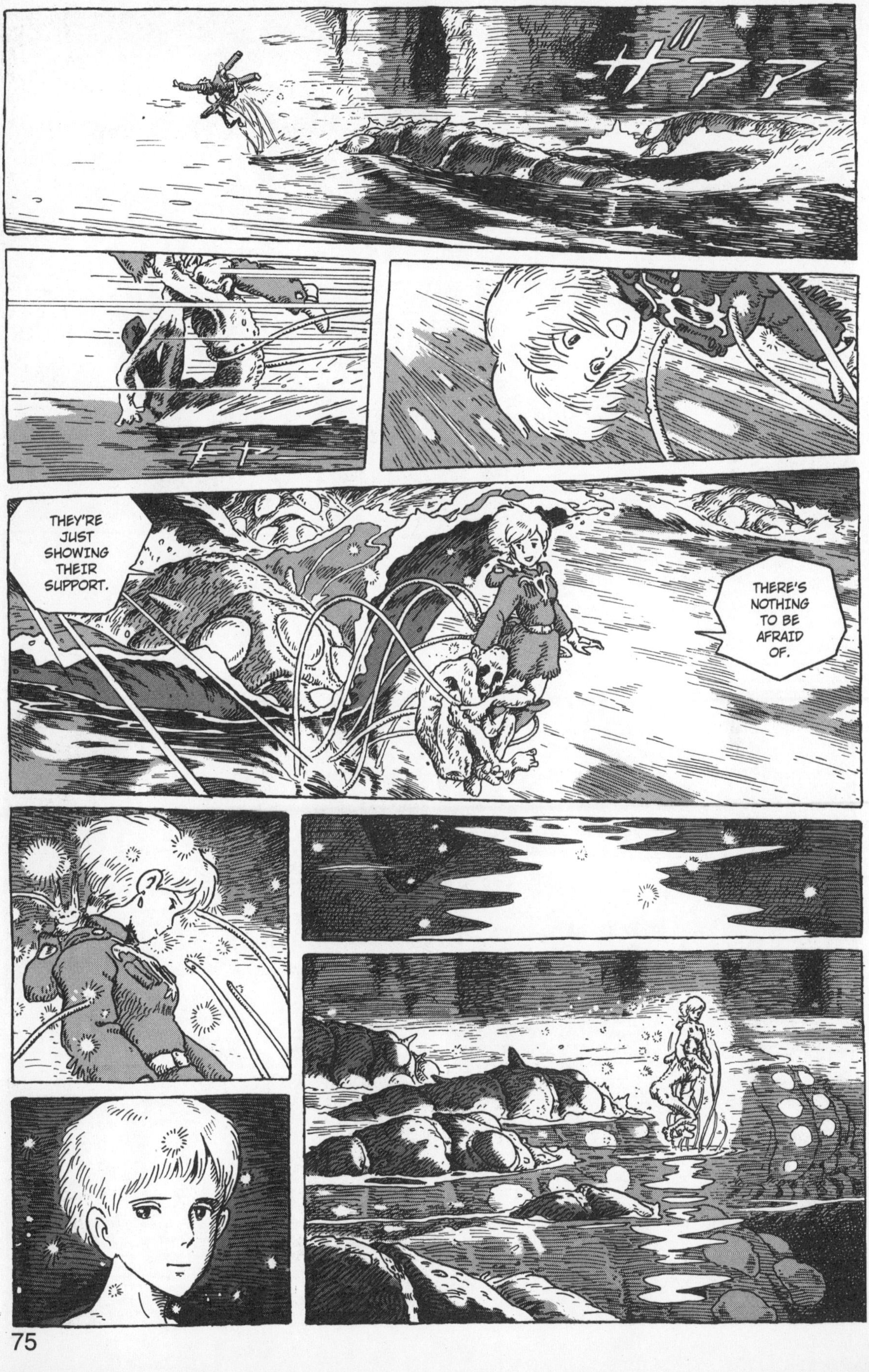
THERE'S NOTHING TO BE AFRAID OF.
THEY'RE JUST SHOWING THEIR SUPPORT.

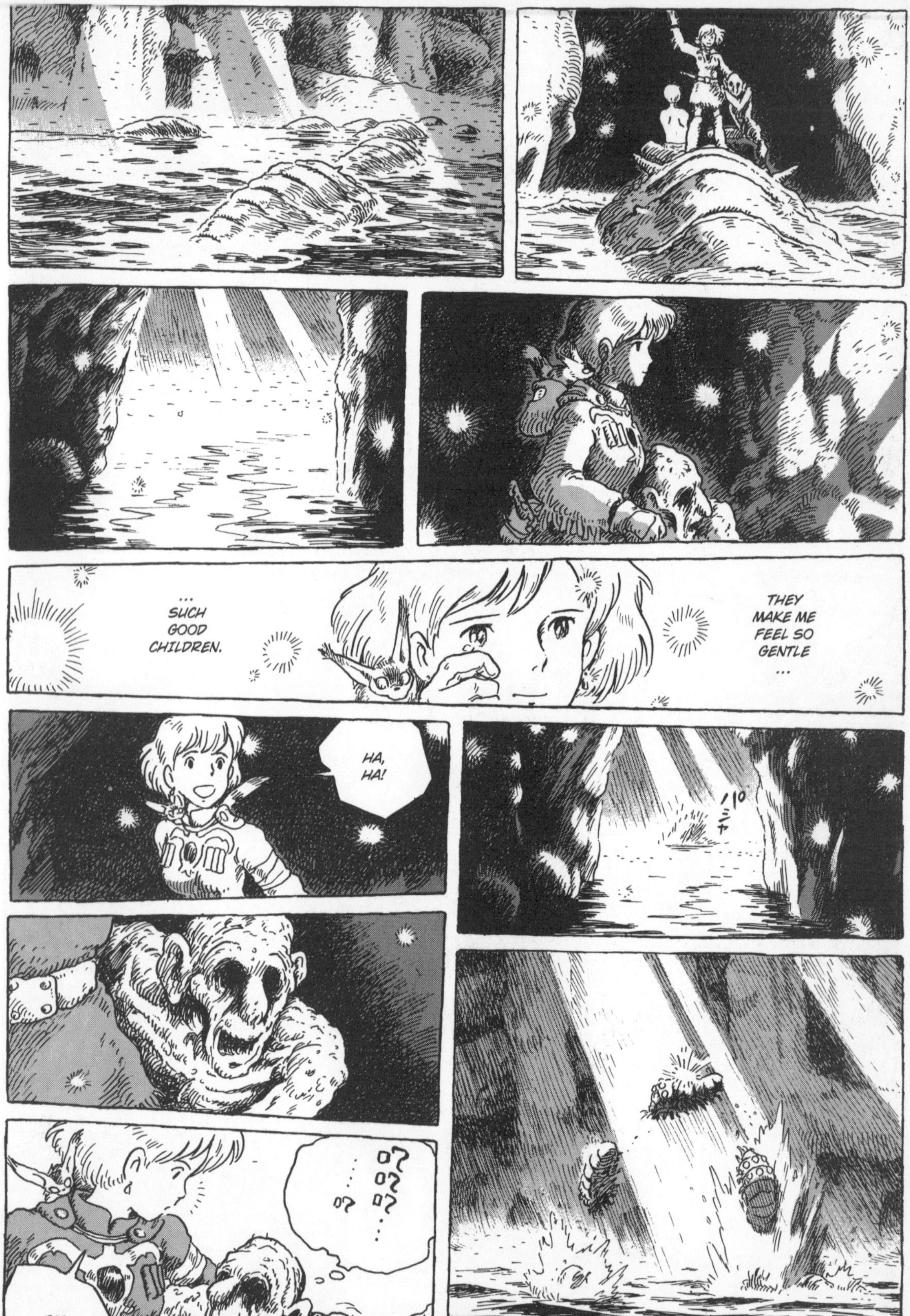
THEY MAKE ME FEEL SO GENTLE ...
... SUCH GOOD CHILDREN.
パシャ
HA, HA!
ロ?ロ?ロ?…
…ロ?
EH !?

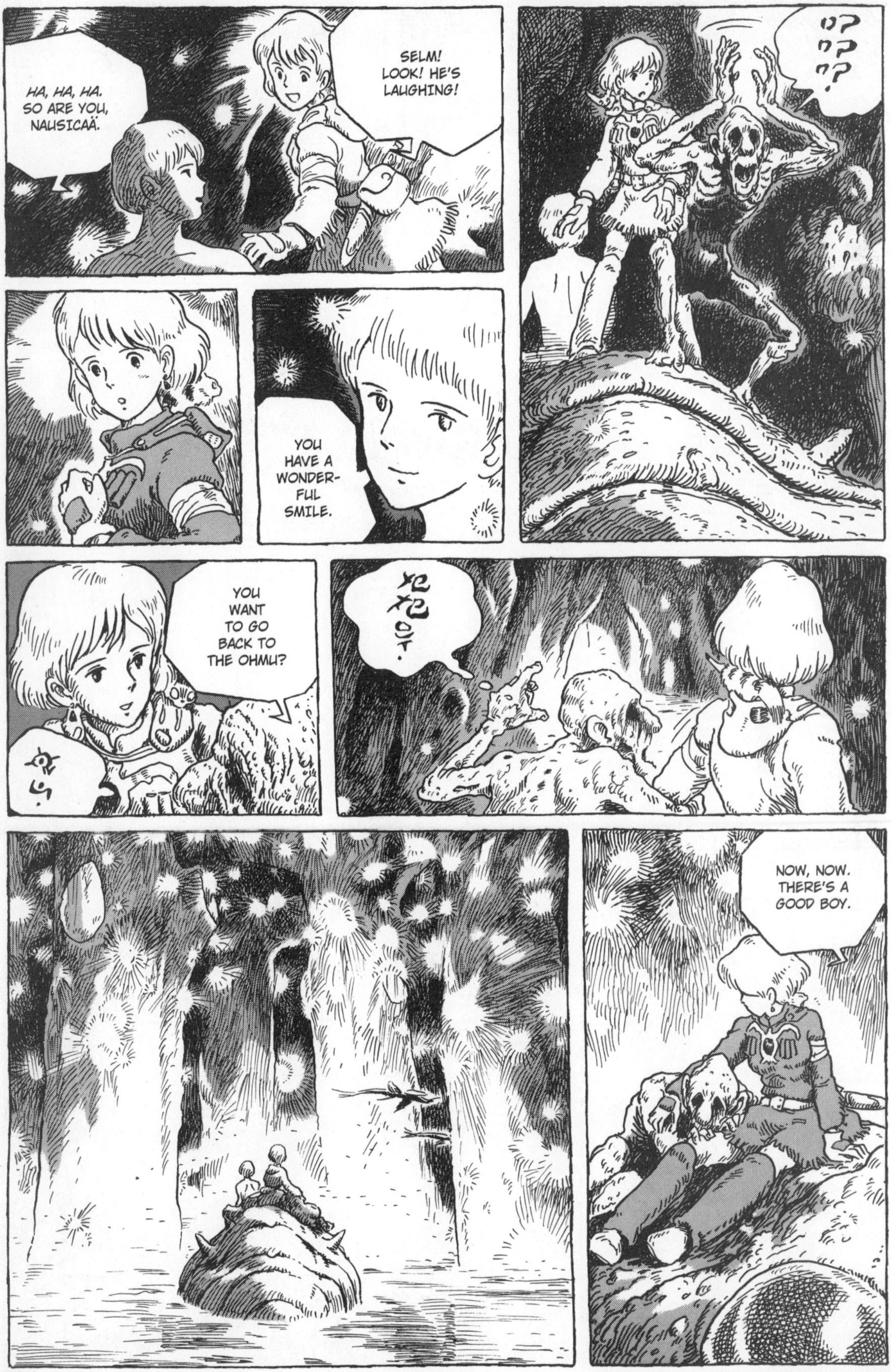

SELM! LOOK! HE'S LAUGHING!
HA, HA, HA. SO ARE YOU, NAUSICAÄ.
YOU HAVE A WONDERFUL SMILE.
YOU WANT TO GO BACK TO THE OHMU?
NOW, NOW. THERE'S A GOOD BOY.

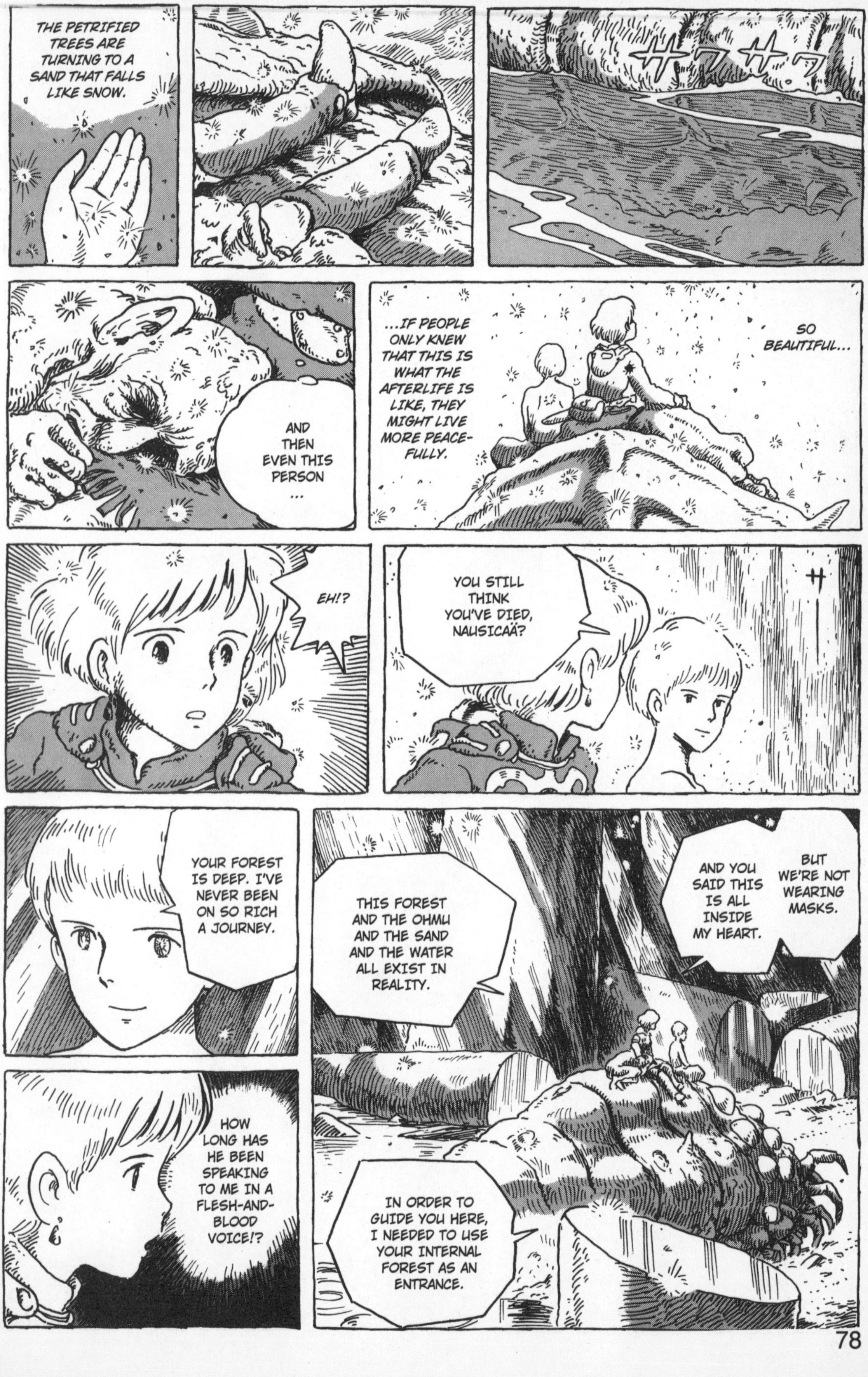
サワサワ
THE PETRIFIED TREES ARE TURNING TO A SAND THAT FALLS LIKE SNOW.
SO BEAUTIFUL...
...IF PEOPLE ONLY KNEW THAT THIS IS WHAT THE AFTERLIFE IS LIKE, THEY MIGHT LIVE MORE PEACE-FULLY.
AND THEN EVEN THIS PERSON ...
YOU STILL THINK YOU'VE DIED, NAUSICAÄ?
EH!?
BUT WE'RE NOT WEARING MASKS.
AND YOU SAID THIS IS ALL INSIDE MY HEART.
THIS FOREST AND THE OHMU AND THE SAND AND THE WATER ALL EXIST IN REALITY.
IN ORDER TO GUIDE YOU HERE, I NEEDED TO USE YOUR INTERNAL FOREST AS AN ENTRANCE.
YOUR FOREST IS DEEP. I'VE NEVER BEEN ON SO RICH A JOURNEY.
HOW LONG HAS HE BEEN SPEAKING TO ME IN A FLESH-AND-BLOOD VOICE!?

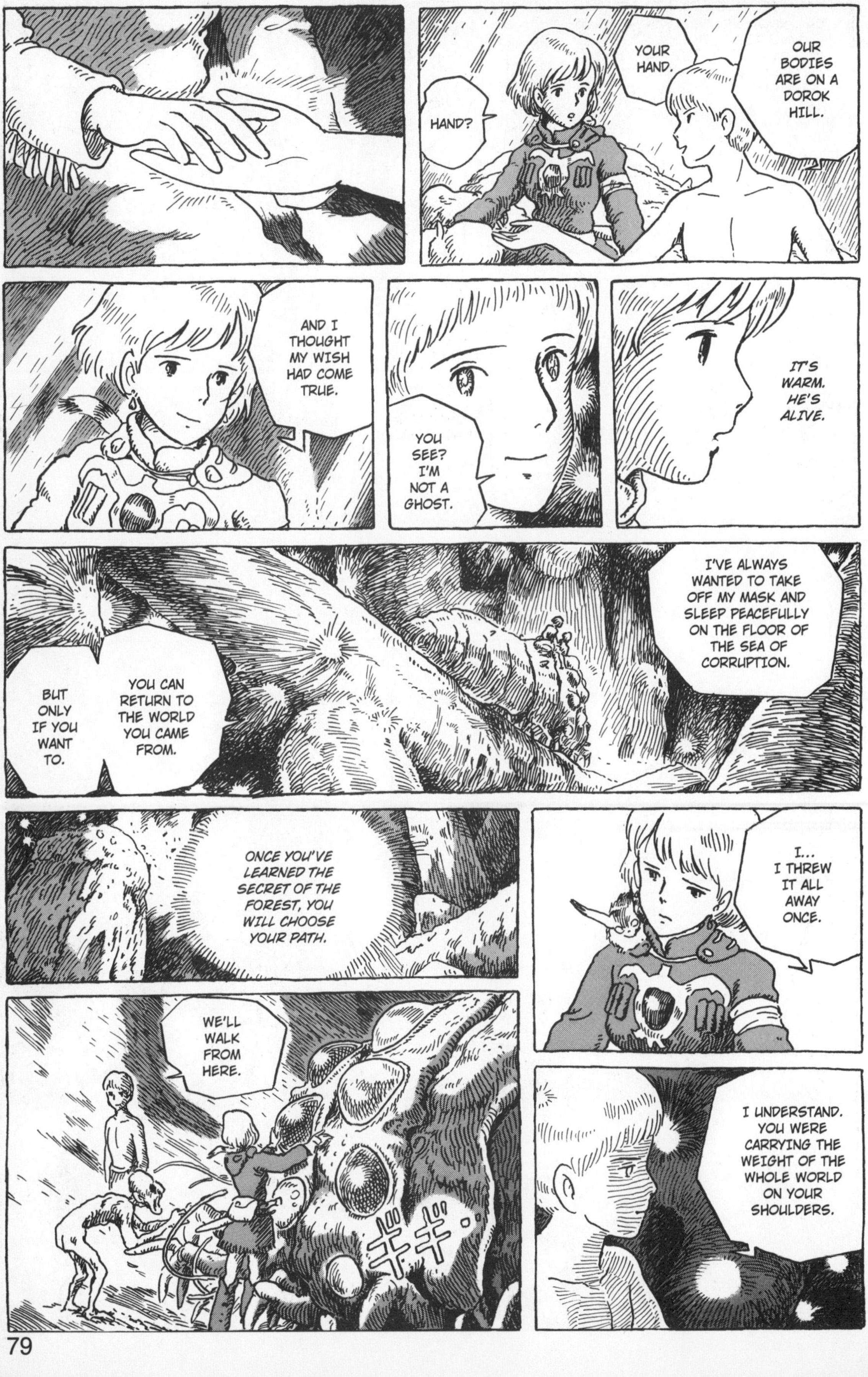

OUR BODIES ARE ON A DOROK HILL.
YOUR HAND.
HAND?
IT'S WARM. HE'S ALIVE.
YOU SEE? I'M NOT A GHOST.
AND I THOUGHT MY WISH HAD COME TRUE.
I'VE ALWAYS WANTED TO TAKE OFF MY MASK AND SLEEP PEACEFULLY ON THE FLOOR OF THE SEA OF CORRUPTION.
YOU CAN RETURN TO THE WORLD YOU CAME FROM.
BUT ONLY IF YOU WANT TO.
I... I THREW IT ALL AWAY ONCE.
I UNDERSTAND. YOU WERE CARRYING THE WEIGHT OF THE WHOLE WORLD ON YOUR SHOULDERS.
ONCE YOU'VE LEARNED THE SECRET OF THE FOREST, YOU WILL CHOOSE YOUR PATH.
WE'LL WALK FROM HERE.
ギギ。

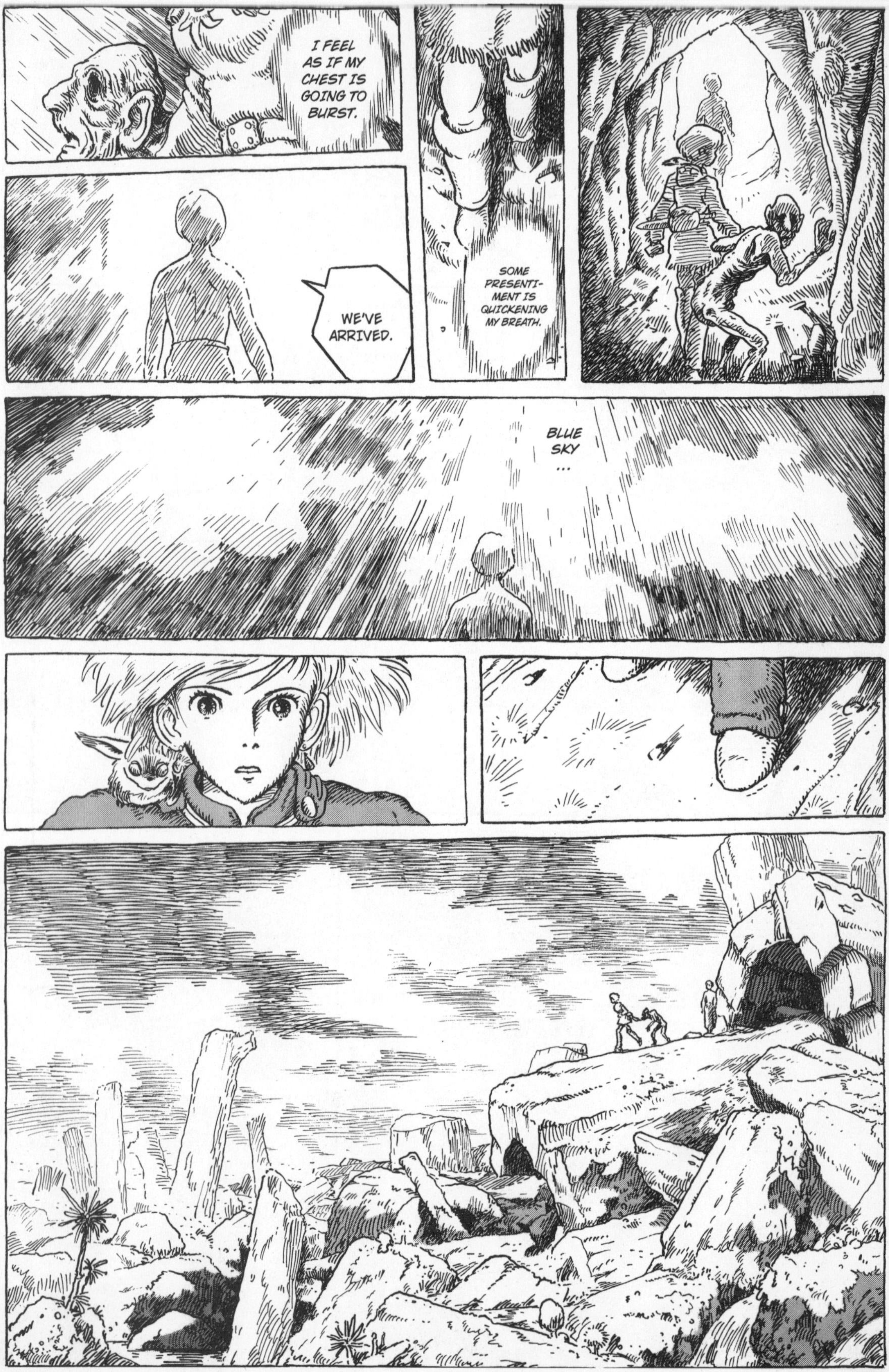
SOME PRESENTIMENT IS QUICKENING MY BREATH.
I FEEL AS IF MY CHEST IS GOING TO BURST.
WE'VE ARRIVED.
BLUE SKY ...

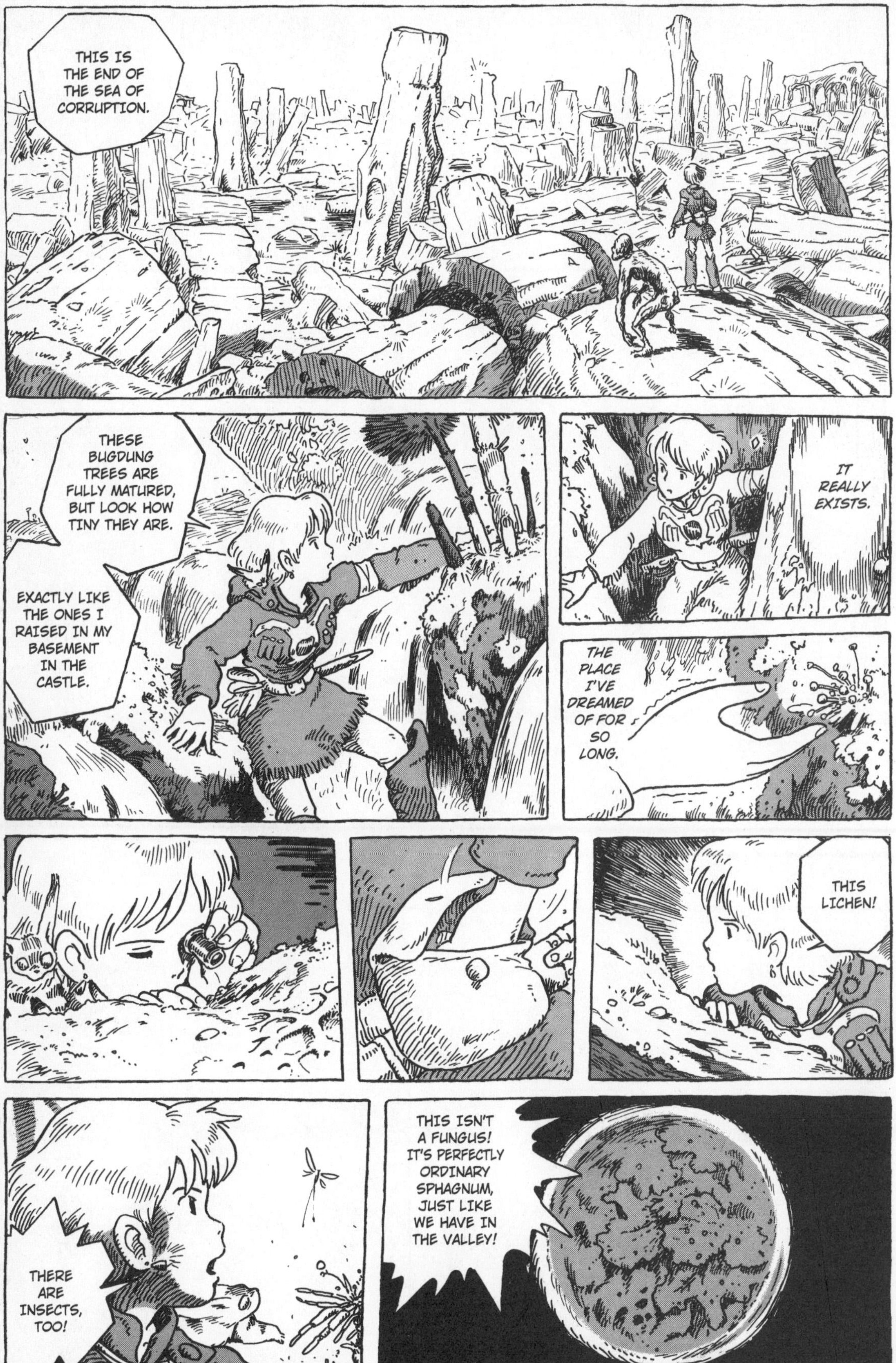
THIS IS THE END OF THE SEA OF CORRUPTION.
IT REALLY EXISTS.
THE PLACE I'VE DREAMED OF FOR SO LONG.
THESE BUGDUNG TREES ARE FULLY MATURED, BUT LOOK HOW TINY THEY ARE.
EXACTLY LIKE THE ONES I RAISED IN MY BASEMENT IN THE CASTLE.
THIS LICHEN!
THIS ISN'T A FUNGUS! IT'S PERFECTLY ORDINARY SPHAGNUM, JUST LIKE WE HAVE IN THE VALLEY!
THERE ARE INSECTS, TOO!

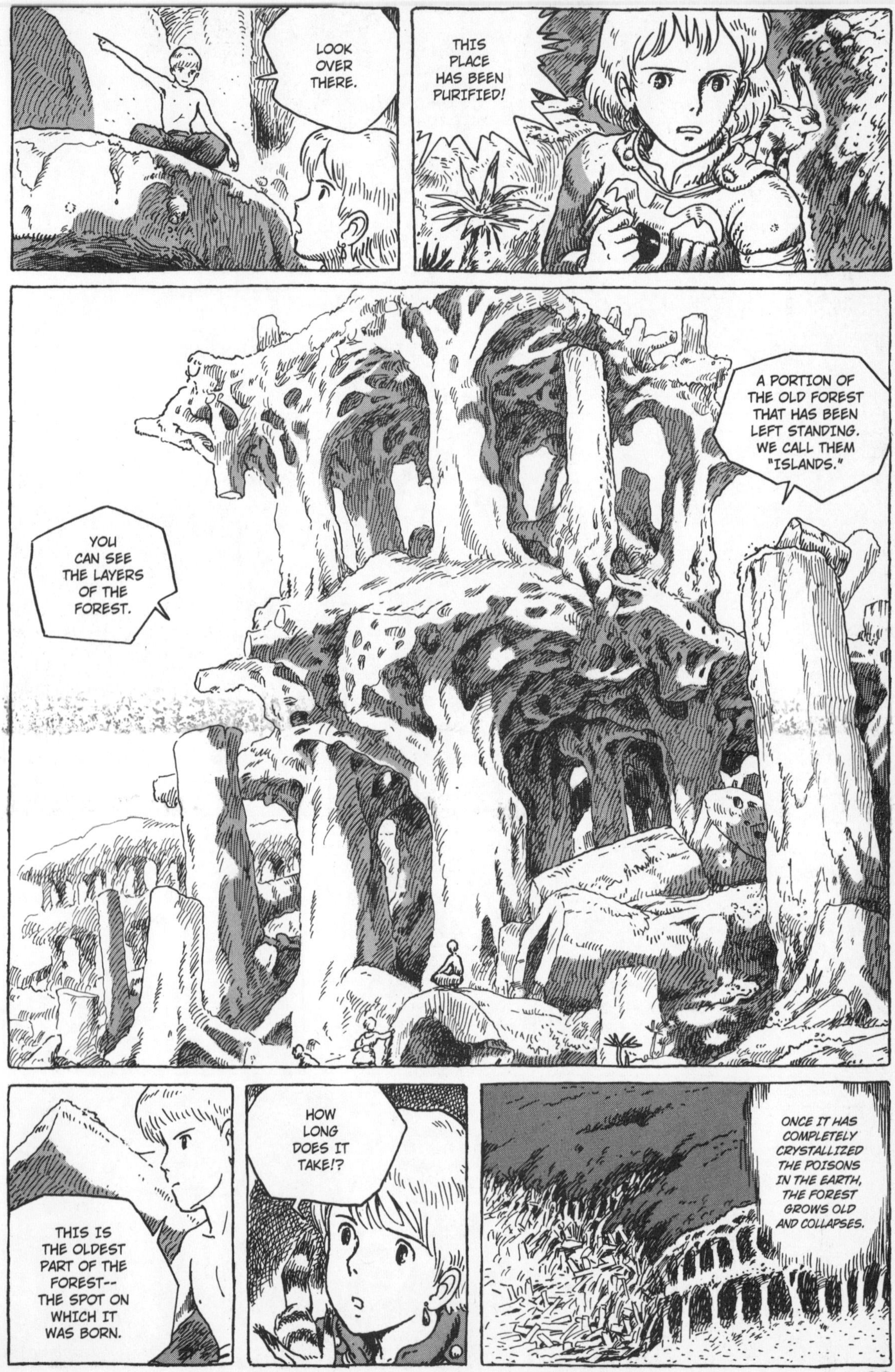
LOOK OVER THERE.
THIS PLACE HAS BEEN PURIFIED!
YOU CAN SEE THE LAYERS OF THE FOREST.
A PORTION OF THE OLD FOREST THAT HAS BEEN LEFT STANDING. WE CALL THEM "ISLANDS."
THIS IS THE OLDEST PART OF THE FOREST-- THE SPOT ON WHICH IT WAS BORN.
HOW LONG DOES IT TAKE!?
ONCE IT HAS COMPLETELY CRYSTALLIZED THE POISONS IN THE EARTH, THE FOREST GROWS OLD AND COLLAPSES.

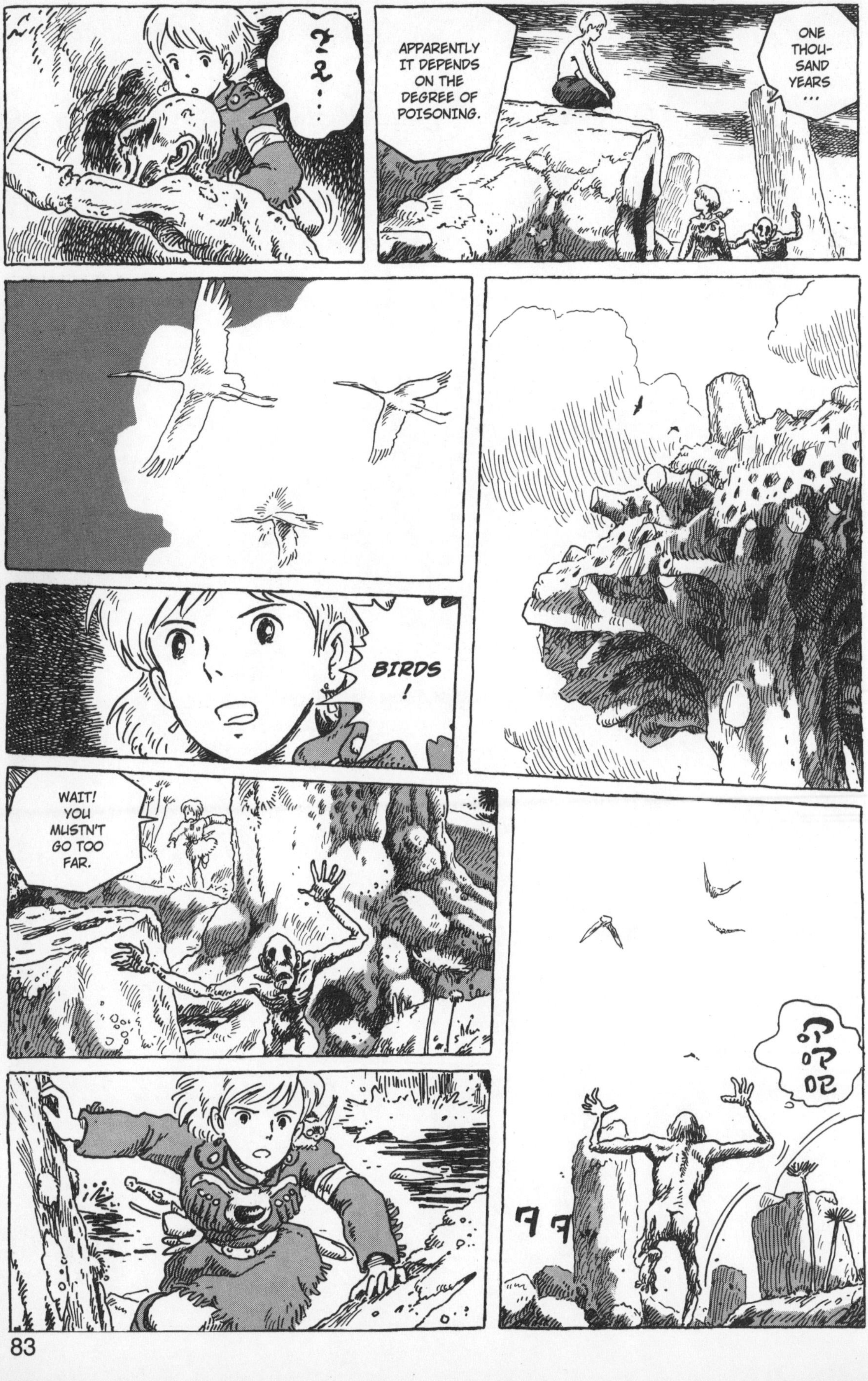
ONE THOU-SAND YEARS...
APPARENTLY IT DEPENDS ON THE DEGREE OF POISONING.
BIRDS!
WAIT! YOU MUSTN'T GO TOO FAR.

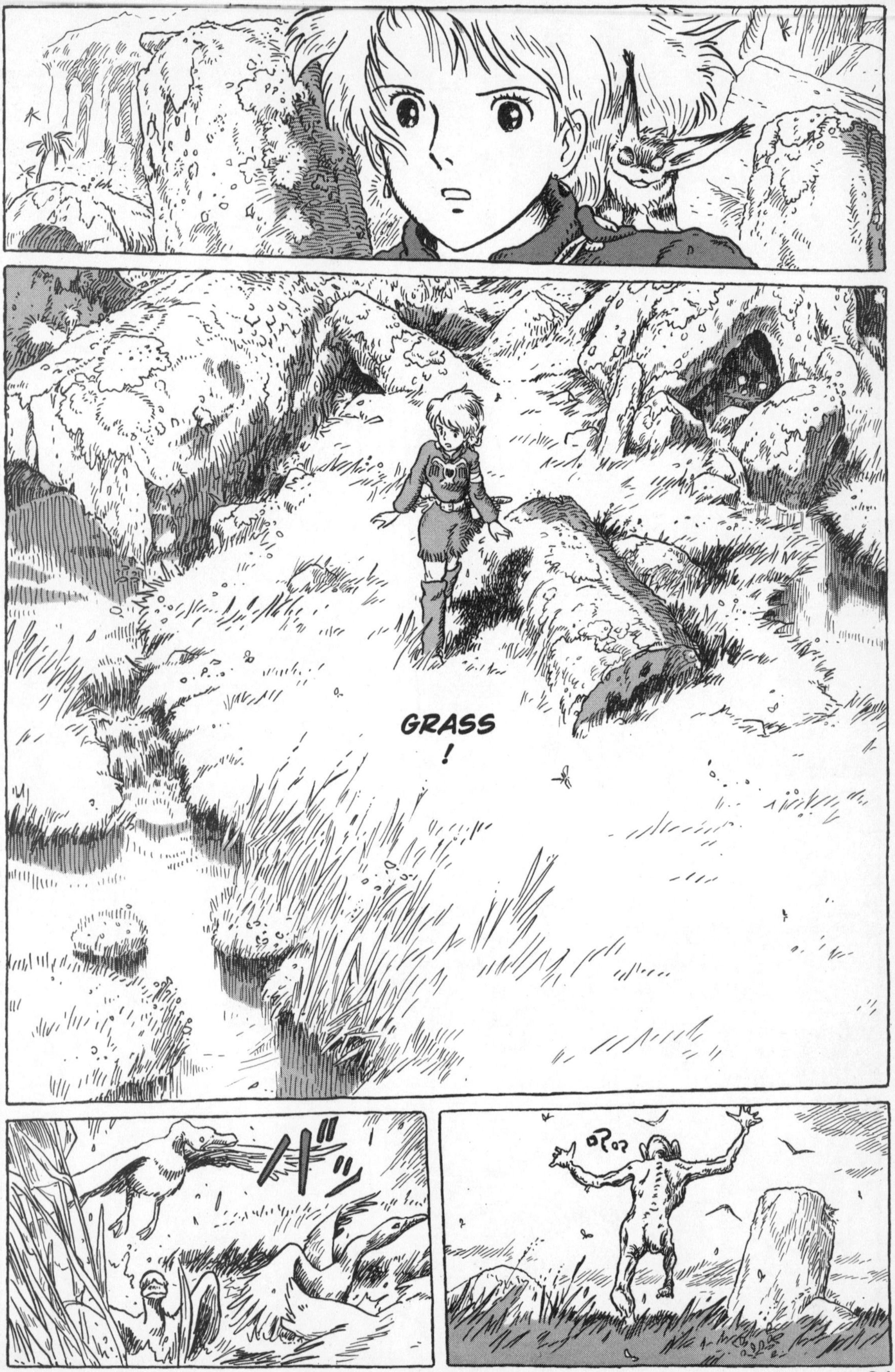
GRASS
!
バッ

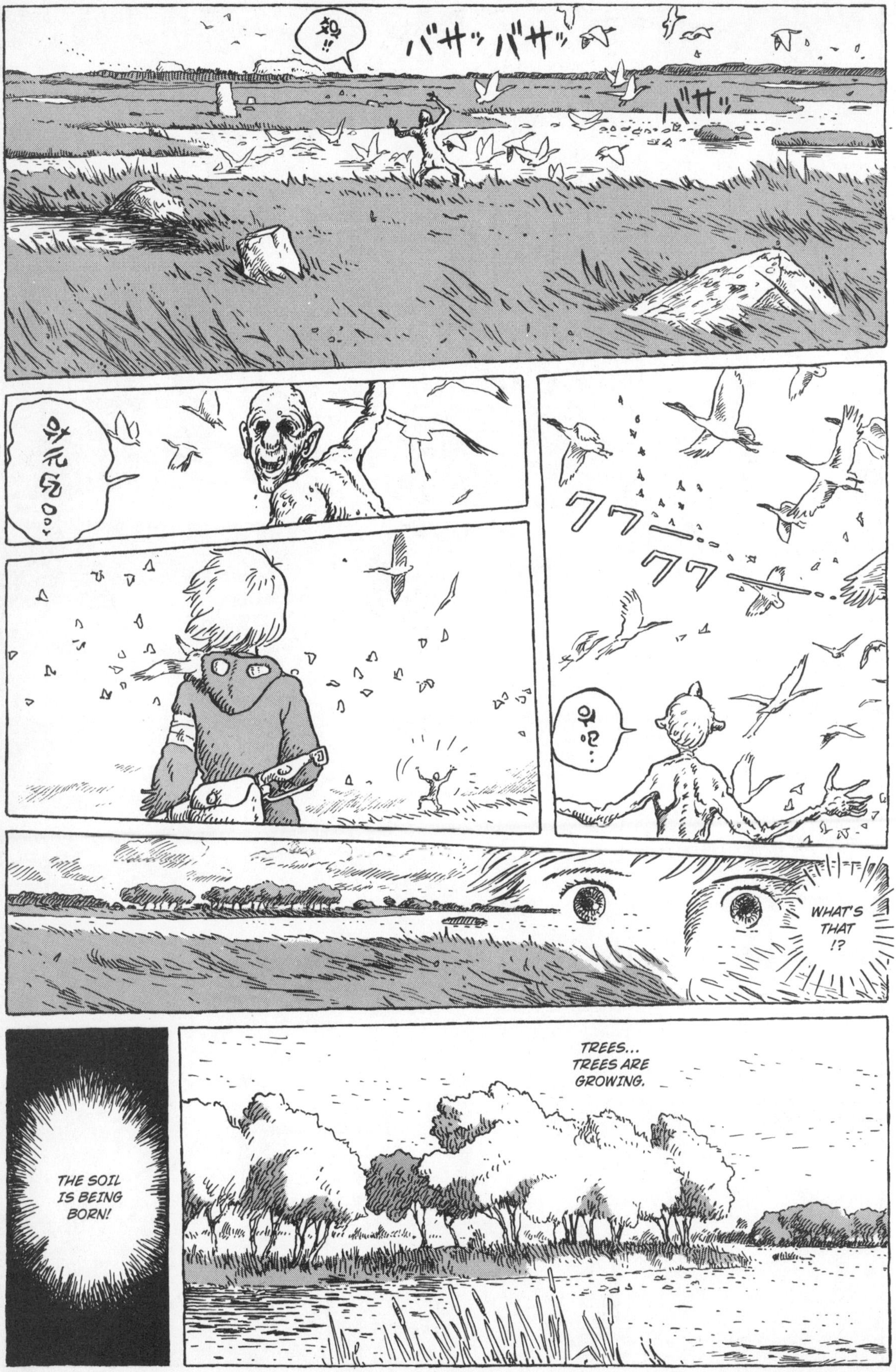

バサッバサッ
バサッ
クワー…
クワー…
WHAT'S THAT !?
TREES... TREES ARE GROWING.
THE SOIL IS BEING BORN!

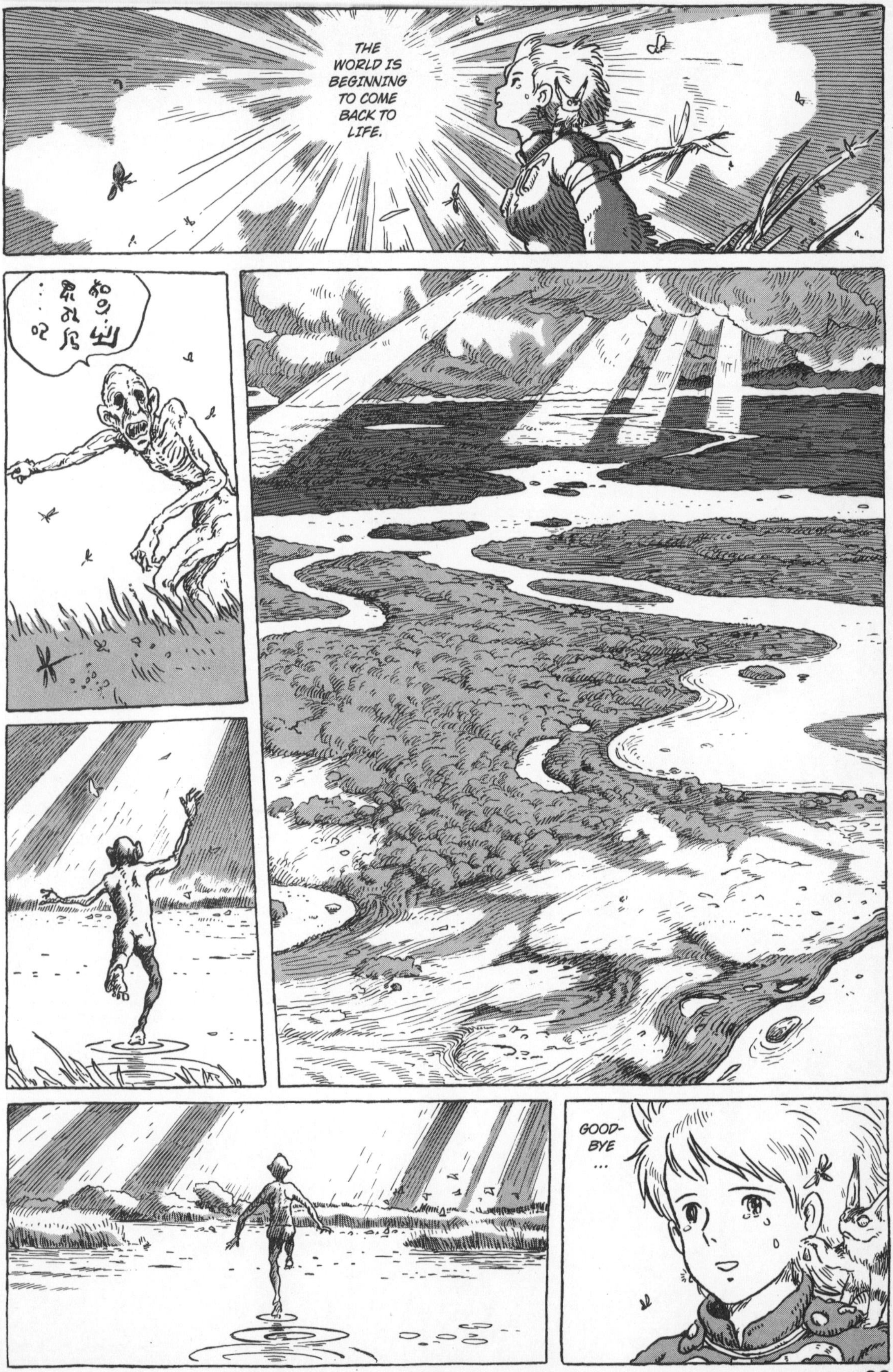
THE WORLD IS BEGINNING TO COME BACK TO LIFE.
GOOD-BYE ...

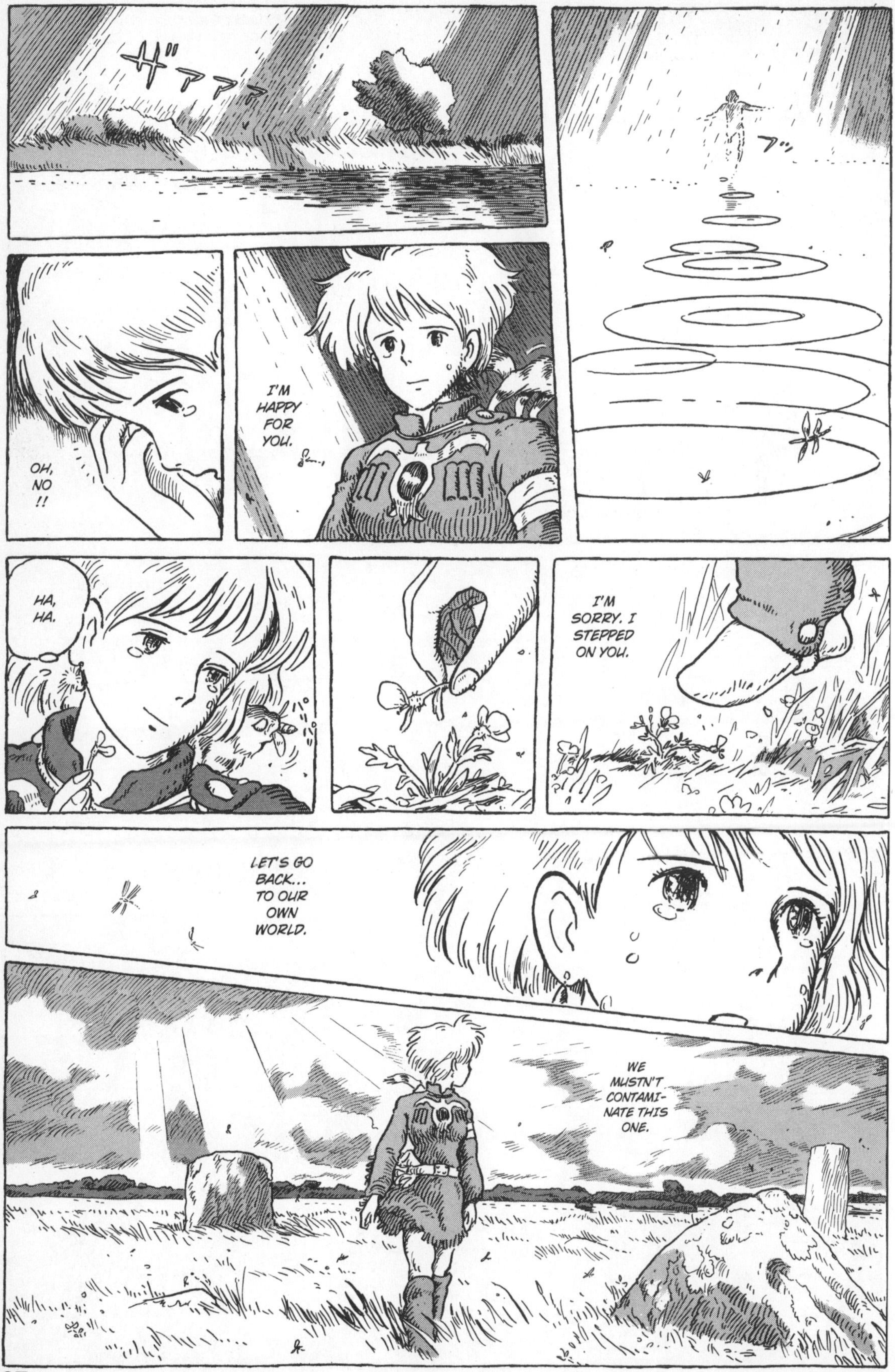
フッ
ザァァァ
I'M HAPPY FOR YOU.
OH, NO !!
I'M SORRY. I STEPPED ON YOU.
HA, HA.
LET'S GO BACK... TO OUR OWN WORLD.
WE MUSTN'T CONTAMINATE THIS ONE.

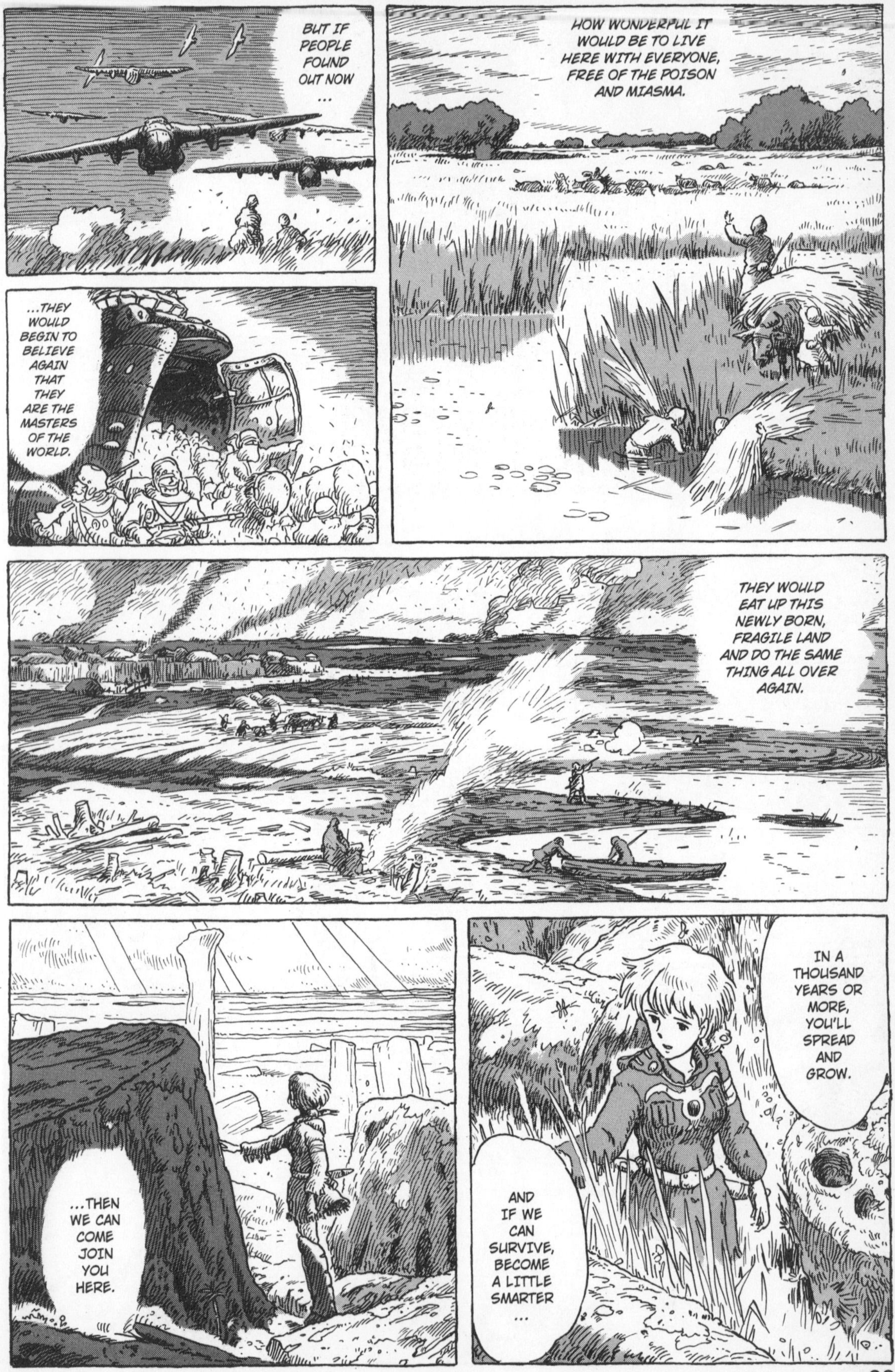
HOW WONDERFUL IT WOULD BE TO LIVE HERE WITH EVERYONE, FREE OF THE POISON AND MIASMA.
BUT IF PEOPLE FOUND OUT NOW ...
...THEY WOULD BEGIN TO BELIEVE AGAIN THAT THEY ARE THE MASTERS OF THE WORLD.
THEY WOULD EAT UP THIS NEWLY BORN, FRAGILE LAND AND DO THE SAME THING ALL OVER AGAIN.
IN A THOUSAND YEARS OR MORE, YOU'LL SPREAD AND GROW.
AND IF WE CAN SURVIVE, BECOME A LITTLE SMARTER ...
...THEN WE CAN COME JOIN YOU HERE.

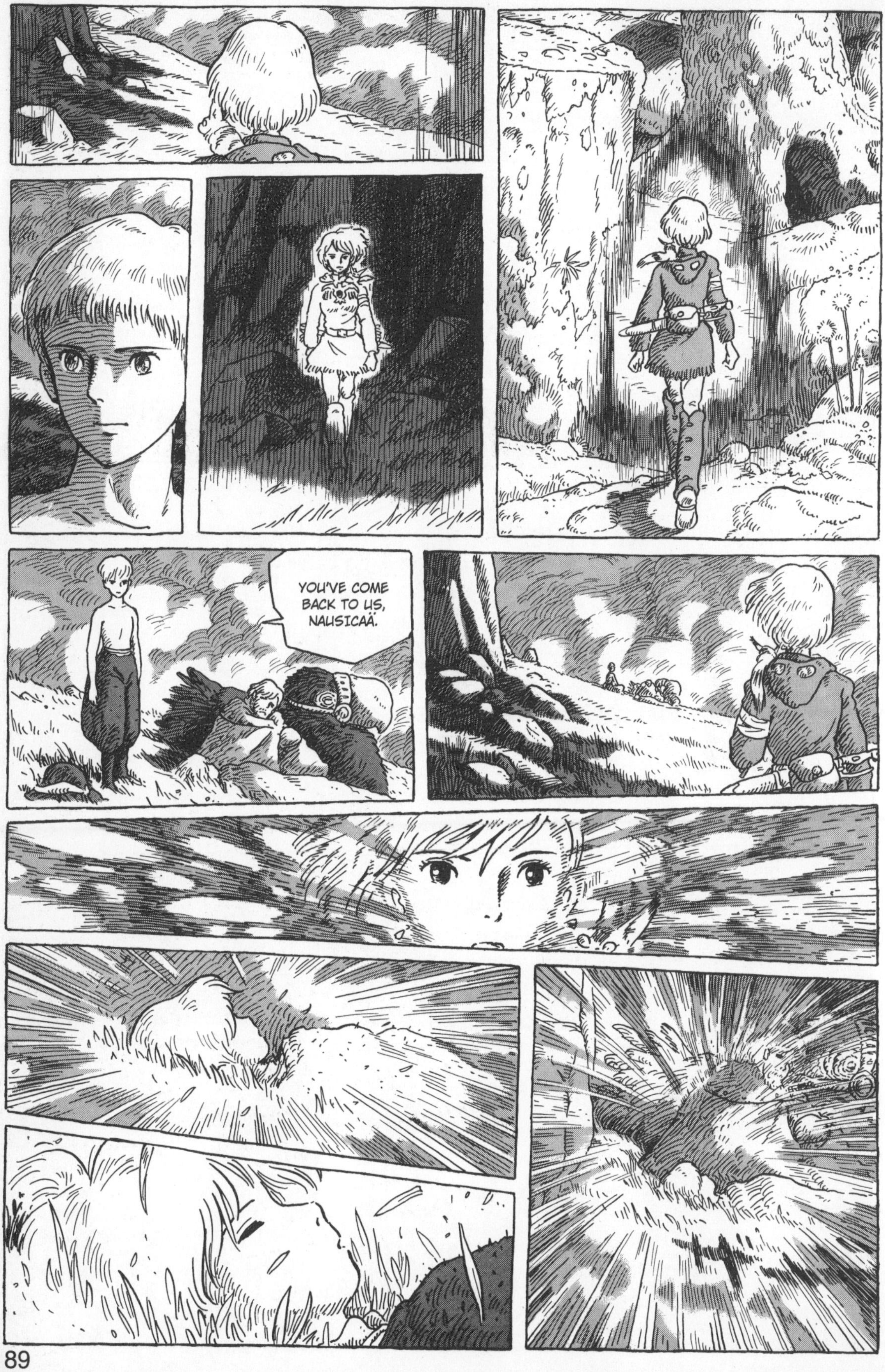
YOU'VE COME
BACK TO US,
NAUSICAÄ.

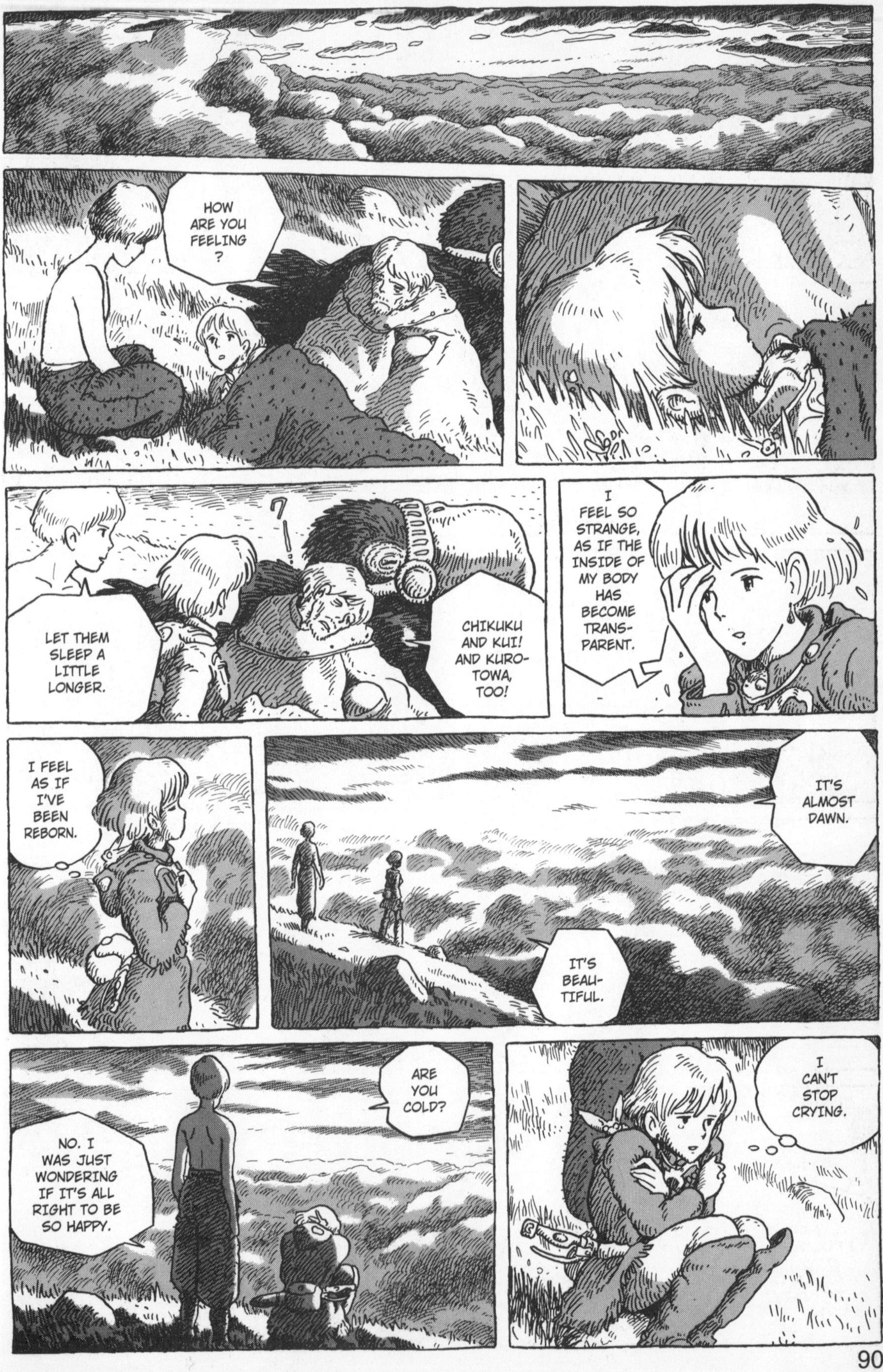
HOW ARE YOU FEELING ?
I FEEL SO STRANGE, AS IF THE INSIDE OF MY BODY HAS BECOME TRANS-PARENT.
CHIKUKU AND KUI! AND KURO-TOWA, TOO!
LET THEM SLEEP A LITTLE LONGER.
IT'S ALMOST DAWN.
IT'S BEAU-TIFUL.
I FEEL AS IF I'VE BEEN REBORN.
I CAN'T STOP CRYING.
ARE YOU COLD?
NO. I WAS JUST WONDERING IF IT'S ALL RIGHT TO BE SO HAPPY.

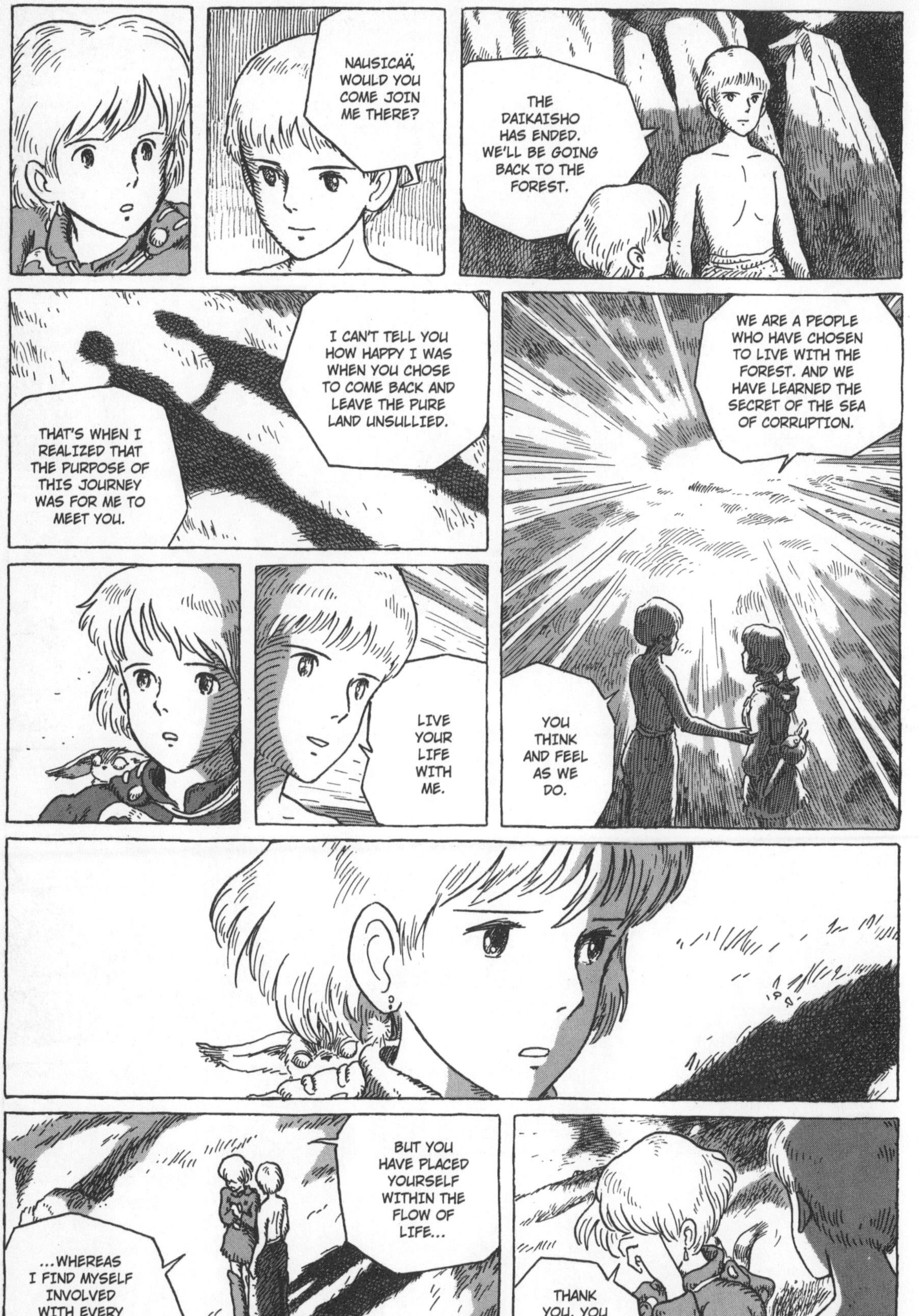
THE DAIKAISHO HAS ENDED. WE'LL BE GOING BACK TO THE FOREST.
NAUSICAÄ, WOULD YOU COME JOIN ME THERE?
WE ARE A PEOPLE WHO HAVE CHOSEN TO LIVE WITH THE FOREST. AND WE HAVE LEARNED THE SECRET OF THE SEA OF CORRUPTION.
YOU THINK AND FEEL AS WE DO.
I CAN'T TELL YOU HOW HAPPY I WAS WHEN YOU CHOSE TO COME BACK AND LEAVE THE PURE LAND UNSULLIED.
THAT'S WHEN I REALIZED THAT THE PURPOSE OF THIS JOURNEY WAS FOR ME TO MEET YOU.
LIVE YOUR LIFE WITH ME.
THANK YOU. YOU MAKE ME VERY HAPPY.
BUT YOU HAVE PLACED YOURSELF WITHIN THE FLOW OF LIFE...
...WHEREAS I FIND MYSELF INVOLVED WITH EVERY INDIVIDUAL LIVING THING.

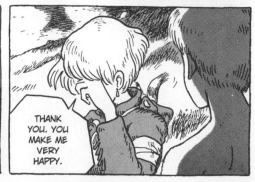

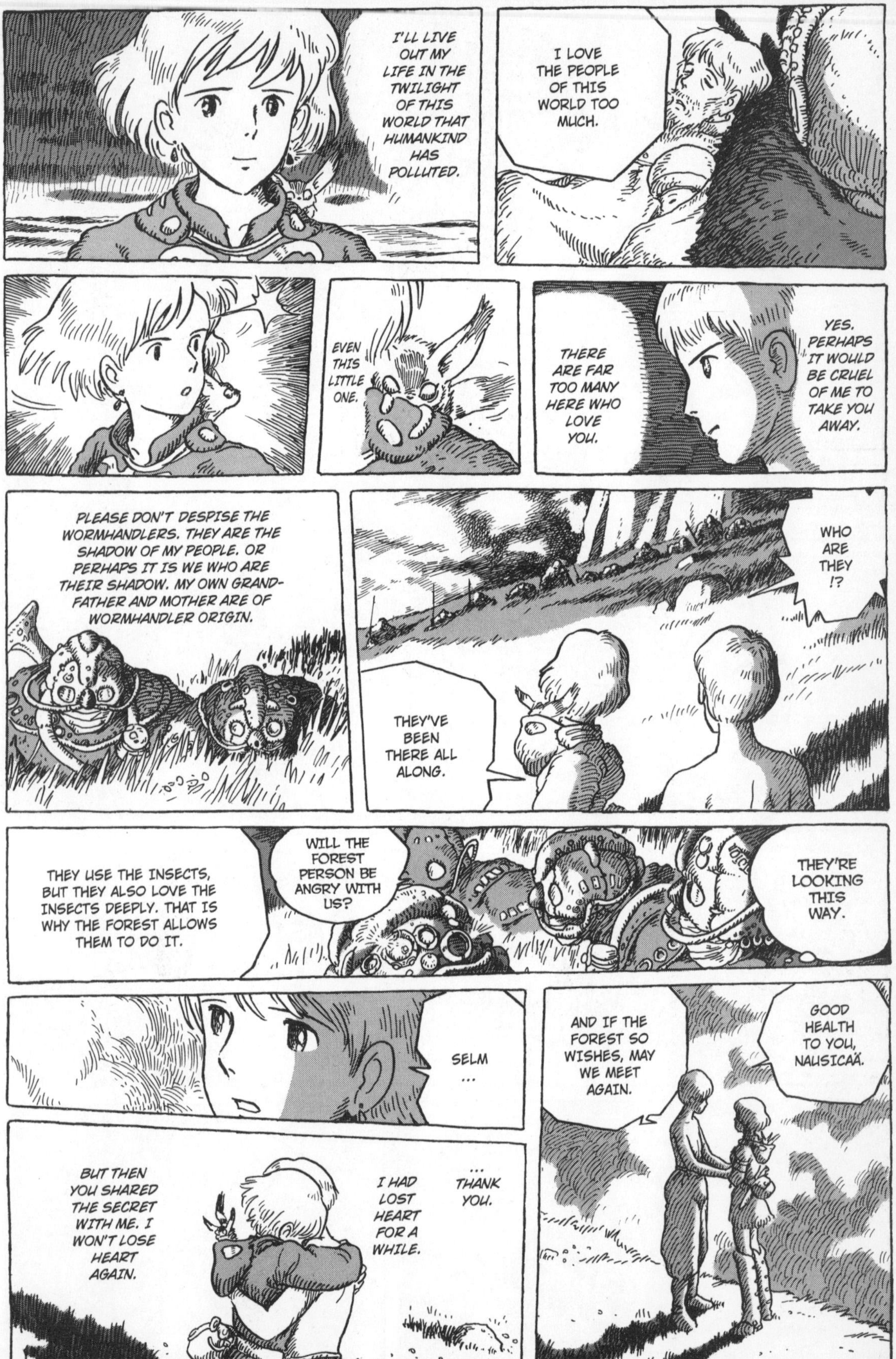
I LOVE THE PEOPLE OF THIS WORLD TOO MUCH.
I'LL LIVE OUT MY LIFE IN THE TWILIGHT OF THIS WORLD THAT HUMANKIND HAS POLLUTED.
YES. PERHAPS IT WOULD BE CRUEL OF ME TO TAKE YOU AWAY.
THERE ARE FAR TOO MANY HERE WHO LOVE YOU.
EVEN THIS LITTLE ONE.
WHO ARE THEY !?
THEY'VE BEEN THERE ALL ALONG.
PLEASE DON'T DESPISE THE WORMHANDLERS. THEY ARE THE SHADOW OF MY PEOPLE. OR PERHAPS IT IS WE WHO ARE THEIR SHADOW. MY OWN GRAND-FATHER AND MOTHER ARE OF WORMHANDLER ORIGIN.
THEY'RE LOOKING THIS WAY.
WILL THE FOREST PERSON BE ANGRY WITH US?
THEY USE THE INSECTS, BUT THEY ALSO LOVE THE INSECTS DEEPLY. THAT IS WHY THE FOREST ALLOWS THEM TO DO IT.
GOOD HEALTH TO YOU, NAUSICAÄ.
AND IF THE FOREST SO WISHES, MAY WE MEET AGAIN.
SELM ...
... THANK YOU.
I HAD LOST HEART FOR A WHILE.
BUT THEN YOU SHARED THE SECRET WITH ME. I WON'T LOSE HEART AGAIN.

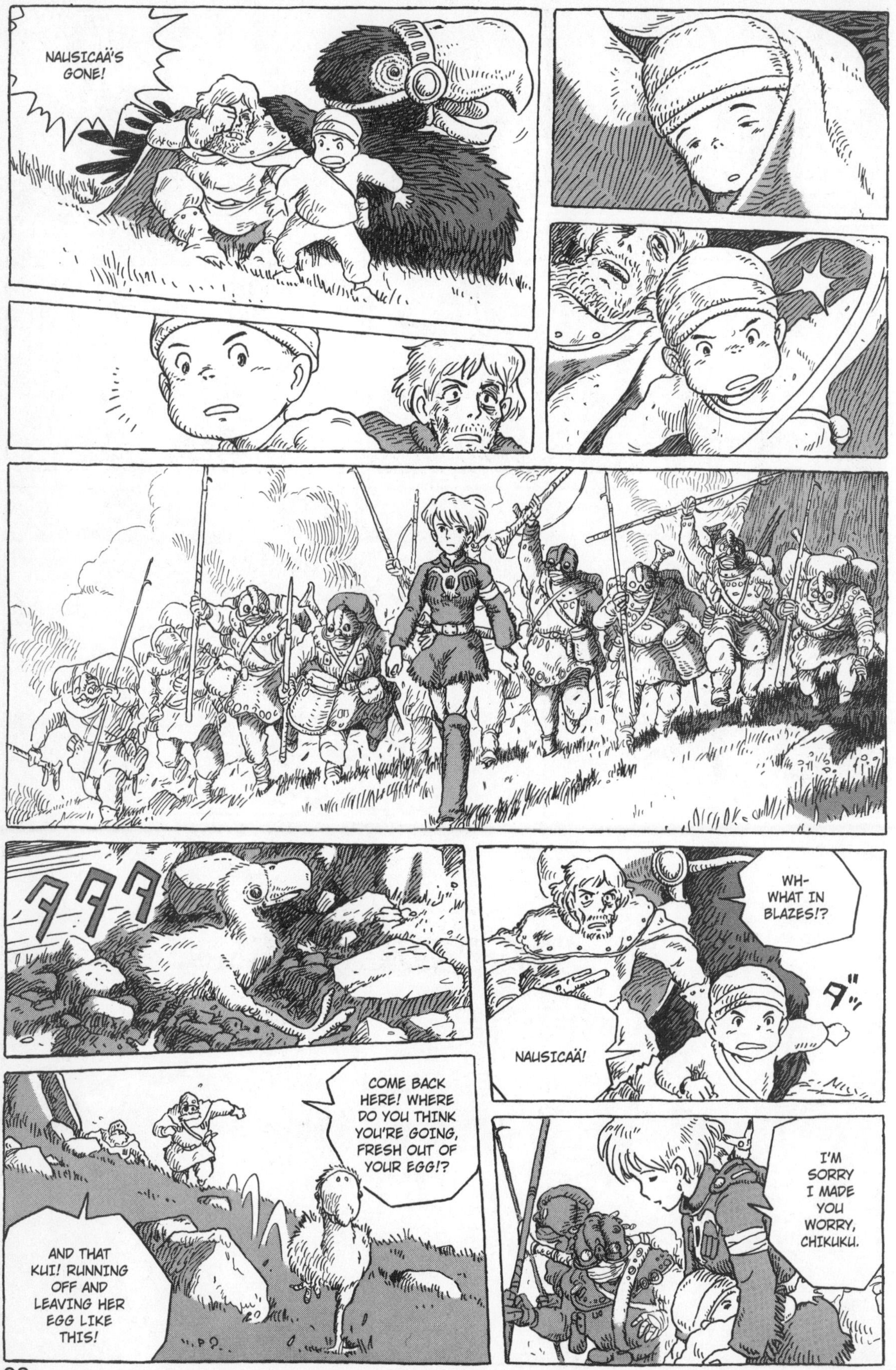

NAUSICAÄ'S GONE!
WH- WHAT IN BLAZES!?
ダッ
NAUSICAÄ!
タタタ
I'M SORRY I MADE YOU WORRY, CHIKUKU.
COME BACK HERE! WHERE DO YOU THINK YOU'RE GOING, FRESH OUT OF YOUR EGG!?
AND THAT KUI! RUNNING OFF AND LEAVING HER EGG LIKE THIS!

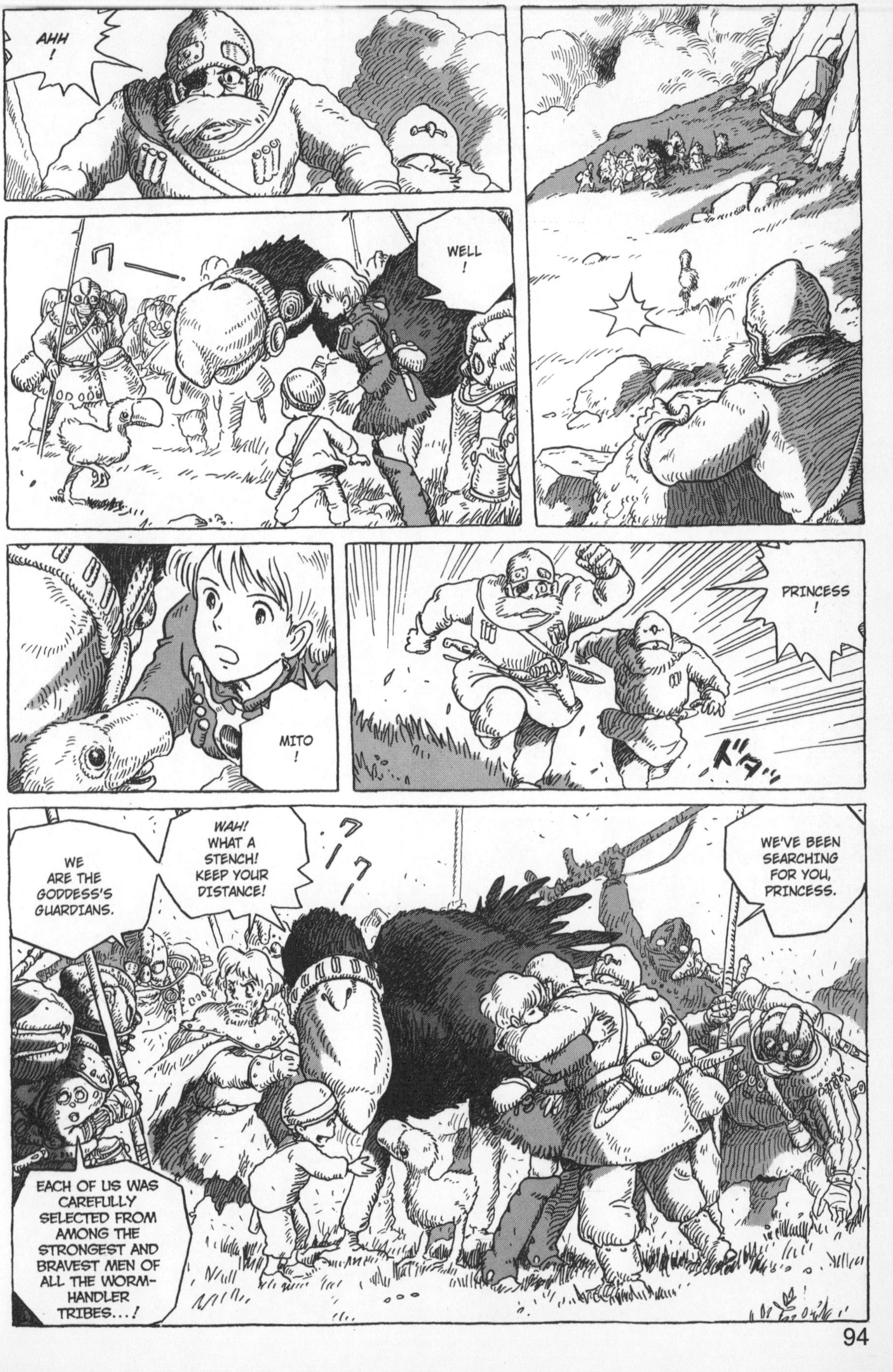
AHH !
WELL !
PRINCESS !
ドタッ
MITO !
WE'VE BEEN SEARCHING FOR YOU, PRINCESS.
WAH! WHAT A STENCH! KEEP YOUR DISTANCE!
WE ARE THE GODDESS'S GUARDIANS.
EACH OF US WAS CAREFULLY SELECTED FROM AMONG THE STRONGEST AND BRAVEST MEN OF ALL THE WORM-HANDLER TRIBES...!

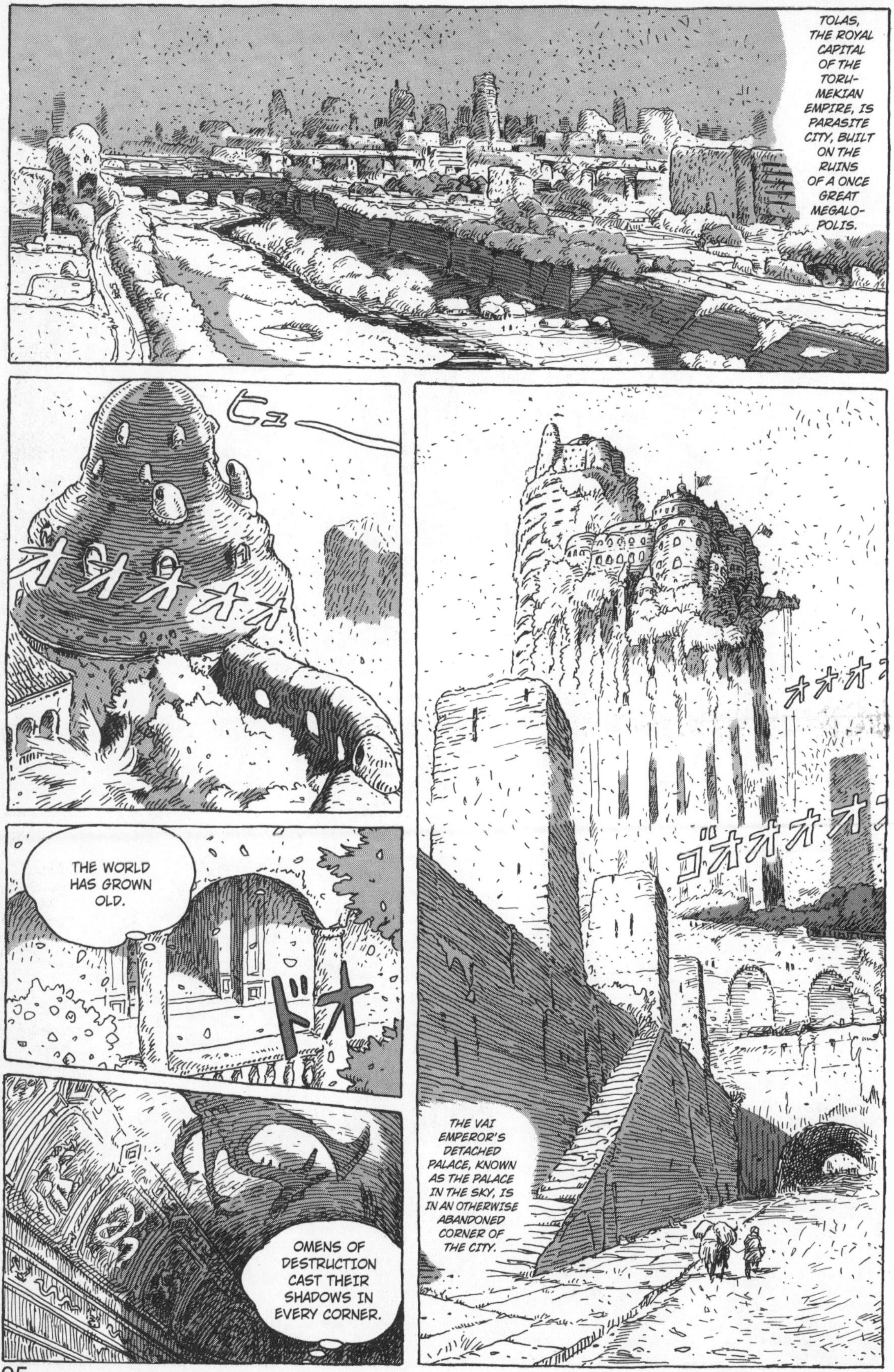
TOLAS, THE ROYAL CAPITAL OF THE TORU-MEKIAN EMPIRE, IS PARASITE CITY, BUILT ON THE RUINS OF A ONCE GREAT MEGALO-POLIS.
オオオ
ゴオオオオ
THE VAI EMPEROR'S DETACHED PALACE, KNOWN AS THE PALACE IN THE SKY, IS IN AN OTHERWISE ABANDONED CORNER OF THE CITY.
ヒュー
オオオオオ
THE WORLD HAS GROWN OLD.
ドォ
OMENS OF DESTRUCTION CAST THEIR SHADOWS IN EVERY CORNER.

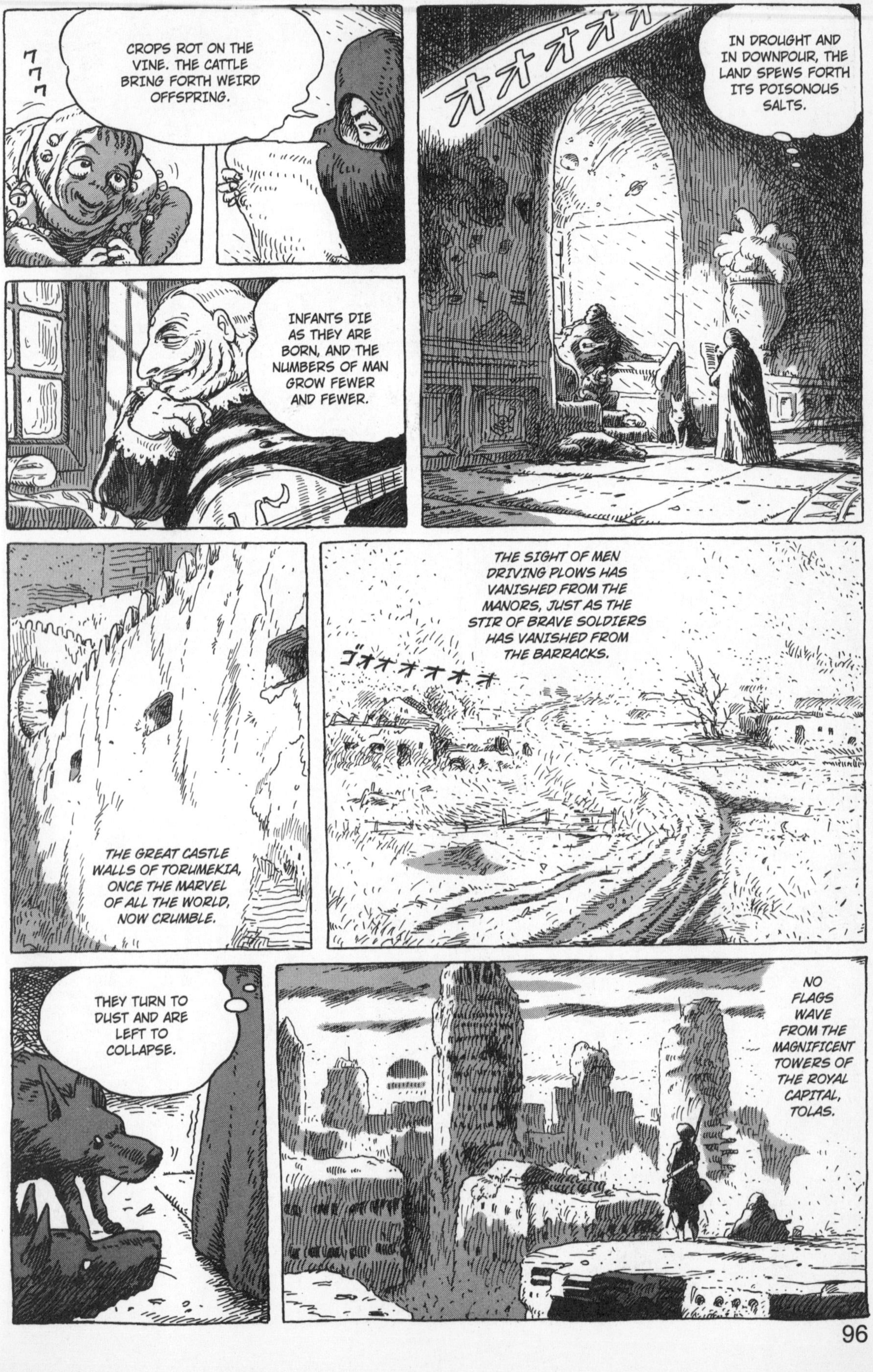

オオオオオ
IN DROUGHT AND IN DOWNPOUR, THE LAND SPEWS FORTH ITS POISONOUS SALTS.
CROPS ROT ON THE VINE. THE CATTLE BRING FORTH WEIRD OFFSPRING.
INFANTS DIE AS THEY ARE BORN, AND THE NUMBERS OF MAN GROW FEWER AND FEWER.
THE SIGHT OF MEN DRIVING PLOWS HAS VANISHED FROM THE MANORS, JUST AS THE STIR OF BRAVE SOLDIERS HAS VANISHED FROM THE BARRACKS.
ゴオオオオオオ
THE GREAT CASTLE WALLS OF TORUMEKIA, ONCE THE MARVEL OF ALL THE WORLD, NOW CRUMBLE.
NO FLAGS WAVE FROM THE MAGNIFICENT TOWERS OF THE ROYAL CAPITAL, TOLAS.
THEY TURN TO DUST AND ARE LEFT TO COLLAPSE.

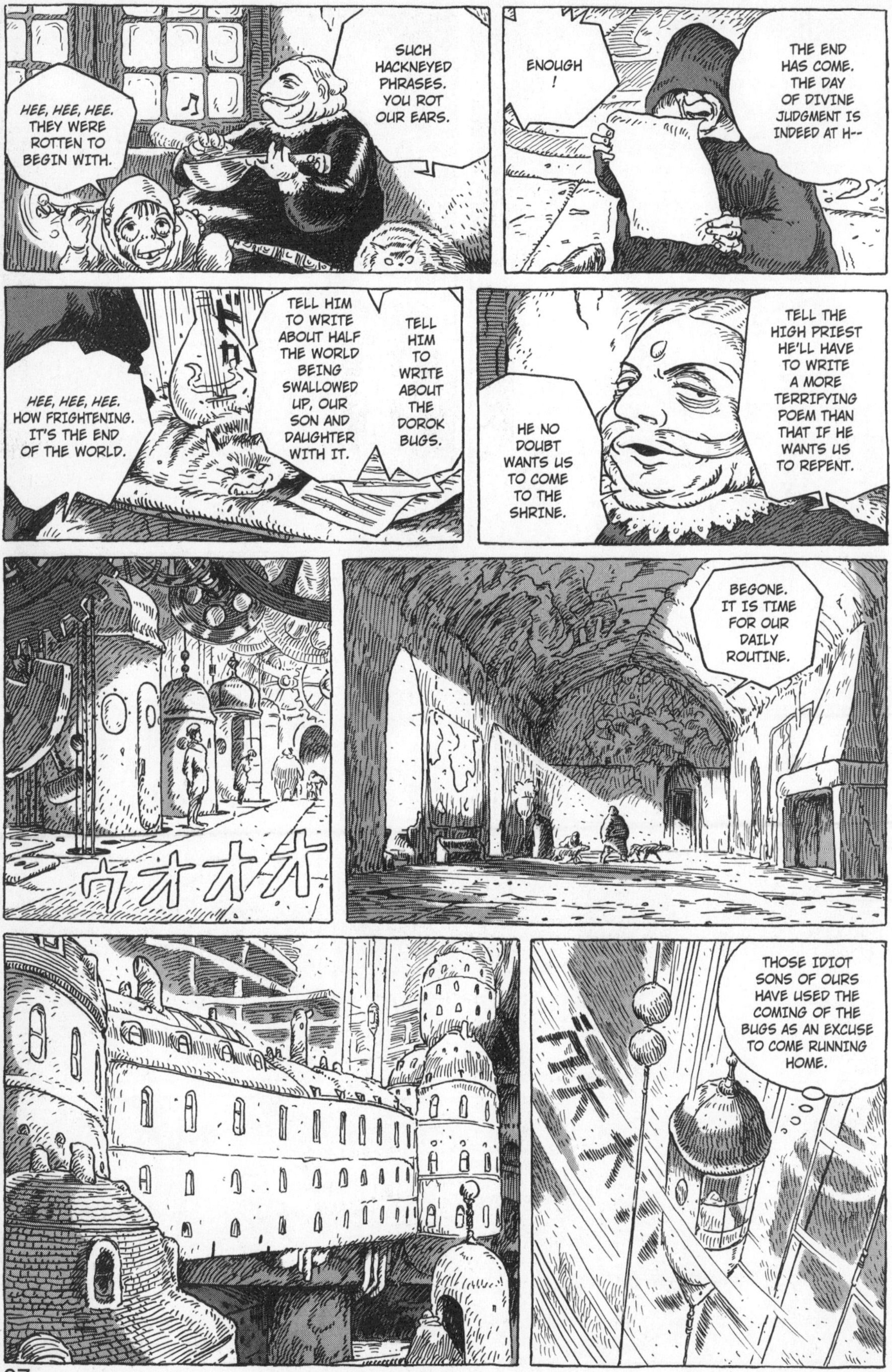
THE END HAS COME. THE DAY OF DIVINE JUDGMENT IS INDEED AT H--
ENOUGH!
SUCH HACKNEYED PHRASES. YOU ROT OUR EARS.
HEE, HEE, HEE. THEY WERE ROTTEN TO BEGIN WITH.
TELL THE HIGH PRIEST HE'LL HAVE TO WRITE A MORE TERRIFYING POEM THAN THAT IF HE WANTS US TO REPENT.
HE NO DOUBT WANTS US TO COME TO THE SHRINE.
TELL HIM TO WRITE ABOUT THE DOROK BUGS.
TELL HIM TO WRITE ABOUT HALF THE WORLD BEING SWALLOWED UP, OUR SON AND DAUGHTER WITH IT.
HEE, HEE, HEE. HOW FRIGHTENING. IT'S THE END OF THE WORLD.
BEGONE. IT IS TIME FOR OUR DAILY ROUTINE.
ウオオオオ
THOSE IDIOT SONS OF OURS HAVE USED THE COMING OF THE BUGS AS AN EXCUSE TO COME RUNNING HOME.

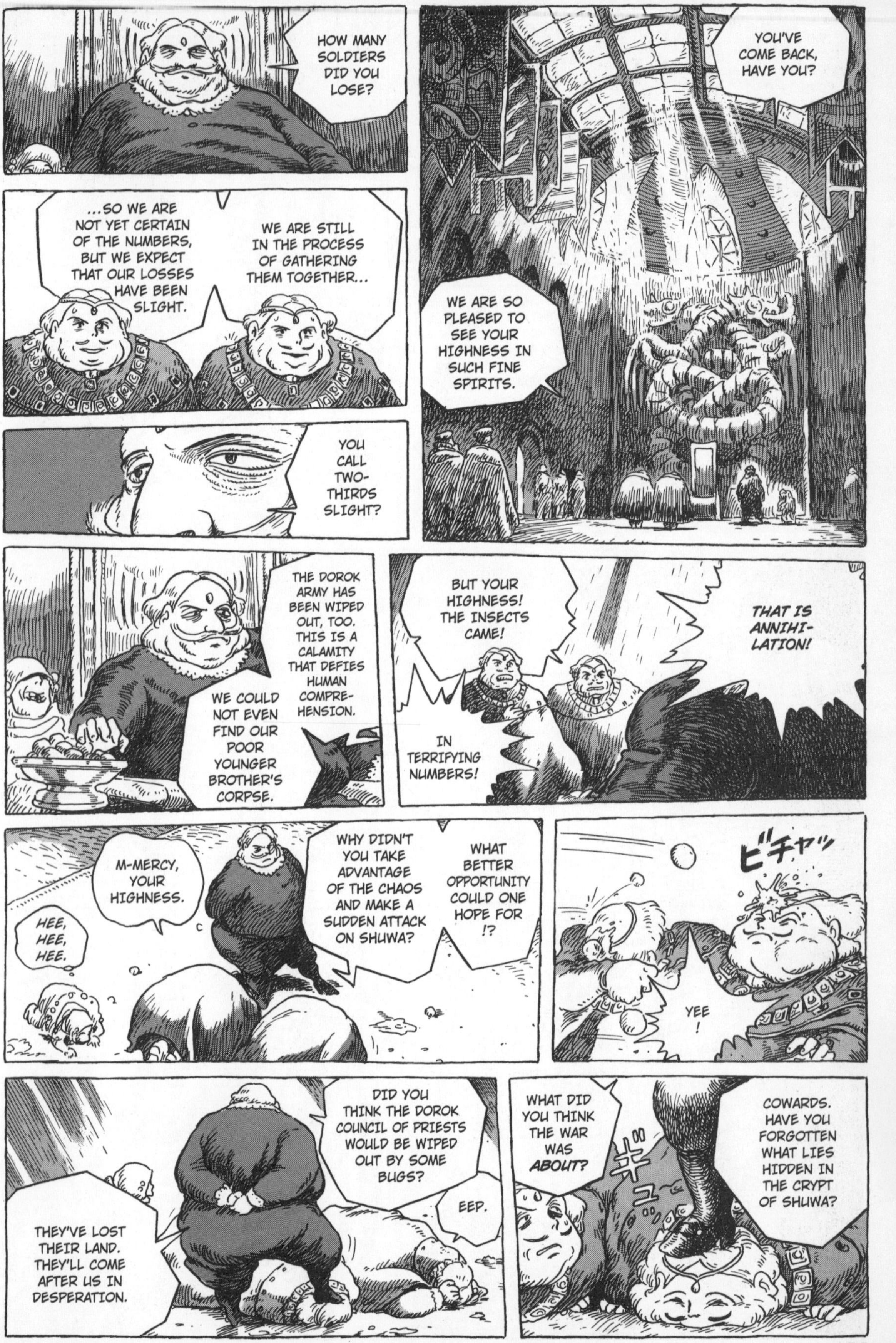
YOU'VE COME BACK, HAVE YOU?
WE ARE SO PLEASED TO SEE YOUR HIGHNESS IN SUCH FINE SPIRITS.
HOW MANY SOLDIERS DID YOU LOSE?
WE ARE STILL IN THE PROCESS OF GATHERING THEM TOGETHER...
...SO WE ARE NOT YET CERTAIN OF THE NUMBERS, BUT WE EXPECT THAT OUR LOSSES HAVE BEEN SLIGHT.
YOU CALL TWO-THIRDS SLIGHT?
BUT YOUR HIGHNESS! THE INSECTS CAME!
IN TERRIFYING NUMBERS!
THAT IS ANNIHILATION!
THE DOROK ARMY HAS BEEN WIPED OUT, TOO. THIS IS A CALAMITY THAT DEFIES HUMAN COMPREHENSION.
WE COULD NOT EVEN FIND OUR POOR YOUNGER BROTHER'S CORPSE.
ビチャッ
YEE!
WHY DIDN'T YOU TAKE ADVANTAGE OF THE CHAOS AND MAKE A SUDDEN ATTACK ON SHUWA?
WHAT BETTER OPPORTUNITY COULD ONE HOPE FOR!?
M-MERCY, YOUR HIGHNESS.
HEE, HEE, HEE.
COWARDS. HAVE YOU FORGOTTEN WHAT LIES HIDDEN IN THE CRYPT OF SHUWA?
WHAT DID YOU THINK THE WAR WAS *ABOUT?*
DID YOU THINK THE DOROK COUNCIL OF PRIESTS WOULD BE WIPED OUT BY SOME BUGS?
EEP.
THEY'VE LOST THEIR LAND. THEY'LL COME AFTER US IN DESPERATION.

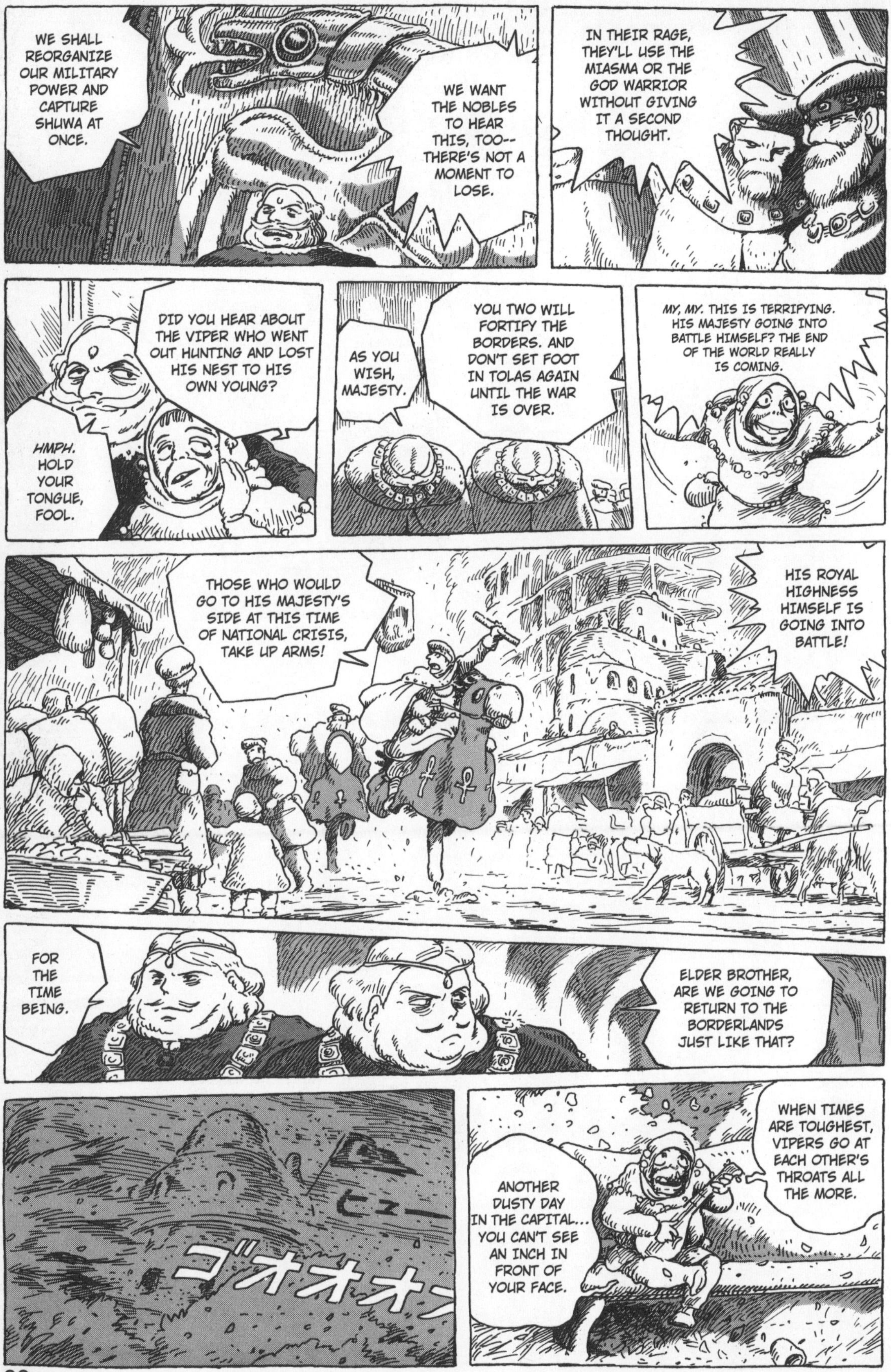
IN THEIR RAGE, THEY'LL USE THE MIASMA OR THE GOD WARRIOR WITHOUT GIVING IT A SECOND THOUGHT.
WE SHALL REORGANIZE OUR MILITARY POWER AND CAPTURE SHUWA AT ONCE.
WE WANT THE NOBLES TO HEAR THIS, TOO--THERE'S NOT A MOMENT TO LOSE.
MY, MY. THIS IS TERRIFYING. HIS MAJESTY GOING INTO BATTLE HIMSELF? THE END OF THE WORLD REALLY IS COMING.
YOU TWO WILL FORTIFY THE BORDERS. AND DON'T SET FOOT IN TOLAS AGAIN UNTIL THE WAR IS OVER.
AS YOU WISH, MAJESTY.
DID YOU HEAR ABOUT THE VIPER WHO WENT OUT HUNTING AND LOST HIS NEST TO HIS OWN YOUNG?
HMPH. HOLD YOUR TONGUE, FOOL.
HIS ROYAL HIGHNESS HIMSELF IS GOING INTO BATTLE!
THOSE WHO WOULD GO TO HIS MAJESTY'S SIDE AT THIS TIME OF NATIONAL CRISIS, TAKE UP ARMS!
ELDER BROTHER, ARE WE GOING TO RETURN TO THE BORDERLANDS JUST LIKE THAT?
FOR THE TIME BEING.
WHEN TIMES ARE TOUGHEST, VIPERS GO AT EACH OTHER'S THROATS ALL THE MORE.
ANOTHER DUSTY DAY IN THE CAPITAL... YOU CAN'T SEE AN INCH IN FRONT OF YOUR FACE.
ヒュー
ゴオオオ

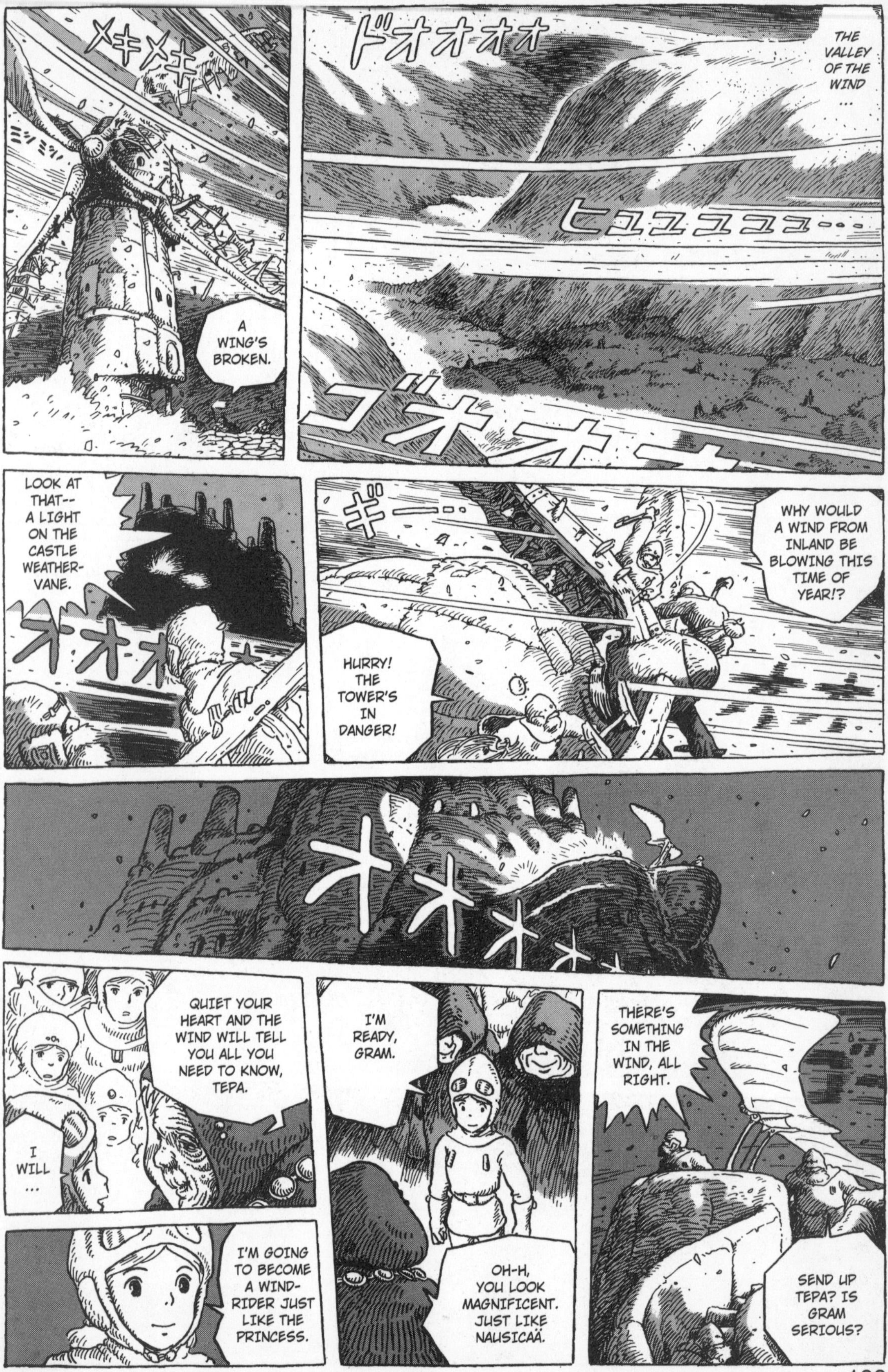
ドオオオオ
THE VALLEY OF THE WIND ...
ヒュュュュュ…
ゴオオオ
メキメキ
A WING'S BROKEN.
ギー…
WHY WOULD A WIND FROM INLAND BE BLOWING THIS TIME OF YEAR!?
HURRY! THE TOWER'S IN DANGER!
LOOK AT THAT-- A LIGHT ON THE CASTLE WEATHER-VANE.
オオオオ
オオオオ
THERE'S SOMETHING IN THE WIND, ALL RIGHT.
SEND UP TEPA? IS GRAM SERIOUS?
I'M READY, GRAM.
OH-H, YOU LOOK MAGNIFICENT. JUST LIKE NAUSICAÄ.
QUIET YOUR HEART AND THE WIND WILL TELL YOU ALL YOU NEED TO KNOW, TEPA.
I WILL ...
I'M GOING TO BECOME A WIND-RIDER JUST LIKE THE PRINCESS.

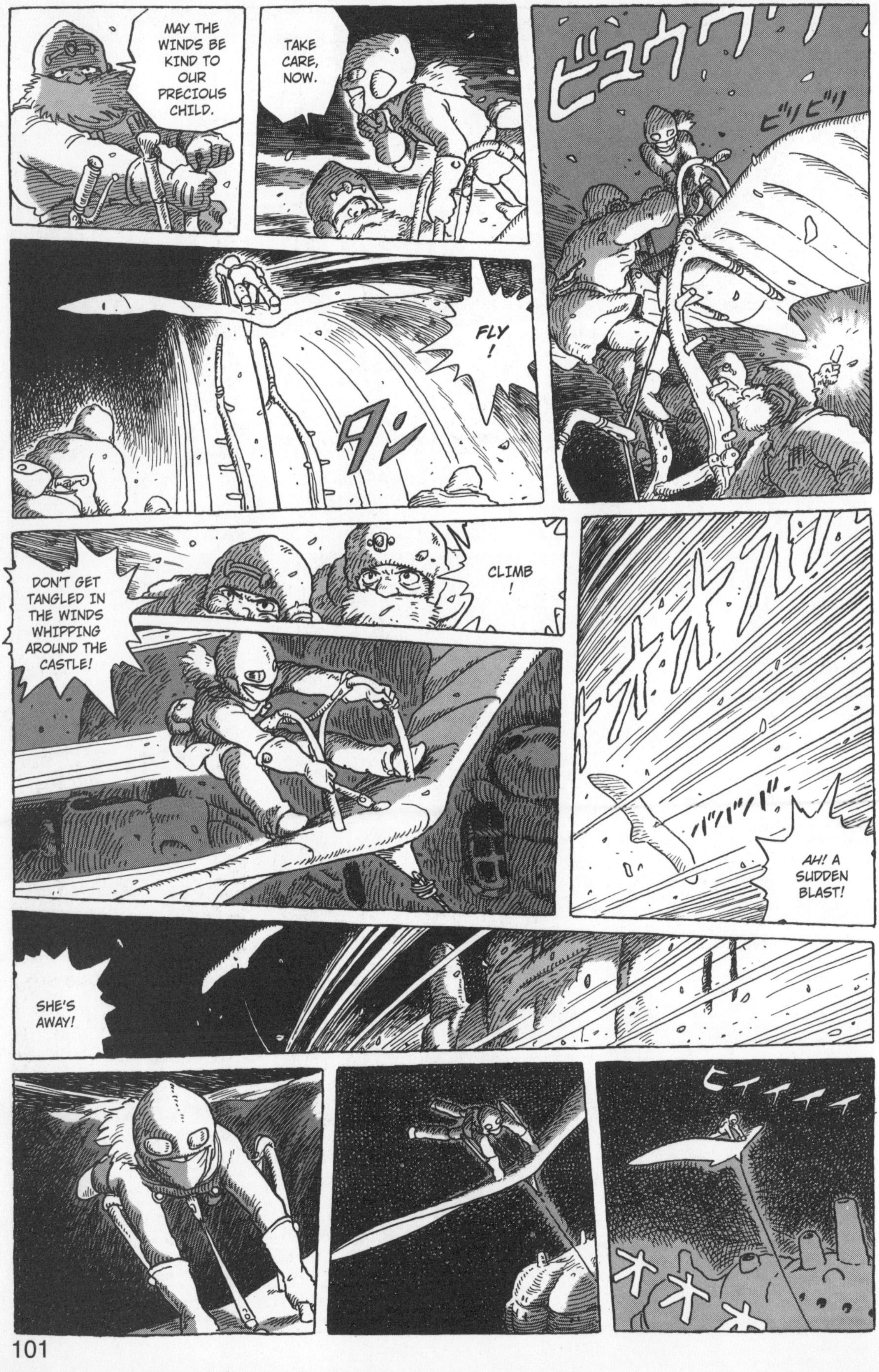
ビュウウ
ビツビツ
TAKE CARE, NOW.
MAY THE WINDS BE KIND TO OUR PRECIOUS CHILD.
FLY!
タン
オオオオ
ババババ
AH! A SUDDEN BLAST!
CLIMB!
DON'T GET TANGLED IN THE WINDS WHIPPING AROUND THE CASTLE!
SHE'S AWAY!
ヒイイイイ
オオオ

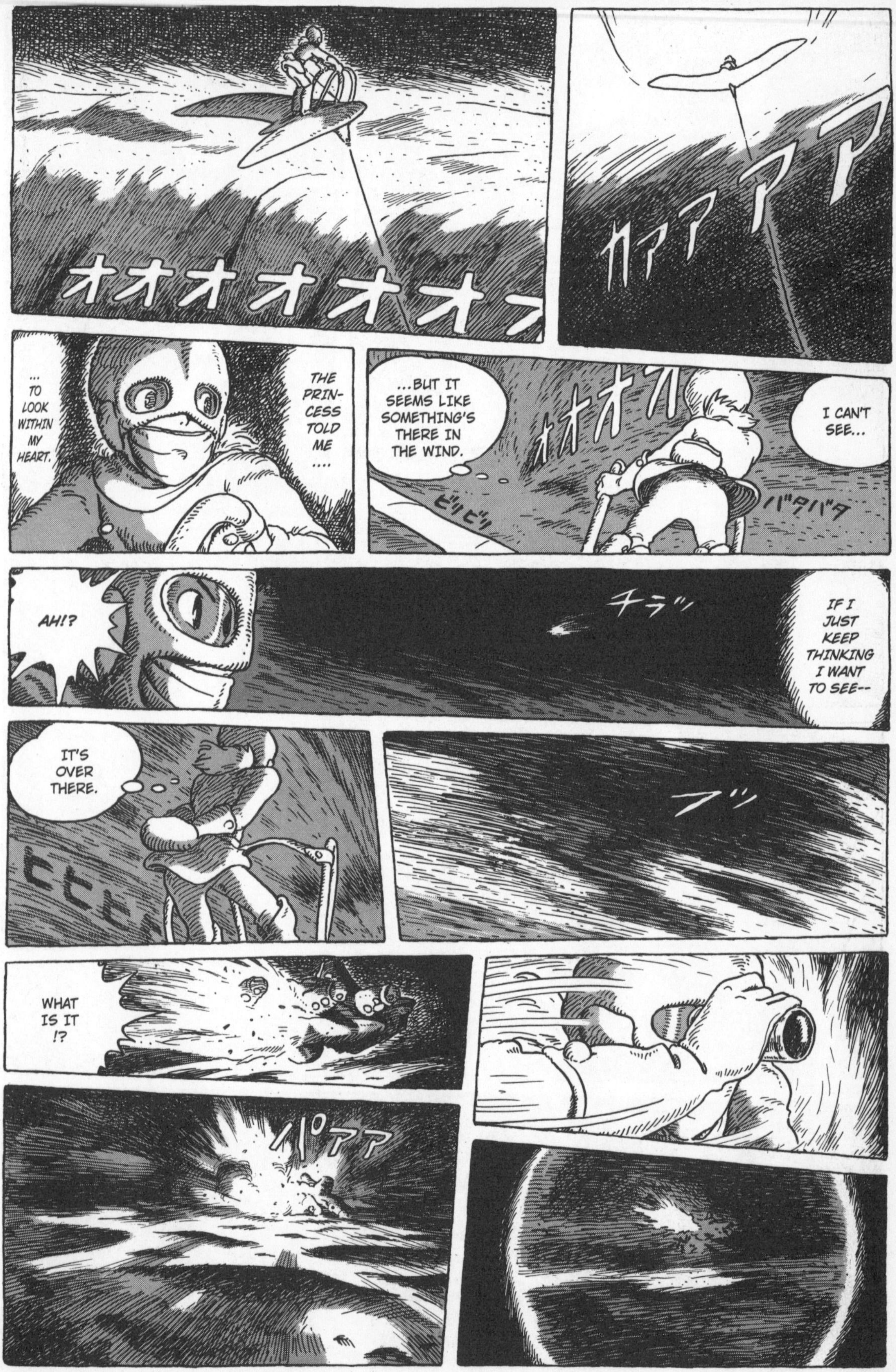
カァアアア
オオオオオオオ
I CAN'T SEE...
...BUT IT SEEMS LIKE SOMETHING'S THERE IN THE WIND.
THE PRIN- CESS TOLD ME ....
... TO LOOK WITHIN MY HEART.
IF I JUST KEEP THINKING I WANT TO SEE--
チラッ
AH!?
ブッ
IT'S OVER THERE.
WHAT IS IT !?
パァア

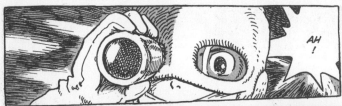

AH
!

AH
!

IT
CRASHED
!!

THE
INSECTS
ARE
COMING!

I'VE
GOT TO
WARN--

AHH
!!

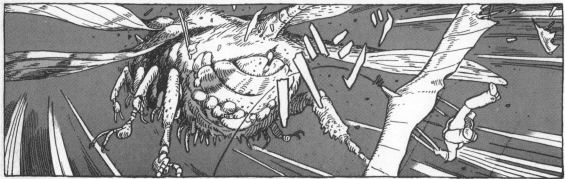

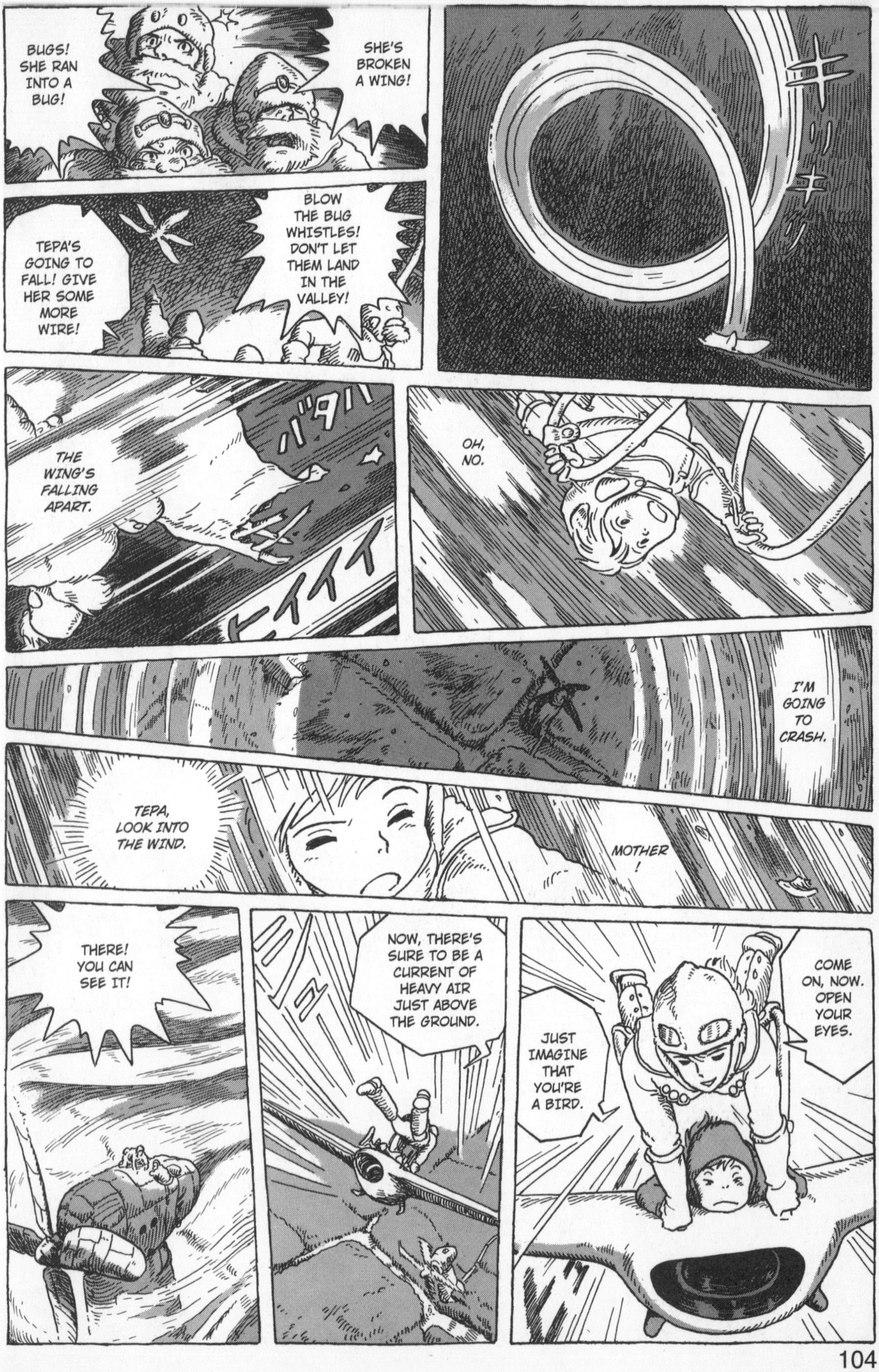
SHE'S BROKEN A WING!
BUGS! SHE RAN INTO A BUG!
BLOW THE BUG WHISTLES! DON'T LET THEM LAND IN THE VALLEY!
TEPA'S GOING TO FALL! GIVE HER SOME MORE WIRE!
OH, NO.
THE WING'S FALLING APART.
I'M GOING TO CRASH.
MOTHER!
TEPA, LOOK INTO THE WIND.
COME ON, NOW. OPEN YOUR EYES.
JUST IMAGINE THAT YOU'RE A BIRD.
NOW, THERE'S SURE TO BE A CURRENT OF HEAVY AIR JUST ABOVE THE GROUND.
THERE! YOU CAN SEE IT!

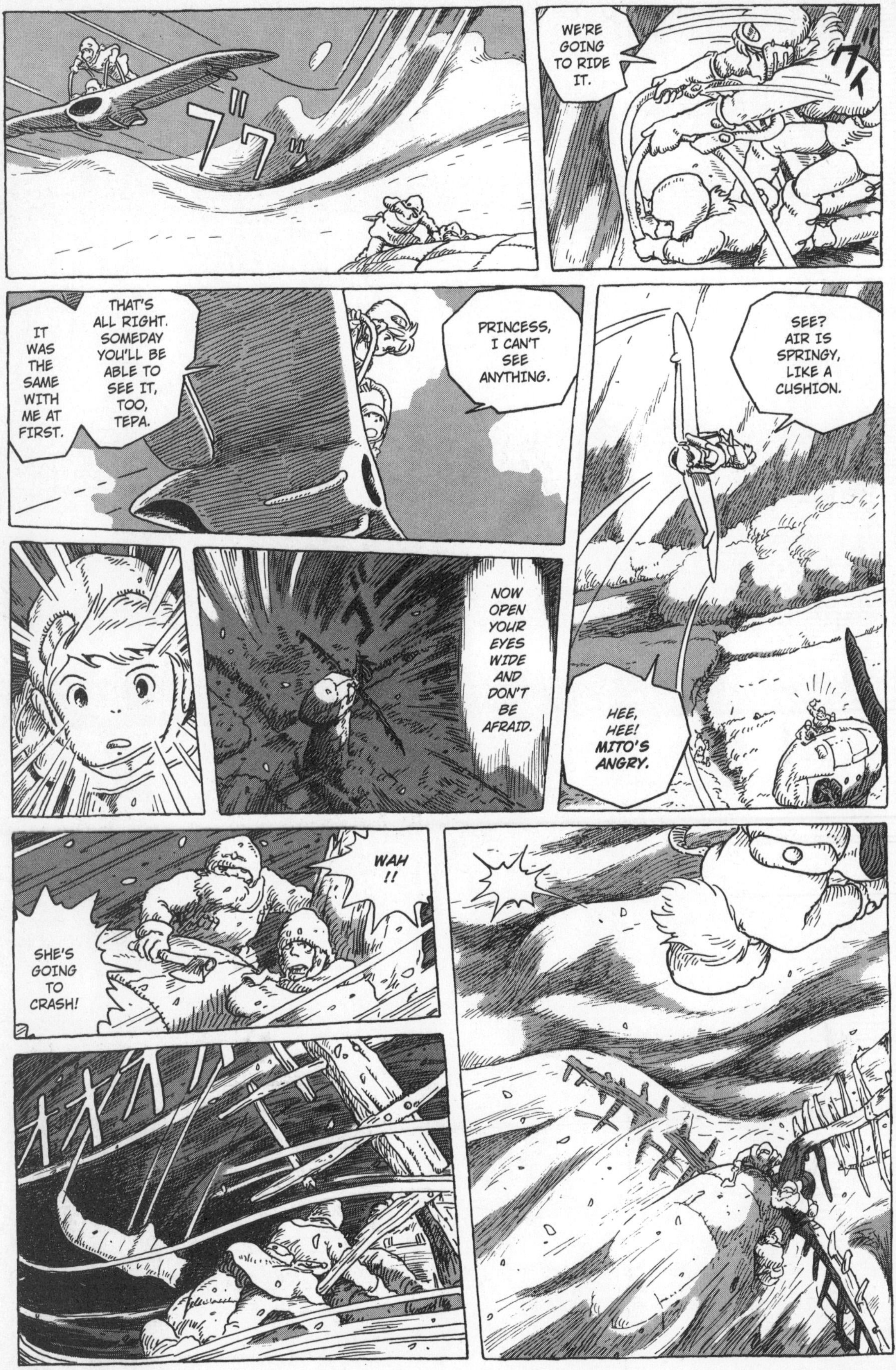
WE'RE GOING TO RIDE IT.
SEE? AIR IS SPRINGY, LIKE A CUSHION.
HEE, HEE! MITO'S ANGRY.
PRINCESS, I CAN'T SEE ANYTHING.
THAT'S ALL RIGHT. SOMEDAY YOU'LL BE ABLE TO SEE IT, TOO, TEPA.
IT WAS THE SAME WITH ME AT FIRST.
NOW OPEN YOUR EYES WIDE AND DON'T BE AFRAID.
WAH!!
SHE'S GOING TO CRASH!

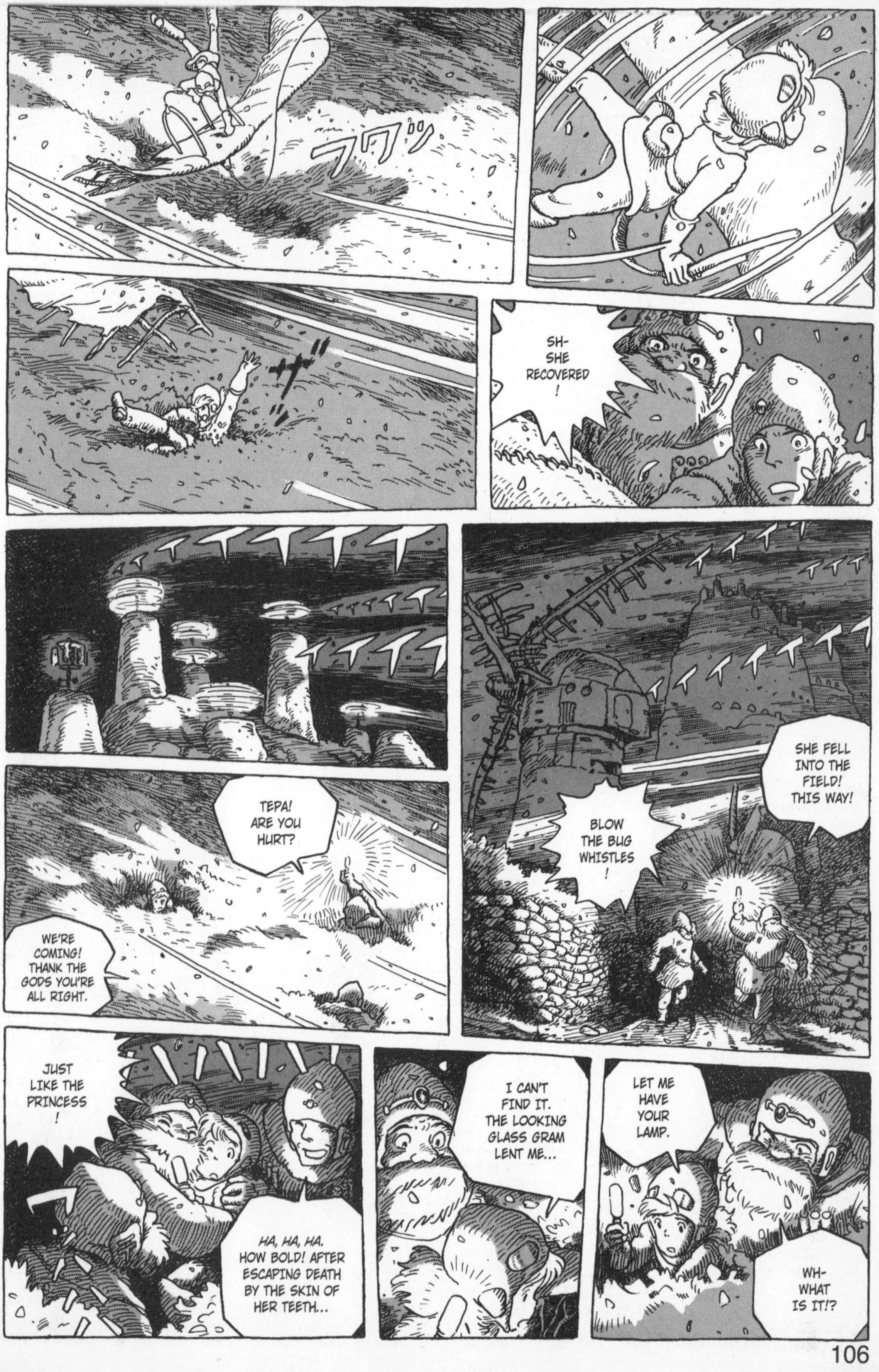
フワッ
SH- SHE RECOVERED !
SHE FELL INTO THE FIELD! THIS WAY!
BLOW THE BUG WHISTLES !
TEPA! ARE YOU HURT?
WE'RE COMING! THANK THE GODS YOU'RE ALL RIGHT.
LET ME HAVE YOUR LAMP.
WH- WHAT IS IT!?
I CAN'T FIND IT. THE LOOKING GLASS GRAM LENT ME...
JUST LIKE THE PRINCESS !
HA, HA, HA. HOW BOLD! AFTER ESCAPING DEATH BY THE SKIN OF HER TEETH...

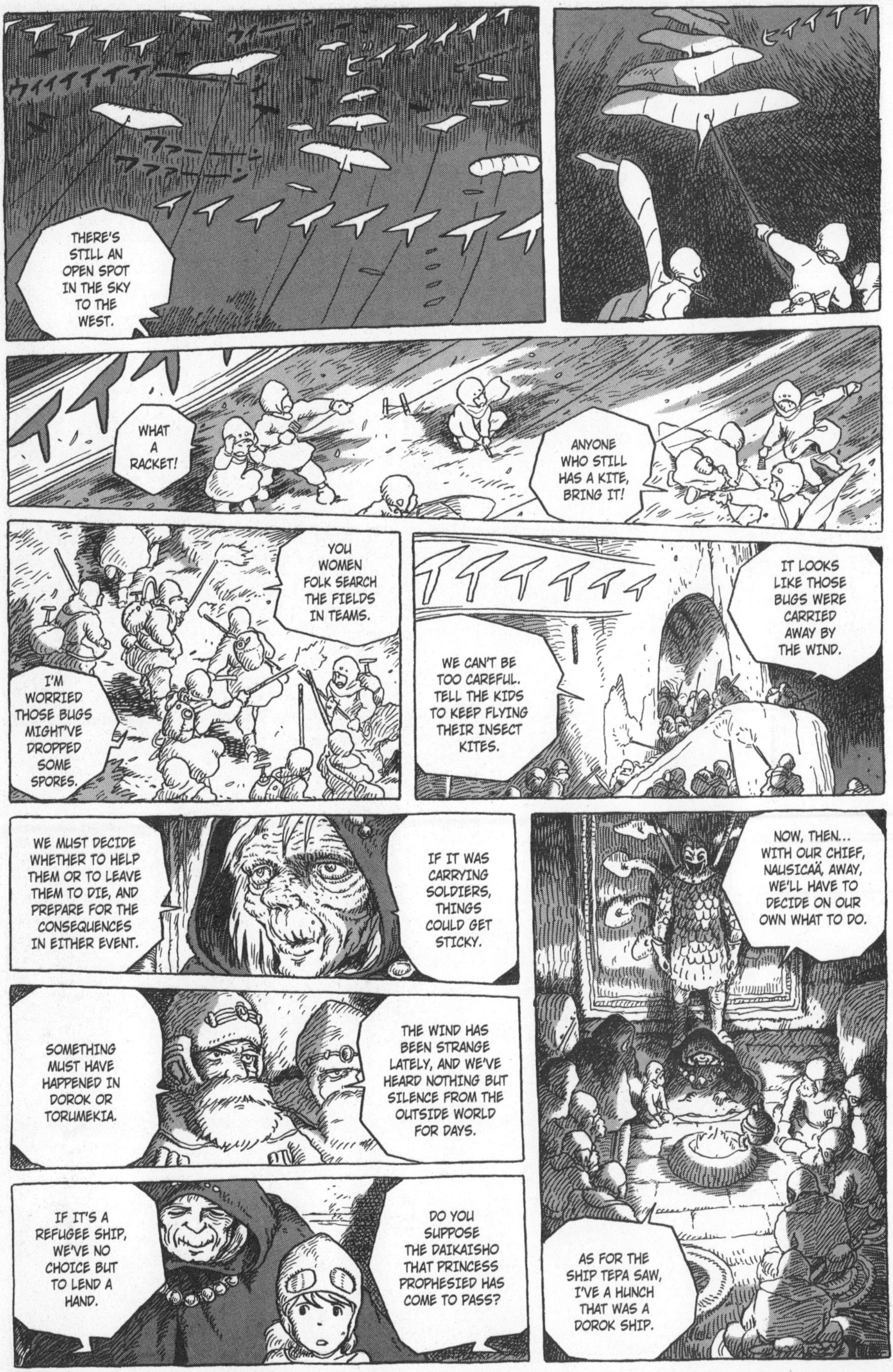
THERE'S STILL AN OPEN SPOT IN THE SKY TO THE WEST.
ANYONE WHO STILL HAS A KITE, BRING IT!
WHAT A RACKET!
IT LOOKS LIKE THOSE BUGS WERE CARRIED AWAY BY THE WIND.
WE CAN'T BE TOO CAREFUL. TELL THE KIDS TO KEEP FLYING THEIR INSECT KITES.
YOU WOMEN FOLK SEARCH THE FIELDS IN TEAMS.
I'M WORRIED THOSE BUGS MIGHT'VE DROPPED SOME SPORES.
NOW, THEN... WITH OUR CHIEF, NAUSICAÄ, AWAY, WE'LL HAVE TO DECIDE ON OUR OWN WHAT TO DO.
AS FOR THE SHIP TEPA SAW, I'VE A HUNCH THAT WAS A DOROK SHIP.
IF IT WAS CARRYING SOLDIERS, THINGS COULD GET STICKY.
WE MUST DECIDE WHETHER TO HELP THEM OR TO LEAVE THEM TO DIE, AND PREPARE FOR THE CONSEQUENCES IN EITHER EVENT.
THE WIND HAS BEEN STRANGE LATELY, AND WE'VE HEARD NOTHING BUT SILENCE FROM THE OUTSIDE WORLD FOR DAYS.
SOMETHING MUST HAVE HAPPENED IN DOROK OR TORUMEKIA.
DO YOU SUPPOSE THE DAIKAISHO THAT PRINCESS PROPHESIED HAS COME TO PASS?
IF IT'S A REFUGEE SHIP, WE'VE NO CHOICE BUT TO LEND A HAND.

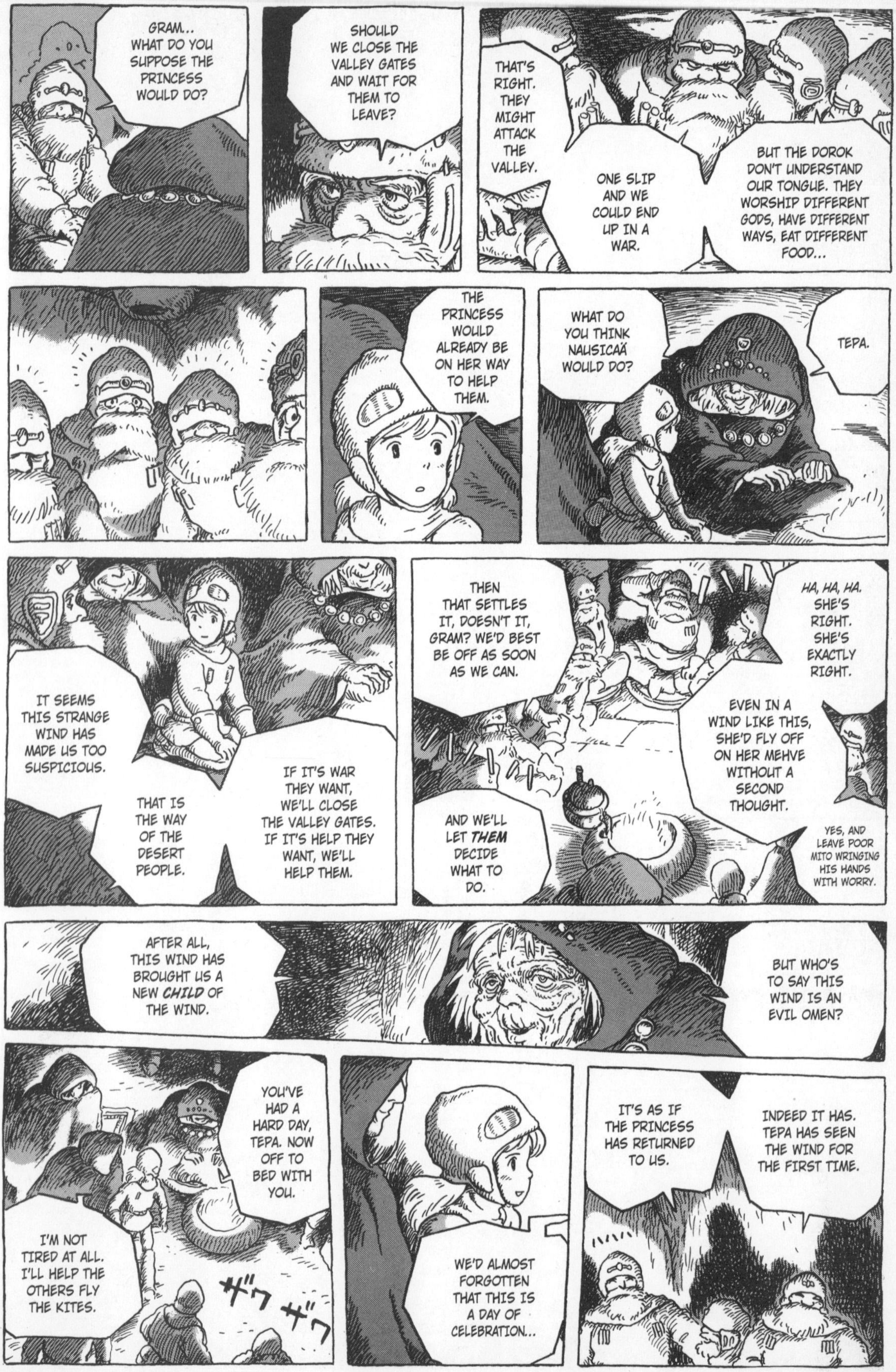
BUT THE DOROK DON'T UNDERSTAND OUR TONGUE. THEY WORSHIP DIFFERENT GODS, HAVE DIFFERENT WAYS, EAT DIFFERENT FOOD...
ONE SLIP AND WE COULD END UP IN A WAR.
THAT'S RIGHT. THEY MIGHT ATTACK THE VALLEY.
SHOULD WE CLOSE THE VALLEY GATES AND WAIT FOR THEM TO LEAVE?
GRAM... WHAT DO YOU SUPPOSE THE PRINCESS WOULD DO?
TEPA.
WHAT DO YOU THINK NAUSICAÄ WOULD DO?
THE PRINCESS WOULD ALREADY BE ON HER WAY TO HELP THEM.
HA, HA, HA. SHE'S RIGHT. SHE'S EXACTLY RIGHT.
EVEN IN A WIND LIKE THIS, SHE'D FLY OFF ON HER MEHVE WITHOUT A SECOND THOUGHT.
YES, AND LEAVE POOR MITO WRINGING HIS HANDS WITH WORRY.
THEN THAT SETTLES IT, DOESN'T IT, GRAM? WE'D BEST BE OFF AS SOON AS WE CAN.
AND WE'LL LET THEM DECIDE WHAT TO DO.
IT SEEMS THIS STRANGE WIND HAS MADE US TOO SUSPICIOUS.
IF IT'S WAR THEY WANT, WE'LL CLOSE THE VALLEY GATES. IF IT'S HELP THEY WANT, WE'LL HELP THEM.
THAT IS THE WAY OF THE DESERT PEOPLE.
BUT WHO'S TO SAY THIS WIND IS AN EVIL OMEN?
AFTER ALL, THIS WIND HAS BROUGHT US A NEW CHILD OF THE WIND.
INDEED IT HAS. TEPA HAS SEEN THE WIND FOR THE FIRST TIME.
IT'S AS IF THE PRINCESS HAS RETURNED TO US.
WE'D ALMOST FORGOTTEN THAT THIS IS A DAY OF CELEBRATION...
YOU'VE HAD A HARD DAY, TEPA. NOW OFF TO BED WITH YOU.
I'M NOT TIRED AT ALL. I'LL HELP THE OTHERS FLY THE KITES.
ザワ ザワ

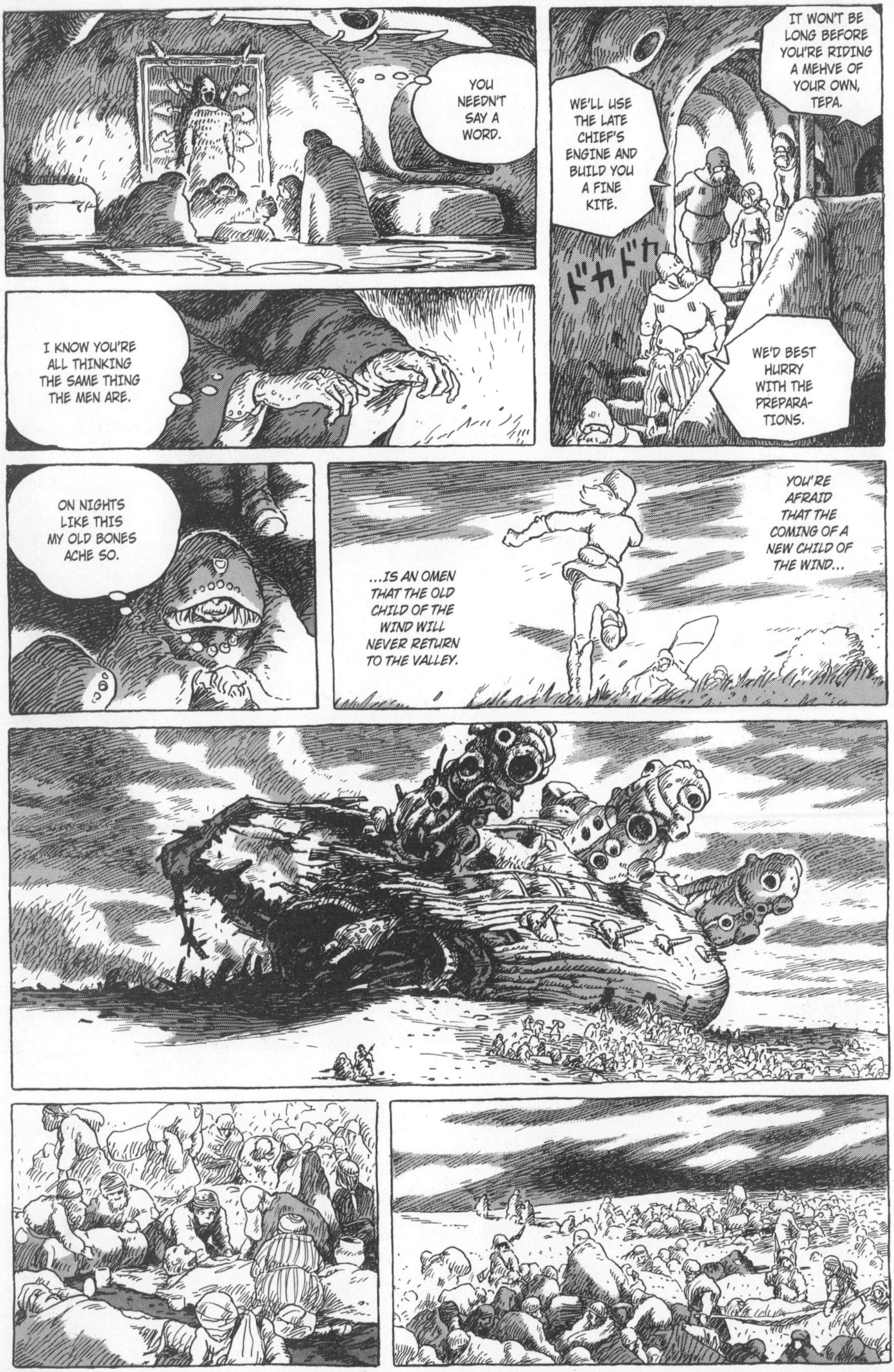
IT WON'T BE LONG BEFORE YOU'RE RIDING A MEHVE OF YOUR OWN, TEPA.
WE'LL USE THE LATE CHIEF'S ENGINE AND BUILD YOU A FINE KITE.
ドカドカ
WE'D BEST HURRY WITH THE PREPARATIONS.
YOU NEEDN'T SAY A WORD.
I KNOW YOU'RE ALL THINKING THE SAME THING THE MEN ARE.
YOU'RE AFRAID THAT THE COMING OF A NEW CHILD OF THE WIND...
...IS AN OMEN THAT THE OLD CHILD OF THE WIND WILL NEVER RETURN TO THE VALLEY.
ON NIGHTS LIKE THIS MY OLD BONES ACHE SO.

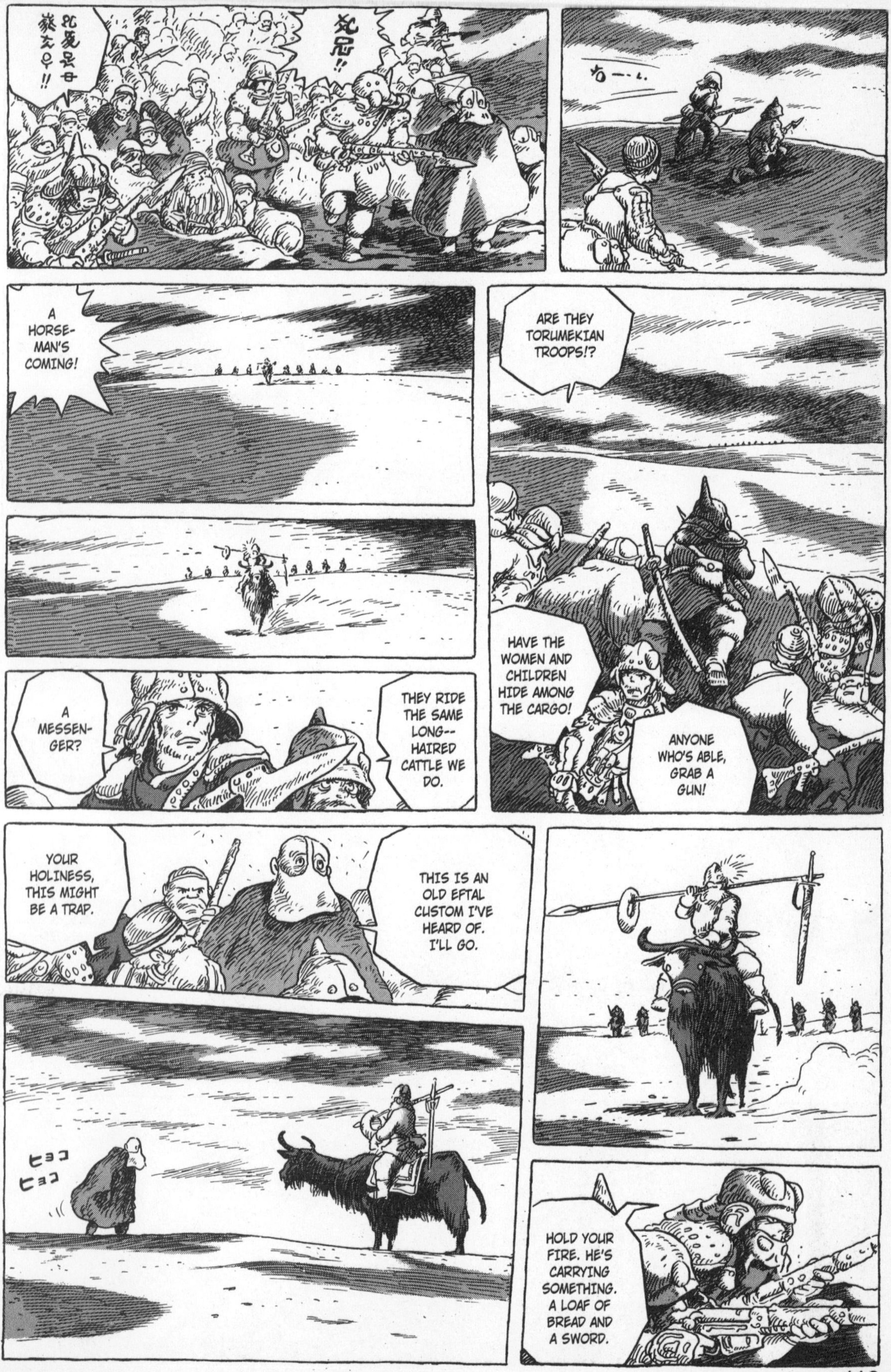
ARE THEY TORUMEKIAN TROOPS!?
HAVE THE WOMEN AND CHILDREN HIDE AMONG THE CARGO!
ANYONE WHO'S ABLE, GRAB A GUN!
A HORSE-MAN'S COMING!
THEY RIDE THE SAME LONG--HAIRED CATTLE WE DO.
A MESSEN-GER?
THIS IS AN OLD EFTAL CUSTOM I'VE HEARD OF. I'LL GO.
YOUR HOLINESS, THIS MIGHT BE A TRAP.
HOLD YOUR FIRE. HE'S CARRYING SOMETHING. A LOAF OF BREAD AND A SWORD.
ヒョコ
ヒョコ

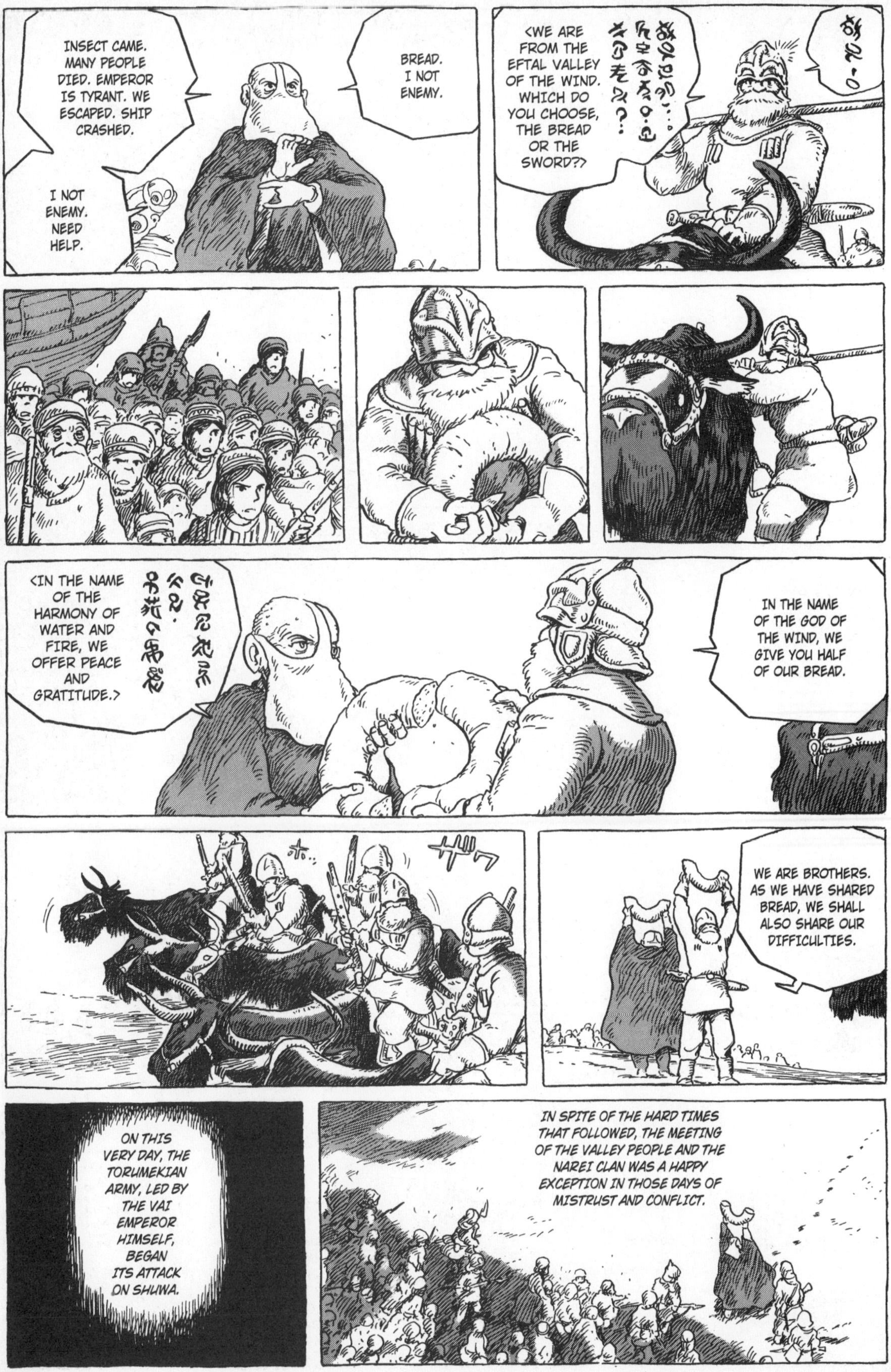
<WE ARE FROM THE EFTAL VALLEY OF THE WIND. WHICH DO YOU CHOOSE, THE BREAD OR THE SWORD?>
BREAD. I NOT ENEMY.
INSECT CAME. MANY PEOPLE DIED. EMPEROR IS TYRANT. WE ESCAPED. SHIP CRASHED.
I NOT ENEMY. NEED HELP.
IN THE NAME OF THE GOD OF THE WIND, WE GIVE YOU HALF OF OUR BREAD.
<IN THE NAME OF THE HARMONY OF WATER AND FIRE, WE OFFER PEACE AND GRATITUDE.>
WE ARE BROTHERS. AS WE HAVE SHARED BREAD, WE SHALL ALSO SHARE OUR DIFFICULTIES.
ザワ
IN SPITE OF THE HARD TIMES THAT FOLLOWED, THE MEETING OF THE VALLEY PEOPLE AND THE NAREI CLAN WAS A HAPPY EXCEPTION IN THOSE DAYS OF MISTRUST AND CONFLICT.
ON THIS VERY DAY, THE TORUMEKIAN ARMY, LED BY THE VAI EMPEROR HIMSELF, BEGAN ITS ATTACK ON SHUWA.

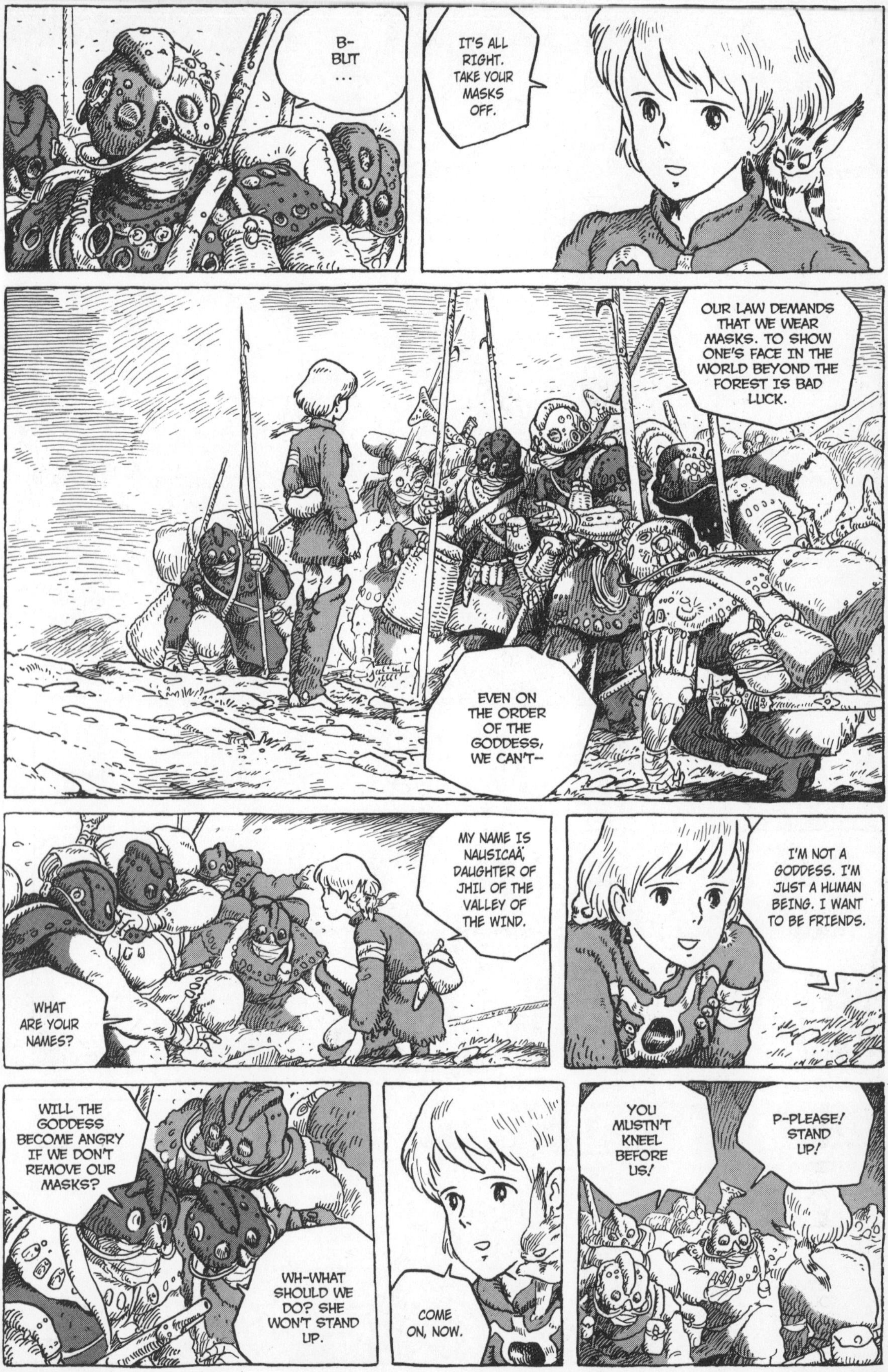

IT'S ALL RIGHT. TAKE YOUR MASKS OFF.
B-BUT ...
OUR LAW DEMANDS THAT WE WEAR MASKS. TO SHOW ONE'S FACE IN THE WORLD BEYOND THE FOREST IS BAD LUCK.
EVEN ON THE ORDER OF THE GODDESS, WE CAN'T-
I'M NOT A GODDESS. I'M JUST A HUMAN BEING. I WANT TO BE FRIENDS.
MY NAME IS NAUSICAÄ, DAUGHTER OF JHIL OF THE VALLEY OF THE WIND.
WHAT ARE YOUR NAMES?
P-PLEASE! STAND UP!
YOU MUSTN'T KNEEL BEFORE US!
COME ON, NOW.
WILL THE GODDESS BECOME ANGRY IF WE DON'T REMOVE OUR MASKS?
WH-WHAT SHOULD WE DO? SHE WON'T STAND UP.

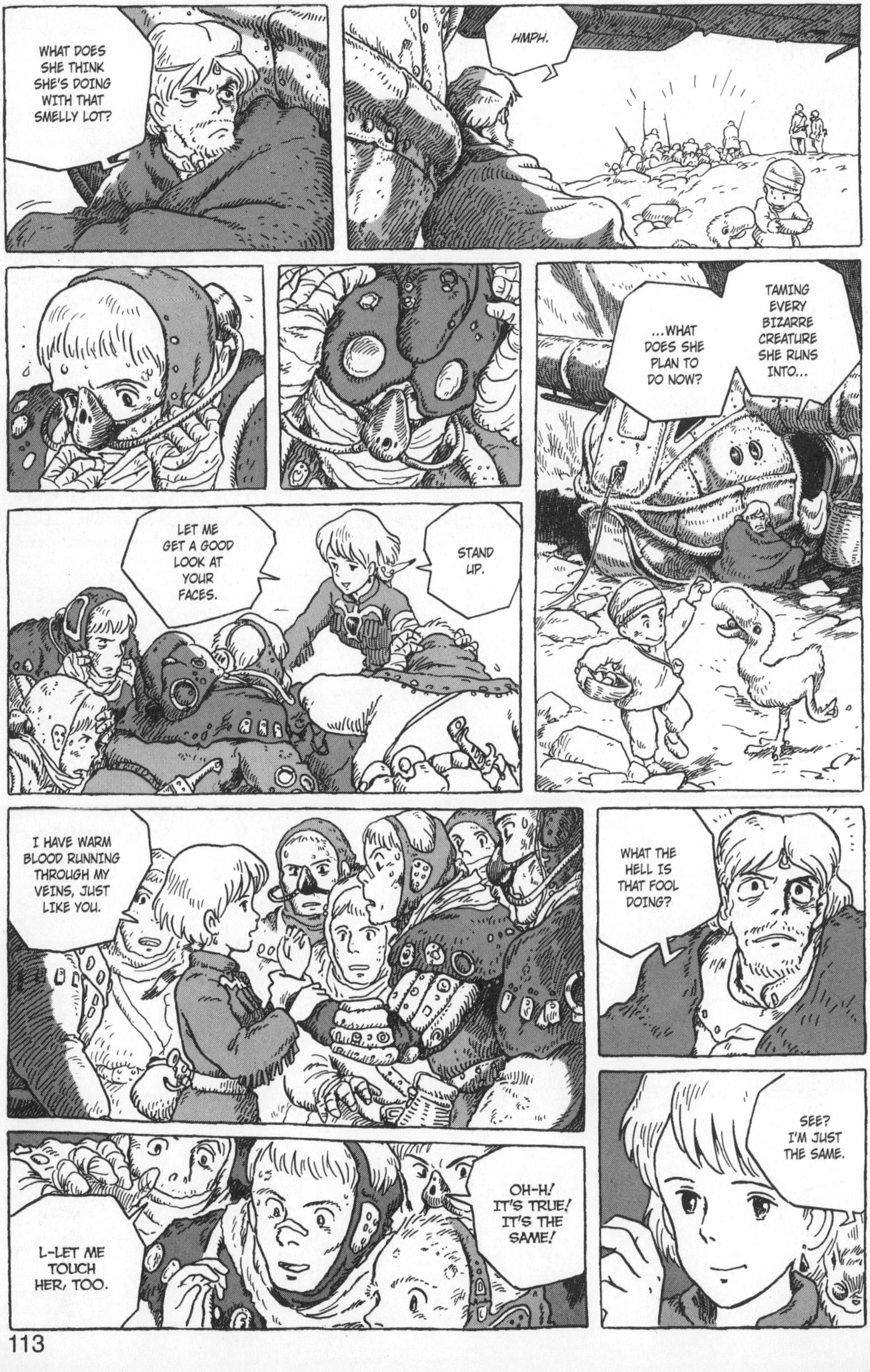
HMPH.
WHAT DOES SHE THINK SHE'S DOING WITH THAT SMELLY LOT?
TAMING EVERY BIZARRE CREATURE SHE RUNS INTO...
...WHAT DOES SHE PLAN TO DO NOW?
STAND UP.
LET ME GET A GOOD LOOK AT YOUR FACES.
WHAT THE HELL IS THAT FOOL DOING?
I HAVE WARM BLOOD RUNNING THROUGH MY VEINS, JUST LIKE YOU.
SEE? I'M JUST THE SAME.
OH-H! IT'S TRUE! IT'S THE SAME!
L-LET ME TOUCH HER, TOO.

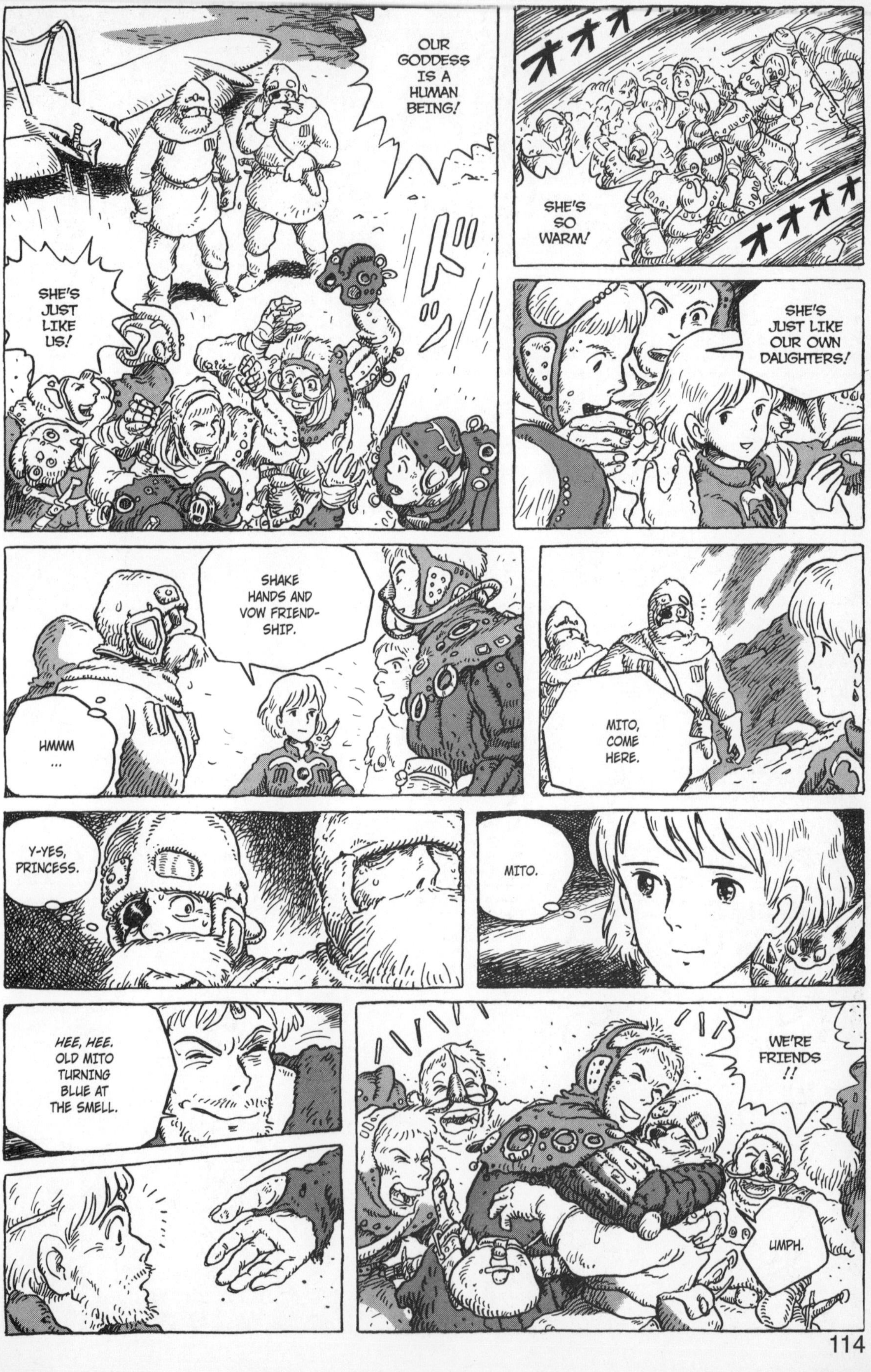
OUR GODDESS IS A HUMAN BEING!
SHE'S JUST LIKE US!
オオオオ
SHE'S SO WARM!
オオオオ
SHE'S JUST LIKE OUR OWN DAUGHTERS!
SHAKE HANDS AND VOW FRIENDSHIP.
HMMM ...
MITO, COME HERE.
Y-YES, PRINCESS.
MITO.
HEE, HEE. OLD MITO TURNING BLUE AT THE SMELL.
WE'RE FRIENDS !!
UMPH.

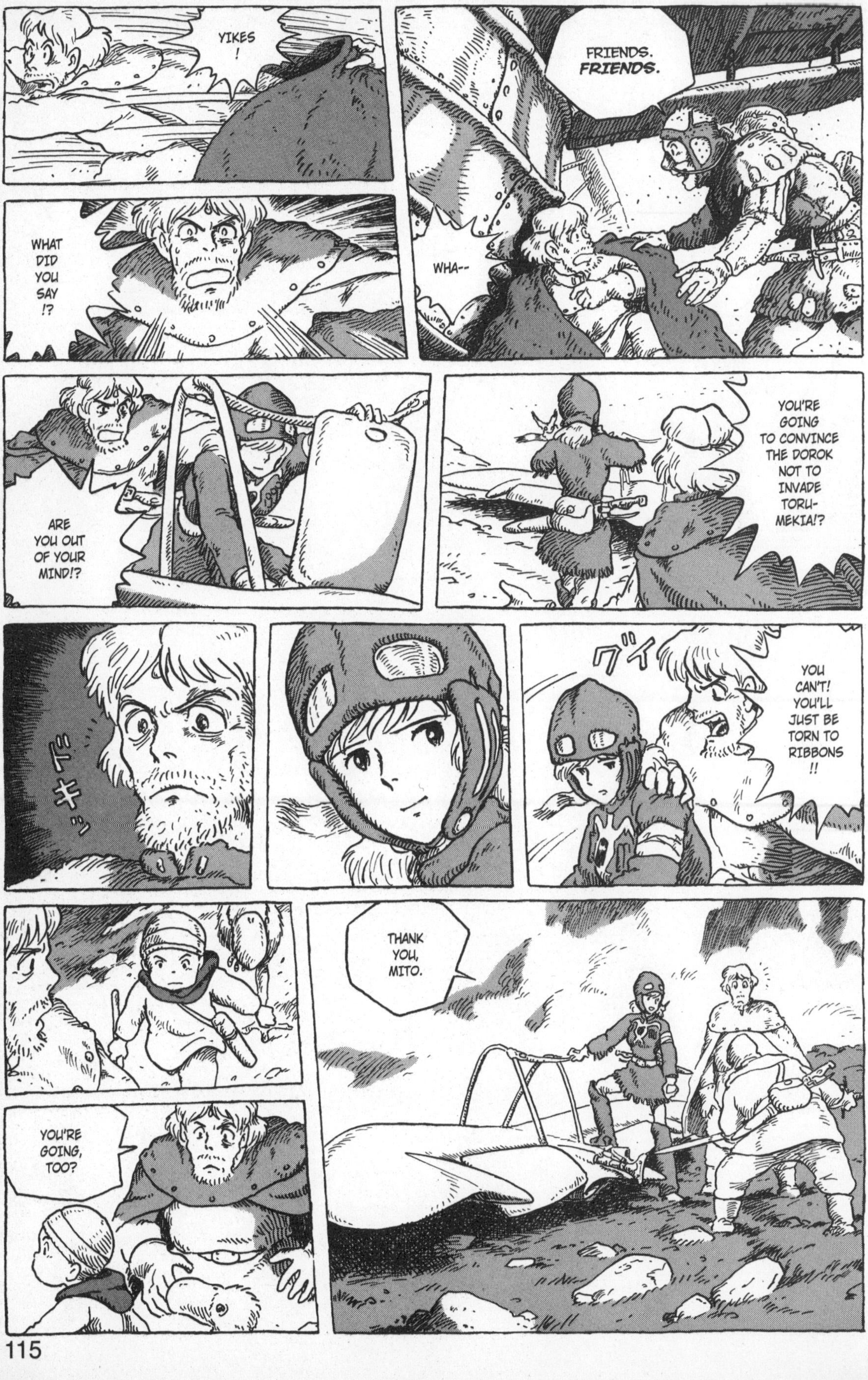

FRIENDS. **FRIENDS.**
WHA--
YIKES!
WHAT DID YOU SAY!?
YOU'RE GOING TO CONVINCE THE DOROK NOT TO INVADE TORU-MEKIA!?
ARE YOU OUT OF YOUR MIND!?
グイ
YOU CAN'T! YOU'LL JUST BE TORN TO RIBBONS!!
ドキッ
THANK YOU, MITO.
YOU'RE GOING, TOO?

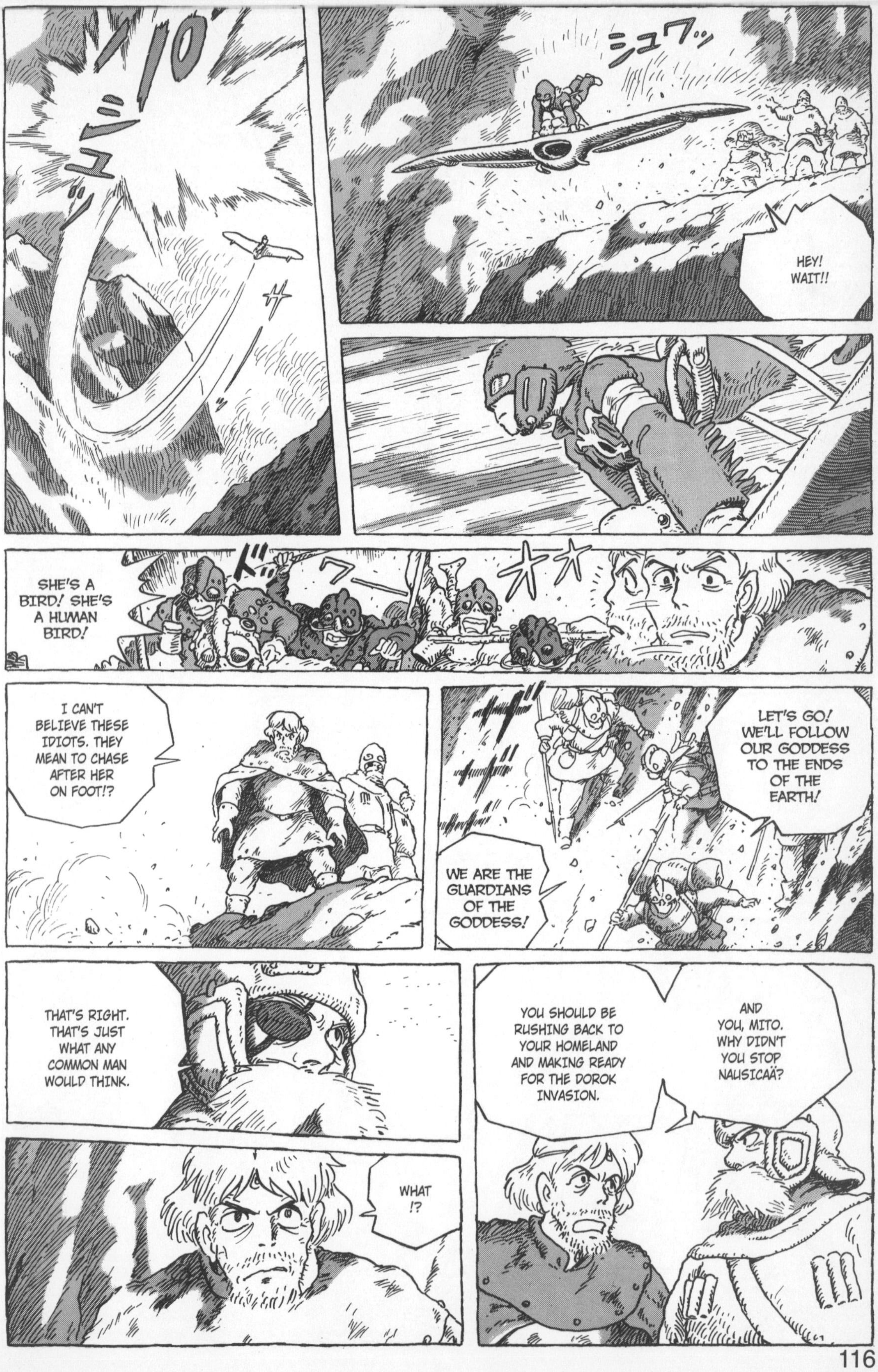
シュワッ
HEY! WAIT!!
SHE'S A BIRD! SHE'S A HUMAN BIRD!
LET'S GO! WE'LL FOLLOW OUR GODDESS TO THE ENDS OF THE EARTH!
WE ARE THE GUARDIANS OF THE GODDESS!
I CAN'T BELIEVE THESE IDIOTS. THEY MEAN TO CHASE AFTER HER ON FOOT!?
AND YOU, MITO. WHY DIDN'T YOU STOP NAUSICAÄ?
YOU SHOULD BE RUSHING BACK TO YOUR HOMELAND AND MAKING READY FOR THE DOROK INVASION.
THAT'S RIGHT. THAT'S JUST WHAT ANY COMMON MAN WOULD THINK.
WHAT !?

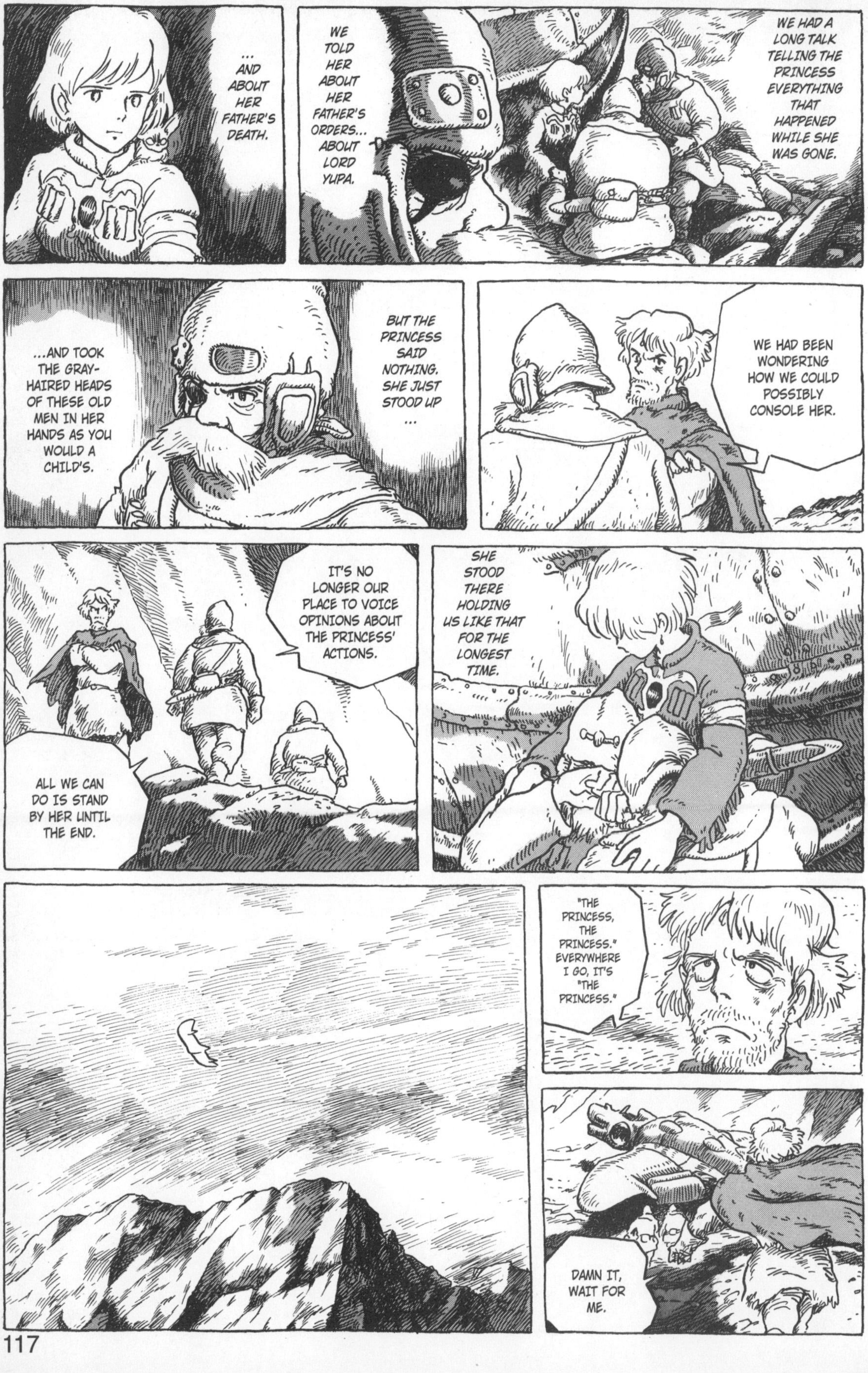
WE HAD A LONG TALK TELLING THE PRINCESS EVERYTHING THAT HAPPENED WHILE SHE WAS GONE.
WE TOLD HER ABOUT HER FATHER'S ORDERS... ABOUT LORD YUPA.
... AND ABOUT HER FATHER'S DEATH.
WE HAD BEEN WONDERING HOW WE COULD POSSIBLY CONSOLE HER.
BUT THE PRINCESS SAID NOTHING. SHE JUST STOOD UP ...
...AND TOOK THE GRAY-HAIRED HEADS OF THESE OLD MEN IN HER HANDS AS YOU WOULD A CHILD'S.
SHE STOOD THERE HOLDING US LIKE THAT FOR THE LONGEST TIME.
IT'S NO LONGER OUR PLACE TO VOICE OPINIONS ABOUT THE PRINCESS' ACTIONS.
ALL WE CAN DO IS STAND BY HER UNTIL THE END.
"THE PRINCESS, THE PRINCESS." EVERYWHERE I GO, IT'S "THE PRINCESS."
DAMN IT, WAIT FOR ME.

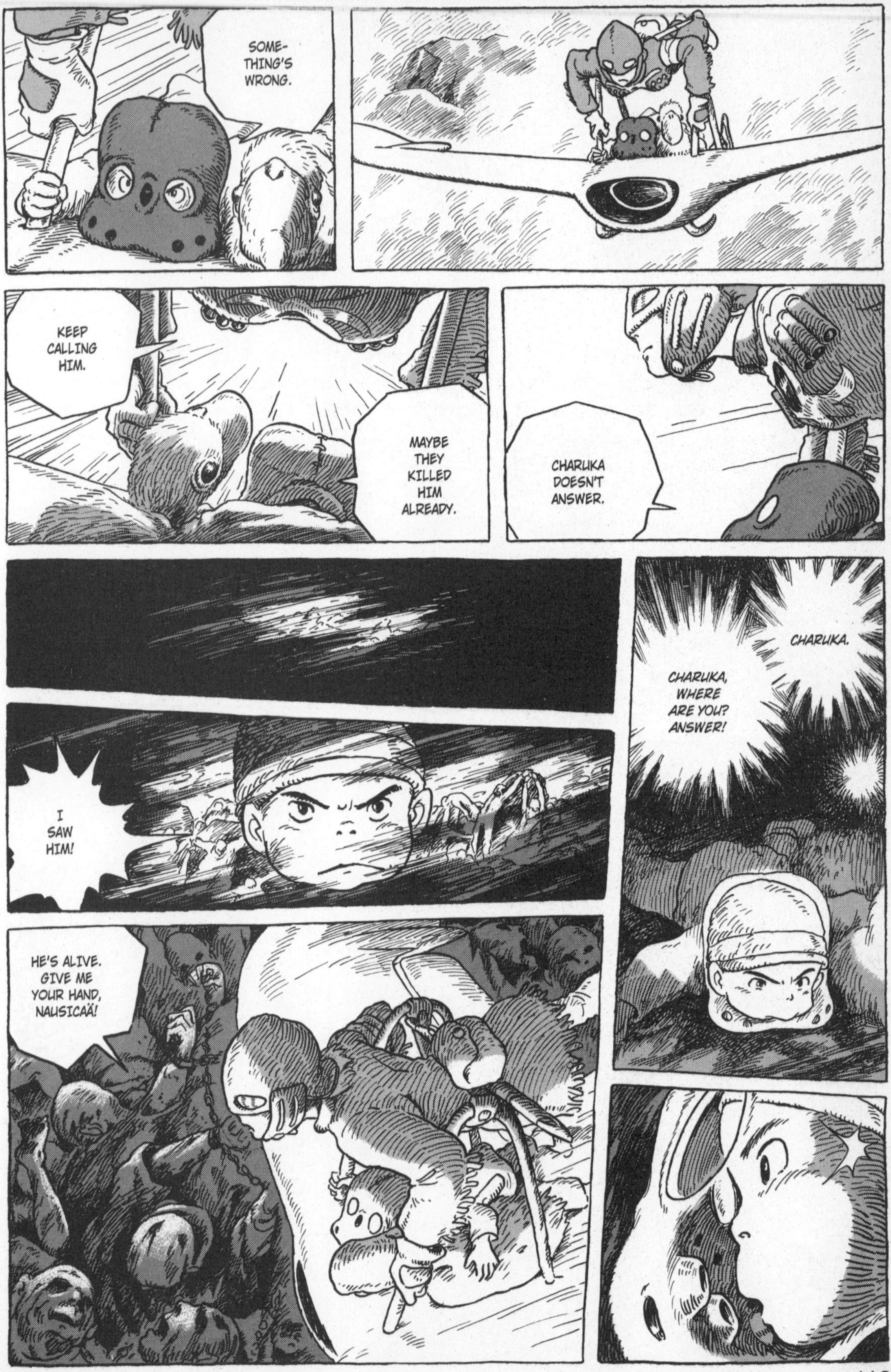
SOME-THING'S WRONG.
CHARUKA DOESN'T ANSWER.
MAYBE THEY KILLED HIM ALREADY.
KEEP CALLING HIM.
CHARUKA.
CHARUKA, WHERE ARE YOU? ANSWER!
I SAW HIM!
HE'S ALIVE. GIVE ME YOUR HAND, NAUSICAÄ!

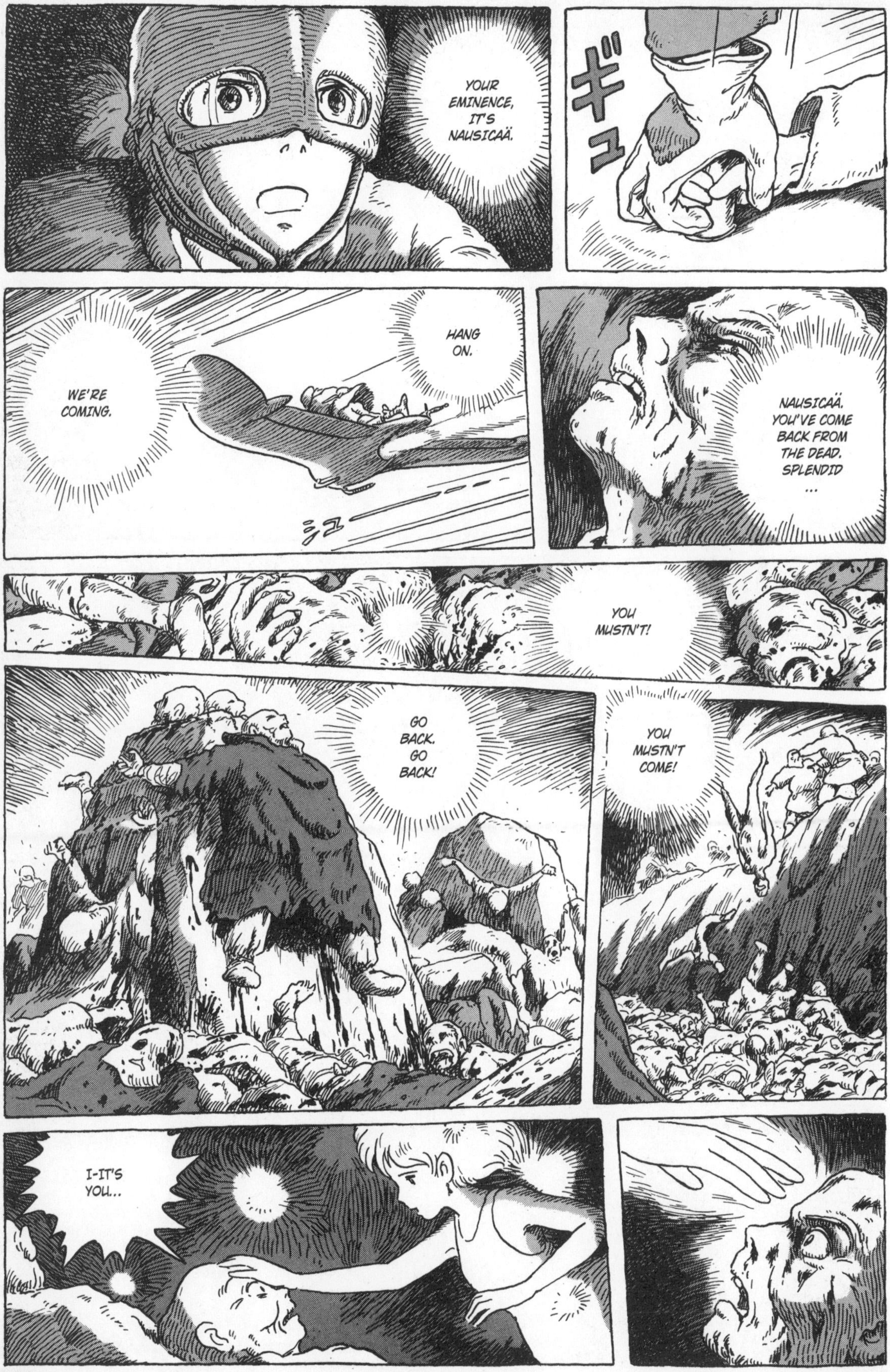
ギュ
YOUR EMINENCE, IT'S NAUSICAÄ.
NAUSICAÄ. YOU'VE COME BACK FROM THE DEAD. SPLENDID ...
HANG ON.
WE'RE COMING.
シュ
YOU MUSTN'T!
YOU MUSTN'T COME!
GO BACK. GO BACK!
I-IT'S YOU...

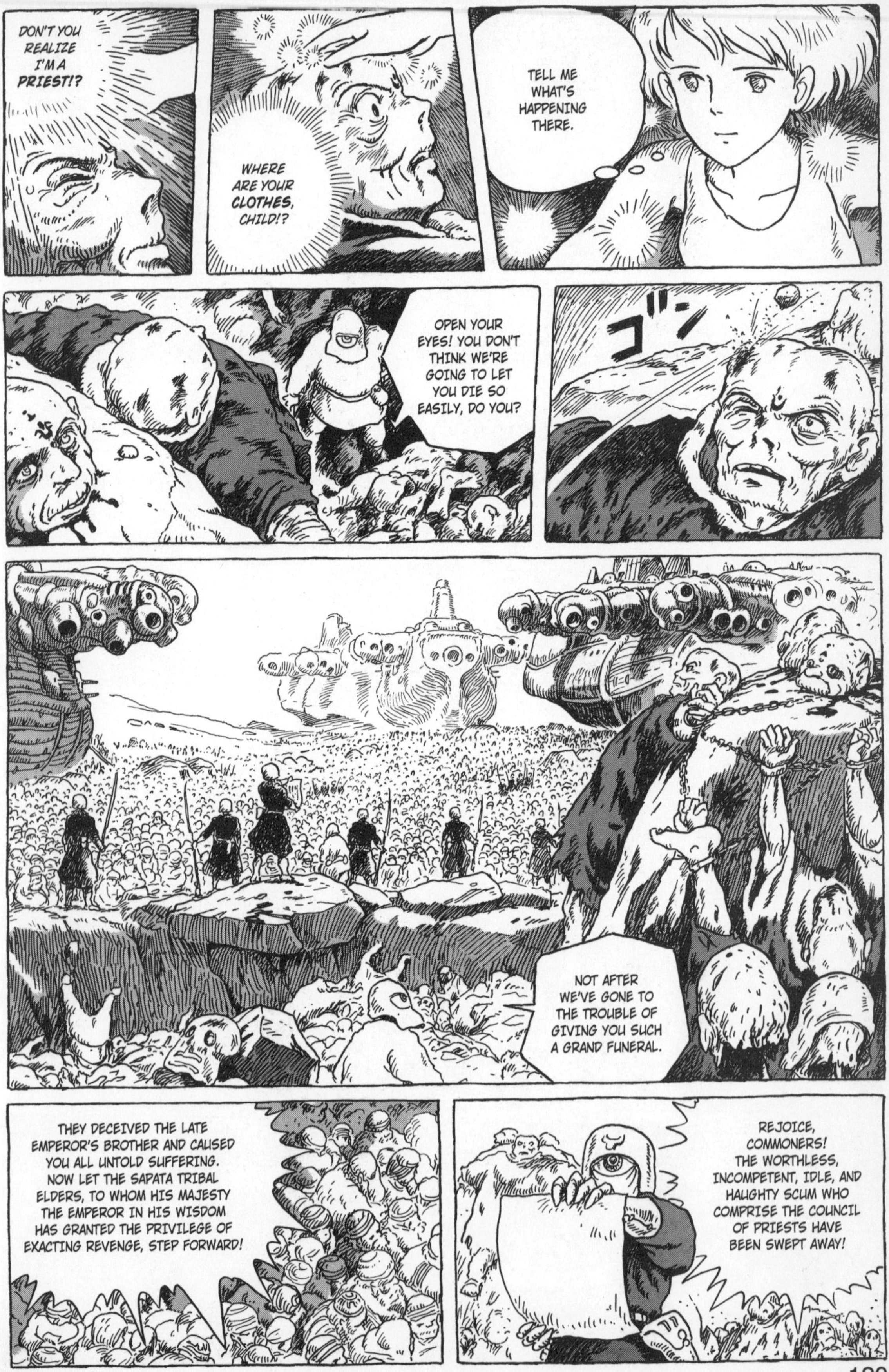
TELL ME WHAT'S HAPPENING THERE.
WHERE ARE YOUR CLOTHES, CHILD!?
DON'T YOU REALIZE I'M A PRIEST!?
ゴン
OPEN YOUR EYES! YOU DON'T THINK WE'RE GOING TO LET YOU DIE SO EASILY, DO YOU?
NOT AFTER WE'VE GONE TO THE TROUBLE OF GIVING YOU SUCH A GRAND FUNERAL.
REJOICE, COMMONERS! THE WORTHLESS, INCOMPETENT, IDLE, AND HAUGHTY SCUM WHO COMPRISE THE COUNCIL OF PRIESTS HAVE BEEN SWEPT AWAY!
THEY DECEIVED THE LATE EMPEROR'S BROTHER AND CAUSED YOU ALL UNTOLD SUFFERING. NOW LET THE SAPATA TRIBAL ELDERS, TO WHOM HIS MAJESTY THE EMPEROR IN HIS WISDOM HAS GRANTED THE PRIVILEGE OF EXACTING REVENGE, STEP FORWARD!

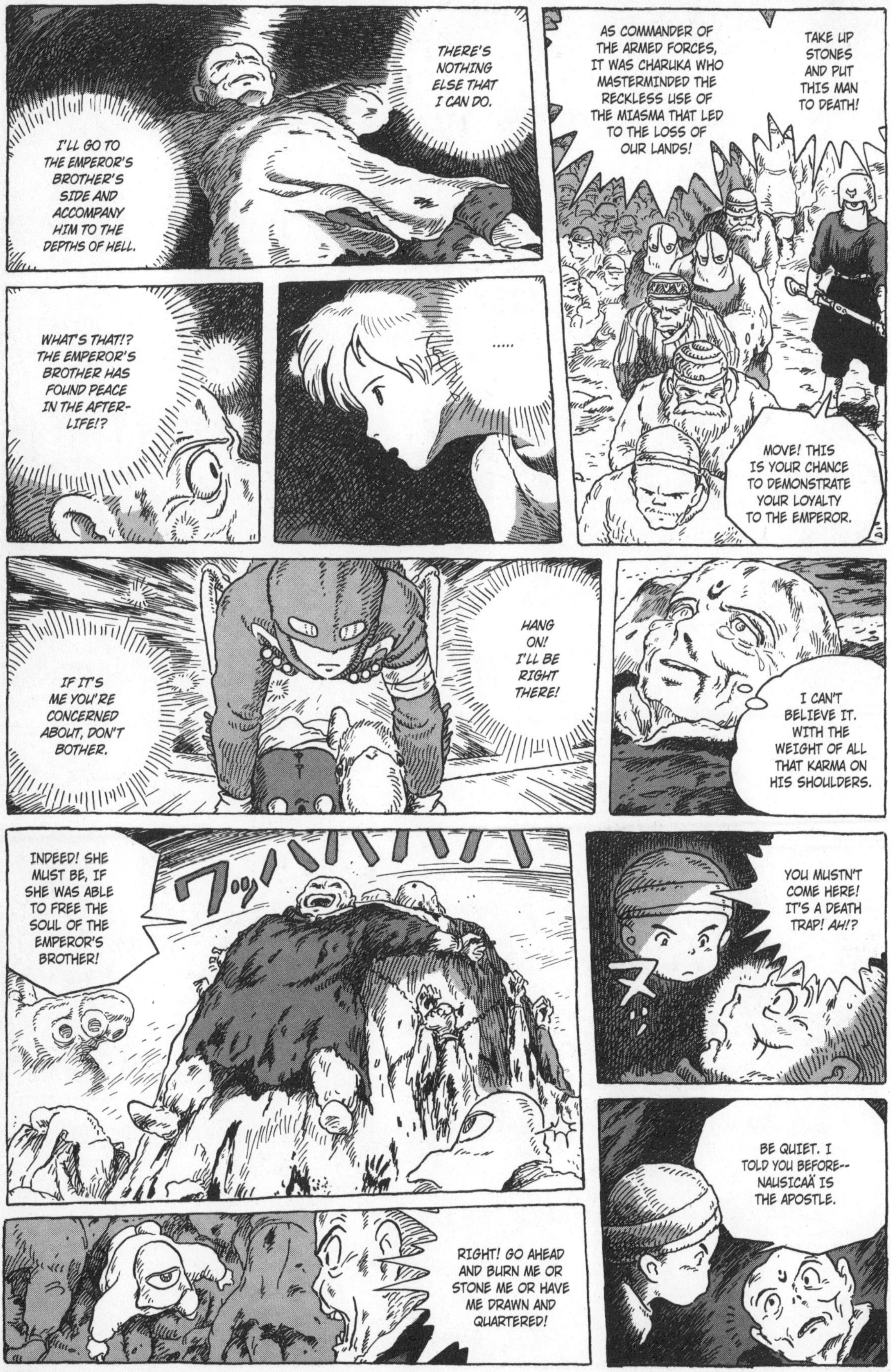
TAKE UP STONES AND PUT THIS MAN TO DEATH!
AS COMMANDER OF THE ARMED FORCES, IT WAS CHARUKA WHO MASTERMINDED THE RECKLESS USE OF THE MIASMA THAT LED TO THE LOSS OF OUR LANDS!
MOVE! THIS IS YOUR CHANCE TO DEMONSTRATE YOUR LOYALTY TO THE EMPEROR.
THERE'S NOTHING ELSE THAT I CAN DO.
I'LL GO TO THE EMPEROR'S BROTHER'S SIDE AND ACCOMPANY HIM TO THE DEPTHS OF HELL.
.....
WHAT'S THAT!? THE EMPEROR'S BROTHER HAS FOUND PEACE IN THE AFTER-LIFE!?
I CAN'T BELIEVE IT. WITH THE WEIGHT OF ALL THAT KARMA ON HIS SHOULDERS.
HANG ON! I'LL BE RIGHT THERE!
IF IT'S ME YOU'RE CONCERNED ABOUT, DON'T BOTHER.
YOU MUSTN'T COME HERE! IT'S A DEATH TRAP! AH!?
BE QUIET. I TOLD YOU BEFORE-- NAUSICAÄ IS THE APOSTLE.
ワッ
INDEED! SHE MUST BE, IF SHE WAS ABLE TO FREE THE SOUL OF THE EMPEROR'S BROTHER!
RIGHT! GO AHEAD AND BURN ME OR STONE ME OR HAVE ME DRAWN AND QUARTERED!

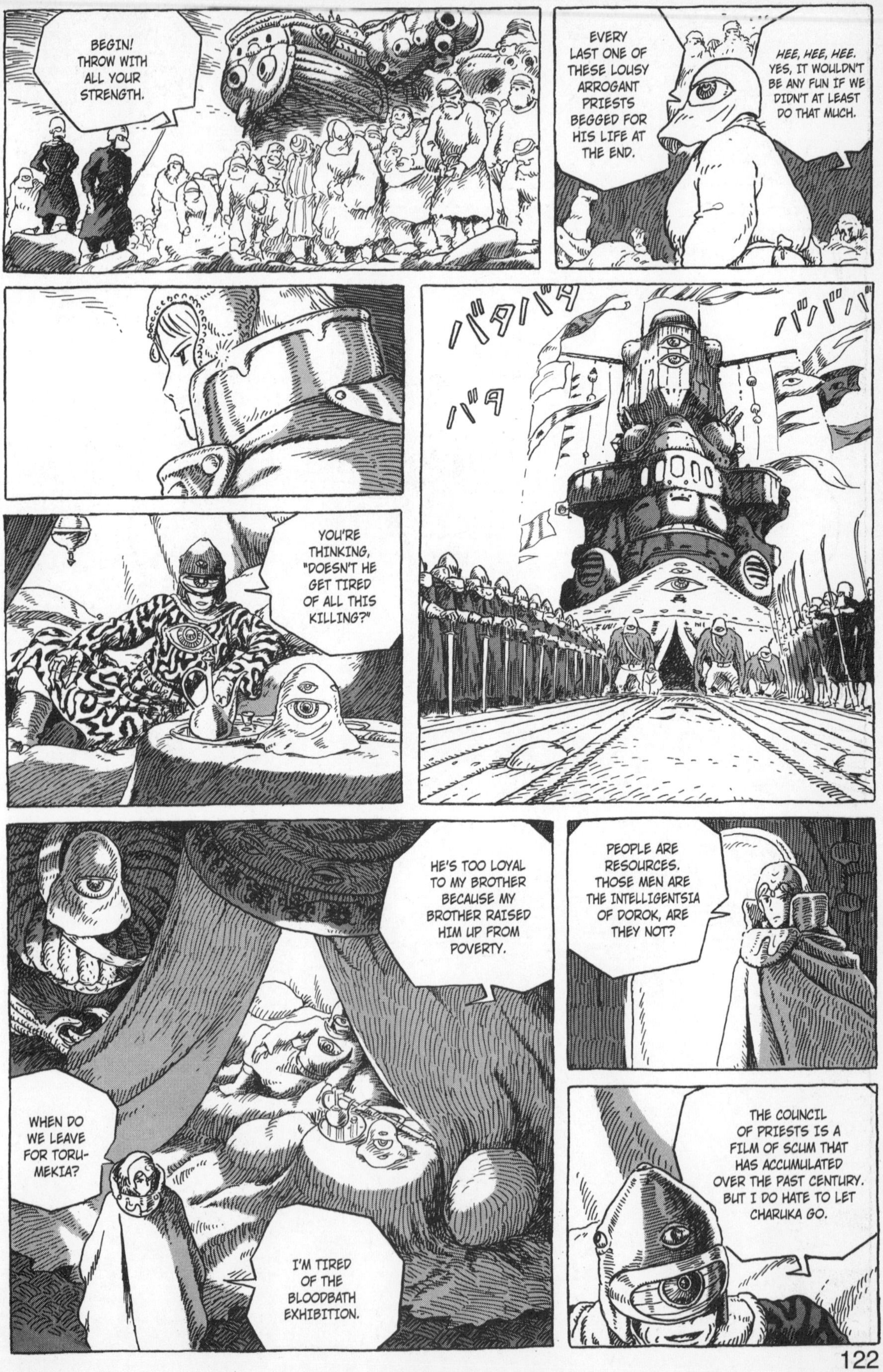
HEE, HEE, HEE. YES, IT WOULDN'T BE ANY FUN IF WE DIDN'T AT LEAST DO THAT MUCH.
EVERY LAST ONE OF THESE LOUSY ARROGANT PRIESTS BEGGED FOR HIS LIFE AT THE END.
BEGIN! THROW WITH ALL YOUR STRENGTH.
バババ
バタバタ
バタ
YOU'RE THINKING, "DOESN'T HE GET TIRED OF ALL THIS KILLING?"
PEOPLE ARE RESOURCES. THOSE MEN ARE THE INTELLIGENTSIA OF DOROK, ARE THEY NOT?
THE COUNCIL OF PRIESTS IS A FILM OF SCUM THAT HAS ACCUMULATED OVER THE PAST CENTURY. BUT I DO HATE TO LET CHARUKA GO.
HE'S TOO LOYAL TO MY BROTHER BECAUSE MY BROTHER RAISED HIM UP FROM POVERTY.
WHEN DO WE LEAVE FOR TORU-MEKIA?
I'M TIRED OF THE BLOODBATH EXHIBITION.

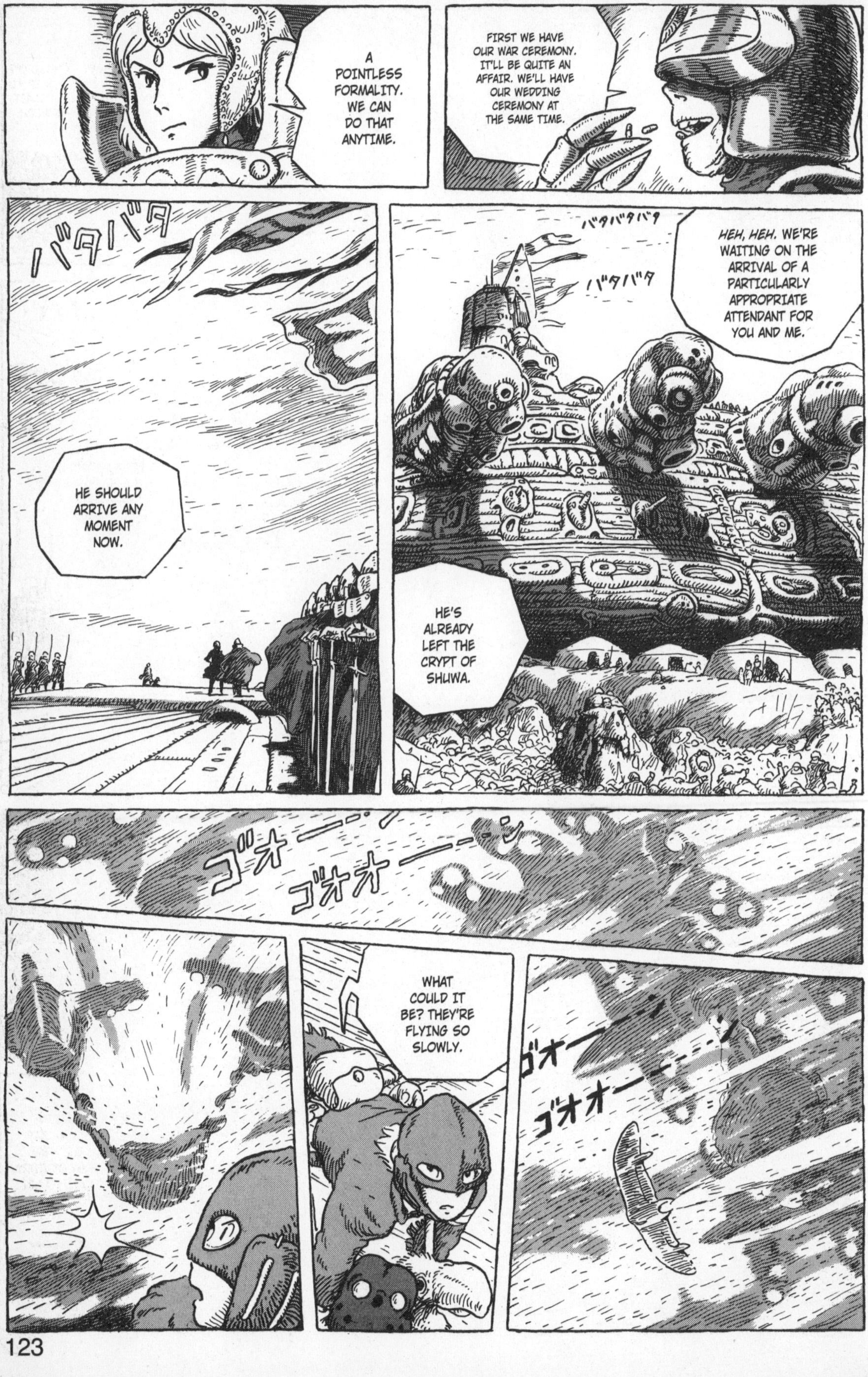

FIRST WE HAVE OUR WAR CEREMONY. IT'LL BE QUITE AN AFFAIR. WE'LL HAVE OUR WEDDING CEREMONY AT THE SAME TIME.
A POINTLESS FORMALITY. WE CAN DO THAT ANYTIME.
バタバタバタ
バタバタ
HEH, HEH. WE'RE WAITING ON THE ARRIVAL OF A PARTICULARLY APPROPRIATE ATTENDANT FOR YOU AND ME.
HE'S ALREADY LEFT THE CRYPT OF SHUWA.
バタバタ
HE SHOULD ARRIVE ANY MOMENT NOW.
ゴオーーン
ゴオオーーーン
ゴオーーーン
ゴオオーーーン
WHAT COULD IT BE? THEY'RE FLYING SO SLOWLY.

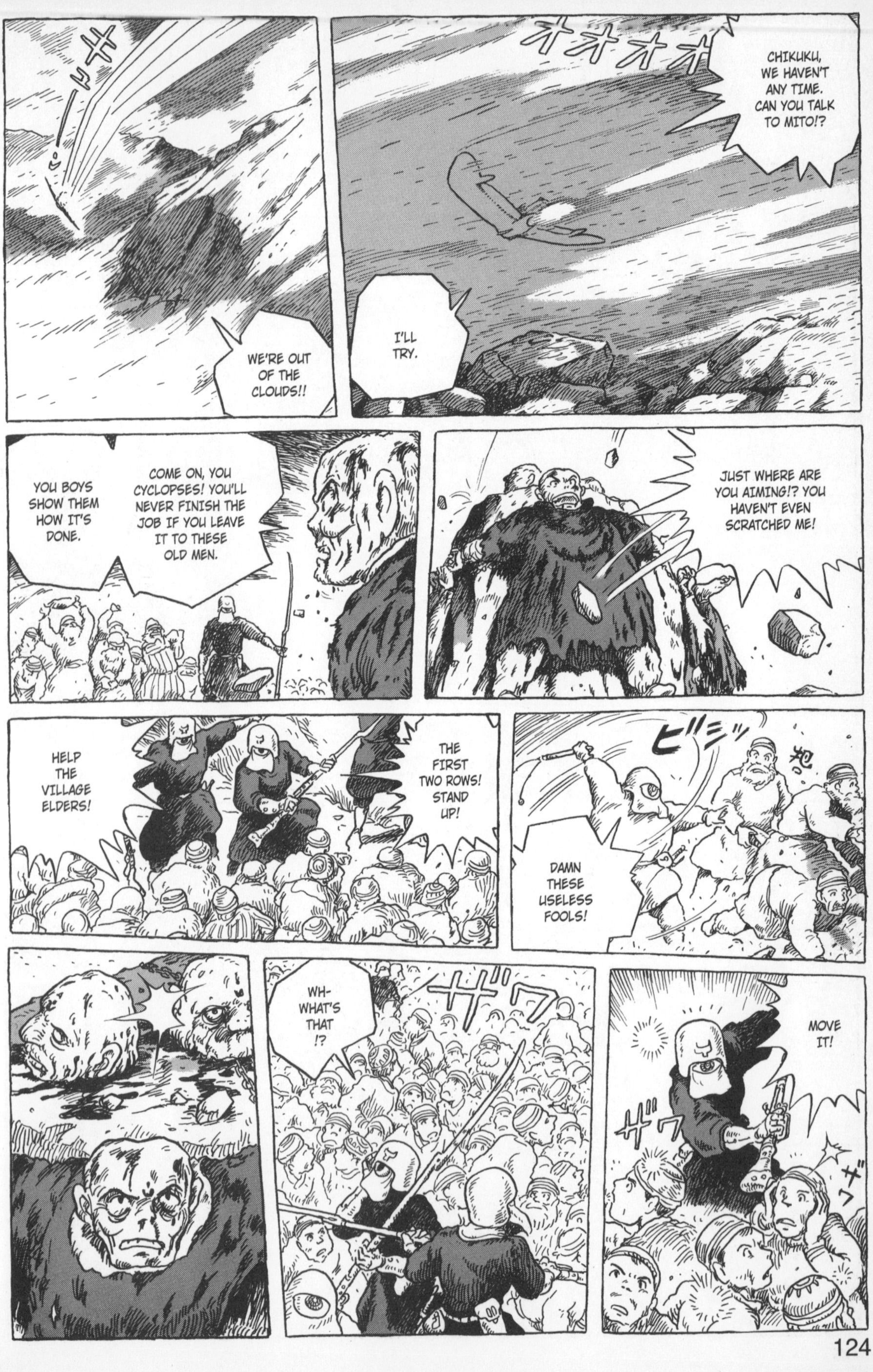

オオオオオ
CHIKUKU, WE HAVEN'T ANY TIME. CAN YOU TALK TO MITO!?
I'LL TRY.
WE'RE OUT OF THE CLOUDS!!
JUST WHERE ARE YOU AIMING!? YOU HAVEN'T EVEN SCRATCHED ME!
COME ON, YOU CYCLOPSES! YOU'LL NEVER FINISH THE JOB IF YOU LEAVE IT TO THESE OLD MEN.
YOU BOYS SHOW THEM HOW IT'S DONE.
DAMN THESE USELESS FOOLS!
THE FIRST TWO ROWS! STAND UP!
HELP THE VILLAGE ELDERS!
MOVE IT!
ザワ
ザワ
WH-WHAT'S THAT !?

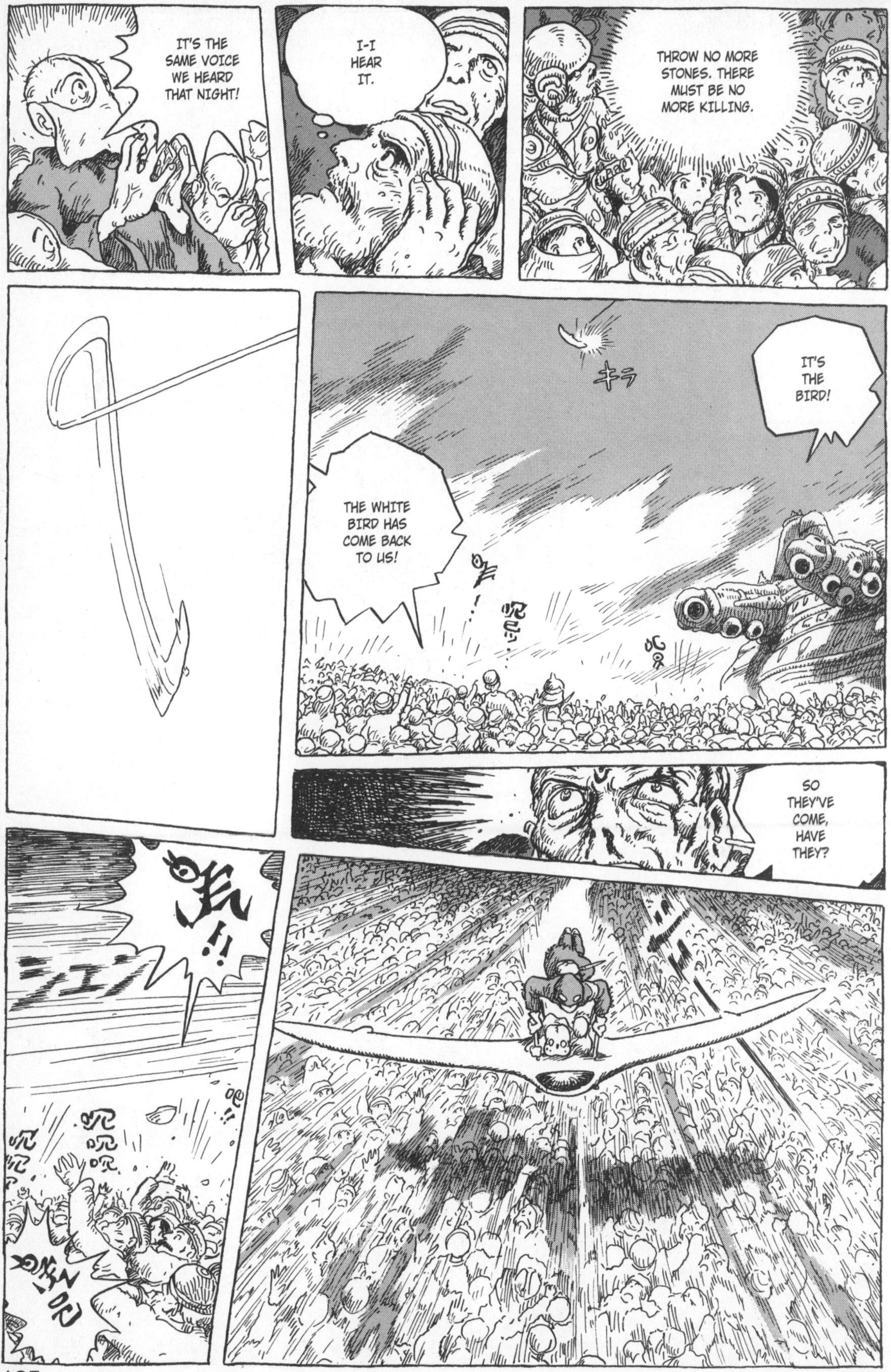

THROW NO MORE STONES. THERE MUST BE NO MORE KILLING.
I-I HEAR IT.
IT'S THE SAME VOICE WE HEARD THAT NIGHT!
IT'S THE BIRD!
キラ
THE WHITE BIRD HAS COME BACK TO US!
SO THEY'VE COME, HAVE THEY?

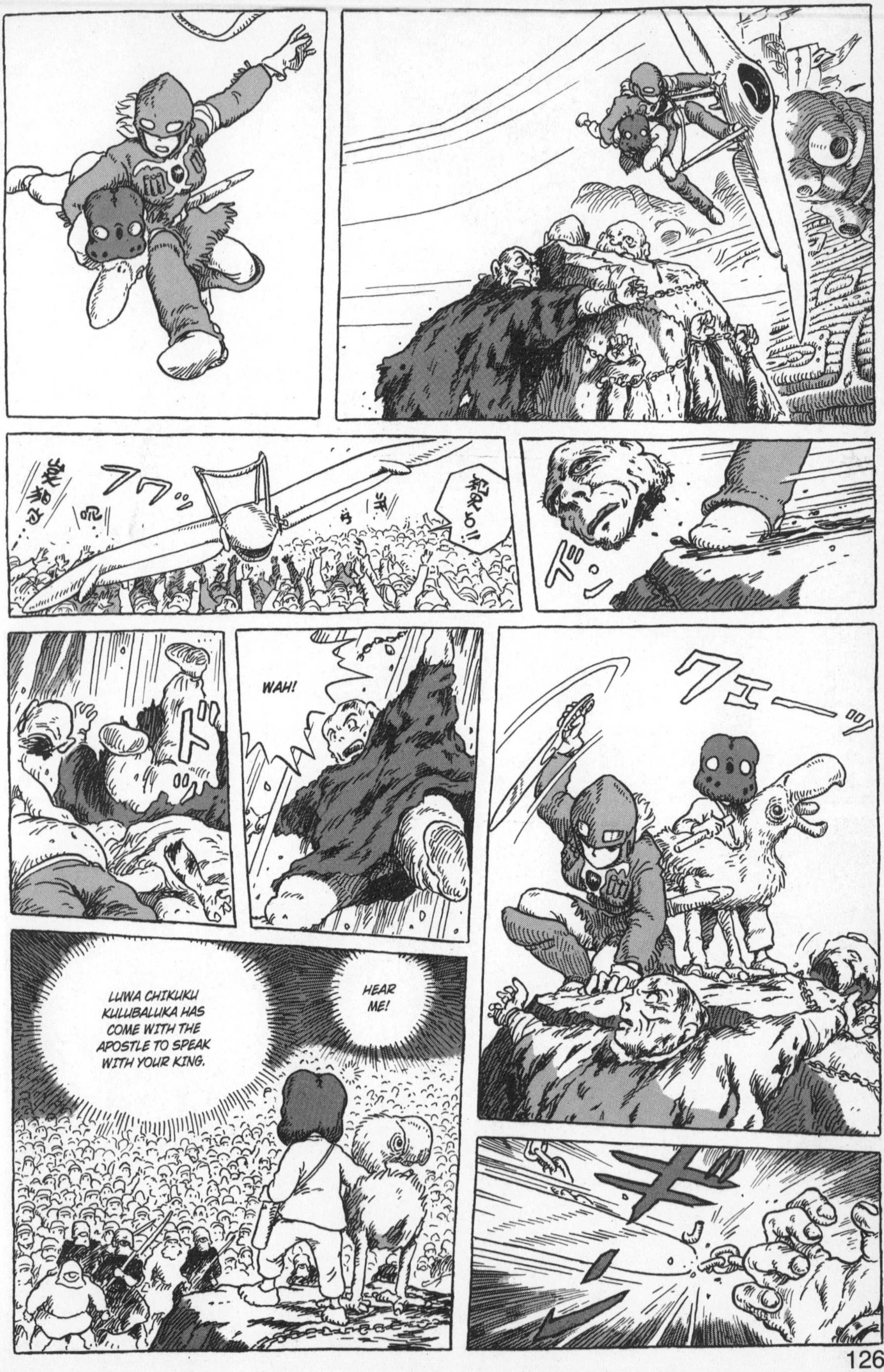
ドン
フワッ
クェーッ
WAH!
ド
HEAR ME!
LUWA CHIKUKU KULUBALUKA HAS COME WITH THE APOSTLE TO SPEAK WITH YOUR KING.

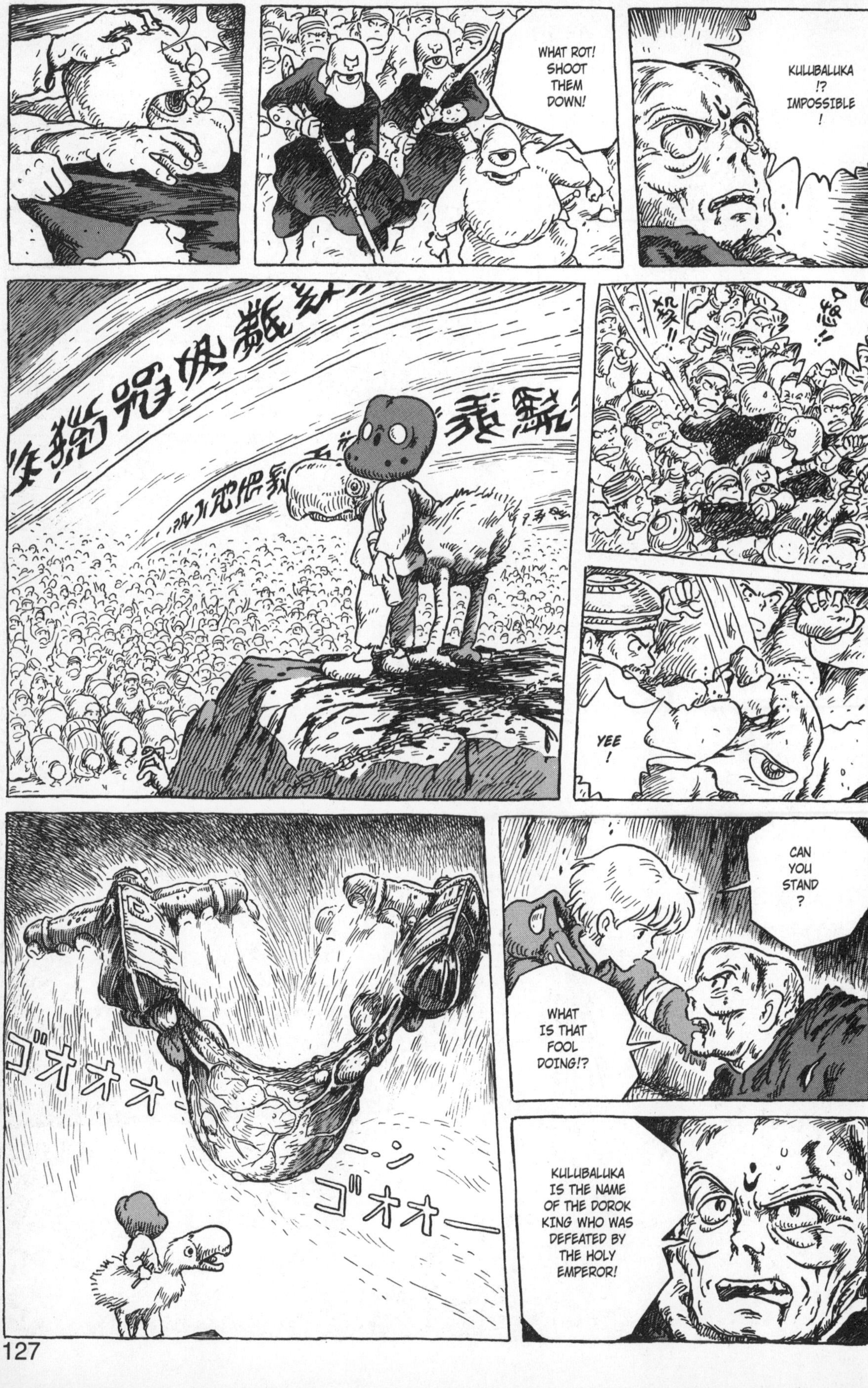
KULUBALUKA !? IMPOSSIBLE !
WHAT ROT! SHOOT THEM DOWN!
YEE !
CAN YOU STAND ?
WHAT IS THAT FOOL DOING!?
KULUBALUKA IS THE NAME OF THE DOROK KING WHO WAS DEFEATED BY THE HOLY EMPEROR!
ゴオオオー
ーン
ゴオオー

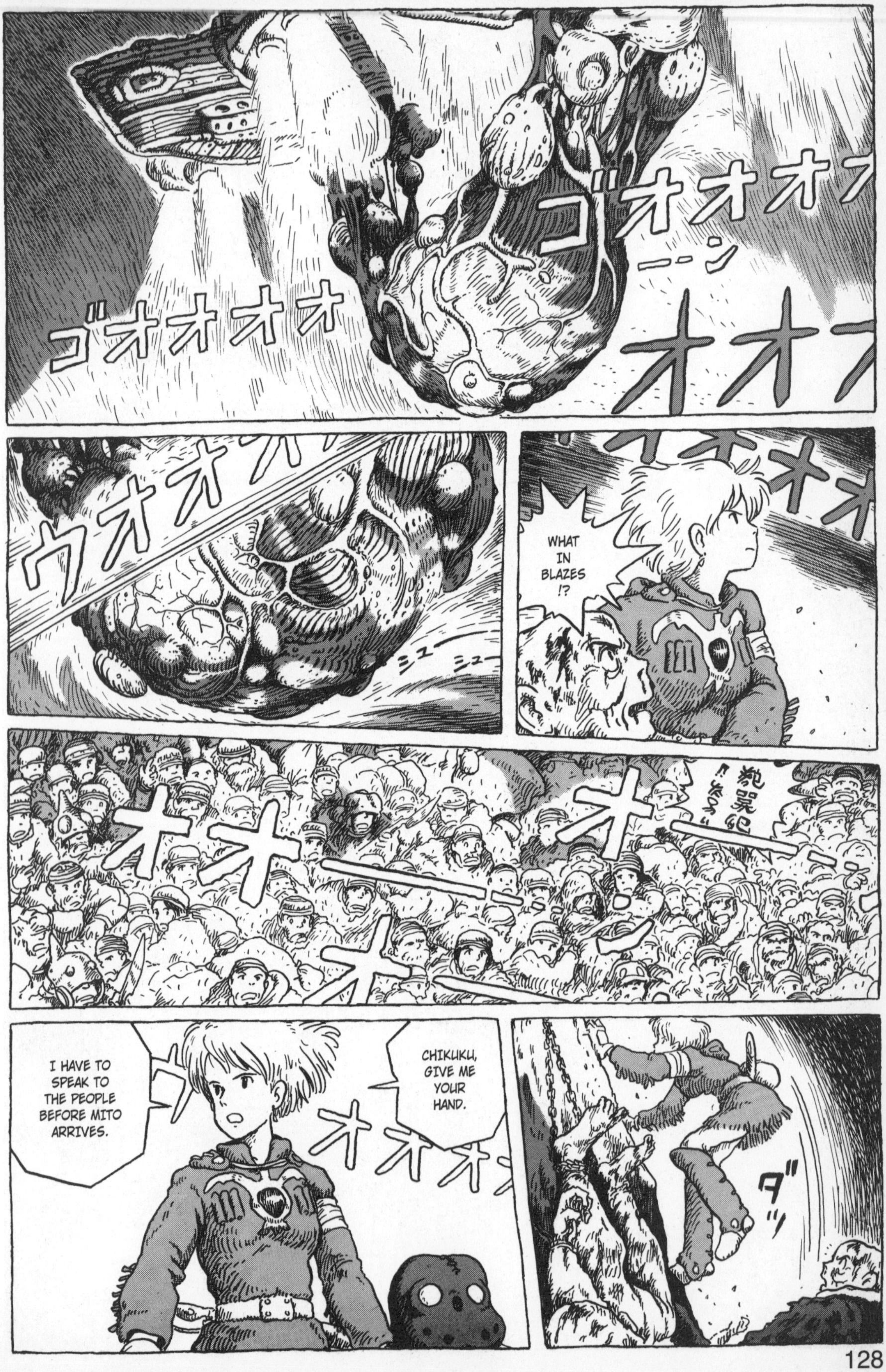

WHAT IN BLAZES !?
CHIKUKU, GIVE ME YOUR HAND.
I HAVE TO SPEAK TO THE PEOPLE BEFORE MITO ARRIVES.

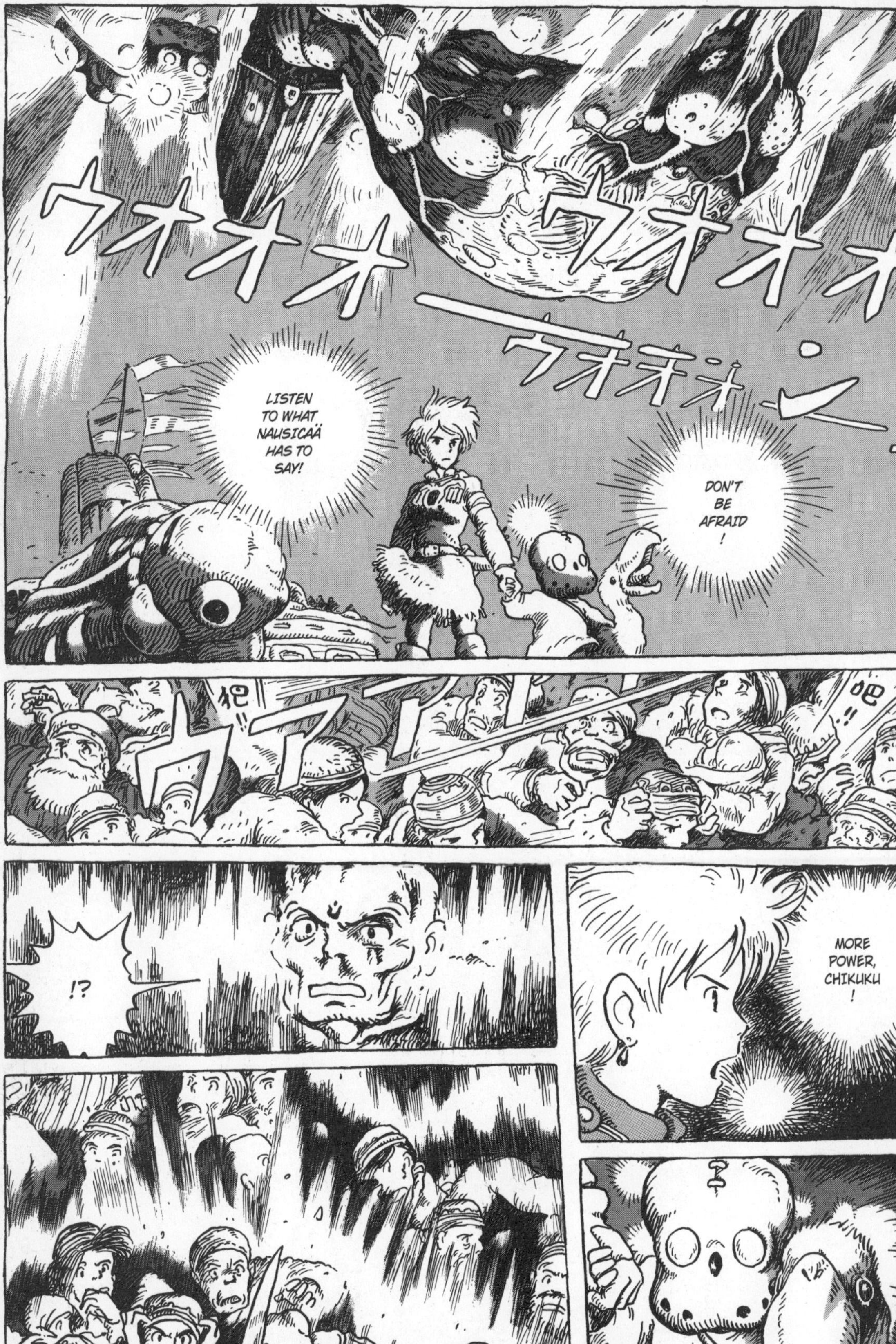
ウオオオーウオオオ
ウオオオオーン
LISTEN TO WHAT NAUSICAÄ HAS TO SAY!
DON'T BE AFRAID!
MORE POWER, CHIKUKU!
!?

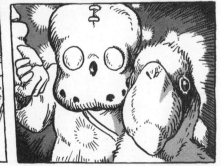

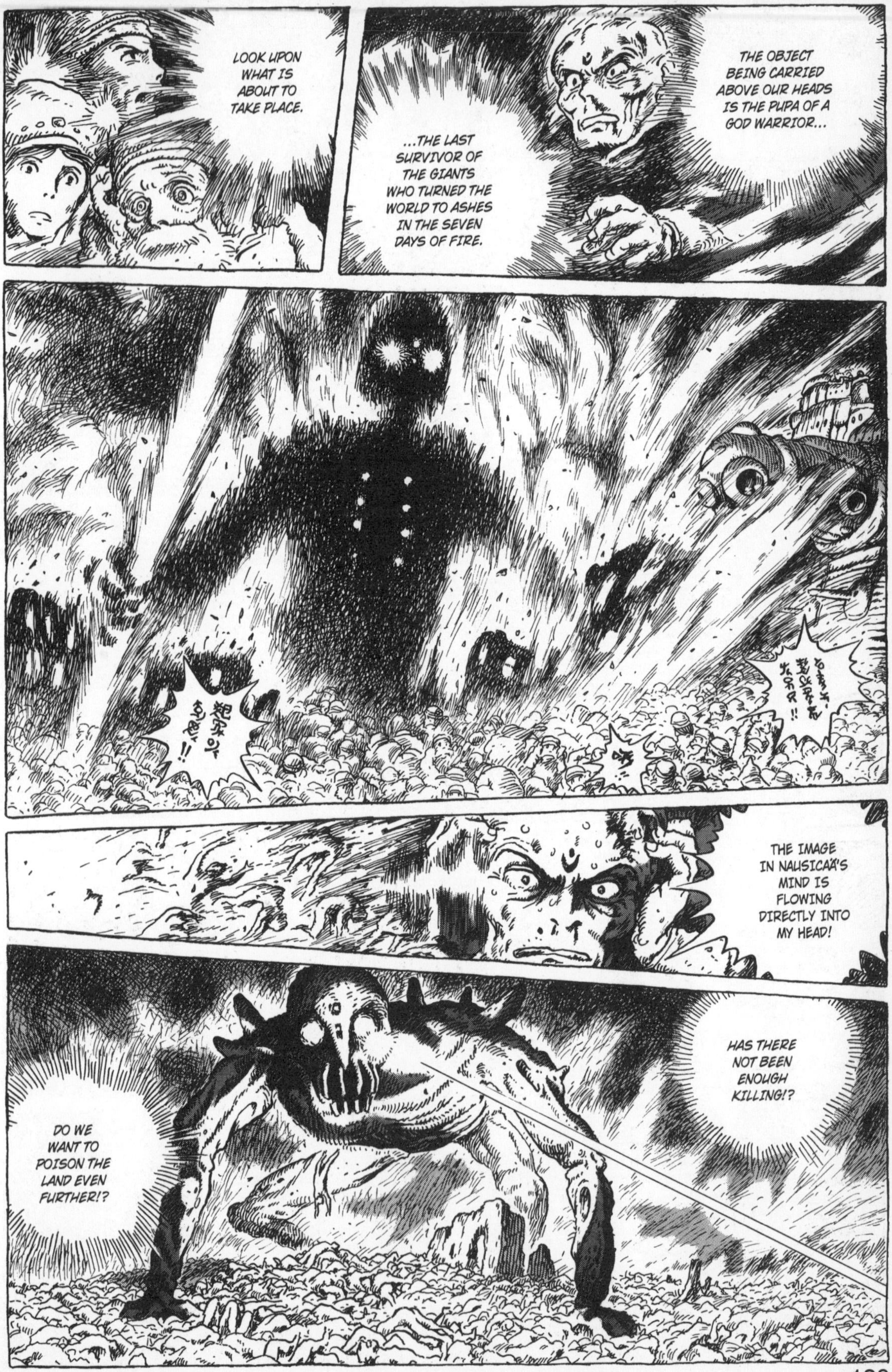
THE OBJECT BEING CARRIED ABOVE OUR HEADS IS THE PUPA OF A GOD WARRIOR...
...THE LAST SURVIVOR OF THE GIANTS WHO TURNED THE WORLD TO ASHES IN THE SEVEN DAYS OF FIRE.
LOOK UPON WHAT IS ABOUT TO TAKE PLACE.
THE IMAGE IN NAUSICAÄ'S MIND IS FLOWING DIRECTLY INTO MY HEAD!
HAS THERE NOT BEEN ENOUGH KILLING!?
DO WE WANT TO POISON THE LAND EVEN FURTHER!?

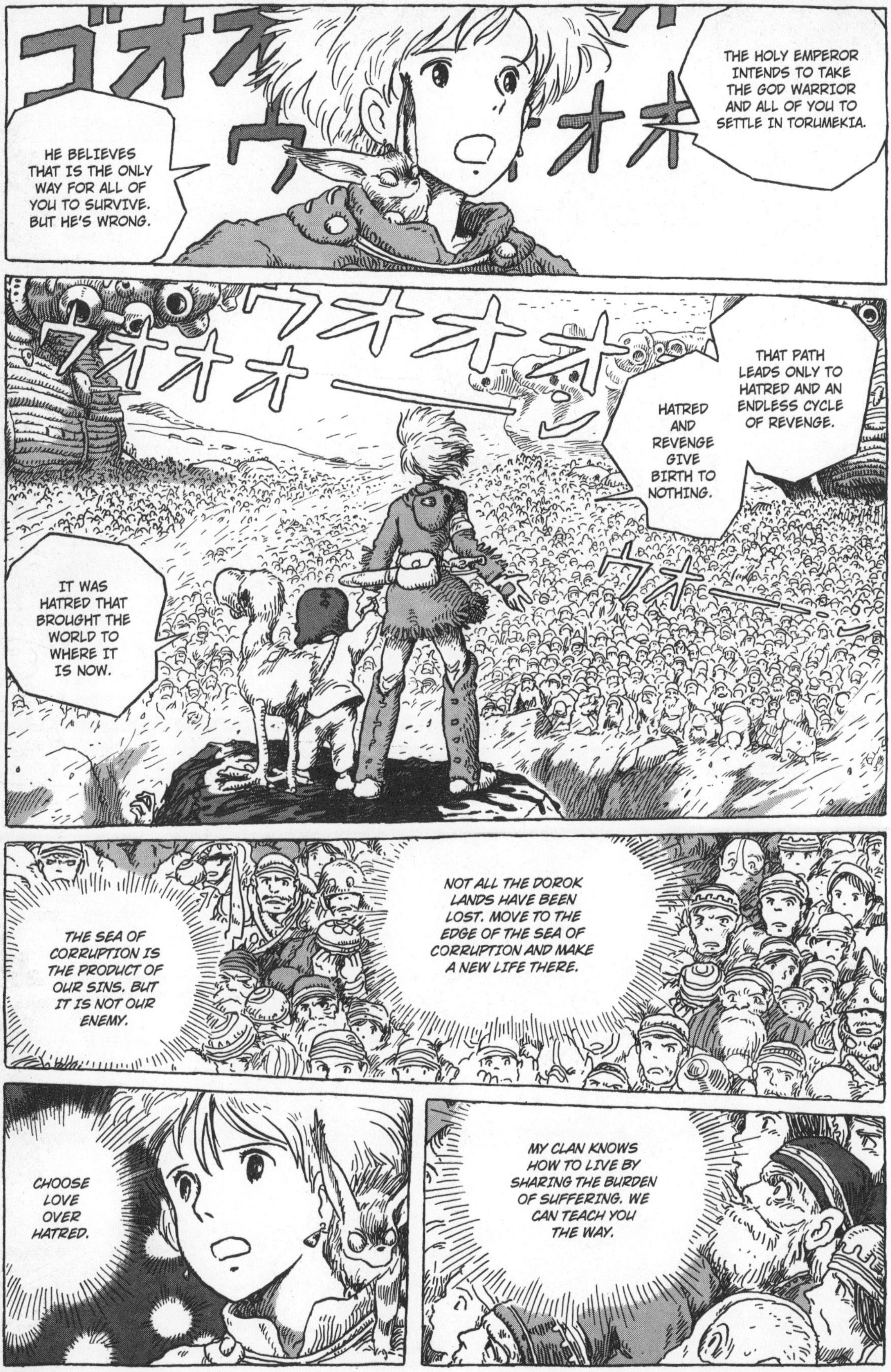
THE HOLY EMPEROR INTENDS TO TAKE THE GOD WARRIOR AND ALL OF YOU TO SETTLE IN TORUMEKIA.
HE BELIEVES THAT IS THE ONLY WAY FOR ALL OF YOU TO SURVIVE. BUT HE'S WRONG.
ウオオオオーン
ウオオオーー
THAT PATH LEADS ONLY TO HATRED AND AN ENDLESS CYCLE OF REVENGE.
HATRED AND REVENGE GIVE BIRTH TO NOTHING.
ウオーーン
IT WAS HATRED THAT BROUGHT THE WORLD TO WHERE IT IS NOW.
NOT ALL THE DOROK LANDS HAVE BEEN LOST. MOVE TO THE EDGE OF THE SEA OF CORRUPTION AND MAKE A NEW LIFE THERE.
THE SEA OF CORRUPTION IS THE PRODUCT OF OUR SINS. BUT IT IS NOT OUR ENEMY.
MY CLAN KNOWS HOW TO LIVE BY SHARING THE BURDEN OF SUFFERING. WE CAN TEACH YOU THE WAY.
CHOOSE LOVE OVER HATRED.

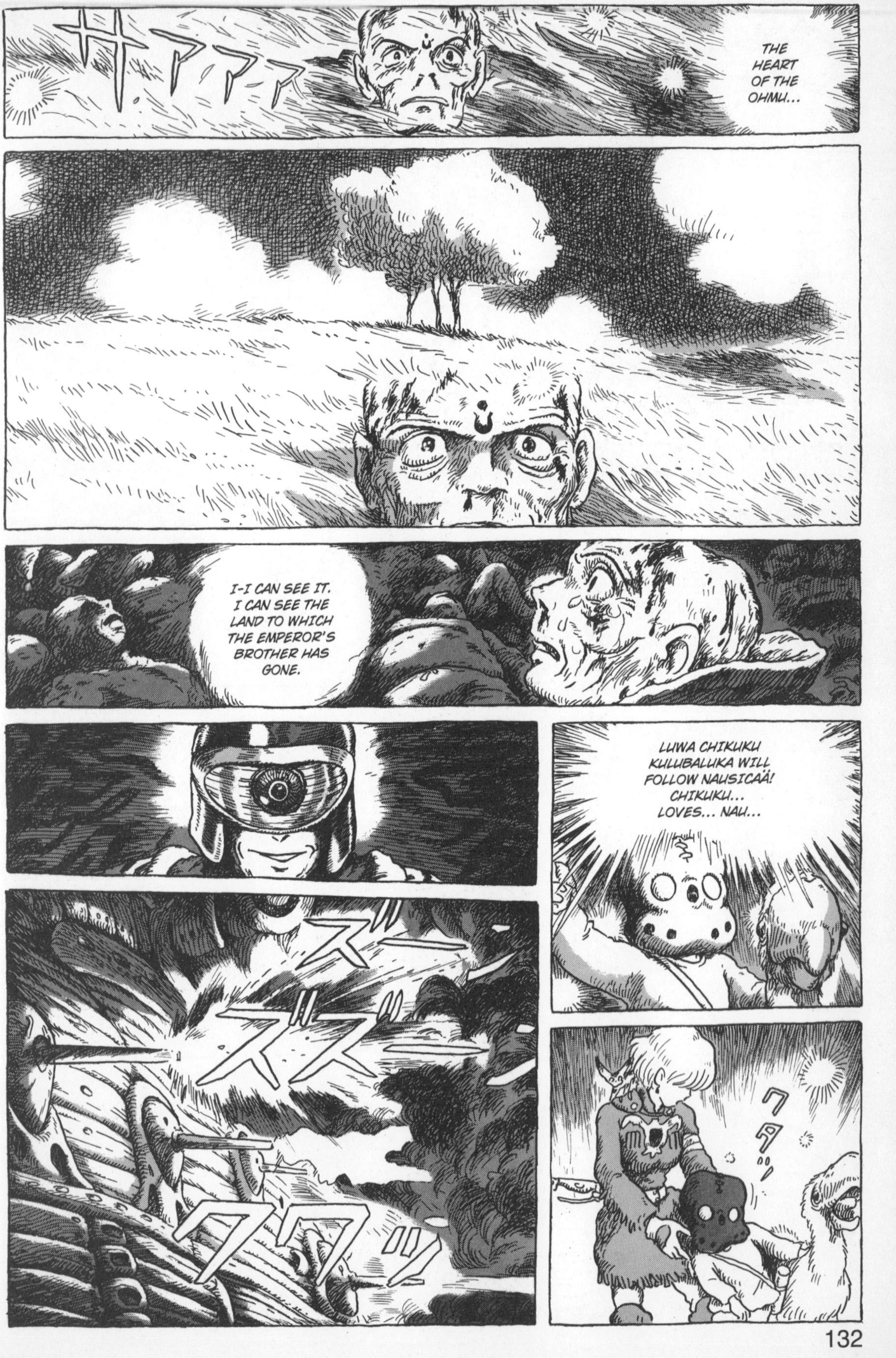

THE HEART OF THE OHMU...
I-I CAN SEE IT. I CAN SEE THE LAND TO WHICH THE EMPEROR'S BROTHER HAS GONE.
LUWA CHIKUKU KULUBALUKA WILL FOLLOW NAUSICAÄ! CHIKUKU... LOVES... NAU...

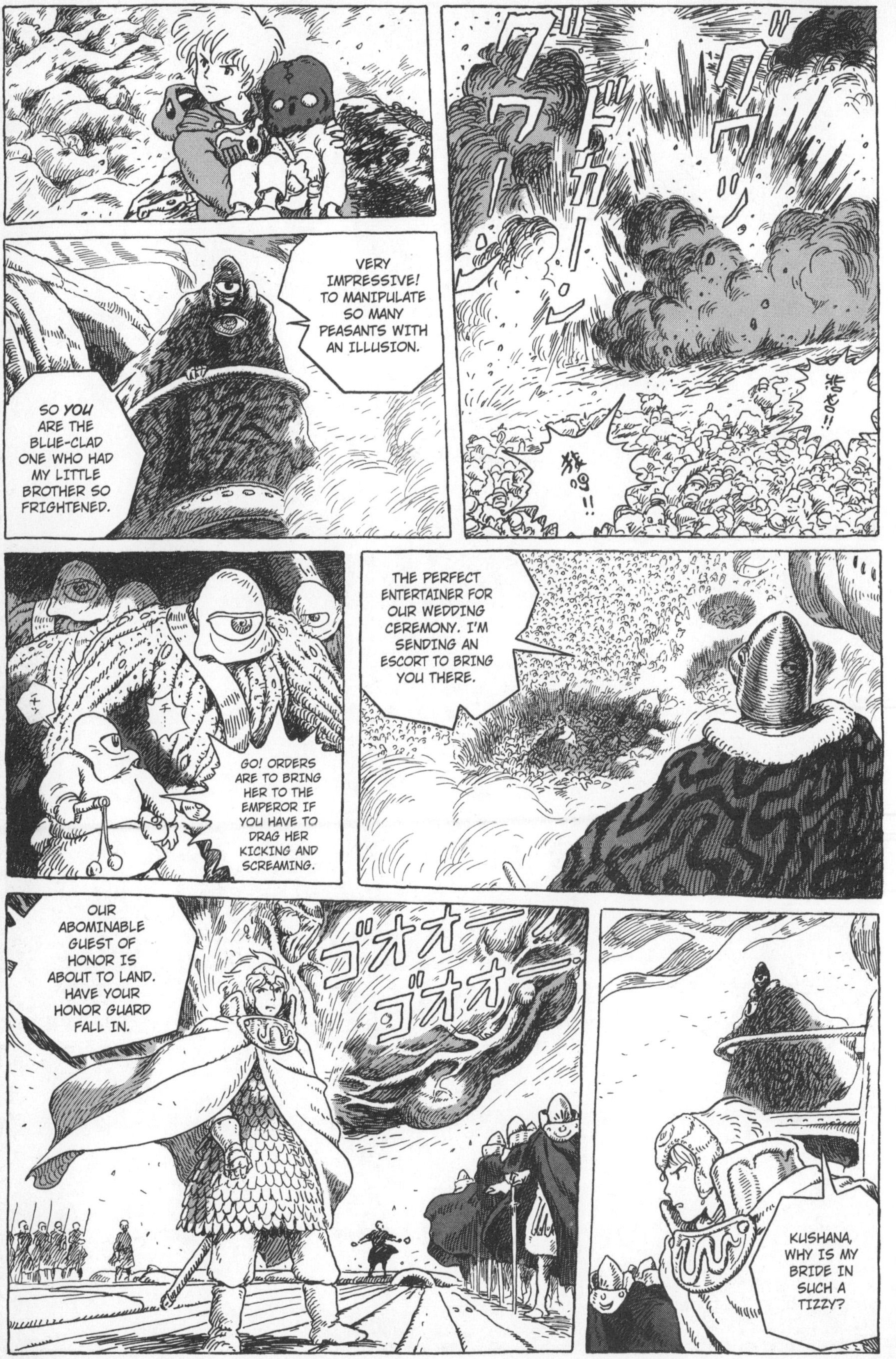
VERY IMPRESSIVE! TO MANIPULATE SO MANY PEASANTS WITH AN ILLUSION.
SO *YOU* ARE THE BLUE-CLAD ONE WHO HAD MY LITTLE BROTHER SO FRIGHTENED.
THE PERFECT ENTERTAINER FOR OUR WEDDING CEREMONY. I'M SENDING AN ESCORT TO BRING YOU THERE.
チ…
チッ
GO! ORDERS ARE TO BRING HER TO THE EMPEROR IF YOU HAVE TO DRAG HER KICKING AND SCREAMING.
KUSHANA, WHY IS MY BRIDE IN SUCH A TIZZY?
OUR ABOMINABLE GUEST OF HONOR IS ABOUT TO LAND. HAVE YOUR HONOR GUARD FALL IN.
ゴオオー
ゴオオー

MOVE BACK! IT'S ME THE HEEDRA ARE AFTER!

TAKE CHIKUKU. HE'S SPENT ALL HIS ENERGY.

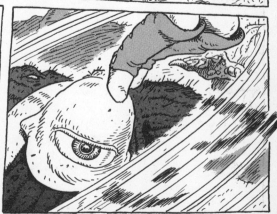

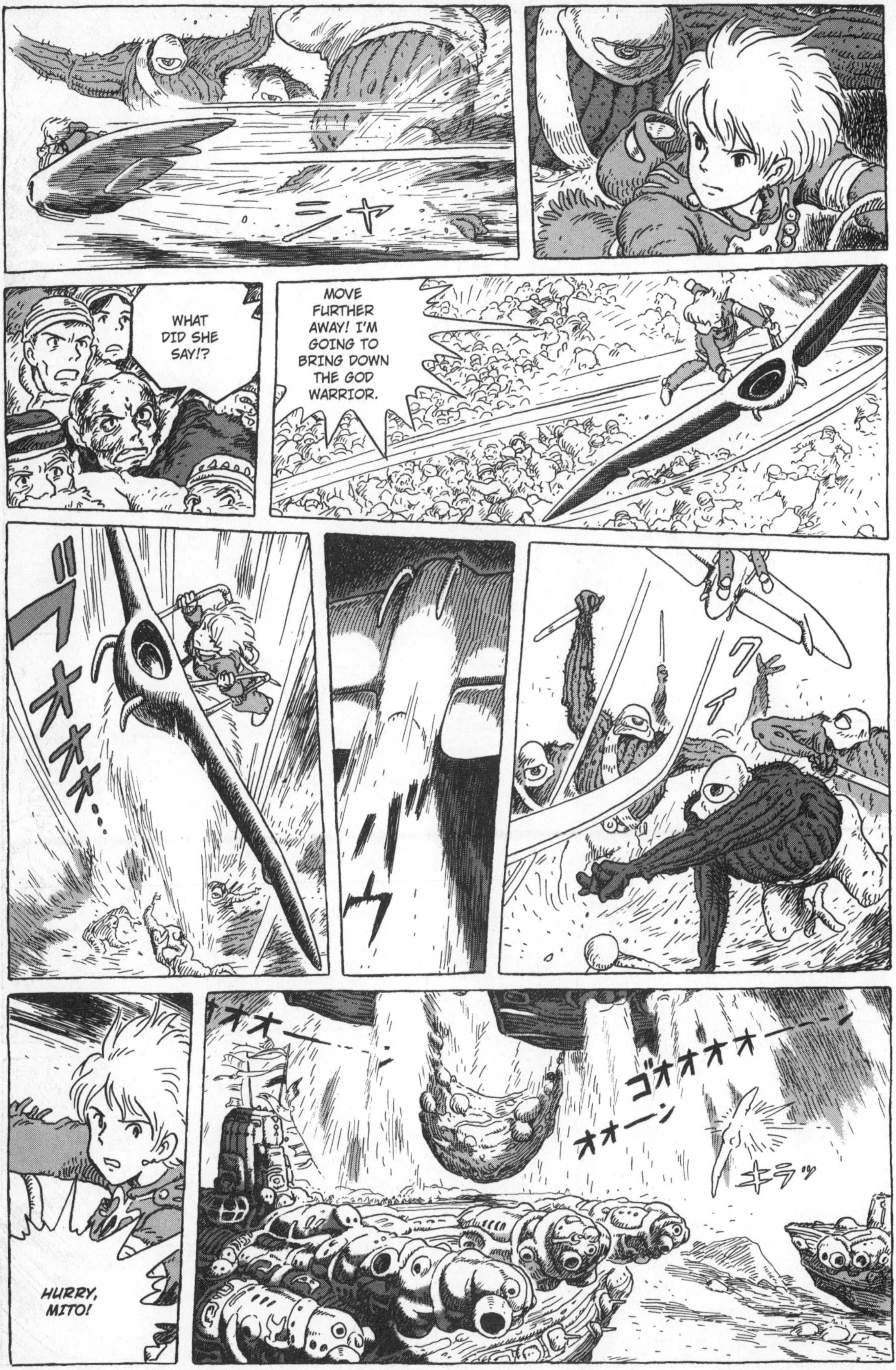
MOVE FURTHER AWAY! I'M GOING TO BRING DOWN THE GOD WARRIOR.
WHAT DID SHE SAY!?
ゴオオオオーーン
オオーン
キラッ
HURRY, MITO!

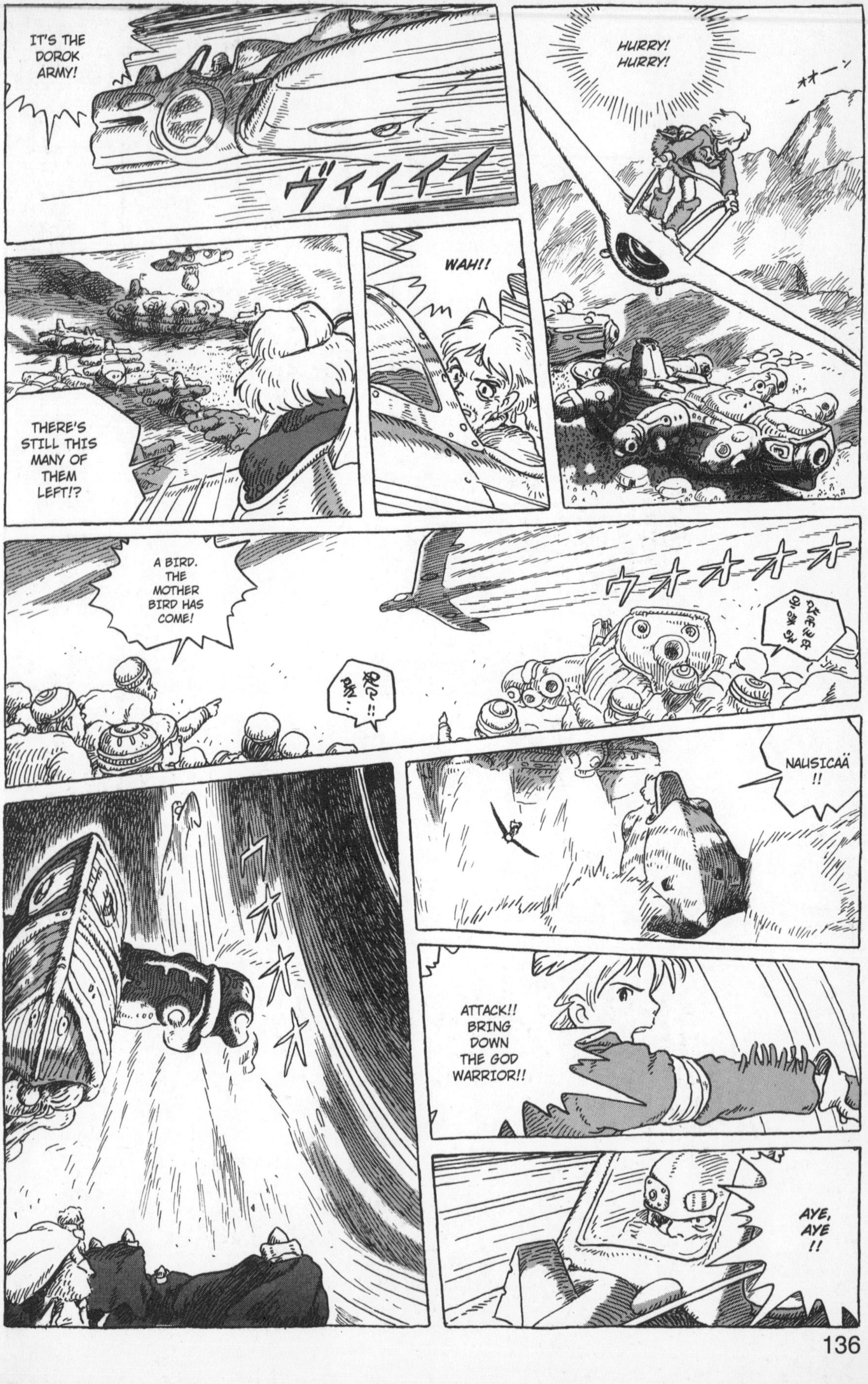
HURRY! HURRY!
オオーン
IT'S THE DOROK ARMY!
ヴィイイイ
WAH!!
THERE'S STILL THIS MANY OF THEM LEFT!?
A BIRD. THE MOTHER BIRD HAS COME!
ウオオオオオ
NAUSICAÄ !!
ATTACK!! BRING DOWN THE GOD WARRIOR!!
AYE, AYE !!
ウオオオオ

RETREAT!

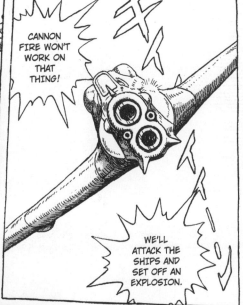

CANNON FIRE WON'T WORK ON THAT THING!

WE'LL ATTACK THE SHIPS AND SET OFF AN EXPLOSION.

THIS IS THE ONLY WAY. EVEN IF IT MEANS...

THERE!!

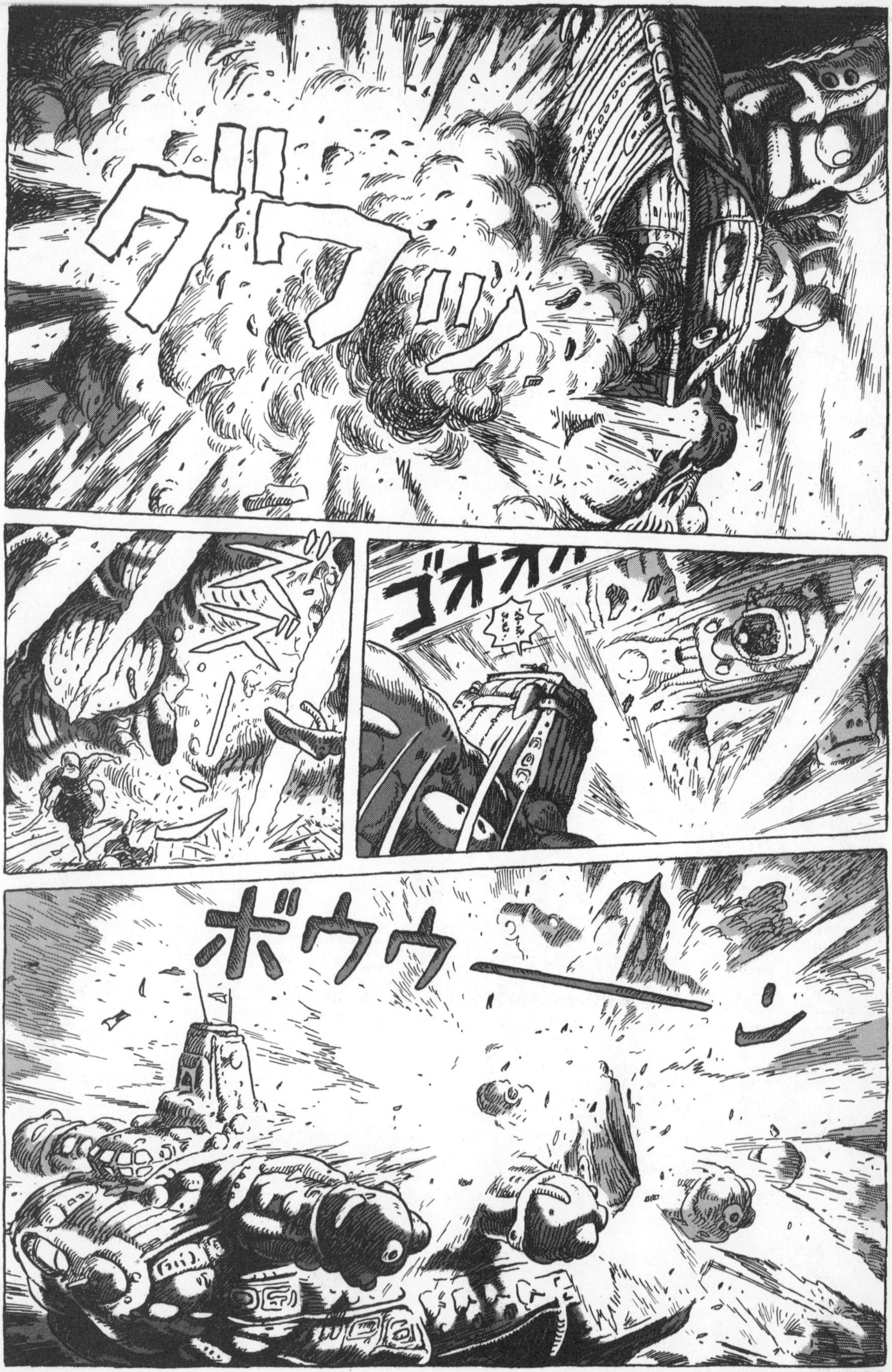
グワッ
ゴオオ
ズズ
ボウウーーン

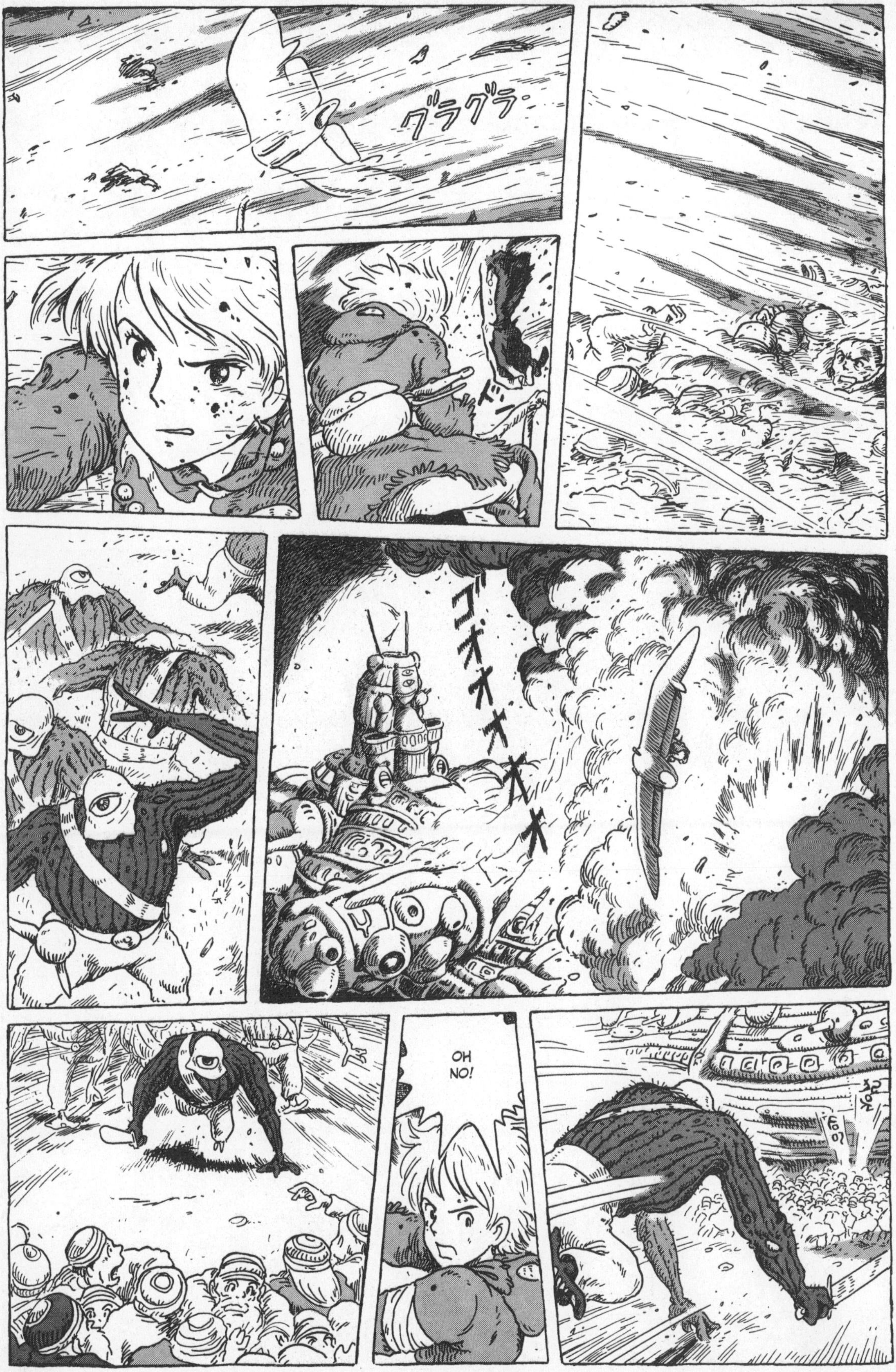
グラグラ
ドー
ゴオオオオオオ
OH NO!

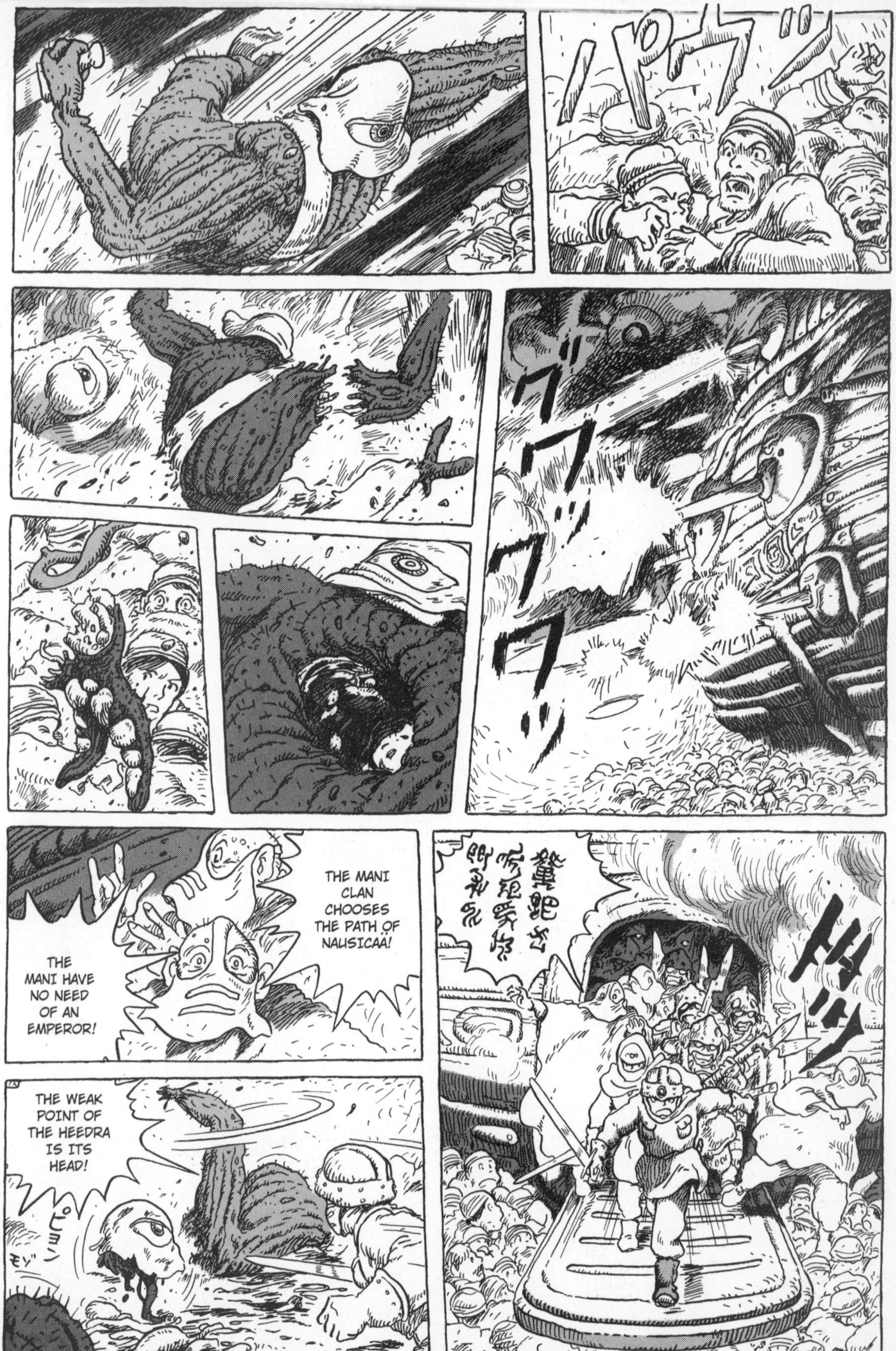
THE MANI CLAN CHOOSES THE PATH OF NAUSICAÄ!
THE MANI HAVE NO NEED OF AN EMPEROR!
THE WEAK POINT OF THE HEEDRA IS ITS HEAD!

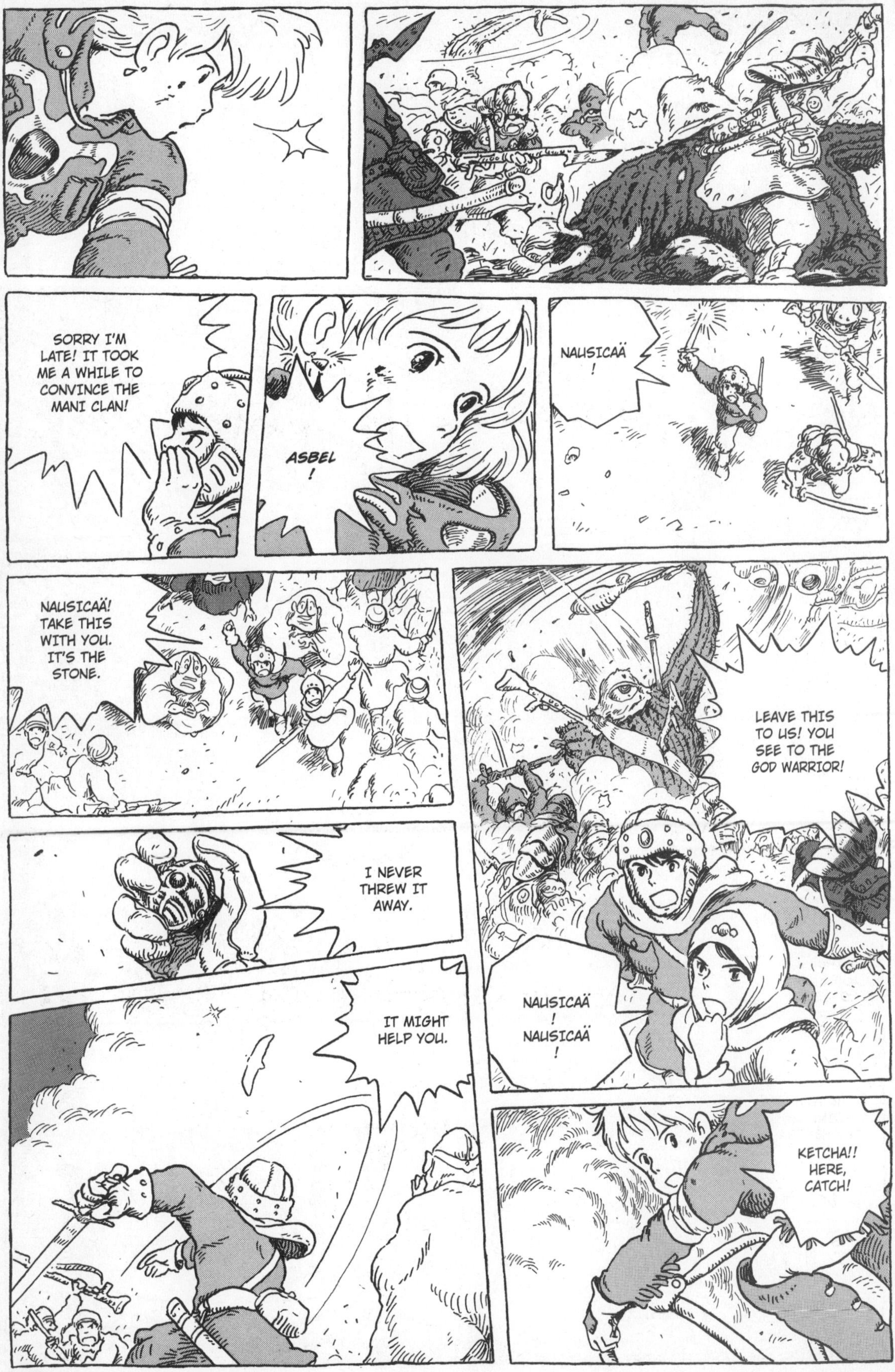

NAUSICAÄ!
ASBEL!
SORRY I'M LATE! IT TOOK ME A WHILE TO CONVINCE THE MANI CLAN!
LEAVE THIS TO US! YOU SEE TO THE GOD WARRIOR!
NAUSICAÄ! NAUSICAÄ!
NAUSICAÄ! TAKE THIS WITH YOU. IT'S THE STONE.
I NEVER THREW IT AWAY.
IT MIGHT HELP YOU.
KETCHA!! HERE, CATCH!

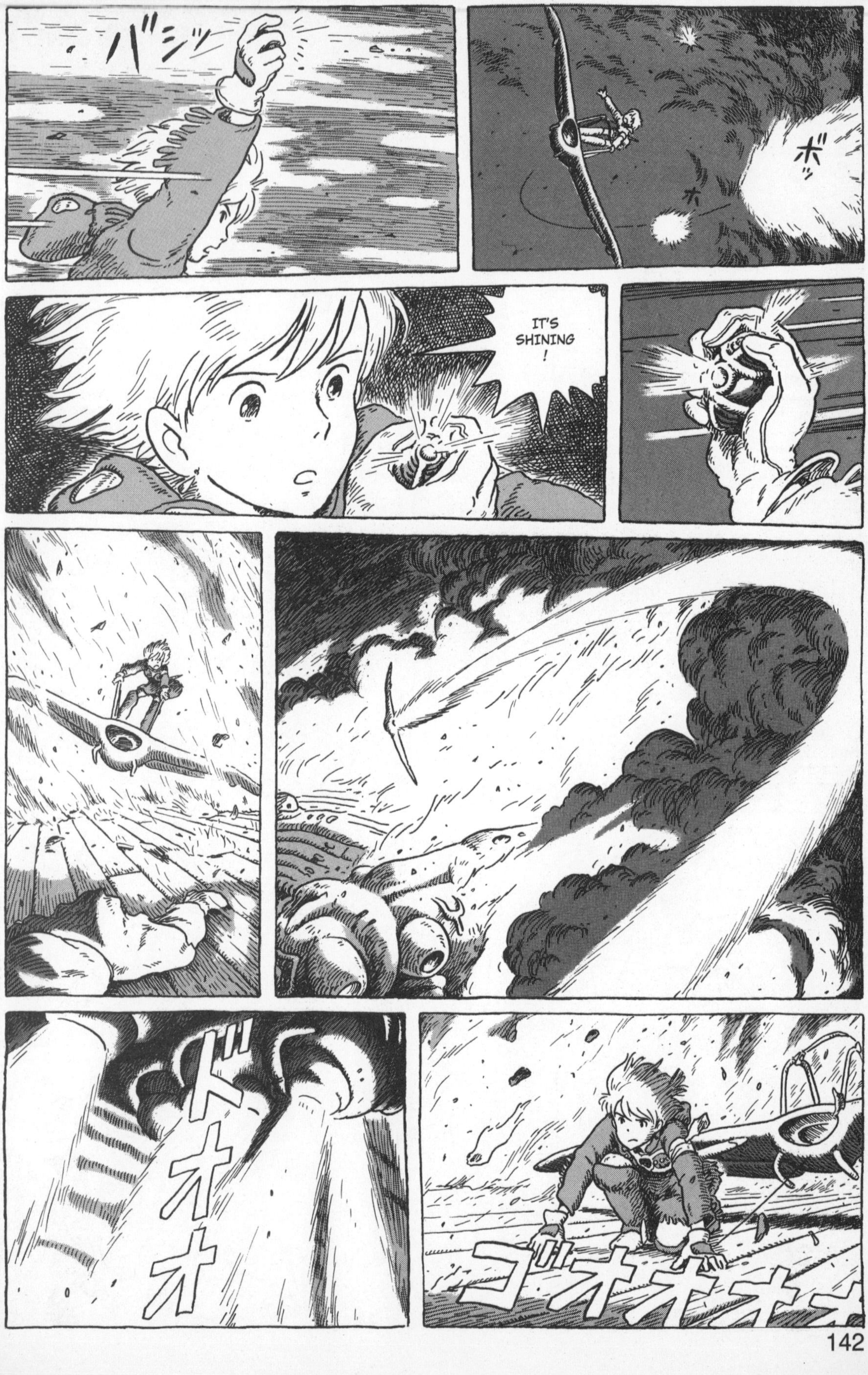
ボッ
IT'S SHINING!
ゴオオオオ
ドオオオ

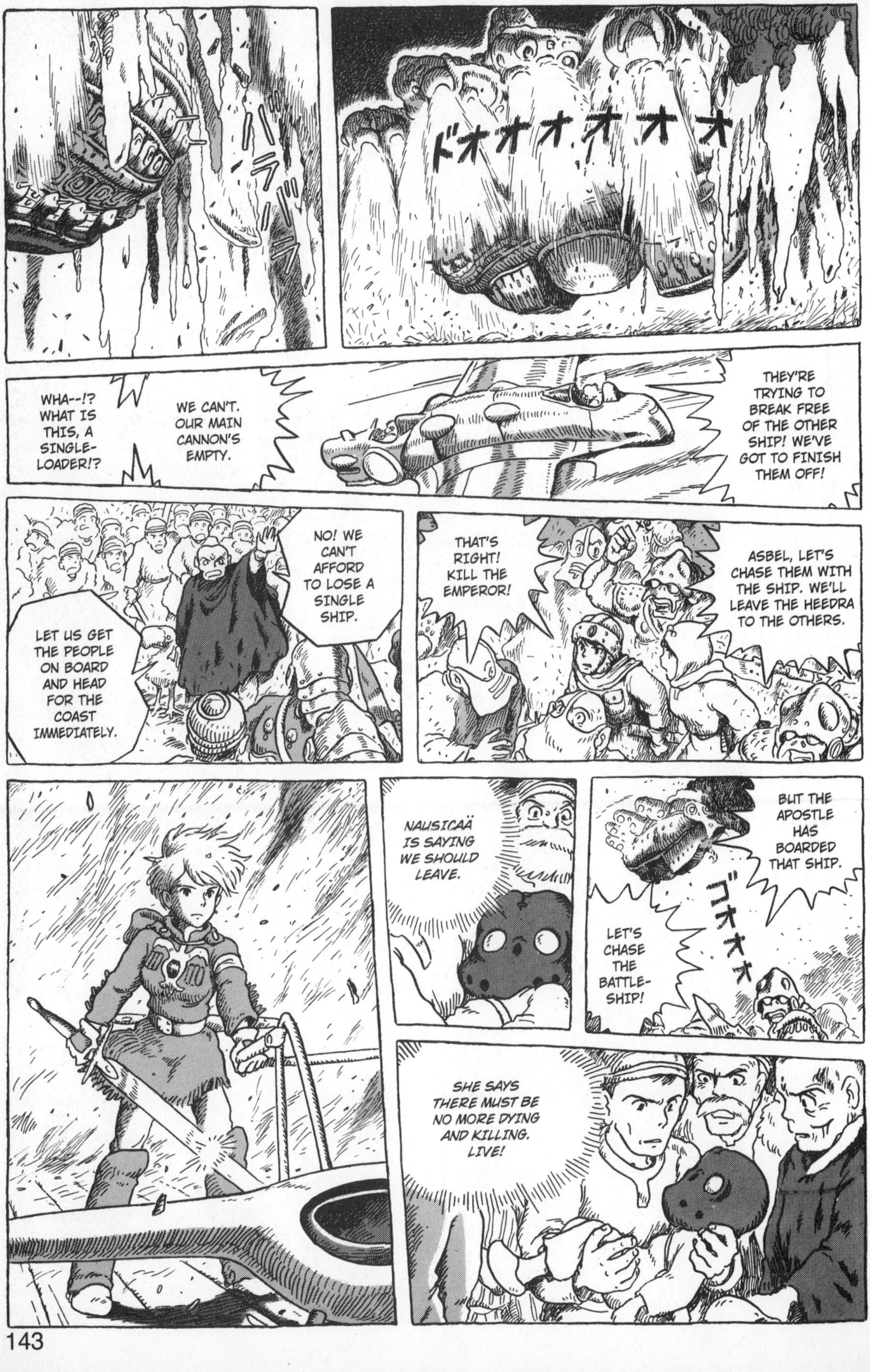
ドオオオオオ
THEY'RE TRYING TO BREAK FREE OF THE OTHER SHIP! WE'VE GOT TO FINISH THEM OFF!
WE CAN'T. OUR MAIN CANNON'S EMPTY.
WHA--!? WHAT IS THIS, A SINGLE-LOADER!?
ASBEL, LET'S CHASE THEM WITH THE SHIP. WE'LL LEAVE THE HEEDRA TO THE OTHERS.
THAT'S RIGHT! KILL THE EMPEROR!
NO! WE CAN'T AFFORD TO LOSE A SINGLE SHIP.
LET US GET THE PEOPLE ON BOARD AND HEAD FOR THE COAST IMMEDIATELY.
BUT THE APOSTLE HAS BOARDED THAT SHIP.
LET'S CHASE THE BATTLE-SHIP!
NAUSICAÄ IS SAYING WE SHOULD LEAVE.
SHE SAYS THERE MUST BE NO MORE DYING AND KILLING. LIVE!

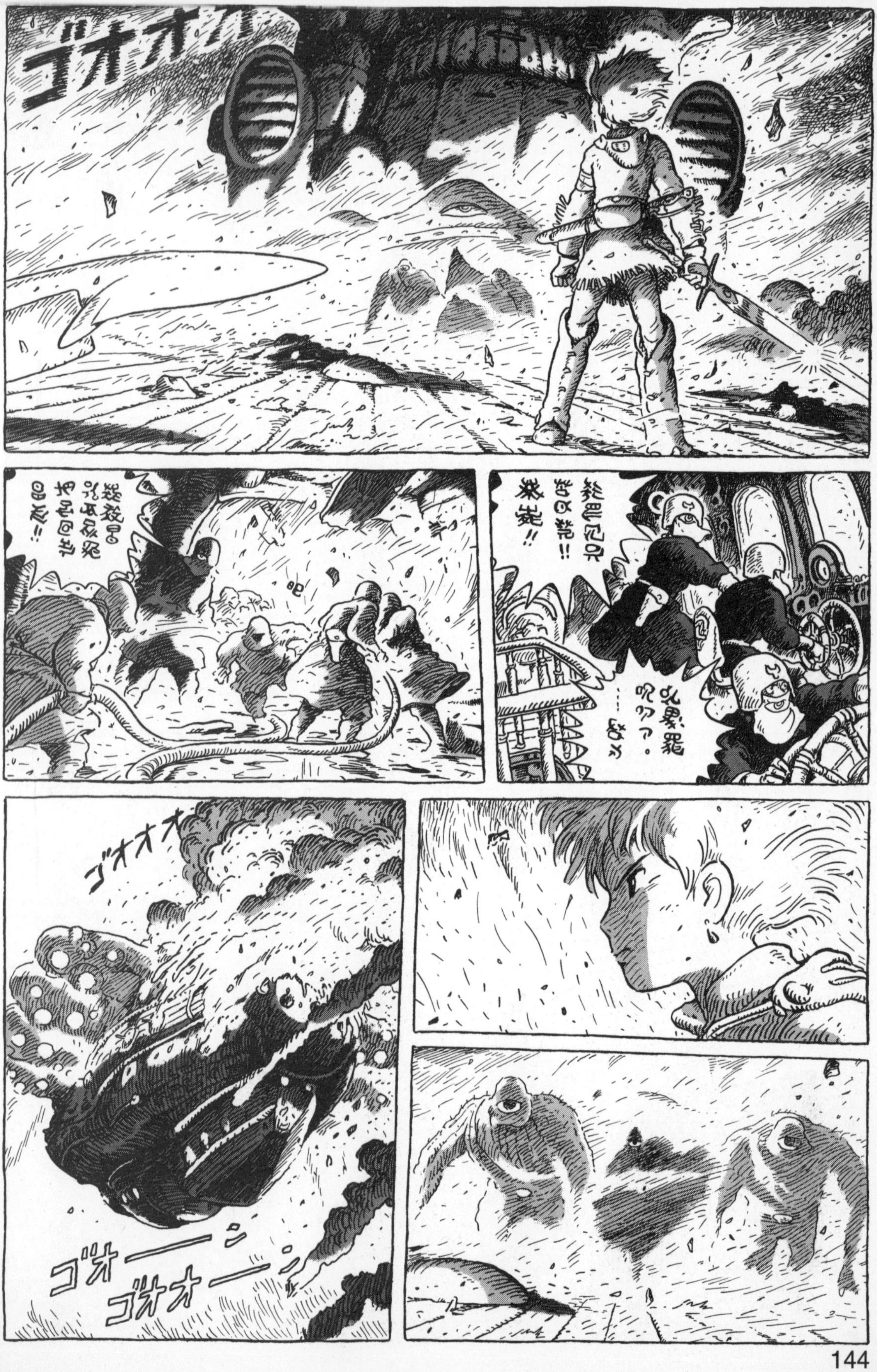
ゴオオオ
ゴオオオ
ゴオーーン
ゴオーーン

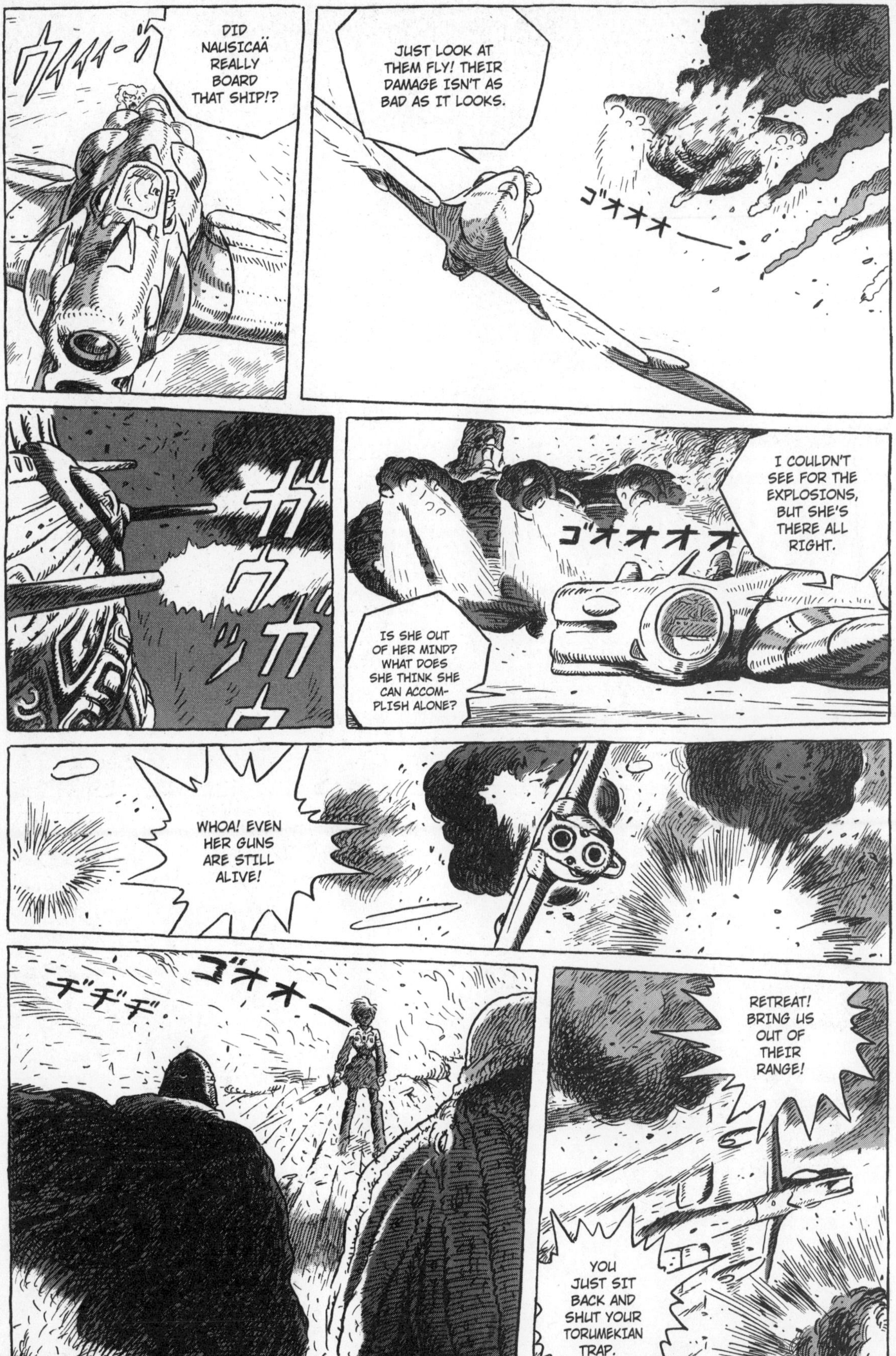
JUST LOOK AT THEM FLY! THEIR DAMAGE ISN'T AS BAD AS IT LOOKS.
ゴオオオーーン
DID NAUSICAÄ REALLY BOARD THAT SHIP!?
ウィィィーン
I COULDN'T SEE FOR THE EXPLOSIONS, BUT SHE'S THERE ALL RIGHT.
ゴオオオオオ
IS SHE OUT OF HER MIND? WHAT DOES SHE THINK SHE CAN ACCOMPLISH ALONE?
WHOA! EVEN HER GUNS ARE STILL ALIVE!
RETREAT! BRING US OUT OF THEIR RANGE!
YOU JUST SIT BACK AND SHUT YOUR TORUMEKIAN TRAP.
ゴオオー
ヂヂヂ

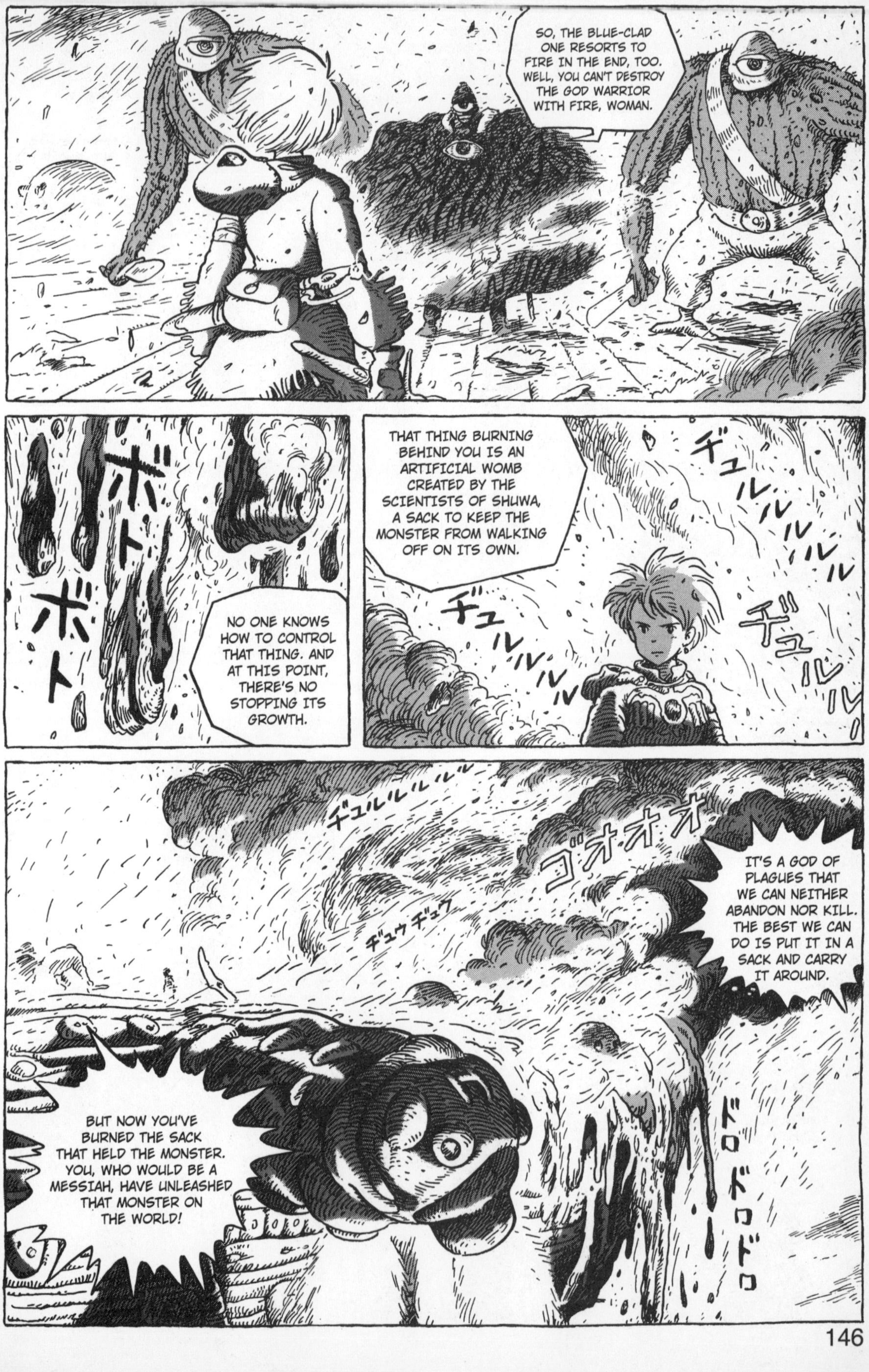
SO, THE BLUE-CLAD ONE RESORTS TO FIRE IN THE END, TOO. WELL, YOU CAN'T DESTROY THE GOD WARRIOR WITH FIRE, WOMAN.
THAT THING BURNING BEHIND YOU IS AN ARTIFICIAL WOMB CREATED BY THE SCIENTISTS OF SHUWA, A SACK TO KEEP THE MONSTER FROM WALKING OFF ON ITS OWN.
ヂュルルルルル
ヂュルルルル
ヂュルルル
NO ONE KNOWS HOW TO CONTROL THAT THING. AND AT THIS POINT, THERE'S NO STOPPING ITS GROWTH.
ボト
ボト
ヂュルルルルル
ゴオオオ
IT'S A GOD OF PLAGUES THAT WE CAN NEITHER ABANDON NOR KILL. THE BEST WE CAN DO IS PUT IT IN A SACK AND CARRY IT AROUND.
ドロ
ドロドロドロ
BUT NOW YOU'VE BURNED THE SACK THAT HELD THE MONSTER. YOU, WHO WOULD BE A MESSIAH, HAVE UNLEASHED THAT MONSTER ON THE WORLD!

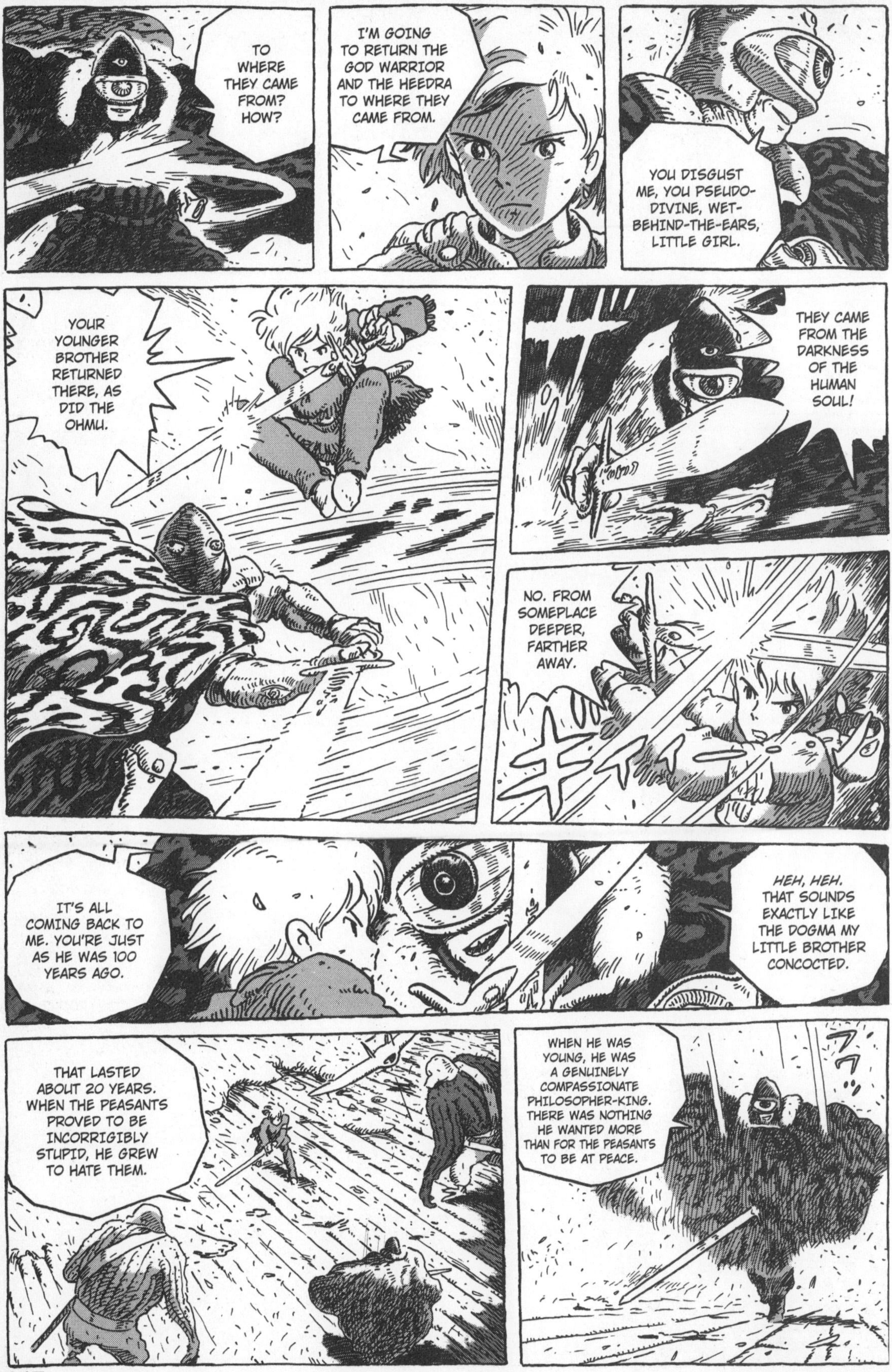
YOU DISGUST ME, YOU PSEUDO-DIVINE, WET-BEHIND-THE-EARS, LITTLE GIRL.
I'M GOING TO RETURN THE GOD WARRIOR AND THE HEEDRA TO WHERE THEY CAME FROM.
TO WHERE THEY CAME FROM? HOW?
THEY CAME FROM THE DARKNESS OF THE HUMAN SOUL!
NO. FROM SOMEPLACE DEEPER, FARTHER AWAY.
YOUR YOUNGER BROTHER RETURNED THERE, AS DID THE OHMU.
HEH, HEH. THAT SOUNDS EXACTLY LIKE THE DOGMA MY LITTLE BROTHER CONCOCTED.
IT'S ALL COMING BACK TO ME. YOU'RE JUST AS HE WAS 100 YEARS AGO.
WHEN HE WAS YOUNG, HE WAS A GENUINELY COMPASSIONATE PHILOSOPHER-KING. THERE WAS NOTHING HE WANTED MORE THAN FOR THE PEASANTS TO BE AT PEACE.
THAT LASTED ABOUT 20 YEARS. WHEN THE PEASANTS PROVED TO BE INCORRIGIBLY STUPID, HE GREW TO HATE THEM.

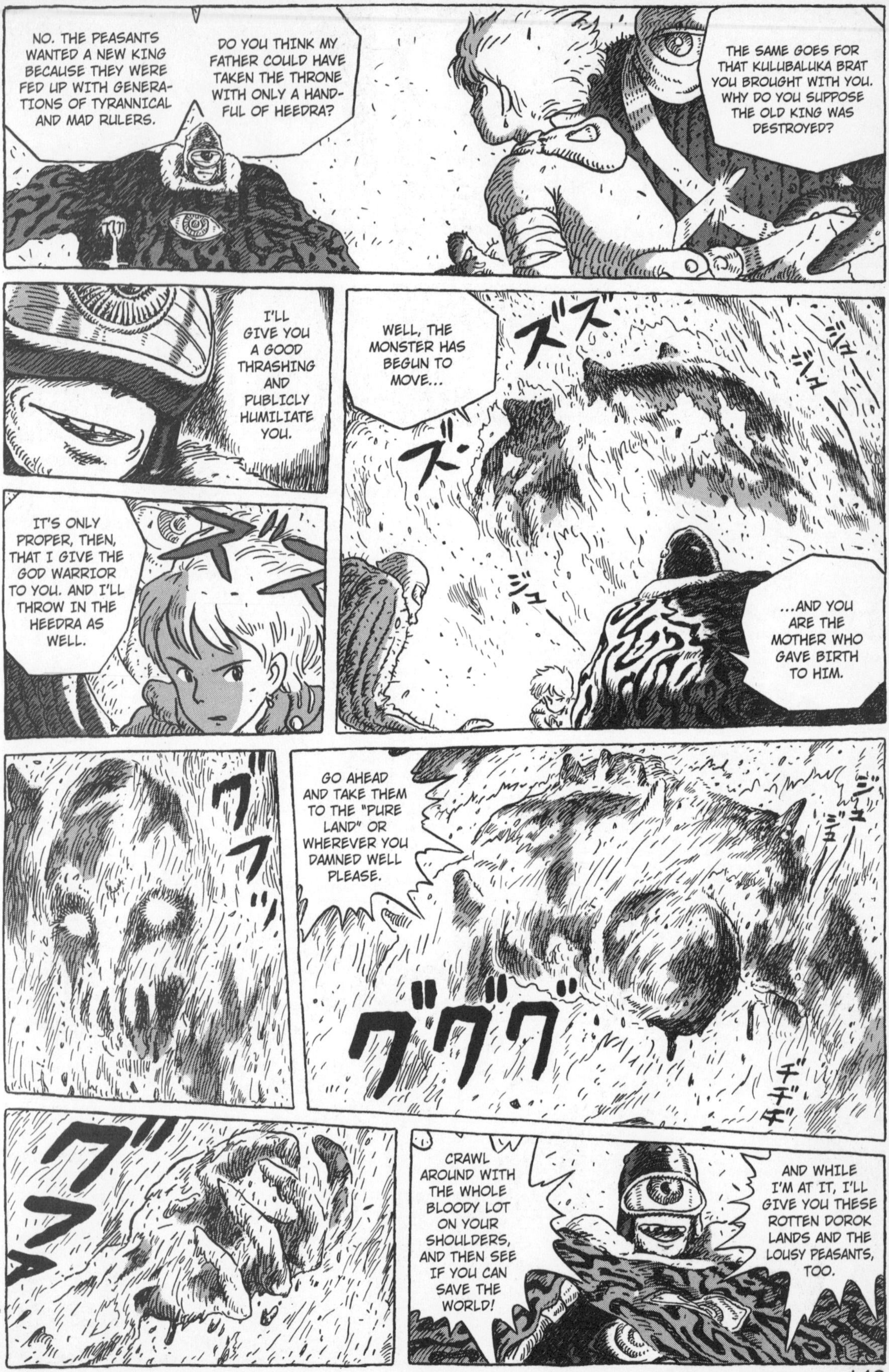

THE SAME GOES FOR THAT KULUBALUKA BRAT YOU BROUGHT WITH YOU. WHY DO YOU SUPPOSE THE OLD KING WAS DESTROYED?
DO YOU THINK MY FATHER COULD HAVE TAKEN THE THRONE WITH ONLY A HAND-FUL OF HEEDRA?
NO. THE PEASANTS WANTED A NEW KING BECAUSE THEY WERE FED UP WITH GENERA-TIONS OF TYRANNICAL AND MAD RULERS.
WELL, THE MONSTER HAS BEGUN TO MOVE...
...AND YOU ARE THE MOTHER WHO GAVE BIRTH TO HIM.
I'LL GIVE YOU A GOOD THRASHING AND PUBLICLY HUMILIATE YOU.
IT'S ONLY PROPER, THEN, THAT I GIVE THE GOD WARRIOR TO YOU. AND I'LL THROW IN THE HEEDRA AS WELL.
GO AHEAD AND TAKE THEM TO THE "PURE LAND" OR WHEREVER YOU DAMNED WELL PLEASE.
AND WHILE I'M AT IT, I'LL GIVE YOU THESE ROTTEN DOROK LANDS AND THE LOUSY PEASANTS, TOO.
CRAWL AROUND WITH THE WHOLE BLOODY LOT ON YOUR SHOULDERS, AND THEN SEE IF YOU CAN SAVE THE WORLD!

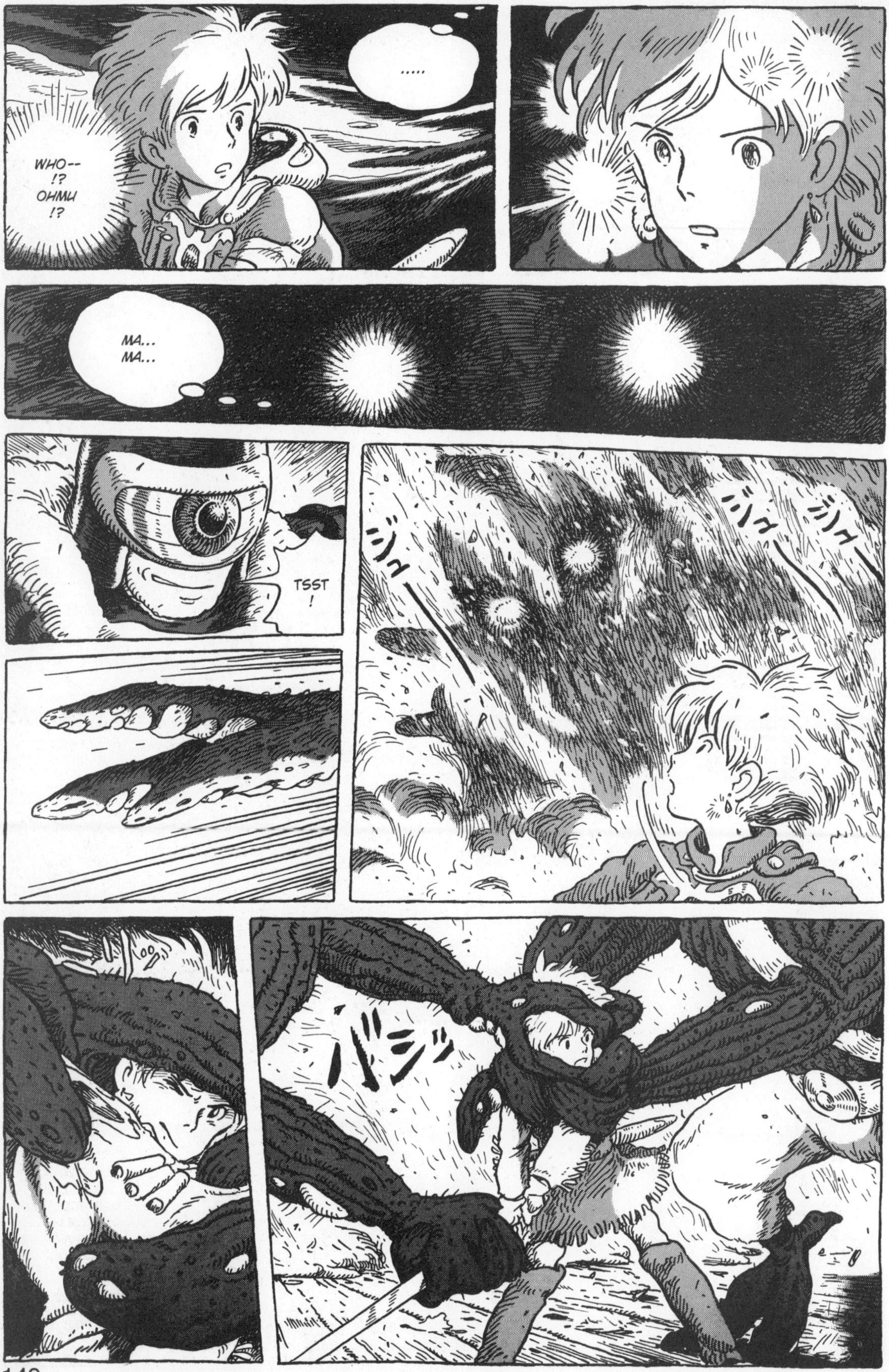
.....
WHO-- !? OHMU !?
MA... MA...
ジュ
ジュ
ジュ
TSST !
バシッ

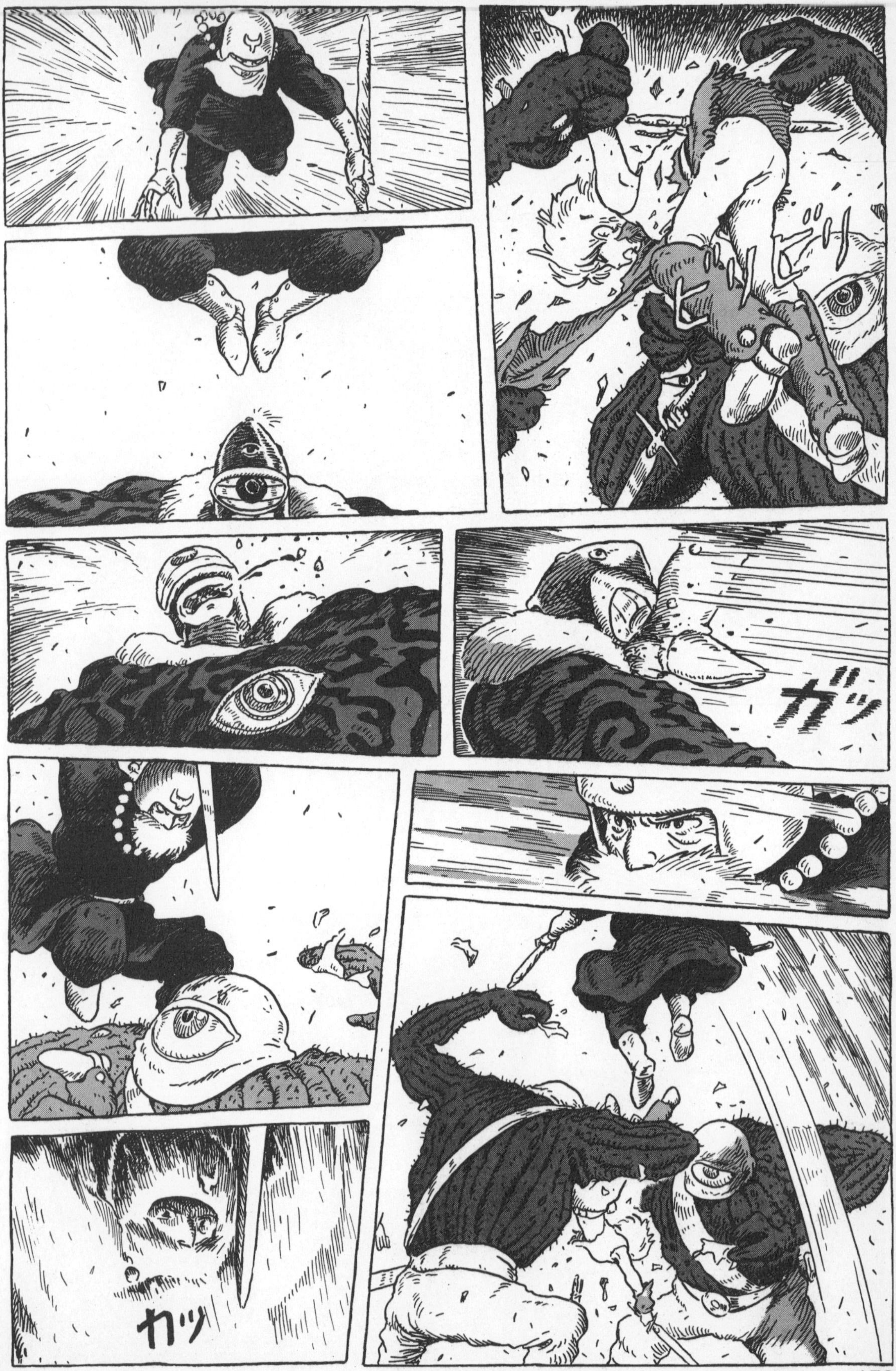
ビリビリ
ガッ
カッ

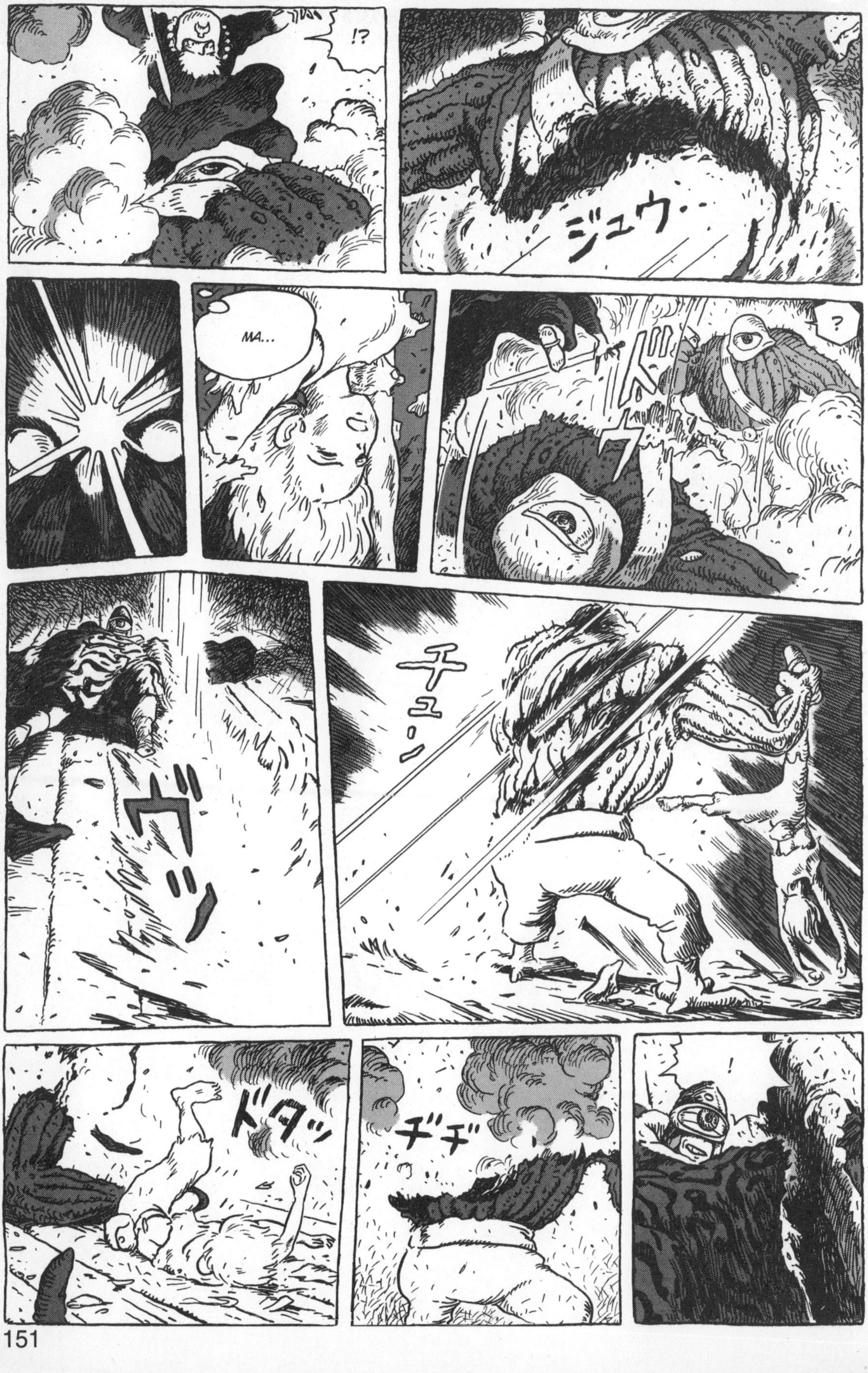
ジュウ・
!?
?
MA...
チュン
!
ヂヂ
ドタッ

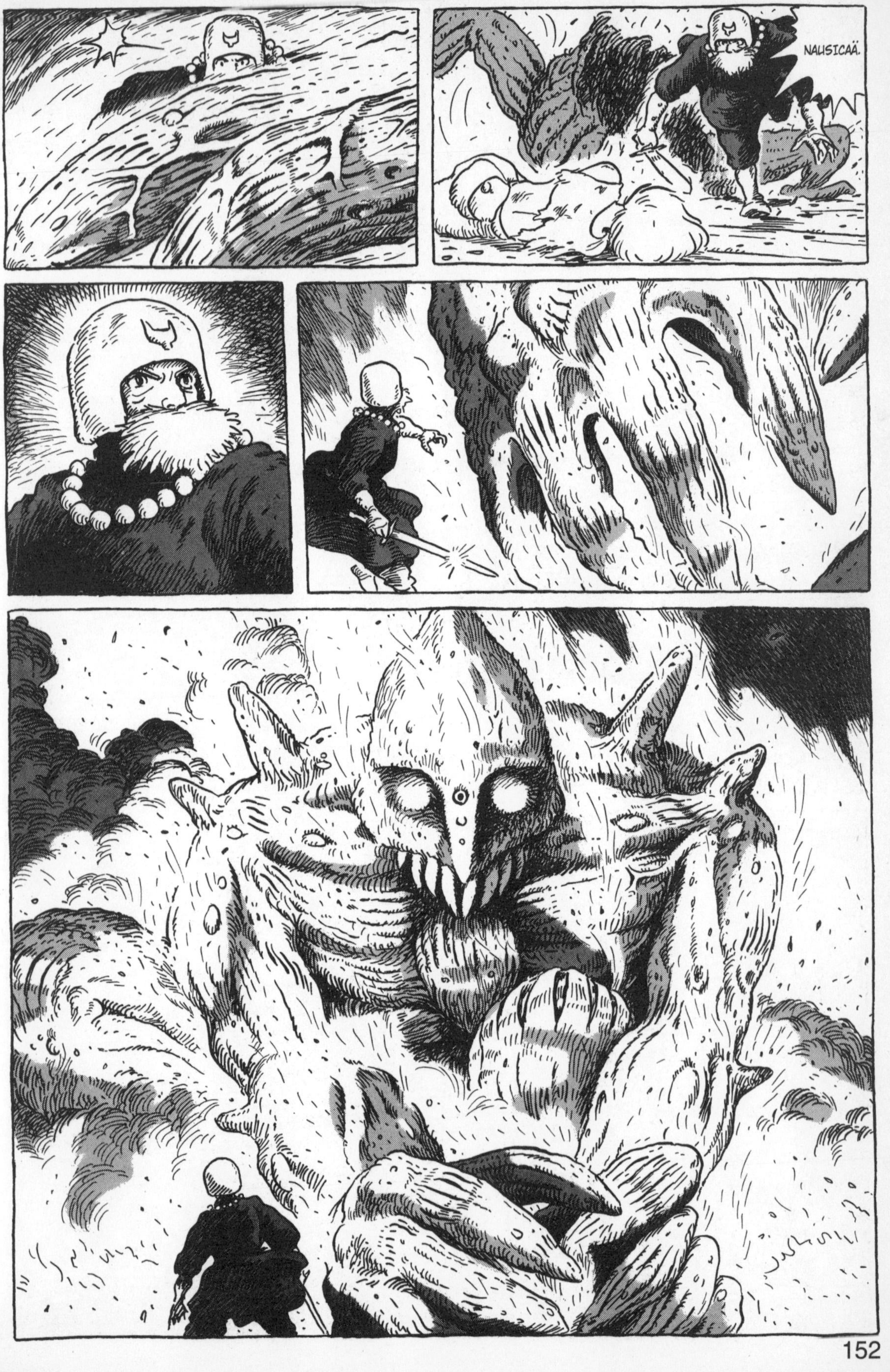
NAUSICAÄ.

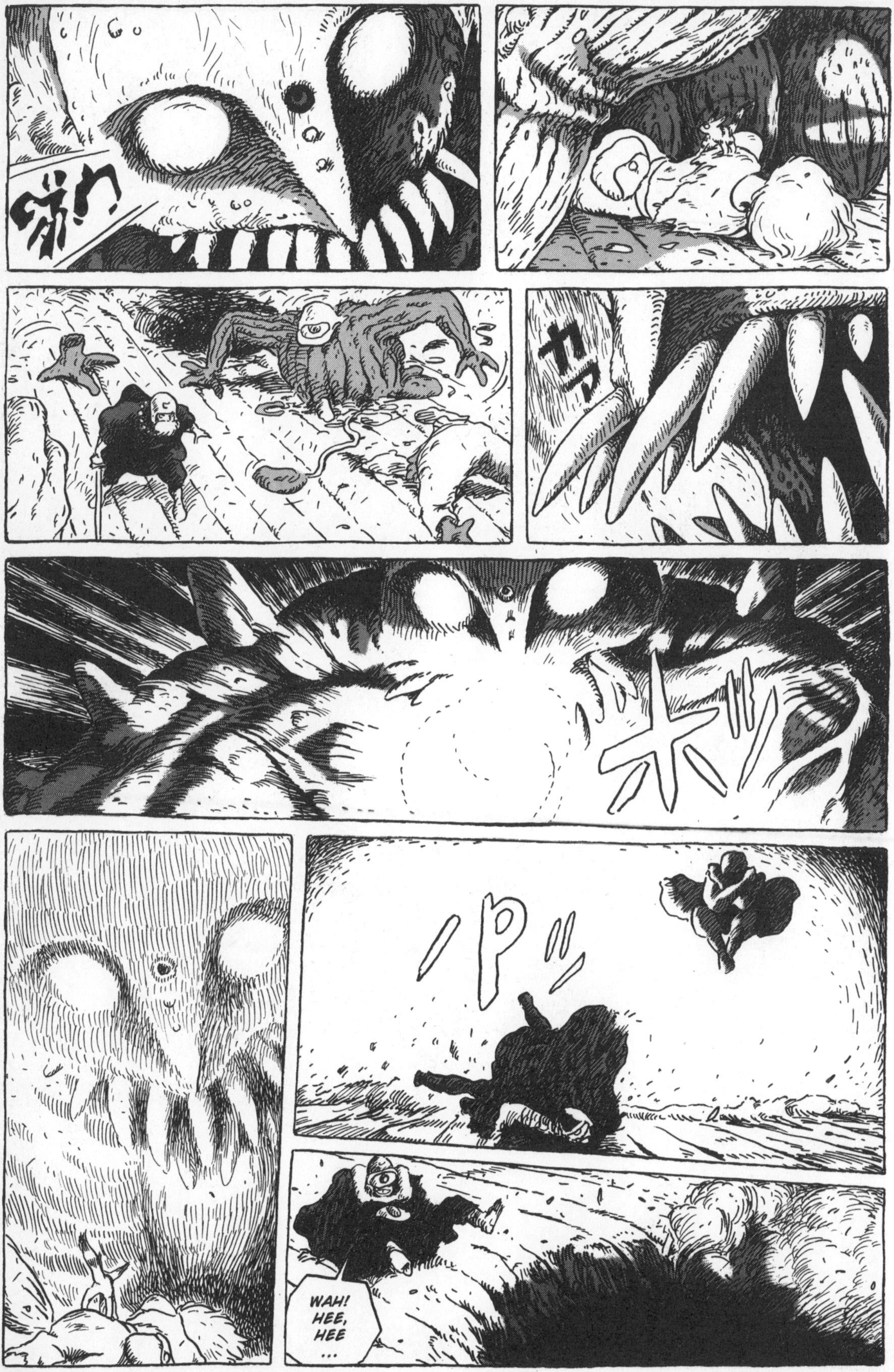
カッ
ボッ
パッ
WAH! HEE, HEE ...

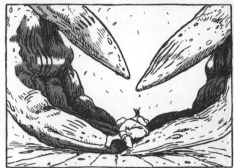

DOES THAT THING REALLY BELIEVE SHE'S ITS MOTHER!?

UNH
...

UNH
!

.....

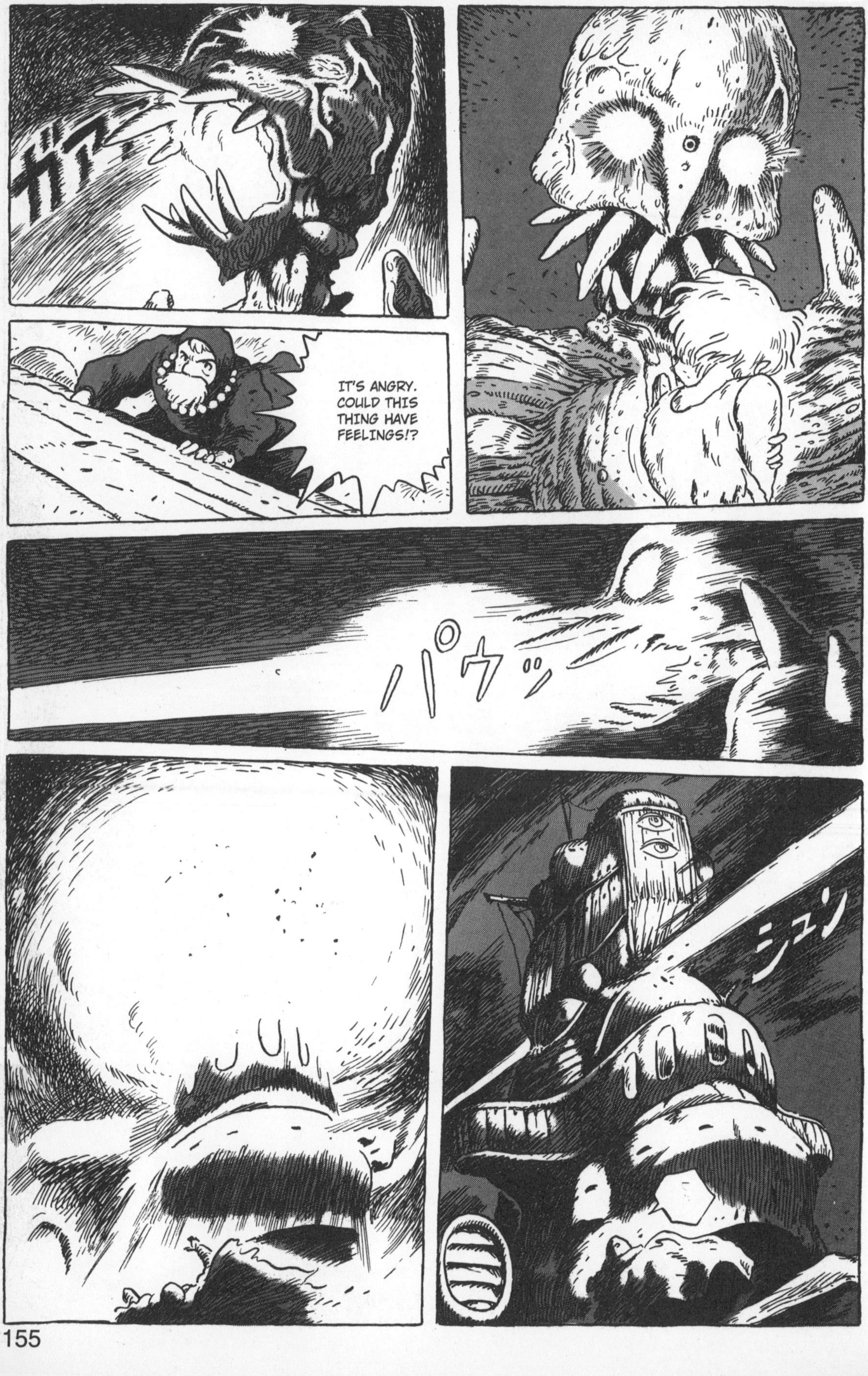
IT'S ANGRY. COULD THIS THING HAVE FEELINGS!?
パウッ
シュン

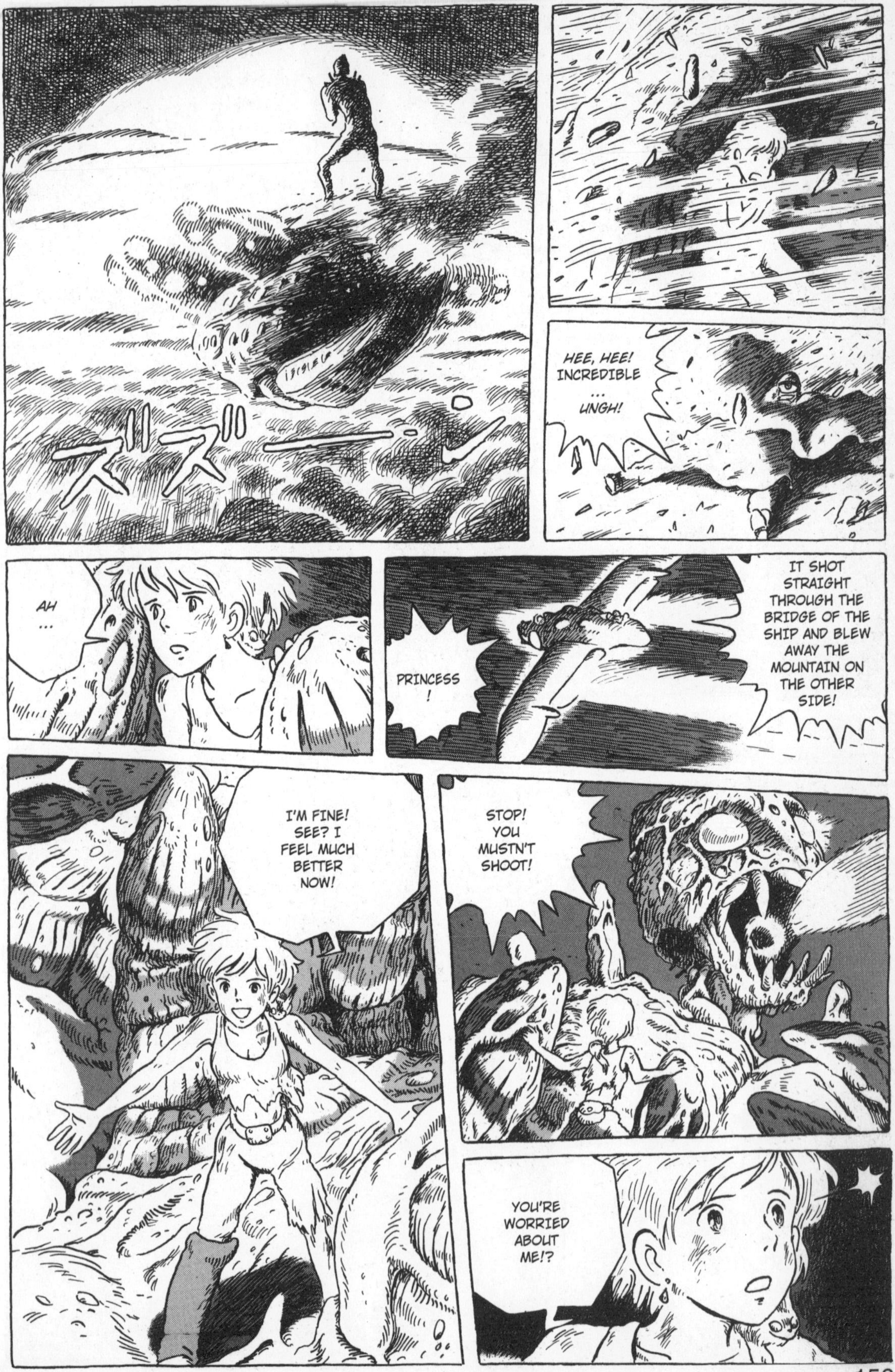
HEE, HEE! INCREDIBLE ... UNGH!
IT SHOT STRAIGHT THROUGH THE BRIDGE OF THE SHIP AND BLEW AWAY THE MOUNTAIN ON THE OTHER SIDE!
PRINCESS!
AH ...
STOP! YOU MUSTN'T SHOOT!
YOU'RE WORRIED ABOUT ME!?
I'M FINE! SEE? I FEEL MUCH BETTER NOW!

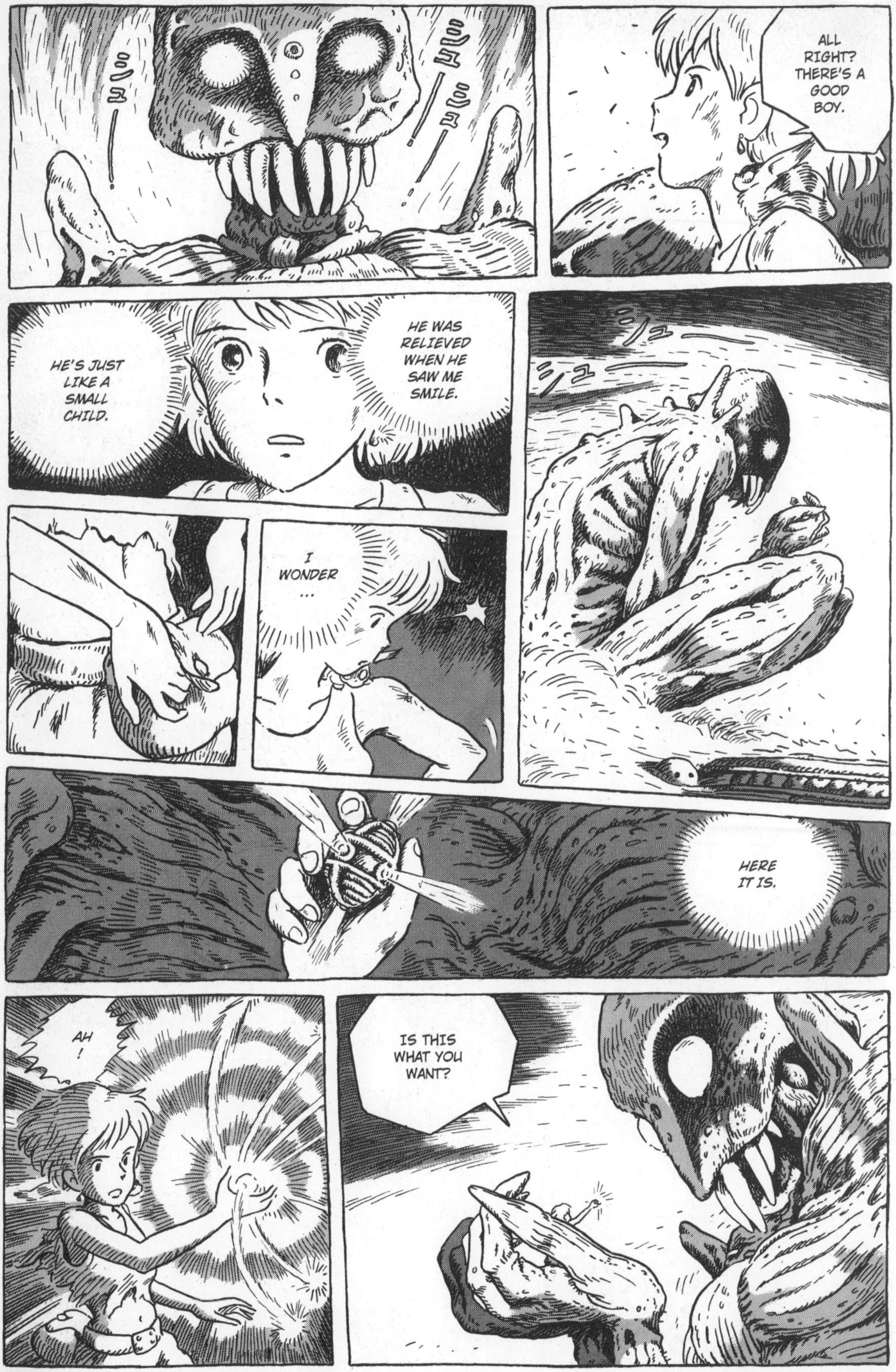
ALL RIGHT? THERE'S A GOOD BOY.
HE WAS RELIEVED WHEN HE SAW ME SMILE.
HE'S JUST LIKE A SMALL CHILD.
I WONDER ...
HERE IT IS.
IS THIS WHAT YOU WANT?
AH !

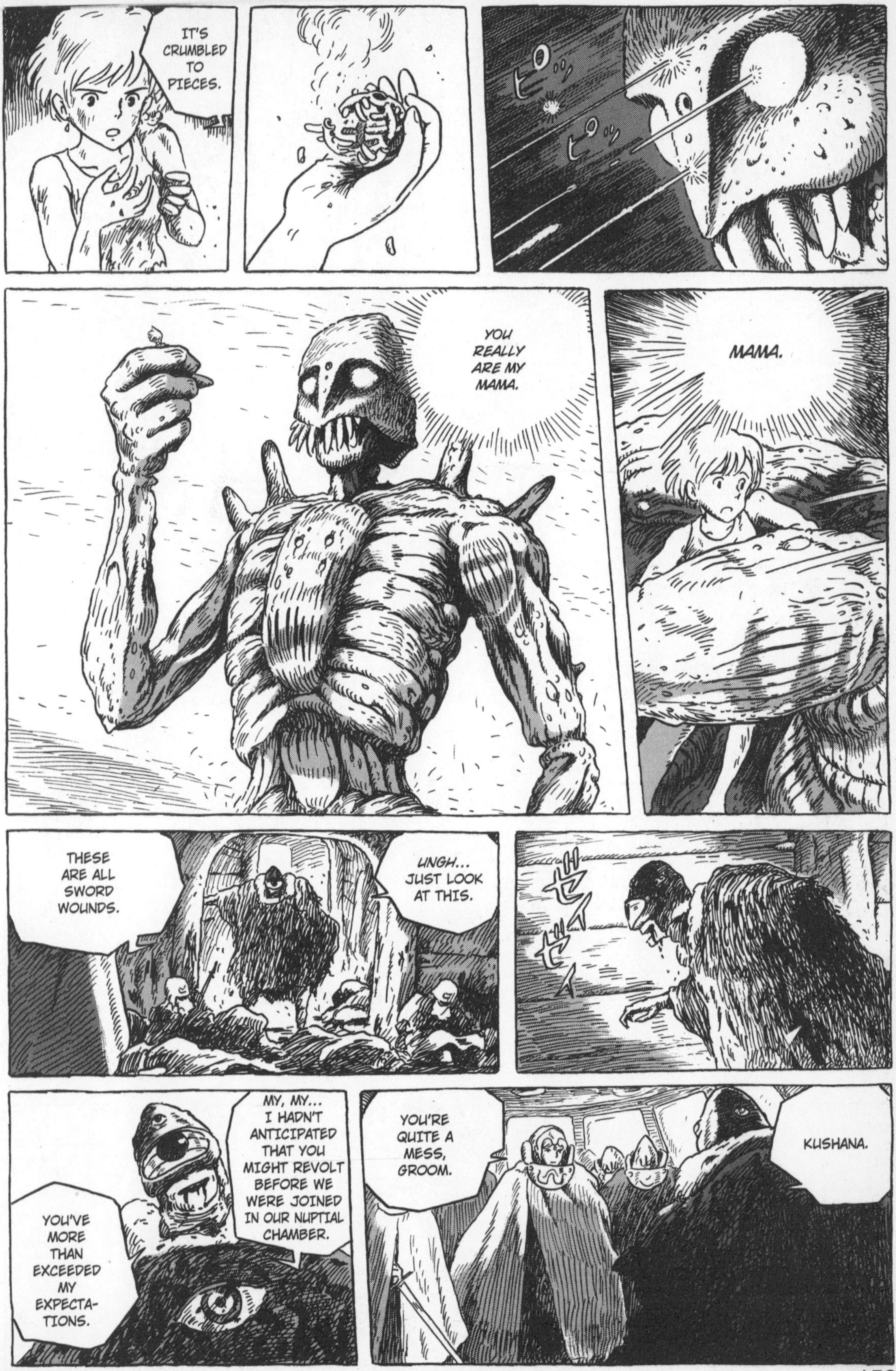
ピッ
ピッ
IT'S CRUMBLED TO PIECES.
MAMA.
YOU REALLY ARE MY MAMA.
ゼイゼイ
UNGH... JUST LOOK AT THIS.
THESE ARE ALL SWORD WOUNDS.
KUSHANA.
YOU'RE QUITE A MESS, GROOM.
MY, MY... I HADN'T ANTICIPATED THAT YOU MIGHT REVOLT BEFORE WE WERE JOINED IN OUR NUPTIAL CHAMBER.
YOU'VE MORE THAN EXCEEDED MY EXPECTATIONS.

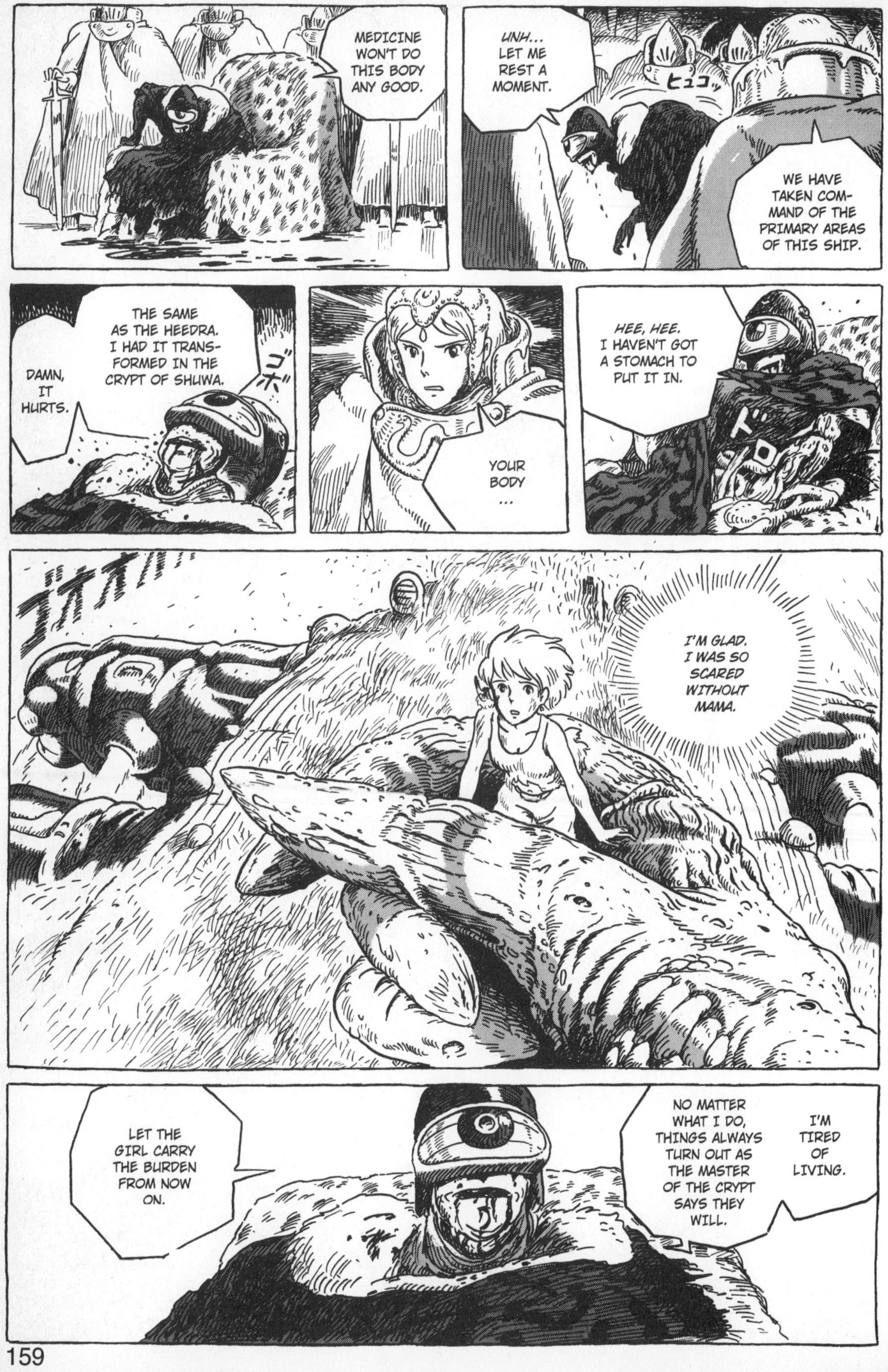

ヒュコッ
UNH... LET ME REST A MOMENT.
WE HAVE TAKEN COMMAND OF THE PRIMARY AREAS OF THIS SHIP.
MEDICINE WON'T DO THIS BODY ANY GOOD.
HEE, HEE. I HAVEN'T GOT A STOMACH TO PUT IT IN.
ドロ
YOUR BODY ...
THE SAME AS THE HEEDRA. I HAD IT TRANSFORMED IN THE CRYPT OF SHUWA.
ゴボ
DAMN, IT HURTS.
I'M GLAD. I WAS SO SCARED WITHOUT MAMA.
ゴオオパ
I'M TIRED OF LIVING.
NO MATTER WHAT I DO, THINGS ALWAYS TURN OUT AS THE MASTER OF THE CRYPT SAYS THEY WILL.
LET THE GIRL CARRY THE BURDEN FROM NOW ON.

Nausicaä of the Valley of the Wind Guide to Sound Effects

VIZ has left the sound effects in *Nausicaä of the Valley of the Wind* as Hayao Miyazaki originally created them – in Japanese. Use this glossary to decipher, page-by-page and panel-by-panel, what all those foreign words and background noises mean. The glossary lists the page number then panel. For example, 6.1 indicates page 6, panel 1.

24.2——FX: Puchipuchipuchi (popoppwip)

24.3——FX: Sawasawasawa zawa (shwrrrsh zshh)

24.5——FX: Kikiki (vwoosh)

24.8——FX: Nuu (nwrrh)

24.8——FX: Puchi (pop)

24.8——FX: Nyuuuu (nwoiii)

25.1——FX: Kachi (click)

25.3——FX: Lulululu (whir)

25.4——FX: Za (zash)

25.5——FX: Zubo (zvoosh)

25.8——FX: Mokumoku (mwkwmk)

26.5——FX: Wahahaha hihahaha kyahaha hahahahaha (laughter)

30.9——FX: Do (dwoomh)

31.5——FX: Lulululu (whirr)

33.4——FX: Gugu (tug)

33.5——FX: Ba (vwah)

33.6——FX: Buuun (vwooomh)

33.6——FX: Waa (aaaah)

33.8——FX: Hyun (hwoosh)

34.5——FX: Lulululu (whir)

34.6——FX: Lululu (whir)

35.2——FX: Jala (rattle)

35.4——FX: Pisha (whip)

35.6——FX: Gala gala (clank clank)

35.7——FX: Busu (poke)

35.8——FX: Dolodolo (pour)

35.9——FX: Gubi (glub)

36.1——FX: Gatan (gatank)

12.8——FX: Hahaha hehe (laughter)

13.9——FX: Gu (strangle)

14.4——FX: Zawazawa (yammer yammer)

14.4——FX: Ota (fluster)

14.5——FX: Walawala (scatter)

14.5——FX: Goho (cough)

14.6——FX: Tatata dada (scurry dash)

15.6——FX: Niko (grin)

15.8——FX: Fu (fwoosh)

15.9——FX: Puuu (pwooooh)

15.10——FX: Puuu (pwoosh)

16.4——FX: Lulululu (whir)

16.6——FX: Lululu (whir)

16.7——FX: Bomu (boof)

17.1——FX: Bamu bamu booumu (boof boof bwoofh)

17.9——FX: Lulululu (whir)

20.4——FX: Nyuu (nwoink)

20.7——FX: Putsun (poink)

20.7——FX: Funywa (squish)

21.1——FX: Nuooo (ooze)

21.2——FX: Zuzu (zashh)

21.5——FX: Dodo (thwud)

22.2——FX: Doyon doyon (bwoink bwoink)

22.6——FX: Tololi (trickle)

23.3——FX: Kaaa (gleam)

24.1——FX: Puchi puchipuchipuchi puchipuchi puchipuchi puchipuchi puchi (pop pwippwippop popup pop pwipwip popup pwip)

24.2——FX: Milimili (mwrrkmwrk)

5.8——FX: Lululu (whir)

6.1——FX: Lulululu (whir)

6.2——FX: Lululu (whir)

6.3——FX: Lulululululu (whir)

6.5——FX: Lululu (whir)

7.1——FX: Lulululu (whir)

7.3——FX: Lulululu (whir)

7.4——FX: Gobo gobo (glub glub)

7.6——FX: Ba (bwah)

7.6——FX: Kichikichi (kch kch)

8.1——FX: Lululu lulululu (whir)

8.3——FX: Lulululululu (whir)

8.4——FX: Lulululululu (whir)

9.1——FX: Lululu (whir)

9.2——FX: Kila (glint)

9.3——FX: Lulululu (whir)

9.4——FX: Kila (glint)

9.7——FX: Hyun hyun (hwoosh)

10.1——FX: Bun (bwoosh)

10.3——FX: Wala walawala (stagger stomp stomp)

10.4——FX: Lulululu (whir)

10.5——FX: Chala (chlink)

10.8——FX: Hahahaha hehehe hahaha (laughter)

11.6——FX: Aaan aaan (waaah waah)

11.7——FX: Da (dash)

11.8——FX: Aaaan (waaah)

12.1——FX: Aaaan (waaah)

12.2——FX: Aaan aaan (waaah waah)

36.1—FX: Zuli (zwish)

36.7—FX: Gala (gatank)

36.10—FX: Jala (chlink)

37.1—FX: Doka (dwak)

37.2—FX: Baki (whack)

37.3—FX: Dote (thud)

37.5—FX: Bali (rip)

37.10—FX: Zowazowazowa (creep slink)

37.10—FX: Zuzu (zgashh)

38.3—FX: Byuuun (vwoosh)

38.4—FX: Ton (tump)

38.5—FX: Boka (bwak)

38.6—FX: Guki (jab)

39.3—FX: Don (boot)

39.4—FX: Gooon goon (gwoom gwoom)

39.6—FX: Gooon (gwooom)

39.7—FX: Chika (glint)

39.7—FX: Gooon (gwoom)

40.2—FX: Kila (flash)

40.4—FX: Lululu (whir)

40.5—FX: Goon goon (gwoom gwoom)

41.4—FX: Kobo kogo (glub glug)

41.5—FX: Shuu shuu (fshh fsh)

41.7—FX: Gobo (glub)

42.1—FX: Gobo gobo gobo (glub glub glub)

42.2—FX: Mowa (mwoooh)

42.5—FX: Tololi (shlorp)

43.3—FX: Kasa (rustle)

43.5—FX: Yulali (waver)

43.6—FX: Kasa kasa (rustle rustle)

44.5—FX: Yula (waver)

44.6—FX: Su (swosh)

44.9—FX: Suu (swash)

44.11—FX: Moya (gloom)

45.3—FX: Fu (fwoosh)

45.9—FX: Zowa (shudder)

46.3—FX: Pita pita (pwap pwap)

46.6—FX: Fuwa (float)

47.1—FX: Gooon goon (gwoom gwoom)

47.2—FX: Goon ooon (gwoom woom)

47.4—FX: Goooo (gwoooh)

47.5—FX: Gu (grip)

47.6—FX: Gooo (gwooooh)

47.7—FX: Ooon oon (wroom wroom)

47.7—FX: Uwaan uwaan (wrrmm wrmmm)

48.2—FX: Chikachika (flash flash)

48.2—FX: Uooon (wroom)

48.2—FX: Goon goon (gwoom gwoom)

48.3—FX: Zuzuun zun (zaggm zaboom)

48.5—FX: Zuba doba guwa guwa (zadum daboom bam boom)

49.1—FX: Goon ooon (gwoom gwoom)

49.4—FX: Goooo (gwhoooh)

49.8—FX: Saaa (shaaa)

50.1—FX: Gooon (gwooom)

50.2—FX: Chikachika (flash flash)

50.2—FX: Gooo (gwhooh)

50.3—FX: Waan wann (wreeeen wreeeen)

52.8—FX: Kuuu (coo)

53.1—FX: Gui (tug)

53.4—FX: Golon (roll)

53.5—FX: Kuwaa (coo)

53.6—FX: Totatata (scamper)

53.7—FX: Yoro (wobble)

53.10—FX: Zei zei (huff wheeze)

53.11—FX: Toto (hop skip)

54.3—FX: Kuu (coo)

54.4—FX: Kuwaa (coo)

54.8—FX: Pa (pounce)

55.1—FX: Zazaza (zshhha)

55.2—FX: Jaaa (gshaaa)

55.3—FX: Gagaga (gatungatun)

55.9—FX: Da (kick)

56.6—FX: Kuu (coo)

56.7—FX: Kuu kuu (coo coo)

57.1—FX: Kuu kuu (coo coo)

57.3—FX: Kuu (coo)

57.9—FX: Mozo mozo (rustle rustle)

57.10—FX: Ki (screech)

57.11—FX: Fuu (yaaawn)

59.3—FX: Kasakasa (rustle rustle)

60.2—FX: Zulu (drag)

62.2—FX: Fuu fuu (hiss hiss)

62.5—FX: Bali bali (scratch swipe)

63.7—FX: Ba (bwah)

63.9—FX: Guhe (gack)

63.10—FX: Ha ha (huff huff)

64.1—FX: Yoro (wobble)

64.3—FX: Kasa (crunch)

64.6—FX: Jili jili (sizzle sizzle)

64.8—FX: Goso goso (scrape scrape)

65.4—FX: Shiku shiku (sob sob)

66.2—FX: Zulu (slip)

66.4—FX: Ha ha (huff huff)

66.10—FX: Ta ta (pitter patter)

66.11—FX: Ha (huff)

66.11—FX: Gasa (crunch)

67.3—FX: Ha ha (huff huff)

69.4—FX: Ki (screech)

70.1—FX: Sala sala sala (shwooh shwooh shwooh)

70.2—FX: Sala sala sala (shwooh shwooh shwooh)

70.4—FX: Sala sala (shwooh shwooh)

73.2—FX: Zaza (splash)

73.7—FX: Zaza (zshaa)

73.8—FX: Zabaa do (splash vashum)

74.1—FX: Dobaa (zwooosh)

74.5—FX: Za dodo (zwoosh vashum)

75.1—FX: Zaaa (zshaaa)

75.3—FX: Chaaaaa (shaaa)

76.6—FX: Pasha (splashing)

78.1—FX: Sawasawa (shwf shwf)

78.6—FX: Saaa (haaa)

79.10—FX: Gigi (gheeh)

83.6—FX: Tata (dash)

84.4—FX: Ba (fwah)

85.1—FX: Basa basa basa (fwap fwap fwap)

85.2—FX: Kuwaa kuwaa (kwaak kwaak)

87.1—FX: Fu (fwsh)

87.2—FX: Zaa (zshaa)

89.8—FX: Zaaa (zshaa)

90.5—FX: Kuuu (zzz)

93.6—FX: Da (dash)

93.8—FX: Tatata (pitter patter)

94.3—FX: Kuuu (coo)

94.4—FX: Dota (dmdm)

94.6—FX: Kuuu kuu (coo coo)

95.2—FX: Ooo gooo (ooom vwooh)

95.3—FX: Hyuu (hwooh)

95.3—FX: Oooo (oooom)

95.4—FX: Doo (dwooh)

96.1—FX: Oooo (oooom)

96.2—FX: Kukuku (hehehe)

96.4—FX: Goooo (gwhoooh)

97.4—FX: Doka (slam)

97.6—FX: Uoooo (wroooh)

97.7—FX: Gooo (gwoooh)

98.7—FX: Bicha (smack)

98.9—FX: Gyu (grind)

99.9—FX: Goooo (gwhooh)

99.9—FX: Hyuu (hwoooh)

100.1—FX: Dooo hyuuu goooo
(dwoooosh hwoooh gwoooh)

100.2—FX: Mekimeki (crack crack)

100.2—FX: Mishi mishi (crunch creak)

100.3—FX: Ooooo (vwooooh)

100.3—FX: Gi (creak)

100.4—FX: Oooo (vwoooh)

100.5—FX: Ooo (vwoooh)

100.6—FX: Gooo (gwoooh)

101.1—FX: Bilibili (rattle rattle)

101.1—FX: Byuuuu (bwoooosh)

101.4—FX: Tan (fling)

101.5—FX: Oooo (vwooooh)

101.5—FX: Bababa (rattle)

101.9—FX: Hiiiii (hweeeee)

101.9—FX: Oooo (vwoooh)

102.1—FX: Kaaa (vwiiiish)

102.2—FX: Ooooo (vwoooh)

102.3—FX: Batabata (flutter)

102.3—FX: Bilibili (rattle)

102.3—FX: Oooo (vwoooh)

102.5—FX: Chila (glint)

102.6—FX: Fu (fsh)

102.7—FX: Hihihihihi (hweeee)

102.9—FX: Bo (bwoh)

102.11—FX: Paaa (glow)

103.1—FX: Zuuun (boom)

103.8—FX: Bashiiii (bwak)

104.1—FX: Kilikili (tumble)

104.5—FX: Batabata (rattle rattle)

104.5—FX: Hiiii (hweeeeh)

104.8—FX: Hyuuu (hwooosh)

104.9—FX: Shuuu (fwooosh)

105.1—FX: Gui (yank)

105.2—FX: Buwa (bwoh)

105.5—FX: Gooo (gwhooh)

105.9—FX: Ooooo (vwoooh)

106.2—FX: Fuwa (fwoosh)

106.4—FX: Za (zsh)

106.5—FX: Iiii iiii iiiiii (high-pitched whistles)

106.6—FX: Iiii iiii iiiiii (high-pitched whistles)

106.10—FX: Hahahaha wahahaha (laughter)

107.1—FX: Hiiii (hweeee)

107.2—FX: Iiii hiiii iiiii (high-pitched whistles)

107.2—FX: Hiii uiiii uiiiiin waaaa waaan
(hweeee weeee wrooom wrooom)

107.3—FX: Iiii (high-pitched whistles)

107.4—FX: Iiii (high-pitched whistles)

108.7—FX: Hahaha (laughter)

108.10—FX: Hahaha (laughter)

108.12—FX: Zawazawa (chatter yammer)

109.1—FX: Doka doka (stomp stomp)

110.10—FX: Hyoko hyoko (hobble hobble)

111.8—FX: Zawa (mumble)

111.8—FX: Ho (whew)

114.1—FX: Oooo oooo (woow ooooh)

114.3—FX: Do (yeah)

114.8—FX: Hahaha haha (laughter)

115.6—FX: Gui (grab)

115.8—FX: Doki (badump)

116.1—FX: Shuwa (shwooh)

116.3—FX: Pashu (pshooof)

116.3—FX: Saaa (shwaaa)

116.4—FX: Ooo waaa do
(oooh yaaaaay woohooo)

116.5—FX: Zazaza (zshaaa)

119.1—FX: Gyu (clench)

119.4—FX: Shuu (shoooosh)

120.4—FX: Gon (gonk)

121.7—FX: Nu (nwoh)

121.9—FX: Wahahahaha (laughter)

122.3—FX: Bababa bata bata bata
(flutter fwap fwap fwap)

123.3—FX: Batabatabata batabata
(fwap fwap fwap fwap fwap)

123.4—FX: Batabata (fwap fwap)

123.5—FX: Goon gooon (gwoom gwoom)

123.6—FX: Goon goon (gwoom gwoom)

124.1—FX: Oooo (wrooom)

124.2—FX: Kyuuun (vwiiiish)

124.5—FX: Bishi (whip)

124.7—FX: Zawa zawa (murmur murmur)

124.8—FX: Zawa (murmur gasp)

125.4—FX: Kila (glint)

125.7—FX: Shuuu (shwoooh)

125.8—FX: Shun (shwoom)

126.3—FX: Don (tonk)

126.4—FX: Fuwa (fwoh)

147.6 —FX: Bun (vwosh)

147.8 —FX: Fuwa (fwut)

148.2 —FX: Jyuu jyuu jyuu zu zuzu (sizzle sizzle sizzle zgshh)

148.4 —FX: Zuzu (zgshh)

148.5 —FX: Jyuujyuu (sizzle sizzle)

148.5 —FX: Jijiji (sizzle)

148.5 —FX: Gugugu (guhhh)

148.6 —FX: Gufu (gwah)

148.8 —FX: Gufaa (graaah)

149.4 —FX: Jyuu jyuu jyuu (sizzle sizzle sizzle)

149.7 —FX: Bashi (seize)

150.1 —FX: Bilibili (rip rrrip)

150.4 —FX: Ga (gwak)

150.9 —FX: Ka (flash)

151.1 —FX: Jyuu (jwoof)

151.3 —FX: Dou (thud)

151.6 —FX: Chun (vzzp)

151.7 —FX: Vu (vwoosh)

151.9 —FX: Jiji (sizzle)

151.10 —FX: Dota (thud)

153.3 —FX: Kaa (kraah)

153.6 —FX: Pa (fwap)

154.9 —FX: Yoro (wobble)

155.2 —FX: Gaaa (graaah)

155.4 —FX: Pau (pashooom)

155.5 —FX: Shun (shwif)

156.3 —FX: Zuzuun (zaboom)

157.2 —FX: Shuu shuu shuu (fshh fshh fshh)

157.3 —FX: Shuu shuu (fshh fshh)

158.1 —FX: Pi pi (vwip vwip)

158.6 —FX: Zei zei (wheeze rasp)

159.1 —FX: Hyoko (hobble)

159.3 —FX: Dolo (slorp)

159.5 —FX: Gobo (cough)

159.6 —FX: Gooo (gwhoooh)

137.7 —FX: Bashi (bazap)

138.1 —FX: Guwa (graboom)

138.2 —FX: Gooo (gwoooh)

138.3 —FX: Zuzuuun (zaggmmm)

138.4 —FX: Bouuuuun (boooom)

139.2 —FX: Gulagula (wobble wobble)

139.3 —FX: Don (whud)

139.5 —FX: Goooo (gwhooooh)

140.1 —FX: Pau (pow)

140.3 —FX: Guwa guwa (bang boom)

140.7 —FX: Do (dwum)

140.9 —FX: Pyon (poink)

140.9 —FX: Mozo (shuffle)

142.1 —FX: Bo bo (bwoh bwof)

142.2 —FX: Bashi (whap)

142.7 —FX: Gooo (gwhoooh)

142.8 —FX: Dooo (dvoooh)

143.1 —FX: Doooo (dvoooh)

143.2 —FX: Bala bala (crumble crumble)

143.6 —FX: Gooo (gwhooh)

144.1 —FX: Gooo (vwoooh)

144.6 —FX: Gooo (vwoooosh)

144.6 —FX: Goon goon (gwoom gwoom)

145.1 —FX: Gooon (gwoom)

145.2 —FX: Uiiiin (vweeen)

145.3 —FX: Goooo (vwoooh)

145.4 —FX: Gau gau (bang bang)

145.7 —FX: Goooo (vwoooh)

145.7 —FX: Jijiji (crackle sizzle)

146.2 —FX: Jyululululu jyululu jylululu (sizzle sizzle sizzle)

146.3 —FX: Boto boto (thud thunk)

146.4 —FX: Jylululu (sizzle)

146.4 —FX: Goooo (vwoooh)

146.4 —FX: Jyuujyuu (sizzle sizzle)

146.4 —FX: Dolodolodolo (vwop gush)

147.4 —FX: Za (zash)

147.5 —FX: Giiin (glank)

126.5 —FX: Kueeee (kreeeeh)

126.6 —FX: Gin (kank)

126.8 —FX: Do (thud)

127.9 —FX: Gooon gooon (gwooom gwoom)

128.1 —FX: Gooo gooooon oooo (gwooom gwoooh oooom)

128.2 —FX: Oooo (wrooom)

128.3 —FX: Uoooo (wrooooh)

128.3 —FX: Shuu shuu (fshh fshh)

128.4 —FX: Ooo ooo ooo (ooooh whooah ooh)

128.5 —FX: Da (jumping)

128.6 —FX: Oooo (wroooooom)

129.1 —FX: Uooooo uoooon uoooon (wroooom ooom wrooom)

129.2 —FX: Uaaaa (aaaagh)

131.1 —FX: Goooo uoooo (gwooom wrooom)

131.2 —FX: Uoooo uooooon uooon (wrooom wroom wrooom)

132.1 —FX: Saaa (shaaa)

132.5 —FX: Kuta (falter)

132.7 —FX: Zuuu zuzuuun kuwa (zgmm zaboom flash)

133.1 —FX: Guwa dokaan guwaaan (graboom boom kaboom)

133.7 —FX: Gooo gooo (gwoooh gwooh)

134.1 —FX: Dodo (dumdum)

135.2 —FX: Sha (swoosh)

135.5 —FX: Kui (vwip)

135.6 —FX: Bau (bwoof)

135.7 —FX: Buooo (vwooooosh)

135.8 —FX: Gooon oon ooon (gwoom wroomwoom)

135.8 —FX: Kila (flash)

136.1 —FX: Ooon (wrooom)

136.2 —FX: Uiiii (vweeeeeh)

136.5 —FX: Uoooo (vwooh)

136.9 —FX: Uoooooo (vwoooooh)

137.1 —FX: Uoooo (wrooooooh)

137.2 —FX: Fu (fwoh)

137.3 —FX: Kiiiin (vweeeeeh)

137.6 —FX: Kuwa (kvoosh)

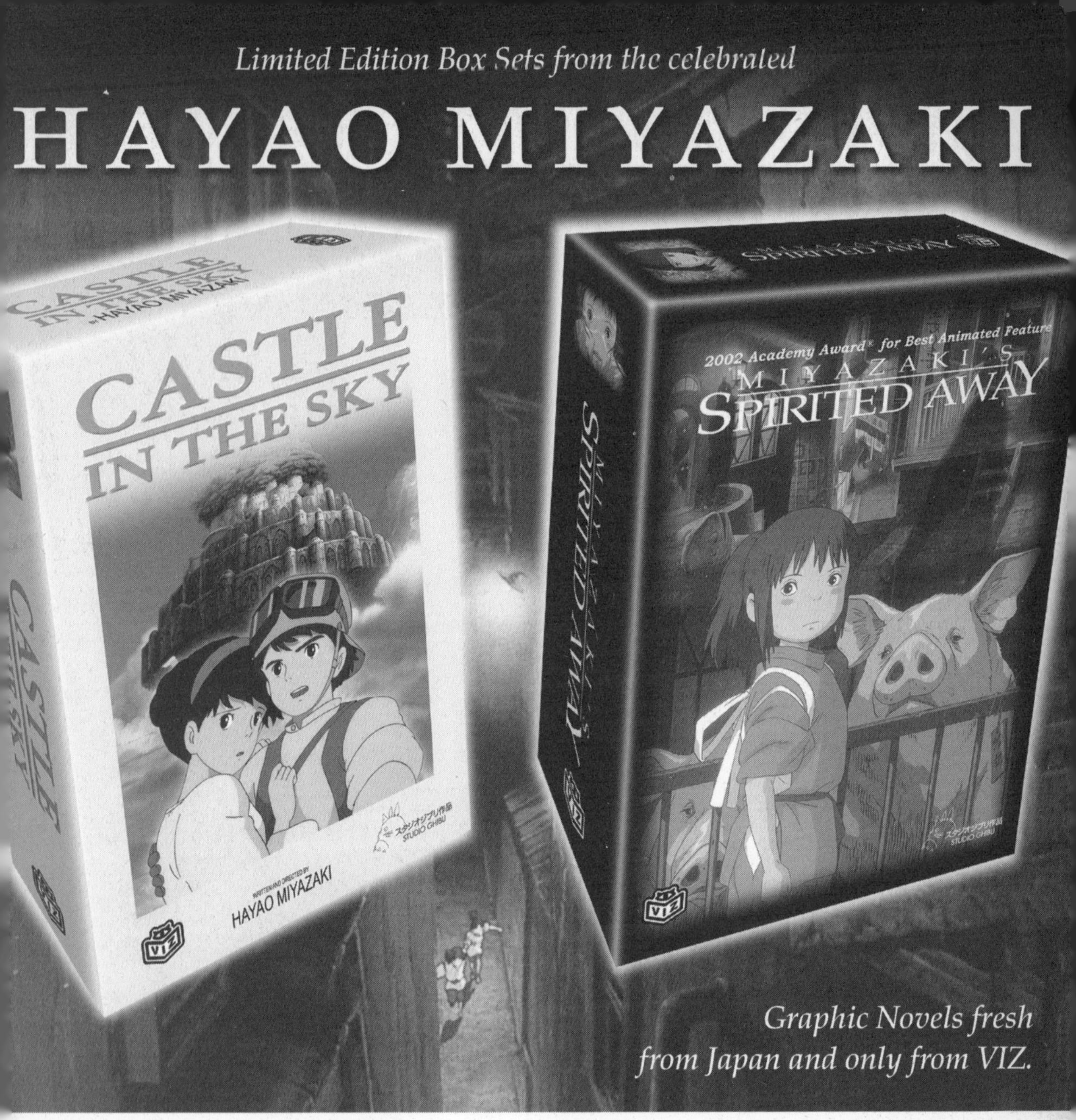

Limited Edition Box Sets from the celebrated
HAYAO MIYAZAKI
CASTLE IN THE SKY
WRITTEN AND DIRECTED BY HAYAO MIYAZAKI
2002 Academy Award® for Best Animated Feature
MIYAZAKI'S SPIRITED AWAY
Graphic Novels fresh from Japan and only from VIZ.

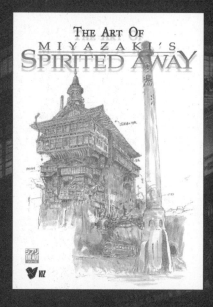